MW01461618

THE REBIRTH OF UZBEKISTAN

POLITICS, ECONOMY AND SOCIETY IN THE POST-SOVIET ERA

For
Yildiz, Muhammed and Evin

THE REBIRTH OF UZBEKISTAN

POLITICS, ECONOMY AND SOCIETY IN THE POST-SOVIET ERA

Resul Yalcin

With a foreword by Bogdan Szajkowski

Durham Middle East Monographs Series

ITHACA PRESS

THE REBIRTH OF UZBEKISTAN
Politics, Economy and Society in the Post-Soviet Era

Ithaca Press is an imprint of Garnet Publishing Limited

Published by
Garnet Publishing Limited
8 Southern Court
South Street
Reading
RG1 4QS
UK

Copyright © Resul Yalcin, 2002

All rights reserved.
No part of this book may be reproduced in any form or by any electronic or mechanical means, including information storage and retrieval systems, without permission in writing from the publisher, except by a reviewer who may quote brief passages in a review.

First Edition

ISBN 0 86372 281 4

British Library Cataloguing-in-Publication Data
A catalogue record for this book is available from the British Library

Jacket design by Garnet Publishing
Typeset by Samantha Barden

Printed in Lebanon

Contents

	List of Tables	vi
	Acknowledgements	vii
	Foreword	ix
	Introduction	1
1	History and People	9
2	Social Transformation: Past, Present and Future	71
3	The Transition to Democracy in Uzbekistan	137
4	The Economic Transformation	179
5	Foreign Policy and External Relations	235
6	Conclusion	295
	Appendices	307
	Interviews	313
	Bibliography	319
	Index	337

Tables

2.1	The national structure of Uzbekistan	106
2.2	The changes in the main ethnic groups	108
4.1	Real GDP growth	197
4.2	Uzbekistan industrial production, 1992–8	198
4.3	Production of selected energy products	199
4.4	Inflation (year-end) and budget deficit	200
4.5	Savings, investment, consumption and wages	201
4.6	Summary of public finance	204
4.7	Balance of payments	207
4.8	Foreign trade	209
4.9	Wages and employment, 1992–8	211
4.10	Sectoral share of NMP	212
4.11	Production of main agricultural products	215
4.12	Production of main industrial products	219

Acknowledgements

The completion of this book has been developed through two different phases of work. The first phase was my doctoral thesis. The second has involved rewriting it for publication. During the thesis, the completion of my work would not have been possible without the valuable contributions and assistance of many individuals. First of all, I would like to express my deepest thanks and gratitude to my supervisor, Professor Bogdan Szajkowski for his guidance, scholarly advice and encouragement as well as his ideas that he did not hesitate to share with me during lengthy discussions.

The research for this book was undertaken in the Republic of Uzbekistan, where I spent over a year conducting my fieldwork. I avail myself of this opportunity to express my thanks and gratitude to local experts, institutions and international organizations for their valuable comments, suggestions and generosity with their time. I am particularly indebted to foreign diplomatic representatives in Tashkent, notably the Embassy of the Russian Federation, the Embassy of the Federal Republic of Germany, the Embassy of France, the Embassy of the Islamic Republic of Iran and the Embassy of the Kyrgyzy Republic for their kind assistance and cooperation. I am also grateful to all the representatives of the ethnic minorities who I had the opportunity to meet and discuss inter-ethnic issues with.

I am deeply grateful to the following individuals and institutions for their valuable contributions and assistance: Mir Botir Mirabdulaev; Hydarov Rawshan Rasuloglu; Jumen Niyazi Komilcan; Aziz Kayumov; Tashpulat Tashlanov; Abdumannob Poulatov; Dr Sergey M. Bozhko, the advisor to the UN Representative Administrative Officer; Mark B. O'Brien, the Residents Representative, International Monetary Fund; Werner Roider, Deputy Chief, Resident Mission, the World Bank; Abdulaeva M. Bahtier; Anatoly Krutov; Elmira Muratova; Michael B. Dan, Project Manager of the European Union's Tacis Programme; Professor Abdul-Kadir Ergashev, Advisor to the UN Development

Programme; Momir Vranes, Technical Officer UNDP project for the Aral Sea; Umaiyeh Khammash, UN population Fund Regional Officer for Central Asia; Chad Breckinridge, Manager of the American Business Centre in Tashkent; Mehmet Arslan, General Director of the Private Uzbek-Turkish Lycee; Mahbuba Ergasheva, a national expert on women's issues; Mikhail Ardzinov, representative of the Human Rights Society of Uzbekistan; Mirhan M. Nazmutdinov; John Macleod, representative of the Human Rights Watch/Helsinki.

I would also like to thank the lecturers and students of the University of World Economy and Diplomacy and the University of World Languages and Uzbek Language Learning Centre for their assistance in 1995–6.

My gratitude also goes to the Uzbek government officials with whom I discussed several national and regional issues, and I am deeply grateful to the people of Uzbekistan for their kindness, generosity and great hospitality given to me. There are many individuals in the region whose names are omitted, but to whom I am no less grateful for valuable help and support. They have given their time and effort to assist in the collection of information and materials for this book.

I would like to thank the University of Exeter in general, and the Department of Politics in particular, for giving me this opportunity to conduct this research. My gratitude must also go to the London School of Economics and Political Science for allowing me to use its Library and IT facilities throughout my study.

After the completion of the thesis, Dr Anoush Ehteshami of the University of Durham and Professor Michael Rush of the University of Exeter both made invaluable suggestions and comments and encouraged me to revise for publication. I am grateful to both of them for their comments and unselfish guidance.

Foreword

Throughout history the area which now constitutes the Republic of Uzbekistan has occupied a central role in the political, social and economic development of Eurasia. The fact that it was subjected to conquests by virtually all of the most important civilizations has had a profound impact on the shaping of its culture, religion and social and political institutions. The people that came with those conquests and settled in the area and mixed with local dwellers continuously added to the complex mosaic of the population. This melting pot of peoples, cultures, religions and types of social and political organization resulted in the development of a high level of civilization in the area.

Modern and now independent Uzbekistan is a successor to this complex process, which not only brings the advantage of serving as a point of reference, but more importantly, in the contemporary environment, engenders the necessity to focus on problems and issues that need to be resolved in globalized settings. The geopolitical position of contemporary Uzbekistan in the intricate system of security, political and economic international relations of Central Asia assures the country's pivotal role not only in this area, but also as a bridge between Europe and Asia, between the Russian Federation in the north and the Islamic world to the south. The tasks are formidable and require economic and political assistance not only from Uzbekistan's immediate neighbours, but also from the world community, particularly the European Union. The success of Uzbekistan depends a great deal on such an overarching assistance.

This, the first comprehensive study of Uzbekistan, is a truly outstanding one. Dr Resul Yalcin traces the intricate history and development of ancient and modern Uzbekistan, the Uzbeks and the peoples of the area with the acute, critical eye of an astute researcher and scholarly investigator for facts and details. The result is an exceptionally high level of focused, refined analysis that contains a major policy prescription pertaining not only to Uzbekistan but also to transitionary societies in general. Yalcin is one of the few Uzbek-speaking British scholars who has managed to understand the profound problems and challenges of Uzbekistan's transition and to disentangle myths from reality.

This notable work is a splendid example of high academic discourse based on deep understanding of the dilemmas and requirements faced by societies in transition as they attempt to become part of the increasingly globalized international environment in political, economic, social and security terms.

Bogdan Szajkowski
Professor of Pan-European Politics
Director, Centre for European Studies, University of Exeter

Introduction

Post-Soviet Central Asia has, strategically and economically, become one of the most important regions of the world and Uzbekistan is the centre point of that region. Until the Arab invasion of Central Asia in the eighth century, the territory that encompasses present-day Uzbekistan was called Transoxiana (meaning 'between the two rivers'). Following the Arab conquest it was called Maverannahr (in ancient Arabic, meaning 'beyond the river'). The country's location in Central Asia made it a natural choice as a trade route and consequently there were frequent struggles for control of this central point, making it the centre of the creation or dissolution of many great empires and dynasties that have existed in this part of the Asian continent since ancient times. As a result, there had always been mass population movements as people were replaced, displaced, expelled or assimilated. These movements and migrations of people, coupled with the long history of conquests, produced a high level of civilization in the region. New conquerors were continually destroying the civilization that existed before them, thereafter restoring the artifacts of ancient cultures. These empires and dynasties included the Medea, Persian, Bactria-Sogdiana, Achaemenid, Macedonian, Kushan, White Huns, Turkish, Sasanian, Samanid, Chinese, Mongol, Uzbek, Tsarist Russia, and finally, the Soviet Union. All the empires formed there had an impact on the people's lives, but none attempted to build a serious civil society.

The boundaries were redrawn many times, with contemporary Uzbekistan as a political entity with its boundaries and organizational structures being created by the Bolsheviks during the 1924–5 'national delimitation' that divided Central Asia into several new ethnically-based units. It became one of the fifteen constituent republics of the Soviet Union in 1924. Uzbekistan was the Soviet Union's most important Muslim community, serving as a model for other Muslim groups in the empire. It was also of special economic importance because it was the world's third largest producer of cotton. After Russians and Ukrainians,

Uzbeks comprised the third largest ethnic group in the Soviet Union, and Uzbekistan was the fifth largest Soviet republic. As recently as 1989, the republic represented the most subservient non-Slavic republic to Moscow in all matters. Yet the government of the Republic of Uzbekistan declared its sovereignty in June 1990, and almost a year later, in August 1991, declared its independence. What brought the country so suddenly to its new status? Unquestionably, the internal forces in Uzbekistan that spearheaded its relatively quiet drive for independence did not emerge overnight. They had been at work beneath the calm surface of the Union since Stalin's days. But the new climate created by Mikhail Gorbachev, played a crucial role.

The Soviet Union disintegrated almost unexpectedly, not because it was threatened with immediate invasion, famine or war, but because of pressures from within. Mikhail Gorbachev, who came to power in 1985, promised to reform the Soviet system. The reform programme he launched – *glasnost* (openness) and *perestroika* (reconstruction) – set in motion revolutionary changes he had never intended. The effects of Gorbachev's reform policies, together with the free atmosphere in Eastern Europe after the fall of the Berlin Wall, were also felt in Central Asia. Thus the consequences of the reform programme marked the beginning of a new era in the USSR. On 19 August 1991, Moscow became the scene of an attempted coup by hardliners in the Soviet Communist Party, the KGB and the army. The coup lasted only three days; its failure sparked an even greater deep-rooted animosity towards the communist regime within the borders of the Soviet Union. This resulted in massive social unrest and movements for independence, which gained impetus and subsequently led to the disintegration of the USSR in December 1991. So ended an extraordinary chapter of history which resulted in the emergence of several new independent states from the Baltic to Central Asia. The movement in Central Asia began in Uzbekistan and later spread to the other republics.

From one perspective, the seventy years of the Soviet period represented an era of tremendous change in Uzbekistan. But this period also marked a totalitarian regime's attempt to realize a peculiar form of political, social, economic and cultural transformation. To go into a detailed analysis of what Lenin might have envisioned as the long-term future for Uzbekistan is beyond the scope of this study. But it is likely that he believed that, under the Bolsheviks, the republic would eventually achieve economic equality and prosperity. The national, religious, and linguistic differences would not serve as bases for inter-ethnic conflict but would eventually give way to a strong Soviet 'community'. Lenin also recognized the need for a strong centralized political power to guide the Central Asian people of the Tsarist Russian Empire towards the communist ideology. Dreams of peace based on economic well-being and ethnic homogeneity, however, were not realized in Uzbekistan. The republic turned out to be one of the poorest countries of the Soviet Union. It became the scene of one of the worst ethnic conflicts in the region in the late 1980s. The Soviet federal structure was based upon the principle of national in form, socialist in content, but in Uzbekistan it ended up socialist in form, national in content. Moreover, the political system established by Lenin imploded in the 1980s and was brought down in 1991.

When Uzbek President Islom Karimov declared the republic's political independence in August 1991, Uzbekistan faced enormous social, political and economic challenges. In response to these problems, the leadership undertook a set of measures to enable the country's transition to a market-oriented economy and political democracy less painful for its people. Uzbekistan does not, however, seem to be willing to adopt the Western model of democracy as it does not fit well to the local conditions. Its adoption in several former Soviet states that experienced political instability, economic crisis and increased social problems, also discouraged Uzbekistan. Therefore, the Uzbek leadership rejected a simultaneous transition from the old totalitarian system to a free democratic society. The idea of a strong state, belief in government as the core of social life and autocracy were fundamentally important in the social consciousness of most, if not all, the countries of the former USSR. The idea of democracy in a modern form in the pre-Soviet Central Asian societies was rarely developed and cultivated. More than seventy years of Soviet totalitarianism thwarted the development of democracy in the lifestyle and consciousness of the whole society. Values of individual freedoms, respect for other views, and tolerance do not seem to have strong roots in society. Therefore cultivation of these values and establishing the structures of a civil society with a single leap would only complicate the task of democratic reform.

On economic transformation Uzbekistan prefered economic 'gradualism' for two main reasons: (1) the economic structure left over from the Soviet era; (2) the economic models of privatization and marketization which were alien models to the local conditions. Despite all the differences and particular features of the countries of the former Soviet Union, almost all of them were advised to adopt a single, rapid, revolutionary form of transition from a planned command economy to a market economy. The implementation of this model in most of the CIS countries without appropriate preparation or creation of effective mechanisms of support for enterprises, aggravated the economic crisis and drove many enterprises to the brink of bankruptcy. In order to minimize possible social, economic and political upheavals and to protect people's livelihoods and well-being during the transition period, Uzbekistan chose a path separate from other CIS countries in its shift away from a centrally planned command economy to a multi-sectoral market economy. The government wanted to avoid social unrest and minimize the threat to stability in the country, while examining various approaches and economic models for the transition to a market economy. Soviet-era economic development left the republic burdened by many problems and, since independence, these problems have accelerated the county's economic decline and complicated the task of economic reform. A new long-term strategy of national development was needed, one that would correspond to the country's fundamental economic, social and cultural characteristics.

Ethnic, religious and cultural factors have assisted in shaping the post-independence pattern of Uzbekistan's foreign policy priorities, its perception of the world outside of the former Soviet Union, and the republic's place in its region and in the world as a whole. But the relative impact of these has been conditioned by other determining factors of Uzbek foreign policy that are geopolitical, political and economic in nature. In addition to these, the republic's regional and international aspirations have also helped to determine its foreign policy priorities.

The demise of the Soviet Union also paved the way for Uzbeks to assert full control over their own state and seek to establish a commanding position in the politics of Central Asia. Uzbekistan is a newly independent country and still in a state of transition. What emerges from the next stage will affect the entire area of Central Asia and across Central Eurasia. Future stability and a democratic community in Uzbekistan will play a decisive role in the politics of neighbouring states. Uzbekistan is the largest republic in its region by population, and lies at the heart of

INTRODUCTION

Central Asia. It has common borders with each of the other four states. The Uzbeks consider themselves the heirs of the great civilizations of the region. Uzbekistan's territory encompasses the heart of old Turkestan, that includes the ancient cities of Bukhara, which had been an important center of Islamic learning, and Samarkand, a crossroads between East and West since the time of Alexander the Great and an important stop on the Silk Road, the main route of trade between China and Europe. The republic's capital is another historic city and an ancient commercial centre on the caravan routes to Europe and Asia. Present-day Uzbekistan also includes much of the territory ruled by the strongest and most sophisticated regimes – the Khanate of Khiva, Bukhara, and Khokand – that the Russians encountered at the beginning of the nineteenth century.

Uzbekistan is now an independent state with its own agenda and ambitions, and since independence a strong sense of nationhood has been developing. Post-Soviet Uzbek politics are shaped within this framework, and earlier approaches describing the republic's politics within a clan or tribal context do not give a clear picture of what is actually going on in the country. If it achieves strong macroeconomic stability and a law-based state with freedom and equality for its citizens, it could play a significant role in Central Asia, and influence the balance of power across Eurasia affecting the direct interests of several major states in the region.

This book is a comprehensive study of Uzbekistan and its people. To my knowledge, this work is thus far the first attempt to study systematically, the social, political and economic changes that have taken place in the republic since independence, as well as its foreign policy and external relations in one volume. It examines the history, politics, economy and society of Uzbekistan, as well as the republic's foreign policy and external relations. The aim is to trace the main direction and developments in the country after the break-up of the Soviet Union. Although many scholars have focused on Soviet and post-Soviet Uzbekistan, there has not been any study that focused on post-Soviet Uzbekistan in such detail as this one. The books and articles published on the republic have consisted of analyses of Uzbekistan's history, political development, its economy, nationalism and identity. But missing was a comprehensive study in one volume of the republic's history, macroeconomic progress, political and social changes, its foreign policy and external relations.

What is more, a similarly rigorous analysis of the transition to democracy in post-Soviet Uzbekistan, its foreign policy and external relations has never been explored by scholars in such detail. Thus this research is the first attempt in the field to fill this analytical gap.

Another novel aspect of this research lies in its study of the political, economic and cultural distinctiveness of Uzbeks and Uzbekistan's historical development. The analysis of the historical conditions that determined the social development of Uzbek society from the time of the first states that were formed on the territory of present-day Uzbekistan also belongs to this study. This research is also a first attempt to study political systems and institutions of democracy in the republic; examining how they have been shaped by historical and cultural factors; and assessing the basic features of the newly-established democratic institutions and the process of democracy in Uzbekistan.

Much of the material, which is derived from articles published in serial literature and chapters in various books, has been thoroughly revised, updated and expanded. I lived in Uzbekistan and conducted extensive field research for over a year in 1995–6. I have also conducted several crucial interviews and had numerous discussions throughout the country with many people, among whom were scholars, leaders of political parties, government officials, journalists, representatives of non-governmental organizations and local government, and leaders of ethnic minorities. To update most of the materials used for the book earlier and explore the most recent changes in the region, I revisited Central Asia for three weeks in April 2000. I have analysed the interviews and discussions as well as my participant observations in the region for both occasions, especially in Uzbekistan, and employed them extensively throughout the study. They provide an important methodological basis of this work.

This book also attempts to find answers to several questions among which are: who are the Uzbeks and what is the significance of their history to contemporary Uzbekistan? What impact did *glasnost* and *perestroika* have on Uzbekistan and its people? What has been the impact of the changing political environment in the country after the demise of the Soviet Union? What were the advantages and disadvantages of over a century of Russian and Soviet rule over Uzbekistan? What is the importance of Islam for Uzbekistan and what role did it play in the socio-political life of Uzbeks throughout the period of Russian and

INTRODUCTION

Soviet rule? What have inter-ethnic relations been like throughout the decades of Russian and Soviet rule, and what sort of ethnic policy is to be pursued in Uzbekistan in order to preserve stability in the country? In the domestic sphere, what kind of political and socio-economic system will replace the communist one-party regime, and can pluralism and social justice prevail in the country? What is Uzbekistan's potential for establishing the foundations of democracy against a background of acute political struggle in a number of countries in the region? Has the leadership role in post-Soviet Uzbekistan changed significantly? With regard to foreign policy, Uzbekistan, like several other states in the region, is being tugged in opposite directions. Which direction would the republic choose, and what effect would this choice have on Uzbekistan's status and role in the international community? How much has Uzbekistan relinquished or altered its sense of regional identity, and would it seek a regional confederation? How would Uzbekistan react to the ambitions of major regional powers?

The study is divided into six chapters. Chapter 1 is a study of Uzbekistan, its history and people: firstly, it presents the country's geography; climate; agriculture; water and natural resources; energy and industry; religions and cultures; environment and the status of women in Uzbekistan. Secondly, it summarizes Uzbekistan's history in three stages – the ancient history of the country until the Russian occupation in the nineteenth century, the modern history until the break-up of the Soviet Union, and the most recent post-Soviet history. Thirdly, it attempts to answer the question 'who are the Uzbeks?' Chapter 2 is devoted to social transformation of the people of Uzbekistan. It comprises two sections. Section one examines the social transformation of the people of Uzbekistan in four stages – their nomadic life, their transformation under the Tsarist Russian administration, the transformation under the former Soviet rule and the post-Soviet transformation. Section two, however, is a study of the minority groups and the inter-ethnic relations in Uzbekistan. Chapter 3 examines the transformation to democracy in Uzbekistan. It gives references to the regimes which ruled the people of Uzbekistan throughout their known history and states the possible impact of these rules as a handicap for modern Uzbek society to develop its own model of democracy in contemporary Uzbekistan. In light of this, chapter 3 analyses the democratic institutions which have been established in the republic and gives a brief account of the country's electoral system. It also studies the party system and the political parties in Uzbekistan.

Chapter 4 discusses the country's transition to a market economy. It gives a brief account of the republic's economic structure during the former Soviet Union, and its after-effects, while stating the republic's macroeconomic performance after the break-up of the union. Reference is given to Uzbekistan's initial desire to remain within a monetary union (the 'rouble zone') with the Russian Federation and its decision to leave the 'rouble zone' and introduce a national currency, the *Sum*. This chapter also examines the 'Uzbek Economic Model' of transition and points out why the leadership is reluctant to introduce a full-scale market economy. It analyses the privatization process; success and the failures of the leadership's macroeconomic policies since independence; and the government's policies in tackling the poverty in the country. Chapter 5 is devoted to the Foreign Policy and External Relations of Uzbekistan. This chapter is divided into two sections. The first section focuses on the republic's foreign policy and 'external' relations during the Soviet era; states its initial steps, the factors that shaped its foreign policy and established the foreign policy principles and priorities after independence. Section two, however, concentrates on the country's post-Soviet external relations. Here Uzbekistan's relations with its neighbouring states, Russia, the US and the UK amongst others are examined.

The last chapter concludes with a brief overview of what has been discussed and provides possible suggestions.

I believe that this study will offer a diversity of information for the general student in an easily accessible form about this increasingly important country of Central Asia and will be used as a textbook for Soviet and post-Soviet Central Asian studies. It will provide source materials for further study for those with a special interest in this field and for social scientists in general specializing in post-Soviet affairs, and it will also assist in acquiring knowledge of the specifics of the culture-change-tradition-modernity and modernization of Muslim Central Asia.

1

History and People

Introduction
Uzbekistan is located in the heart of Central Asia, and lies between two 'sister rivers', the Amu Darya (Oxus) and the Syrdarya (Jaxartes), the largest and deepest rivers in Central Asia. The republic lies along a north-west to south-east axis and its eastern extremity, the Fergana Valley region, borders Kyrgyzstan to the east, Tajikistan to the south-east, Afghanistan to the south, and Turkmenistan to the south-west and the west. The north-west of the country consists of the Aral Sea, and beyond that lies Kazakstan, which forms the entire northern border (see Appendix A, Map 1). Uzbekistan covers an area of 447,400 square kilometres (172,741 square miles), of which the Karakalpak Autonomous Republic covers 164,900 square kilometres. The republic is divided into 12 provinces and subdivided into 162 districts, in which there are 118 cities, 116 towns and 1,332 villages. The entire territory spans 930 kilometres from north to south and 1,425 kilometres from east to west. Until the Arab invasion of Central Asia, modern-day Uzbekistan was named *Transoxiana* (meaning the territory between two rivers), and the Arabs called it *Maverannahr* (the land beyond the river).

Most of the territory of Uzbekistan is flat country and desert, including the south-western part of the Kzyl Kum (Red Sands). The south-east of the republic presents a contrasting picture with clay deserts, foothills and mountain ridges belonging to the Western Tien-Shan and Hissar-Alai ranges, which are cut by valleys. Some peaks rise as high as 4,643 metres above sea level. The rivers of the region have their source in the high altitude glaciers that rush down into the lowlands as foamy streams. The Amu Darya and the Syrdarya rivers both arise in the mountainous regions of the Tien-Shan and flow north-westwards to drain into the Aral Sea. The region between these two rivers, especially in the valleys and those areas suitable for the construction of irrigation canals, is an ancient seat of civilization. Several thousand years ago, there appeared six valleys and six oases surrounded by boundless deserts and foothills on the territory of Uzbekistan and today, the Zaravshan, Kashkadarya, Surkhandarya, Tashkent, Fergana and Khorezm Valleys are the major agricultural centres of the republic. A high level of seismicity (sometimes up to 8 points on the Richter scale) is also characteristic for the republic. Among the most destructive earthquakes were those in Fergana (1823), Andijan (1889 and 1902) and Tashkent (1866 and 1868). A strong earthquake on 26 April 1966 severely damaged some of the capital Tashkent's residential areas, particularly in the centre, killing thousands of people.

The climate of Uzbekistan is continental, with low precipitation, relatively high temperatures and a large number of cloudless days during the year. In summer the temperature rises to between 40 and 50 degrees Celsius at noontime in the south. The northern regions of the republic lie within the temperate zone while the southern regions are in the subtropical zone. The position of the sun and the large number of cloudless days ensure higher solar radiation than in the Mediterranean or California, with an average of 140–160 kilocalories for every square centimetre of surface. Precipitation is very low, particularly in the plains, where in some years there is not a drop of rain from June to October.

In contrast to the summer, the relatively short winters are characterized by capricious weather. The frequent alteration of warm and cold air masses cause considerable fluctuation in temperature and air humidity. The sky is often overcast and it rains and snows occasionally. The snow cover, which appears almost every year, is shallow and frequently thaws during the winter in the south. The usual January temperature in the extreme north, on the Ustyurt plateau and the lower reaches of the Amu Darya, ranges from -7 to -37 degrees Celsius. On the greater part of the plains it is close to zero and about 3 degrees Celsius in the Termez region in the south. Spring begins during the first days of March. In the Plains it lasts not more than a month, but in the mountains it lasts three months. In the spring there is occasional rainfall and sharp temperature fluctuations. Autumn is long and cloudless. It arrives in the mountains in September and descends into the Kzyl Kum and the valleys at the beginning of October. The first autumn frosts arrive at the end of October. Occasional rainfall precedes a fall in temperatures and a period of dry, fine weather sets in. After that it gets hot again. Such changes in the weather occur several times during the year.

The abundance of sun, high temperatures and fertile soil in the valleys of Fergana, Zaravshan and Chirchik encourages the production of such heat-loving crops as cotton, kenaf, figs, grapes, melons, watermelons, apricots, cherries, peaches and pomegranates. The vineyards of the Fergana and Tashkent regions produce grapes. Samarkand and Tashkent are also famous for vegetables, fruits and gourds. Of course all these grow only on irrigated land – without water the merciless sun reduces any plantation to barren desert – with the water for the irrigation coming from the rivers. In Uzbekistan the planting of cotton is the mainstay of the country's economy. The republic is still one of the world's major producers of cotton, most of which is grown in the northwest, in the east and along the valley of the Amu Darya. Once it was called 'white gold', because of the money it supplied for the USSR's economy. But it has also wrought enormous environmental damage to the region's water and soil because of the lack of modern technology needed to water and harvest the cotton properly. Now the Uzbek authorities are reassessing the irrigation and harvesting systems. The country also leads in the cultivation of kenaf, a plant used to make rope, sacks and other heavy materials. The raising of livestock is important in northern and western Uzbekistan. The breeding of Karakul sheep is also very important. In the foothills and mountainous areas of the country, cattle and goats provide meat and dairy products, while chicken farms are common throughout the country. The breeding of horses and camels occurs in the western areas of the country. The Karakalpaks raise muskrat, mink and silver foxes for their fur. Uzbekistan also produces over half of the total silk cocoons produced in the CIS.

Water is vitally important for Uzbekistan. The surface water is distributed over the territory in an inefficient way and a lot of it is wasted. Most of the rivers originating in the republic take most of their water from the mountains with the greatest precipitation and the lowest evaporation. Snow and glaciers provide water for all the rivers of Central Asia, and for those of Uzbekistan too. The Amu Darya and the Syrdarya are the biggest and longest rivers, not only in Uzbekistan but also in the whole of Central Asia, at 1,437 and 2,137 kilometres long respectively. The two rivers take their source outside Uzbekistan. The Amu Darya is a confluence of the rivers Pyanje and Vakhsh, and the Syrdarya is the confluence of the Narin and Kara Darya rivers. The latter is longer than the former, but it has less water.

The Syrdarya and the Amu Darya form two river basins. The Syrdarya basin contains the rivers Narin, Kara Darya, Chirchik, Akhangharan, Sokh, Isfara, Akbura, Isfairamsai, Shakhimardan, Gavasai and Kasansai. The Amu Darya basin contains the rivers Zaravshan, Kashkadarya, Surkhandarya, Tupolangdarya and Sherabad. Only the middle and lower reaches of the Amu Darya and Syrdarya tributaries are within the republic's territory. The Amu Darya water is mainly used in the territory of Uzbekistan for the irrigation of the Khorezm oasis and Karakalpakistan. Some water in the middle reaches, however, is taken to the Amu Darya canal for irrigating the Bukhara and Kashkadarya oasis.

Agriculture in Uzbekistan is based on artificial irrigation. The significance of the rivers and the water reservoirs is great not only for the preservation of the existing oases but also for exploration and irrigation of new, previously uncultivated lands. In ancient times canals of different dimensions were built. Modern canals serve not only for irrigation, but also to some extent for hydropower plants. These canals include Narpai, South Fergana, North Fergana, Big Fergana, Eskiangar, Amu-Bukhara, Big Namangan and others.

Uzbekistan has a few lakes on its territory, the largest of which is the Aral. As it occupied a large area, it was called a 'sea'. Among the other comparatively big lakes are the Sudochye and Arnasai. The streams of warm and humid air originating above the Aral Sea, according to scientists, previously formed a natural obstacle to the air going to the south from Russia and Kazakstan. This obstacle is being destroyed with the drying up of the Aral Sea and heavy industrial pollution, causing one of the most serious environmental crises in the world. So nothing can prevent the cold air from rushing to the Central Asian states and bringing unexpected hail and heavy rain showers to the farmland. Thunderstorms can occur now even in midsummer and can cause huge damage. All these factors reduce the vegetation period of heat-loving crops and create many complications. During the past four decades big water reservoirs in Chavrak, Akhangran, Tuyabuguz, Yuzhno-Surkhandarya, and Cimkurgan were built in Uzbekistan, but the materials used are now out of date. The water is highly polluted and too much water is wasted when it is used for irrigation.

There is also underground water. The territory of Uzbekistan is an arid area that has a serious shortage of water resources. That is why this water is widely applied for water supply, cattle breeding and irrigation too. According to a 1995 World Bank assessment, only 85 per cent of the urban population and 52 per cent of the rural population have access to piped water. One-third of the water delivered by pipe in cities and over half of that provided in villages does not meet government quality standards. Two large water treatment plants located near the Aral Sea have been equipped with new laboratory and chlorination equipment under a US $5 million technical assistance grant. The project was started in 1994 and completed at the end of 1996. Other than these two plants, virtually all of the 25 metropolitan plants and two hundred smaller stations in towns and rural areas require substantial improvement and upgrade.

Uzbekistan is rich in mineral water and due to its chemical composition it has a medicinal effect. Especially valuable among the mineral water sources prospected recently are waters with hydrogen sulphide, iodine, radon and thermomineral water with a low content of mineral alkaline. Many sources of mineral water are used for balneological purposes.

Industry
The predominant industrial activity is the extraction and processing of Uzbekistan's considerable mineral wealth. More than 750 types of mineral resources have been found in the depths of the republic. International experts value the investigated resources at approximately US $3 billion. The share of Uzbekistan constitutes a major part of the mineral and raw-mineral resources of the whole Central Asian region. Thus it controls 70 per cent of gas condensate, 31 per cent of oil reserves, 40 per cent of natural gas and 45 per cent of coal reserves. The investigated resources of gas constitute about two billion cubic metres, those of coal over two billion tons, and those of oil about 350 million tons. There are large deposits of salts, aluminium raw materials, ashlar, decorative and precious stones, some types of rare metals, and raw materials for construction items on the territory of the republic. Other significant deposits include gold, uranium, copper, tungsten, silver and aluminium ore. In addition to the established industry of the extraction and refining of gold, and the developing of the hydrocarbons sector, the most promising resource is copper. Uzbekistan is also one of the world's top gold producers, with 65–70 metric tonnes annually. Gold deposits deserve special attention. Uzbekistan stands in second place not only in

gold production, but also in per capita production of gold among the CIS states. Most of the gold mining is done in the deserts of central Uzbekistan, to the north of Bukhara including Muruntau, which is claimed to be the largest single gold mine in the world. There are also some gold deposits in Tashkent, Jizzakh, and the Namangan provinces (Marjanbulak, Zarmitan and Chardak).

Hydrocarbon reserves are another significant resource. Uzbekistan is the third largest natural gas producer in the CIS and the tenth largest exporter in the world. The prospects for the mining and energy sectors are in general quite good. Uzbekistan exports cotton fibre, raw silk, fabrics, karakul pelts, agricultural machinery, vegetables, fruits, rice, marble, gas, gold and tungsten. The country imports petroleum products. Although hydropower electric plants exist, thermal stations fuelled by natural gas generate most of the country's electricity. At the same time, hydropower potential is not fully utilized.

Language
Under Soviet rule the official languages in Uzbekistan were Russian and Uzbek. Since independence, Uzbek has been the only official language in the country and fluency in Uzbek is now a requirement for holding a government post. The Uzbek language belongs to the East-Turkic group. The vocabulary of Uzbek is basically Turkic, with little difference in grammar, but it contains important elements of Arabic, and Persian loan-words. Russian words have also entered the language since the mid-nineteenth century.

Before the revolution the people of Uzbekistan, and indeed in Central Asia as a whole, had never been subjected to anything approaching a linguistics policy. It was only after the revolution that an attempt was made by the government to change and regulate by legislation established languages and methods of writing them. The Tsarist regime's attitude towards national languages was one of indifference – during the time of this regime, all official business was conducted in Russian and therefore Russian officials were not required to study the local languages, nor did they force the local people to learn Russian.

It is known that until the Soviet revolution scholars used Arabic characters to write Uzbek. The Arabic language was used in religion and official writing and Persian was functioning as the language of poetry, though common people spoke Turkic dialects in everyday life. Mir

Alisher Navoi was the first man to work out the foundations of Turkish vocabulary. Ironically all of the arguments raised against the Persian language are within the conventional idioms of Persian literature. Both the grammar and presentation of *The Muhakamad-al-lughatayn*, as well as his other works written in Turkish, are largely dependent on Persian forms, with their structure making it Turkish in vocabulary only.

Just before the October revolution, the *Jadid* Movement proposed to create a single Turkish literary language written in a modified Arabic script for the use of all the Turkic people of Russia. However, lacking the cooperation of the Russians, their plan failed. The Soviet nationalities policy, however, as originally conceived, emphasized the differences rather than similarities among the nationalities. Consequently, the Soviet officials concentrated on the creation of distinct languages and literatures for various nationalities in Central Asia with the evident object of reducing the possibility of their rising up against the new regime. As a first step, the Soviets introduced the Latin alphabet in place of Arabic for the writing of all Central Asian languages, including Uzbek in 1924. In the late 1930s, however, this in turn was replaced by a series of modified Cyrillic alphabets. This emphasized the phonetic and grammatical differences among the languages by allotting certain special letters to each of the languages. The introduction of Cyrillic rather than Latin characters served a dual purpose. On the one hand, it facilitated the learning of Russian; on the other hand, it differentiated the Turkic languages of Central Asia, including Uzbek, from that of Turkey which had adopted Latin characters in 1928. The Soviets were concerned that Soviet Central Asia might develop deeper ties with Turkey, and thus Cyrillic, in which the Russian language was written, became the means for writing all Turkic languages spoken in the then Soviet Union. This method of change was one of the ways in which the Soviets attempted to Russify Central Asian people. The Cyrillic script is still in use today but independent Uzbekistan reintroduced a Latin alphabet all over Uzbekistan starting with the primary schools in the 1996–7 academic year. Russian remains a widely spoken language, particularly in urban areas.

Religion and culture
Until the Arab conquests in the seventh and eighth centuries AD, the people of Uzbekistan followed a number of different religions, including

Buddhism, Shamanism and Zoroastrianism; the latter began at about the same time as Buddhism and became the official religion of the Sasanian Dynasty. Judaism and Nestorian Christianity arrived in the region around the fourth and fifth centuries having spread from the Middle East. The majority of the people of Uzbekistan have been Muslims since the Arab conquest and, up to the establishment of the Soviet regime, Islam was unquestionably the strongest and most durable cultural influence to have taken root in the area. Before the arrival of the Russians, Islamic culture not only survived but was actually embraced by all non-Muslim invaders such as the Karakhandis and Mongols. Only a small part of the population, mainly the upper classes, was influenced by Russian culture under the Tsarist regime. Although it generally adopted a fairly tolerant and indifferent attitude towards Islam, from time to time the Tsarist regime would become rather hostile towards Islam and its followers. Even the openly hostile Soviet attitude towards the Islamic creed and way of life failed to eradicate the Islamic influence. Its effect would have been even less if the start of the Soviet regime had not coincided with the collapse of the Ottoman Empire and the abolition of the Caliphate in Turkey.[1]

Islam had its apogee in Uzbekistan during the Samanid Dynasty, under which Bukhara became an important centre of Islamic learning. It was here that the *Madrasah* (Muslim higher educational establishment) had its origin. The heyday of Islamic culture in this region, however, was during the fourteenth and fifteenth centuries with Samarkand at its centre. At this time, learning and the arts were inseparably associated with Islam and derived great benefit from the close contacts that the region was able to maintain with the rest of the Muslim world. The state of learning, even of popular education, was probably on a par with that of Western Europe. It was far above that of Russia, which was then under the domination of the Mongols who, although converted to Islam, communicated nothing of their spiritual culture to the Russian people. After the fall of the Temurid Dynasty at the beginning of the sixteenth century the creative power of Islamic culture declined. However, the influence of Islam and particularly of the clergy on the lives of the people increased. Later, although the Soviet regime discouraged religious practices, people of faiths continued to practise their religions. The Uzbek government after its independence lifted most religious restrictions. The majority of people in the republic are Muslims, mostly Sunni, but there are also various religious minorities. The Russians brought Russian Orthodox Christianity; a small number of the Korean population follow Buddhism; the Jewish community practises its faith; there are a couple of villages where the inhabitants still practise the Zoroastrian faith; and there is also a small number of Polish communities practising the Catholic faith.

As Bukhara and Samarkand became the cultural centre of the Muslim world from the ninth to the fifteenth century, the people of Uzbekistan also gave the world eminent scientists and famous poets and writers, among whom are the famous astronomer Ferghani, and Muhammed Al-Khorezmi, one of the founders of modern algebra, whose astronomical tables served as a guide for scholars of many generations. Abu-Raikhan Al-Beruni is also regarded as a genius of the medieval East. He wrote 120 works on various branches of science including geography, geology, mineralogy, mathematics, astronomy, history and linguistics. He was the first person to estimate the dimensions of the Earth, and came up with the hypothesis of the rotation of the Earth and its subordinated position in relation to the Sun. Abu Ali Ibn Sina (known as Avicenna in the West), who was born outside Bukhara, was a worldly renowned scholar and physician. His main work, *Canon of Medicine*, had a great impact on the development of medicine. Ulugbek also occupies an important place in the world catalogue of famous scientists.

Environment
The environmental problems in the Central Asian states of the former Soviet Union reflect the region's combination of heavy industrial pollution, equivalent in some areas to that found in developed countries, coupled with sanitation and infrastructural problems on a level with many developing countries. The region is home to one of the greatest environmental tragedies of all times – the drying up of the Aral Sea, which threatens to have a global impact.[2] The extent and rapidity of this process bears testimony both to the Soviet Union's success in implementing massive projects, for example a cotton-monoculture in Uzbekistan, and to its total disregard for environmental issues. The Aral Sea basin covers an area of 690,000 square kilometres. All the Central Asian republics own a greater or lesser share of the basin. Uzbekistan and Kazakstan share the sea itself. Water-rich Kyrgyzstan and Tajikistan contain the sources of

the Syrdarya and Amu Darya respectively, while Uzbekistan, Kazakstan and Turkmenistan together with Afghanistan share the lower reaches. In 1960 it was the fourth largest inland lake in the world, but today the Aral Sea is less than half its original size. The small amount of water reaching the sea is highly salty and heavily polluted with pesticides, fertilizers, and defoliants. Some of these polluted waters are diverted to the adjacent deserts, creating new salt swamps and causing ground water to rise. The rising ground water, in turn, causes logging water that has adverse effects on the development of agricultural land, and adds to the overall salinization of the region. Ground water in most areas is no longer suitable for drinking. The decline of the Aral Sea is inextricably linked to the fate of its two main rivers, the Amu Darya and the Syrdarya. The Amu Darya spans 2,540 kilometres from the confluence of the Pyanje and Vakhsh in Tajikistan to the Aral Sea. The Syrdarya stretches for some 2,200 kilometres from the Naryn River in Kyrgyzstan through the Fergana Valley, Hungry Steppe and Kzyl Kum Desert. These two rivers account for 90 per cent of the average river flow of Central Asia, totalling 122 cubic kilometres per year. Half of this flow is lost naturally through filtration and evaporation. Until the late-1950s, approximately 50 to 60 cubic kilometres of water per year reached the Aral Sea.[3]

When the Russians conquered the Khanates of Turkestan in the late nineteenth century, they introduced new irrigation technologies and began large-scale cotton cultivation. With the consolidation of Soviet power in the 1920s, irrigation was extensively developed in the area of the most favourable thermal, water and soil conditions in the territory of the former Soviet Union. Irrigation lands grew by more than 3.5 million hectares between 1950 and 1988, mostly in the territory of Uzbekistan. In order to support this massive increase of irrigated lands, water was withdrawn indiscriminately. Ninety-six per cent of annual water resources were consumed, leaving only four cubic kilometres of flow for the Aral Sea. In some dry years in the 1980s, no water flowed into the Aral at all.[4] Until 1960, the volume of the Aral Sea was generally in equilibrium, as evaporation from the surface was counterbalanced by inflow from rivers, ground water and rainfall. Since the 1960s, demand for the water resources of the basin has risen dramatically. The irrigated area expanded by over one-third between 1965 and 1988, while the consumption of water tripled to meet the needs of the rise in agriculture and population. The use of water often exceeded the stream flow of the rivers. Much water, even today, still goes to waste, due to an inefficient distribution system and very high water application rates on farms. Irrigation efficiencies account for about 45 per cent. The main reason for the fall in the quantity of river water, however, was not the increase in the area under cotton cultivation, but the damming of the two main rivers and the large water losses in the Karakum Canal. Hence, the balance was disturbed through filtration and evaporation even before water reached the fields. The 1,200-kilometre Karakum Canal, in Turkmenistan, flows directly over loose sand, and overall losses through filtration are estimated to total one-third of all the water used for irrigation in the region. While cotton needs only 8–10,000 cubic metres of water per hectare, average per hectare withdrawals in Central Asia were around 18,700 before falling to 13,700 cubic metres in 1986.[5]

The reason for this above-average usage was mainly the heavy salinization of soils in the region. This caused intensive leaching or washing of fields recently under irrigation, and the periodic leaching of almost all irrigated lands. Poor drainage made the leaching process less effective and consequently wasted further water. This almost complete extraction of water destined for the Aral Sea resulted in severe consequences for the Sea, its tributaries, and surrounding ecosystems. Historically, the natural fluctuations of the sea level due to climatic changes in its basins were between 1.5 and 2 metres. The volume of water fluctuated by only 100–150 cubic kilometres and the surface area by 4,000 square kilometres. Since 1960, the Aral Sea has lost 75 per cent of its volume, while its surface area has shrunk by 50 per cent of its previous surface. Its shores have declined dramatically, in some places by more than 120 kilometres, leaving ecological devastation in its wake, and over 33,000 square kilometres of former seabed uncovered.[6] The exposed seabed is thick with agricultural chemical residues and salt, which are carried by strong winds and deposited over a wide area, affecting crops, natural vegetation, soil quality, water supply, air quality, and the health of animals and people. On the desertified bed of the Aral Sea, an area of about 36,000 square kilometres, a white alkali soil has developed. There, an estimated 75 million tons of toxic salt and dust are dispersed every year. This windborne dust, which can move in belts as wide as 40 kilometres, is a serious threat to plants and soils in the agricultural areas of the basin. An average of over 500 kilograms of salt and sand fall every year on each hectare of the Amu Darya delta, and affect to some extent lands much farther away. This contributes to spreading desertification in the Aral region, where moving sands are encroaching upon agricultural land and residential areas. Erosion is increasingly serious, especially in the southern Kazakstan steppe and in mountain valleys.

Water and soil quality is seriously damaged by the excessive use and dumping of agricultural chemicals. Huge quantities of herbicides, pesticides, fertilizers and defoliants were used to combat pests and diseases. On cotton fields in Karakalpakistan, pesticides were used at ten times the USSR average, and overall use of pesticides in Uzbekistan exceeded normal requirements by six times. By the end of the 1980s, more than three billion cubic metres of drainage water contaminated with agricultural chemicals from Uzbek and Turkmen fields were being dumped every year into the Amu Darya.[7] Industrial sources also played a part in the chemical contamination of natural resources in the Aral basin, though to a far lesser extent due to the relatively underdeveloped state of industry in the region. However, the basin does contain numerous industries, including oil and gas refining, ferrous and non-ferrous metal refining, chemical, and machinery industries. Each contributed to pollution by discharging wastewater runoff from waste dumps, and air pollution resulting from deposition. In Uzbekistan alone, the annual volume of polluted industrial waste reached 300 million cubic metres, up to 70 per cent of which was discharged without any purification.

The level of salinity of the Aral Sea tripled to 30 grams per litre, transforming completely the nature of the marine ecosystem and the organisms that can survive in the Sea. Vast areas of coastal waters lost their natural plant and animal life, and fish life was devastated. The land around the Sea and in cultivated areas of the lower basin has become more saline, less fertile, and increasingly threatened by desertification. The water resources of the basin were contaminated with chemicals from pesticides and fertilizers drained from the fields, as well as other pollutants from upstream users. By the time the two main rivers reach the Sea, there is little water left for those at the end of the line. The low quality of the water in this region causes high rates of intestinal diseases, hepatitis, throat cancer, liver ailments, kidney failure and even typhoid. Illness rates are appalling, and infant mortality rates are the highest in the former Soviet Union.[8]

Although the countries of the Aral Sea basin are committed to pursuing a path of sustainable development and improving the environmental conditions of the affected regions, independence has further complicated the process. Ironically, while the disintegration of the former Soviet Union paved the way for wider recognition of the disastrous environmental condition of the Aral Sea region, the dissolution of the Union made it more difficult to address the environmental crisis in an integrated manner. Moreover, drastic economic changes have limited the capacity of the Central Asian states to address the situation effectively. However, with wider global recognition of the problems faced by the region, international commitment to assistance has grown. An international conference on the sustainable development of the Aral Sea basin, held in Karakalpakistan in September 1995, was a landmark event bringing together the representatives and citizens of the Central Asian states, and mobilizing international support for the rehabilitation efforts. The Nukus Declaration, signed by the five Heads of State, expressed a high-level regional commitment to jointly address the problems.[9] In order to coordinate regional efforts and to deal with basin-wide problems, two apex organizations were established by the five basin countries: the Interstate Council for the Aral Sea (ICAS) is responsible for deciding on the policies and projects to be pursued; and the International Fund for the Aral Sea (IFAS) was established to provide a vehicle for managing financial resources devoted to the crisis by the founding states, international organizations, donor countries and others. The initial phase of a multi-sectoral programme of action to address the ecological and social aspects of the Aral Sea crisis began implementation in early 1995. Subsequent phases will support a long-term, large-scale programme to address a wide range of environmental issues. International funding will be provided by multilateral, bilateral, private sector and non-governmental organizations. Halting the degradation and repairing the damage will take many years and require high levels of investment.

Women in Uzbek society

The population of Uzbekistan is young, with 43 per cent under 16 years of age. Over half of the population is female and the life expectancy of women is 72 years, exceeding that of men by six years. As a result of the Soviet legacy, Uzbek women today enjoy higher levels of literacy, a legal system that does not discriminate against them and better social protection than women in other countries of comparable income levels.[10]

The Constitution of the country includes several provisions aimed at securing the equality of women before the law. Article 18 disallows all forms of discrimination based on creed or gender. Article 117 provides the right to vote and to be elected to public offices at all levels. It has also placed great importance on family obligations. The civic law that regulates marriage and divorce is based on the Soviet Family Code. It contains provisions aimed at securing the equality of partners in the marital union. The legal age for marriage is 17 for women and 18 for men. Younger unions are also possible but subject to special dispensation to be obtained from *Hokimiyat* authorities. Marriage is monogamous and divorce is extremely rare, though partners have equal rights with respect to initiating divorce. The equal rights accorded to women in civic law, however, have little bearing on the customary practices for the rural majority. Girls, in most cases, marry into the households of their husband's fathers and the only form of property they bring to marriage usually consists of their trousseau – namely household implements, linens and jewellery. Although women may work hard for their households they normally have no claim on their husband's family property. In dual-breadwinner urban households, the law may find more direct application. The Labour Code includes many items of protective legislation directed to women. They are excluded from occupations considered heavy or hazardous and from working on night shifts. Pregnant women and women with children under three years old are offered special protection at work. Provisions for maternity leave and benefits are also generous in Uzbekistan. The maternity allowance is 100 per cent of the mother's wage regardless of length of service. The payments begin after thirty weeks of pregnancy and continue for about five months. Women are entitled to up to three years of unpaid leave. All women caring for children under two years of age receive a monthly benefit of 20 per cent of the minimum wage.

There are nine registered women's organizations in the republic. The National Women's Committee is a semi-governmental organization, established in 1991, and has about three million members. It acts on women-related issues and policies, and its main aims are to improve women's health and related issues, their economic situations, establish contact with international organizations dealing with women's issues, and increase awareness of gender issues and develop related expertise. The Business Women's Association is a non-government organization (NGO) and was also created in 1991. It aims to support women's entrepreneurial activities. It has five branches in Uzbekistan – in Tashkent, Bukhara, Samarkand, Fergana and Surkhandarya. These comprise about three thousand members who pay a membership fee. The Women's Resource Centre is also an NGO and was set up in late 1995. It aims to provide information and enlighten women in the republic as well as to establish contacts with other women's organizations in the region and other international women's organizations. The organization acts at the city level, researching women's issues in the *mahallas*. To support professional and scholarly women in the republic, a semi-governmental National Association of Olima (women scholars) was set up in 1996. Its main aim is to support women's scholar activities as well as assist those who wants to set up their own businesses. It works in close contact with the National Women's Committee and receives almost all the assistance it needs from this organization. To assist and support women in the Karakalpak autonomous republic, a Family Planning Association of Karakalpakistan was created in late 1995 as an NGO. The aim of this association is to improve women's health and deal with the health issues which result from the Aral Sea disaster. It also aims to deal with family planning in the region. There is also a Women's Committee of Karakalpakistan, which also acts on women-related issues and policies in the region. There has been a campaign by the government 'For a Healthy Generation' to improve mother and child health throughout the country. For this purpose a National Foundation for a Healthy Generation was founded. Its campaign not only seeks measures for adequate birth spacing and rational family planning; it is also a reflection of a gradualist approach to reverse the strongly pro-nationalist policies of the Soviet times. There is a Red Crescent Society, which acts to provide help to women in general. The Centre for Young Women Leaders was created in late 1996 by Mahbuba Ergasheva, a national expert on women's issues. The centre acts to improve women's legal and socio-economic status in Uzbekistan. It has become a non-governmental volunteer organization, and aims to support women of all ethnic groups regardless of their age and race. It also seeks to strengthen the status of women and their role in the solving of issues at the State level, and to increase women's social activity.

    The role of the Uzbek women in politics has declined since the 1980s, marked by the elimination of representation through a system of quotas. The number of elected women at both national and local levels has decreased. 'This shows the largely tokenistic nature of the former Soviet system and the low level of acceptance of women's involvement in politics'.[11] In 1985 the proportion of women in the decision making level of government was about 35 per cent but by 1996 it had fallen to just 8 per cent. On 2 March 1995, with a presidential decree, the chairperson of the National Women's Committee became a deputy Prime Minister. There were 15 women deputies in the parliament. The chairperson of the election committee of the president Sayora Rashidova is also a woman. There were 12 deputy *hokims* of the large *oblasts* (regions), such as Tashkent, Samarkand, Bukhara, Navoi, Khorezm, and a number of deputy *hokims* in city and small district levels. Women's representation in the judicial bodies is also high. One judge in every five is a woman.

All these initiatives will clearly contribute to achieving the necessary changes to mobilize a concerned public around women's interests and tackle the problems that Uzbek women face during the transition to a market economy and a society based on democratic principles. Most of the problems Uzbek women face today are socio-economic. Women in Uzbekistan comprise over 52 per cent of the country's total population and 61 per cent of them live in rural areas working mainly in the agricultural sector for the associations of cooperatives of farmers. Most are involved in hard manual work. They earn very little money and in most cases payments are delayed for months. Women who live in big cities such as Tashkent, Samarkand and Bukhara have more opportunities and better facilities regarding employment, information and education. The growth of active governmental and non-governmental women's organizations and advocacy groups is a positive move towards improving the status and position of women in the republic. They have good networks, a huge number of members, the power to deal with women's issues and are eager to learn new ideas. But they lack funding, have no clear mission or plan, are not able to use their power, are weak, need to reform the existing system and themselves and suffer from a lack of training. In addition, the organizations are not cooperating with each other, but competing against each other.

The ancient history of Uzbekistan
Uzbekistan is one of the world's earliest inhabited places and was the

home of an ancient and highly developed civilization. It was in the agricultural areas that the first comparatively large-scale political organizations were formed. The country's location in Central Asia made it a natural choice for trade routes. There were always struggles for control over this central point and this, since ancient times, made it the centre of the creation or dissolution of many great empires that existed in this part of the Asian Continent.

In ancient times human beings lived in the territory now known as Uzbekistan, hunting and gathering their food until about 2000 BC. Then the first settled agricultural societies started developing farming, sheep breeding, and growing barley and millet. In mountainous regions, where little cropland was available, the raising of livestock was particularly important. The first urban settlement in the south of Uzbekistan appeared around 1500 BC and it is believed that this was founded by people of Iranian origin. In the seventh century BC the region came under the economic and political domination of more cultured peoples, first of Medea and later of Persia. Under these influences the primitive communal establishments in the region were gradually dissolved. So the area of modern-day Uzbekistan was subsumed under several ancient Persian states, including Bactria in the south and Khorezm (the territory of modern Karakalpakistan) in the north-west. The capital of this Kingdom of Bactria-Sogdiana was at Maracanda (Samarkand) in the south-east. From the sixth century BC Uzbekistan had come under the authority of Cyrus, the first King of Persia's Achaemenid Dynasty (family of rulers), and remained under Achaemenian control until the fourth century BC. Cyrus introduced the Zoroastrian religion and expanded the Persian Empire's borders far to the west and east.[12]

Around the end of the fourth century BC Alexander the Great of Macedonia invaded the region and overthrew the Achaemenians. He had crossed the Hindu Kush Mountains, marched into Central Asia and occupied Bactria (now Balkh) and Sogdiana (the ancient name of the territory now covered by the districts of Samarkand and Bukhara). During this campaign Alexander destroyed the chief town of Sogdiana-Marakand, and he and his successors introduced a new element, that of Hellenism, to the region; subsequently, from the middle of the third century BC, the present-day Uzbekistan formed part of the Greco-Bactrian State. His marriage to Roxana, a Bactrian princess, brought Greek influence to the region. After his death in 323 BC his empire crumbled and was divided by his generals, with Seleucus taking the old Persian land in Uzbekistan. The Seleucuid Kingdom lasted a few centuries until, in 159 BC, Mongolian tribes (Scythians) invaded Sogdiana and, in 139 BC, Bactria. During the first century AD a union of nomadic tribes was formed under the rule of the Kushan tribe of the Hindu Kush Mountains of northern Afghanistan and these pushed into Uzbekistan. Kushan Kings adopted the faith of Buddhism and spread its message. The Kushan Empire's economy depended on trade and the overland caravan routes. The entire region of Central Asia was linked by the 'Silk Road' of the transcontinental trade routes, which for almost two millennia served an economic network encompassing China, India, Europe, the Middle East and the Black Sea basin. The principal seat of the Kushan was Bactria, and their power was at its zenith at the end of the first and the beginning of the second centuries AD.

At the end of the second century, Kushan rule began to decay, and in the middle of the fifth century a related tribe, the Ephthalites, or White Huns, conquered Bactria and put a complete end to Kushan rule in Central Asia. But the rule of the White Huns did not last very long. Their power was undermined by the attacks of the nomadic Turks, and their rule collapsed in the late sixth century.[13] When they started threatening the security of Persia, the then Sasanian Emperor, Khosrau Anoshirvan (AD 531–79) allied himself with the Turks and crushed the Hephthalites in a fierce battle soon after AD 557. Their lands were partitioned along the river of the Oxus (Amu Darya) between the Sasanians, who took the southern part while the Turks took all that lay to the north (see Appendix A, Map 2). The founder of the Turkish Empire was the chief called, in Chinese sources, Tu-men (Bumin in the Turkish inscription). The residence of the Turkish Khan was established in the Aq Tagh (Akdag) to the north of Kucha. The western expansion of the Turkish realm reached as far as the Oxus and the Caspian Sea, and the area came under the virtually independent rule of Istemi the brother of Tu-men (called Sinjbu, or Silzibul, in the western sources). It was he who formed an alliance with Khosrau Anushirvan I of Persia, which resulted in the destruction of the Hephthalite Kingdom, and established the Turkish Empire. In AD 576 Istemi died, but Turkish influence remained strong in Sogdiana, even though both parts of the Turkish Empire made nominal concessions to the T'ang Dynasty of China, the eastern Turks in AD 630, and the western Turks in AD 659. However, the first record of the presence of the Turks in Central Asia dates from the mid-sixth century. The Turks rapidly gained control of a vast territory including part of the route of the 'Silk Road'. After settling in the agricultural areas of Uzbekistan, they changed their nomadic way of life and turned to farming and trade. Their Empire survived in one form or another, despite frequent attacks from the Chinese, until the mid-eighth century, when they were overthrown by yet another wave of Turkish tribes, the Uighurs. The progress of Turkish incursions into the region continued up to the early sixteenth century. By the tenth century, however, the earlier inhabitants had been either expelled or overwhelmed to the extent that much of Central Asia came to be known as 'Turkestan' (land of the Turks).[14] This does not imply that the region was united under a single ruler, which indeed was not the case, but that the vast majority of the population spoke 'Turkish'. Some of the Turk tribes remained nomadic, but others in the south and the west adopted a sedentary way of life and were converted to Islam.

After invading the Sasanids Dynasty of Persia, the Arabs conquered the entire land of Uzbekistan in the eighth century. By introducing Islam, they not only brought to the region a new belief system, but also a new social order and a new 'epistemology'. The ancient cities of Khiva, Bukhara and Samarkand had become important centres of Muslim learning. In time they produced some of the greatest scholars and finest buildings in the world. The Arabs soon withdrew, but administratively the region remained under the jurisdiction of Khorasan (Northern Persia) working for the Arab Dynasty. In the ninth century, however, the first independent Muslim State in Uzbekistan was founded by a Persian Dynasty from Khorasan. In 875 Samankhoda, a Persian noble, founded the Samanid Dynasty with Bukhara as its capital. Under Samanid rule, Samarkand, Termez, Khorezm and Tashkent became major commercial, religious and educational centres. Caravans continued to travel through Uzbekistan, bringing leather, silk, wool and livestock from areas as far north as the Baltic Sea.[15]

At the end of the tenth century the Samanid state was overthrown by the Turkish tribes of the Karakhandis (932–1165) who established themselves in Bukhara but extended their borders further to the east, to the Ili and Chu rivers (Modern Xinjang). Karakhandis became the first Turkish Muslim State. The settled Turks in the cities of present-day Uzbekistan were heavily influenced by Muslim culture, and in the

Bukhara-Samarkand regions, *Farsi* (Persian) continued to be the main vehicle for administration, literature and trade, despite the emergence of Turkish literary languages, such as Karakhandis and later, Chagatai.[16] The Karakhandis State was overrun by Qara-Khitay of the nomadic Liao dynasty of China. This had been driven out of China by rival tribes and had crossed Central Asia to win control of the declining empire of the Karakhandis, which had decayed as a result of inter-tribal frictions and the arrival of the Selchuk Turks. A new independent kingdom emerged, including the Ghaznavid State in what is now south Uzbekistan and the Khorezm State in the north-west. Thus, on the eve of the invasion of Chinggis Khan, the empire of the Qara-Khitay was dissolving and by the late eleventh century Khorezm had become the most powerful domain in the region. The Khorezm Shah was exercising sole rule over all the Central Asian territories. Khorezm's power, however, did not last long. In 1211 a huge army of Mongols under Chinggis Khan marched on Central Asia, accompanied by his best commanders and his four sons, Jochi, Chagatai, Ogetei and Tolui (see Appendix B). He crossed the Jurchid frontiers and swept through northern China. The Mongols attacked in 1220, massacring much of the population and destroying cities, farms and irrigation works in Central Asia. The rule of the Mongols in this region, in various vicissitudes and forms, lasted for several centuries. After the death of Chinggis Khan in 1227, the Mongols intermingled with the local people and adopted their language and culture. Chinggis's death greatly affected the course of Mongol expansion, and the momentum of his initial conquests was sustained for more than half a century.[17]

Before his death, Chinggis Khan had divided his conquests among his four sons; Jochi, the eldest, was allotted as his *Ulus* (fief) the Mongol conquests west of the Irtysh (part of modern-day Kazakhstan and Western Siberia). As Jochi predeceased his father, this immense area passed to his son Batu, who enlarged it at the expense of his western neighbours, founding an empire which became known as the *Altin Orda* (Golden Horde), and expanded his kingdom by invading southern Russia, Poland and Hungary. Chinggis Khan's second son, Chagatai, was allotted Uiguristan (East Turkestan), Maverannahr, Kashgaria (Ili river oases) and Semirechie (the lands of the Seven Rivers). After Chagatai's death in 1241, his descendants ruled for nearly a century and in the early fourteenth century the *Ulus* disintegrated. In modern-day Uzbekistan, Chagatai khans fought each other in the name of rival puppet khans of Chinggiskhanid stock until the emergence of Temur (Timurlane) as ruler of this land in the second half of the fourteenth century. The third son, Ogetai, received eastern Jungaria, Mongolia and the Chinese provinces already conquered. In accordance with Mongol custom, the fourth son, Tolui, took charge of his father's household, including the treasury and the ancestral pastures together with the 'crack-troops' of the Empire. This territorial division was a traditional Mongol family arrangement, in order to preserve the unity of the Empire on the basis of family cooperation.[18] As Chinggis Khan's eldest son, Jochi received as his share of his father's Empire the lands west of the Irtysh together with Khorezm; to the west of Jochi's *Ulus* and the north of the Caspian and the Black Sea lay the unconquered Dasht-i Qipchaq, inhabited by several other Turkish tribes such as Cumans. To the north of that lay the Bulgar Khanate of the upper Volga and the Russian principalities. During the lifetime of Jochi, the Mongols took little interest in these peoples. Between 1237 and 1242 Jochi's second son Batu, assisted by the veteran Subetei, extinguished the Bulgar Khanate, subdued the tribes of the Dasht-i Qipchaq and the Russians. Kiev was sacked in 1240 and penetrated deep into Poland and Hungary in 1241. During this period, the Mongol ruling class and its Turkish troops gradually assimilated themselves with the original inhabitants of the Dasht-i Qipchaq to become the Tatars of later times. Islam became the dominant religion, and the Tatar language began to evolve as a *lingua franca*. Meanwhile the death of Ogetai, the last surviving son of Chinggis, in 1241 produced the first signs of strain in the unity of the Mongol Empire. In 1255 Jochi's second son Batu died and, except for the five-year reign of his brother, Berke, the Golden Horde (*Ulus* of Batu) was ruled for over a century by his direct descendants, until 1359, when the throne passed to descendants of the other sons of Jochi. By 1258 Berke was the undisputed ruler. A man of restless ambition, energy and great ability, he was one of the most outstanding Mongol rulers of the thirteenth century and the first to become an avowed Muslim.[19]

His successor, Mongke-Temur (1267–80), a grandson of Batu, inherited from Berke the Mamluk alliance, the struggle for the Caucuses and a tenuous friendship with the Chagatai Khans based upon mutual hostility towards their relatives in Persia and China. These factors further intensified the isolation of the Golden Horde from the rest of the Mongol World, and drew it closer to the commerce and culture of the Mediterranean.[20] During the reigns of Ozbeg(k) Khan (1312–42), Mongke-Temur's grandson, and his own son Jonibeck (1342–57), the Golden Horde became a fully-fledged Islamic state, which was thereafter called Uzbek Khanate. The conversion of the Golden Horde to Islam was an event of crucial importance in the history of both the Tatars (as the Muslims of the Golden Horde will henceforth be called) and the Russians, since thereafter the two peoples were divided from each other by religion and culture, making future assimilation impossible. After Uzbek Khan's death in 1342 and his son Jonibek's death in 1357 the dynastic stability that the Golden Horde had enjoyed for almost a century ended. Following this a period of twenty years' anarchy ensued while various descendants of Jochi struggled for power. The Golden Horde (the Uzbek Khanate) was experiencing a period of instability until the emergence of Tuqtamush, a descendant of Batu's eldest brother Hordu, who by 1381 was the Khan of the *Ak Horde* (White Horde), and who became the undisputed ruler of the Uzbek Khanate.[21] Before he had gained control of the Uzbek Khanate he had to engage in a bitter struggle for leadership with his kinsmen of the White Horde (the original *Ulus* of Hordu). To succeed in this he needed the assistance from Temur (Timurlane), a nominal vassal of the Chagatai Khan of present-day Uzbekistan, who was trying to establish his own empire. War later broke out between Temur and Tuqtamush between 1389 and 1395. Subsequently, in 1395 Temur himself marched through the Caucuses from Azerbaijan and defeated Tuqtamush.[22]

Amir Temur (1369–1405) was born in 1336 in the village of Khodja-Ilgar, near Shahrisabz. His father was Taraghai, a Turkish amir of the Barlas tribe, a devout Muslim and a friend to scholars and dervishes alike. In 1370, after bitter struggles with rivals, the Mugholistan Khan Tuglug-Temur, Temur, the fourteenth-century potentate defeated his uncle, Hoji Barlas, proclaimed Amir Temur the ruler of Kesh and sent his son Ilias-Hodi to rule present-day Uzbekistan. Temur did not like Ilias-Hodi. After the death of Tuglug-Temur, he invaded Balkh with the help of Turkish Amir Kozagan's grandson Husein. Amir Temur repaired the Mongolian destruction, erected superb buildings, encouraged science and the arts, and yet retained restless ferocity. During the 1360s he established a large military following and a position of exceptional strength among the amirs and chieftains of the Turkish-Mongol Chagatai

Ulus, who had dominated Maverannahr since the Mongol conquest of a century and a half earlier. In 1370 he was *de facto* ruler of Maverannahr.[23] He continued to extend his rule and finally, in 1395, he defeated the already weakened Uzbek Khanate of the Golden Horde, which at that time held sway over a large part of Russia. Between 1381 and 1404, Amir Temur took Persia, Azerbaijan, Iraq, Syria, India and defeated the Ottoman Sultan Yildirim Beyazid I, sacking his land and then starting preparations for a big expedition to China. Amir Temur deemed that 'if there is one God in the world, then there must also be one ruler'.[24] He then conquered territory from the Black Sea in the west, to India in the east, and formed his own empire. Bukhara became his empire's religious and educational centre, while Samarkand became its capital. After the death of Temur in 1405 the unity of his empire collapsed and in 1447 it began breaking up.

The overthrow of Tuqtamush after 1395 also cleared the way for the emergence of the last important figure in the history of the Golden Horde: Idiku, a Nogay Tatar of the Mangit clan. In 1395 he restored the prestige of the Uzbek Khanate of the Golden Horde with its western neighbours and with the Russian princes after defeating Grand Duke Vitold of Lithuania (1377–1430). In the east, he recaptured Khorezm from the Temurids in 1405–6, and advanced as far as the neighbourhood of Bukhara. His unfortunate death in 1419 precipitated a struggle among the Tatar chieftains who aspired to take his place. The Uzbek Khanate began to decline because of these conflicts and, as a result, during the fifteenth century the Golden Horde disintegrated. By the middle of fifteenth century the original *Ulus* of Batu (the Golden Horde) had completely disappeared and in its place were the independent Khanates at Kazan and Astrakhan, on the Volga and in the Crimea. In addition to the White Horde in modern-day Kazakstan, there was the Nogay Horde, with its capital near the future city of Tobolsk, and ruled by the descendants of Batu's brother Sibagan (Shayban) in 1380.[25]

In 1428, Abu-l Khayr Khan, a descendent of Shayban, having become paramount chieftain of the Shaybanid *Ulus*, succeeded in uniting all the nomadic tribes between the Ural river, the Syrdarya, Mugholistan and the Tobol (see Appendix A, Map 3). He then formed a new state and called it Uzbekistan, named after his grandfather, Uzbek Khan. An energetic ruler, Abu-l Khayr tried to extend his possession and, in 1430, attacked his southern Temurid neighbours, taking possession of part of Khwarazm and sacking the ancient city of Urgench. In 1447 he seized the Syrdarya region from the Temurids. This region was held to be the key to the conquest of Maverannahr and its thriving cities provided an important market for the exchange of goods between the nomads from the north and the sedentary population from across the river to the south. He made one of these cities, *Sighnaq*, his capital. At its height, the Uzbek Empire of Abu-l Khayr extended from the Syrdarya to the Siberian forests where another Shaybani prince, Ibak, had founded the allied Khanate of Sibir.[26]

To consolidate his authority, Abu-l Khayr sought to establish a centralized system of government, which would entail crushing the quasi-independent position of the Chinggiskhanid chieftains, who were his vassals. However, such a goal in a nomadic society was doomed to failure. Rather than bringing about unity, it caused division and, as a result, two Jochid princes, Koray and Janibek, broke free and followed by a large number of tribes, sought refuge with Esenbuqa, the Chagatai Khan of Mugholistan. These dissident tribes received the name of 'Kazak', meaning free people. Such major defections left Abu-l Khayr susceptible to the Mongol Empire of the Oirats. In 1450 the Buddhist Oirats launched their first raids in the direction of the Muslim steppes, and such raids were thereafter repeated periodically, and with the utmost ferocity. In 1456–7 the Oirats penetrated deep into the steppes and inflicted upon Abu-l Khayr a crushing defeat that caused irreparable damage to the Uzbek Empire. The Syrdarya region was ravaged from end to end. The Khans Koray and Janibek with their Kazak tribes were quick to take advantage of the situation. Following the departure of the Oirat Hordes, they returned to the steppes in force and in 1468 defeated and killed Abu-l Khayr in a great battle. The son of Abu-l Khayr, Shaykh Haydar, was also killed in the same year by Yunus Khan of Mugholistan. Thus, from the race of Shayban there remained only a young grandson of Abu-l Khayr, Muhammad Shaybani. He was born around 1451 and, after taking power, he seized, one by one, the petty principalities that were all that remained of Temur's original conquests. The last generations of Temurid princes were too deeply involved in quarrels among themselves to be able to offer a concerted front against the usurper. Maverannahr was the scene of continual conflicts among Temur's remaining descendants, including Babor himself, descended from Temur through his paternal grandfather, Abu Said. While Babor and his cousins were fighting for the thrones of Fergana and Samarkand, a formidable new power had established itself between the Syrdarya and the Amu Darya, that of the Uzbeks under Muhammad Shaybani, grandson of the unfortunate Abu-l Khayr. By 1500, therefore, he was the undisputed master of Maverannahr, having taken in that year Bukhara, Qarshi and Samarkand. He founded on the ruins of the Temurid Empire the last great Empire of Turkestan, the Uzbek Khanate over which his family were to rule for nearly a century. Muhammad Shaybani extended his conquest even further with the capture of Balkh and Qunduz while the defeat of his old patron, Muhammad, brought him Tashkent and the Fergana Valley, and during 1505–6 he captured Khorezm.[27]

The migration of the Shaybanid tribes into Maverannahr left a vacuum on the steppes north of the Syrdarya. This vacuum was rapidly filled by the 'Kazak' tribes which had originally followed Koray and Janibek into Mugholistan and which now returned to their homeland. During the reign of Burunduk Khan (1488–1509), the son of Koray, and especially during that of Kasym (1509–18), the son of Janibek, the Kazak tribes spread rapidly throughout the territory of the former Khanate of Abu-l Khayr. From this time onwards the terms 'Kazak' and 'Uzbek' assumed a new significance. The former designated the tribes remaining north of the Syrdarya, and the latter those that had followed Muhammad Shaybani and established themselves south of the river. However, both were derived from the same ancestral tribes.

As the Uzbek Empire replaced the Mongol Empire, the Safavid Dynasty came to power in Persia. The founder of the Safavids, Shah Ismail (1502–14) established the Shiite form of the Islamic faith as his state's religion. The Uzbeks, who followed the Sunni branch, fought many wars with the Safavids. At the same time there was a series of conflicts between Kazaks and Uzbeks. Although the Kazaks generally seemed to have emerged victorious, they were no nearer to their objective of conquering Maverannahr. Although the Kazaks occasionally dominated the Uzbeks, the conflicts not only gave Shah Ismail a great opportunity to attack the Uzbeks in 1510, but also gave the Oirats and later the Kalmuyks the chance to attack both the Kazaks and Uzbeks, until the Kazaks became the nominal vassal of Russia in 1724.

In December 1510 the armies of Shaybani and Shah Ismail met near Merv and after fierce fighting, Muhammad Shaybani, along with his exhausted army, was defeated and killed. Shah Ismail ordered Shaybani's skull to be set in gold and made into a drinking cup and the skin of his head, stuffed with straw, to be sent to the Ottoman Sultan Bayazid II, ruler of the Sunni faith and the nominal allay of the Uzbeks. Such was the end of Muhammad Shaybani, a brilliant leader in the great tradition of Central Asian conquerors who was also a man of considerable culture and versatility. This act of Shah Ismail towards Shaybani's death angered the Ottoman Sultan Yavuz Selim (Bayazid II) and he marched into Persia and inflicted a heavy defeat on the Safavid Dynasty. Shah Ismail was killed there in 1514.

Nevertheless, the Uzbeks, under the Shaybanid Dynasty, held on to their land and Sunni faith and continued farming, cultivating crops and intermingling with the local population. The city's economy, however, still depended on overland trade. In the 1500s, as European merchants and explorers found routes to Asia by sea, the caravan trails lost favour. As commerce in Central Asia declined, the Uzbek Empire, weakened by the loss of trade, broke into independent Khanates each of which was headed by a Khan. The Khanates of Bukhara and Khiva emerged in the sixteenth century and the Khanate of Khokand was formed in the eighteenth century. Thus, the disunity and frequent internal struggles and revolts by nomads reduced their ability to resist foreign powers including the Russian Empire. The rise of Russian power, however, coincided with growing weakness and disunity in the states of western Central Asia, promoting the Russian invasions.

The modern history of Uzbekistan
The invasion of Central Asia also allowed Russia to annex land from the Turks and the Persians in the region. The Russians' goals were primarily economic and strategic. One was to make money at the expense of the Central Asian people; the other was to block any attempt by the British to expand their sphere of influence from their imperial base in India. Indeed it was not until the nineteenth century that the Russians tried to expand into Turkestan. By this time, however, imperial Russia feared British expansion in the area. The British Empire was the leading world power and wanted to make sure that the Russians did not threaten Afghanistan and the empire in India. Eventually Russia decided that it could not allow Turkestan to fall into British hands. The British,

though, had nothing to say as long as Russia did not go further than Central Asia and become a threat to their empire, as the Ottoman Empire was in decline.[28] Thus, the invasion of Turkestan was launched. It was in 1714 that Peter the Great ordered a Russian expedition to penetrate the Trans-Caspian steppes for the first time. Three years later another expedition, led by Prince Bekovich-Cherkasskii, tried to reach Khiva from Astrakhan, but his column was ambushed and destroyed in the desert and he was killed there. In 1715 another column commanded by Bukholz set out from Tobolsk in Siberia, and tried to reach Turkestan from the north. There it came into contact with the Oirats and was compelled to turn back. In 1840 General Perovskii led a strong Russian detachment against Khiva but the expedition was a total failure. In 1847 the Russians built near the mouth of the Syrdarya the Fourth of Raim, which became their first military base on the frontiers of Khiva. In 1855 they won from the Khanate of Khokand the fortress of *Aq Mechet* on the middle course of the Syrdarya. At the same time another offensive, starting from Semipalatinsk threatened Turkestan from the north-east. This resulted in the building of *Verniy* (now Almaty) in 1854.[29] However, the three principalities into which the land was divided, the Bukhara Emirate, and the Khokand and Khiva Khanates, were weakened by internal conflicts. The Russian invasion of the region was also delayed by the Crimean War, the resistance of the Kazak tribes and by the war in the Caucuses. It was only after the final defeat of the Imam Shamil in Daghstan that the invasion was undertaken in a systematic manner. In 1864 a column under General Cherniev, setting out from Verniy, captured the town of Turkestan (*Yasi*), then Chimkent and in May 1865 Tashkent, which had belonged to the Khokand Khanate. Two years later the Russians attacked Bukhara and in 1868 they took Samarkand and defeated Bukharan troops at the battle of Zerabulak. The Amir of Bukhara signed a treaty that placed his state under a Russian protectorate. In 1873 it was the turn of Khiva. The capital of the Khanate was taken and in August a treaty put an end to its independence. Consequently, Khokand was invaded in 1875. The capital surrendered on 29 August and on 19 February 1876 the Khanate, the most dangerous opponent of Russia in Central Asia, was extinguished. Its territory was annexed to the governor-generalship of Turkestan, which placed under military administration responsible to the Ministry of War. It included the total land of Central Asia taken by the Russians.[30]

The Russians maintained a colonial attitude towards these Muslim populations. Contrary to the means (which were very brutal) employed in other Muslim states taken in the west and north of Central Asia, they did not attempt to Russify the indigenous population in Central Asia, nor even have them initiated into European civilization. The Turkestanis were not considered citizens of the empire, nor were they considered as eligible for military service. The Russians particularly opposed contact between the Turkestanis and their more advanced co-religionists the Volga Tatars, and rejected the claims of Tatars to extend to Turkestan the jurisdiction of the Muslim Spiritual Assembly of Orenburg. For all these reasons the awakening of national consciousness among the Turkestanis was far slower than among the other Turks of Russia.

The Russian Tsar abolished the Khokand Khanate in 1876 and added its territory to Russian Turkestan. In late 1880, the Tsar divided the invaded land of Central Asia among Turkestan, Khiva and Bukhara. The Tsarist administration strengthened economic links between the 'centre' and the Central Asian 'periphery', constructed a railway network, and served security and defence needs. However, resistance to Russian colonization began in the 1880s and movements assumed a religious character, a 'Holy War' against 'infidels', which were all crushed. The first of these rebellions was that of the dervish Khan Tore in the Fergana Valley in 1885, followed in 1891 by disturbances in Namangan and in 1892 by riots in Tashkent and in the neighbourhood of Khokand. In 1898 growing disaffection led to a more important movement organized by the Sufi Brotherhood of Naqshi-bandis, the revolt of Ihsan Madali.[31]

Despite censorship, reformist and pan-Turkish ideas began to penetrate Turkestan at the end of the nineteenth century, in the first place deriving impetus from the personal initiative of Ismail Bey Gaspirinski and his Crimean disciples. From 1905 onwards the movement was activated by the Volga Tatars and after 1908 it finally came under the influence of the native disciples. In early 1919 the local Jadid reformer, following the Bolshevik Revolution, formed the local bureau of the Communist Party branch – the 'Muslim Bureau'. Initially Muslim Turkic native communists, led by Turar Ryskulov and Tursun Khojaev, tried to create a supranational state based on the unity of the region's people. They sought to combine local differences in a larger Turkic identity and establish a Communist Turkestan. Lenin was initially in favour of the idea of creating a united Communist Turkestan, but he demanded it be fully dependent on Moscow. On 30 April 1918, the Tashkent Soviets formed the Turkestan Autonomous Soviet Socialist Republic, which encompassed most of the territory of modern Kyrgyzstan. Bukhara and Khiva became the nominally independent People's Republic in 1920. However, disagreements between the local Soviets in Tashkent and Moscow regarding the latter's plan for a division of Turkestan into Uzbek, Turkmen and Kyrgyz (Kazak) parts, led to the removal of Ryuskulov, Khojaev and their associates from the Party in July 1920. A temporary Central Committee was established under General Frunze, and the Muslim Bureau as an organization thereafter vanished. The removal of Ryuskulov, Khojaev and their associates gave rise to young native Bukharan Jadids, like Faizulla Khojaev, Akmal Ikramov and his followers. Once Moscow had fallen into dispute with the local leaders of the Turkestan Communist Party in Tashkent, who were in favour of a Soviet Turkestan, a larger multinational entity, the new players were probably in favour of smaller units based on ethnic or regional differences. The Jadid reformist movement attempted to unite all the Turkic people of Tsarist Russia in Central Asia under the flag of the Turkestan Autonomous Soviet Socialist Republic, but the leaders were largely out of touch with the masses. The pan-Turkist ideas that they sought to insert in people's minds in the region simply led to the emergence of different ethnic consciousness – Uzbek, Turkmen, Kazak, Kyrgyz and Tajik. This was because of the regional divisions and mutual animosities, plus the power and personal ambitions of the Central Asian politicians. In concert with the young Bukharan radicals, Moscow wanted to establish state units in order to encourage emerging or artificial nations. According to the Soviet nationalities policy, these would later give way to a stronger 'Soviet nation'. Hence, in 1924 the Bolsheviks, together with local native politicians, proposed the partition plan known as the 'national delimitation' of borders. Local factions in Central Asia who opposed the policies of the 'national delimitation' and who wanted instead an independent Turkestan, formed an anti-Soviet resistance group known as the *Basmachi* Movement, centred in the Fergana Valley. The 'national delimitation' took place in 1924 and the movement was finally defeated by the Soviet Red Army in 1926.[32] This process drew new borders, which created five Central Asian Soviet Socialist Republics (SSRs). Uzbekistan was formed consisting of the Fergana region with the exclusion of districts with a predominantly Kara-Kyrgyz (i.e. Kyrgyz) population; the Bukharan state, with the exclusion of parts of the Chärjew and Kerki regions; the Samarkand region, with the exception of the five nomad towns in Jizzakh region; the Khorezm state with the exception of regions with Turkmen and Kyrgyz (i.e. Kazak) population; and the city of Tashkent and Mirzachol district of Syrdarya region. It was immediately given full Union Republic status on 27 October 1924, while Tajikistan was created as an autonomous republic within Uzbekistan. In 1929, however, Tajikistan acquired Union Republic status, and Karakalpakistan, originally part of the Kazak Republic, became an autonomous republic within the jurisdiction of Uzbekistan in 1936. Today it enjoys semi-independent status. The Khujand province was also transferred from Uzbekistan to Tajikistan in 1929. The physical creation of the Soviet Central Asian Republics was followed by comprehensive campaign to modernize and Sovietize the region in ways that enabled them to convey the material and ideological concepts relevant to Soviet society.

After the creation of the various republics in Central Asia, Moscow undertook a policy of 'korenizatsia' (nativization) of cadres. The motivation for this policy was the belief that local administration needed local support, which could come most easily from local leaders. The main aim, however, was to establish the Soviet ideology and all its organizations, and win local peoples' support for Bolshevisk values. In Uzbekistan, by 1928, 'korenizatsia' came to be identified as 'Uzbekizatsia'. It meant that natives would rule their country, but they would do so in accordance with Moscow's designs. Following this, Akmal Ikramov became the first Uzbek Communist Party boss, while Faizulla Khojaev became the first Uzbek Prime Minister in 1925. Both men cooperated with Moscow, partly out of a shared ideological commitment and partly in the interests of their people. The careers of both men, however, ended during the Stalinist purges of 1937. They were suddenly removed from power, tried publicly in Moscow and summarily executed in March 1938. Usman Yusupov, who succeeded Ikramov as first secretary of the party in September 1937, and Abduljabbar Abdurakhmanov, who became the Prime Minister in 1938, remained in their posts until 1950 when they were transferred to Moscow. They belonged to a new Soviet generation whose emergence marked a distinct break with its predecessors, the Jadids. The career of Amin Irmatovich Niyazov, who became first secretary of the Uzbek Communist Party in 1950 and remained in his post until 1955, illustrates a slightly different pattern. His army credentials helped him to survive and prosper when so many of his compatriots fell by the wayside.

The death of Stalin in March 1953 opened the succession struggle, the rise of Khrushchev in Moscow and his de-Stalinization campaign in 1956. In Uzbekistan the first secretary of the Communist Party, Niyazov, was assigned to a lower position in December 1955 after Khrushchev became the first secretary of the Communist Party in Moscow. Niyazov was succeeded by Nuriddin Akramovich Mukhiddinov, who was the chairman of the Uzbekistan Council of Ministers under Niyazov. He served as secretary for two years before being brought to Moscow as a member of the presidium of the CPSU Central Committee, where he remained until 1961. His successor was Sabir Kamalovich Kamalov, who was chairman of the Uzbekistan Council of Ministers before being appointed first secretary of the Communist Party of Uzbekistan in December 1957. His career lasted little more than a year before he was ousted from the party in March 1959, for 'misusing' his power. Then there was the unexpected emergence of Sharef Rashidov, who was appointed as first secretary of the Communist Party in 1959 and who retained it until October 1983. In 1949, Rashidov had been the chairman of the writer's union, before filling Niyazov's former position of Chairman of the Supreme Soviet. His appearance signalled the emergence of a younger generation of Uzbek politicians with weaker political credentials than their predecessors.

The demise of the Soviet Union
When Mikhail Gorbachev became General Secretary of the Communist Party of the Soviet Union on 11 March 1985, the Soviet Union's long status as a global superpower and its formidable military arsenal were creating an immense domestic economic crisis and an enormous budget deficit. The country was manifestly failing to meet the needs of the ordinary people. Almost everything was in short supply and the goods that were available were of extremely poor quality. The general quality of life for most people had deteriorated considerably. The political system was inadequate in responding to the needs, demands and interests of ordinary people. Thus, because of its inefficiency, the official planned economic system was riddled with corruption and crime in most parts

of the Union.[33] Gorbachev represented the modern Soviet intelligentsia, which was committed to addressing the corruption, inefficiency and incompetence of the Soviet system. Gorbachev therefore promised to reform the Soviet political and economic system. He wanted to give people more say and achieve significant economic growth. In 1986, he introduced his reform programme policies, which were known as *glasnost* (openness), and *perestroika* (reconstruction).[34] His liberal stance also led to warm relations with the West and put an end to the Cold War, at least in the old form, which resulted in moves towards disarmament in both East and West. He wanted to achieve a significant improvement in economic performance which would lead to accelerated growth at all levels of the system. Gorbachev believed that life in the Soviet Union had become too routine, so he resolved to find an answer to the question of how people should live. He then introduced a formula: more democracy, more *glasnost* and more humanity. The idea of more freedom and more humanity spread quickly all over the Union and it was hoped that it would contribute to exposing corruption. However, it resulted in an unexpected weakening of the central authority and led to the rise of nationalism throughout the Union. With the weakening of the central authority during the early years of Gorbachev, the local institutions in Uzbekistan, as in other republics, realized a new measure of autonomy. A 'national awakening' began to take place, promoted in large measure by anger at the manner in which the republic was treated as a 'scapegoat' for the corruption. *Glasnost* and *perestroika* allowed freer expression of opinion, cultural identity and religious beliefs, but they also unleashed ethnic tensions. In Central Asia, in 1989, more than a hundred people were killed in the Fergana Valley when Uzbeks attacked Meskhetian Turks who had been exiled from the Meskhet region of Georgia by Stalin during the Second World War. The following year, unrest exploded between Uzbeks and Kyrgyz in the same region, claiming about 320 lives, mostly Uzbeks.

During 1985–6, the Soviet government wanted to rationalize, though not necessarily reform, the country's administrative command system. Mikhail Gorbachev, however, was convinced at this stage that the Soviet system was basically sound. The major problem in Gorbachev's eyes was that the people were not acting as they were supposed to. Thus, he put forward some plans to address this problem, including disciplining individuals to work properly rather than changing institutions, and streamlining the administrative command system to make it work faster and more efficiently. To achieve this he imposed an ambitious five-year plan which became the 'Twelfth five-year plan' of the Soviet Union. The experience of the 1985–6 period, however, did not augur well. It resulted in neither accelerated economic growth nor a properly functioning command system. In fact decline continued apace and the measures adopted severely exacerbated the shortages and imbalances in the Soviet economy, leading to the explosive growth of the Soviet budget deficit.[35] The failure of these early measures convinced Gorbachev to change direction. In order to generate the power needed to run through basic reforms of the institutional structures inherited from the past, in 1987 he shifted towards a new political strategy that emphasized political liberalization. In essence, this strategy was expected to encourage expanded public participation in political life. To this end, Gorbachev engineered a sweeping relaxation of censorship and appealed to the artistic and professional intelligentsia to serve as a spearhead of reform. He also introduced an element of electoral competition into the selection of State and Party officials. Following the Nineteenth Party Conference in June 1988 several constitutional amendments were adopted. Among the measures agreed were:

- new electoral laws
- the creation of a new two-tier parliamentary structure at the all-Union level (the directly elected congress of People's Deputies)
- a proper division of functions between legislative and government bodies and between the Party and the State, thus laying the basis for the creation of a law-based state.[36]

The primary function of the first two amendments was to elect the new 'semi-permanent' Supreme Soviet that was to be a proper working parliament unlike the old one. The USSR Supreme Soviet ratified these amendments on 1 December 1988, and they were to be implemented in 1989. The effects of these measures on the system were revolutionary, contrary to Gorbachev's intentions. The launching of democratization and greater *glasnost* in 1987 led to rapid changes in the general political climate and unleashed 'spontaneous processes' that ultimately became impossible to control. The reform proposals induced enormous opposition from within the Party. After the Nineteenth Party Conference in June

1988, the Party was divided into 'conservative' anti-reformists, Gorbachev supporters, and radical 'pro-democracy reformers' who wanted to go much further and faster than Gorbachev was prepared to go.[37]

These divisions widened and deepened as *perestroika* proceeded. The reforms also led to a slow but unstable 'revolution from below'. People began to organize to defend and promote these reform plans for their own interests. Many groups, large and small, sprang up across the country. Most importantly, in 1988 there was the emergence of radical pro-democracy and pro-independence coalition movements in the Baltic republics, as 'Popular Fronts', which quickly became very effective. This idea of the Popular Front also spread and gained momentum in other republics after 1988. In 1988 and 1989 the vast majority of the social movements and parties that were emerging in the Western border lands, and in Russia itself, were favourably disposed towards Gorbachev and his campaign to restrict the power of the Communist Party 'apparatus'. But following the national elections to the new USSR Congress of People's Deputies, in March 1989, Gorbachev, and the CPSU in particular, increasingly began to lose control over the reform process, so much so that the events came to a critical head. By the end of 1990 Gorbachev and the Party had become almost irrelevant to the spontaneous revolution that was sweeping through the republics. Soon, radical Russian democrats and non-Russian nationalists joined forces to challenge the authority and legitimacy of the Soviet State.

In allowing the 1990 republican legislative elections, which were much freer and consequently more democratic than the federal legislative elections of 1989, and postponing the first direct election for his own federal presidential post until 1994, Gorbachev unintentionally paved the way for an electoral alignment between democratic and separatist forces.[38] The elections to the republic Supreme Soviets and local Soviets that began at the end of 1989 and continued throughout most of 1990 resulted in a genuine transfer of political power from the Party to Sovereign legislatures, and the effective abolition of 'democratic centralism'. The consequence of popular sovereignty was that republican and local politicians were no longer responsible to Moscow but to their electorates. They increasingly began to disobey the central authorities and the overall effect was to promote the disintegration of the political system. The CPSU was the only unifying political force in the country. As it was overrun, there seemed to be no coercive power that could make anyone stay within the restrictive limits of the reforms. The disintegration of the political system also resulted in the rapid disintegration of the economic system, and this effectively transformed the Soviet Union into an anarchic state. The result was the adoption of local strategies for survival and the republics began to assert their independence.

Gorbachev was well aware of the crisis in the Soviet Union and the collapsing executive power of the Party, so he established a new executive Presidency in March 1990. This was his overall attempt to stem the crisis. His belief was that it would replace the collapsing executive authority legitimately vested in the State, and that only a strong leader with extensive powers could pull the country back from the brink of collapse. This also secured Gorbachev's personal position. It meant that even if the Party's hardliners succeeded in ousting him as the General Secretary of the Party he could still continue to rule as President. The authority of this new executive Presidency, however, was undermined by a number of factors. These included the lack of a new constitution, which was still being drafted, and the fact that the responsibilities between the new presidency and the other institutions of government were not clearly defined. Also, the President had no administrative structures or clear chains of command at his disposal through which to govern, and the USSR Congress of People's Deputies, the USSR Supreme Soviet and the old USSR Councils of Ministers had their own sources of authority and operated independently of the President. Gorbachev tried to solve this problem by demanding ever greater powers from the Supreme Soviet. In November and December 1990 he managed to secure these from the Supreme Soviet and unilaterally abolished the Council of Ministers, and the government of the Prime Minister Nikolai Ryzhkov, who was originally a Gorbachev appointee. Ryzhkov was sacked and replaced by bodies such as the new Cabinet of Ministers which was directly responsible and accountable to Gorbachev alone. However, these measures did little to help re-establish Gorbachev's control over the country.

By the end of 1990, all fifteen union-republics had popularly elected governments that had more credible legitimacy than the Central authorities. Every union-republic had declared its independence or sovereignty one way or another, and the governments of these republics fiercely resisted the demands of the centre, as well as Gorbachev's attempts to impose executive control. Gorbachev found it extremely difficult to have his decrees implemented. He failed to stand for popular election, refused to give up the post of CPSU General Secretary, and his persuasion of the Congress to elect him as President in March 1990 on the basis of an uncontested ballot, rather than by going to the country, greatly undermined his own principles. Consequently he lost what was left of his authority in the country at large, and his bargaining position with respect to the democratically elected Presidents of the republics was enormously reduced. Gorbachev tried to improve his position by manoeuvring between the conservatives and the 'democratic forces'. He was coming under pressure from the 'democratic forces' whose interests were informally represented by a powerful and very popular leader in the shape of Boris Yeltsin, who had all the popularity and legitimacy that Gorbachev lacked. Yeltsin had been democratically elected as President of the RSFSR in a Russia-wide competitive election in mid-1991 and became the democratically elected President of the largest and most powerful republic in the Union, giving him a clear political advantage over Gorbachev. Yeltsin who had made himself the champion of liberal Russian nationalism, put forward a program to challenge the authority of Gorbachev and the federal government on the grounds of national self-determination for Russians and the other Soviet nations.[39]

Gorbachev hoped that he could stop the growing paralysis of power in the USSR. Therefore he persuaded the reluctant republican leaders and parliaments to sign a new Union Treaty by holding a referendum on the preservation of the Soviet Union. On 17 March 1991, he initiated a carefully worded referendum so that it produced substantial majorities for the preservation of the Soviet Union. Although a majority voted in favour in all of the nine republics that participated, the referendum had brought the signing of a new Union Treaty no closer.[40] In April 1991, Gorbachev, who was under pressure from Boris Yeltsin and the presidents of eight other republics, left his hard-line government to its own devices and engaged in intense negotiations with the group of republican leaders. During the talks, Yeltsin and the other eight Presidents managed to convince Gorbachev that he would have to cooperate with them if the Union were to be preserved in any form at all.[41] In the spring and summer of 1991, successive drafts of the new Union Treaty were produced. Each conceded more and more powers to the republics, but still described the prospective new Union as a federal state. On 23 April, against a background of growing crisis, Gorbachev had a meeting in Novo-Ogarevo, outside Moscow, with the leaders of the nine republics that had held the referendum. At this meeting he finally recognized their declarations of sovereignty. He also agreed to Yeltsin's demand that the autonomous republics should not sign the treaty on their own account but as part of their respective union republican delegations. Yeltsin agreed to sign it only after Gorbachev had given in to his demands that the concept of federal taxes be dropped and that all union enterprises on the territory of the RSFSR be transferred to its jurisdiction as soon as the treaty was signed.[42]

Gorbachev had been keen to have the treaty signed before it was too late and also before the G-7 meeting in London in mid-July 1991, in order to persuade the heads of the leading industrial nations that the Soviet Union was not falling apart. This, however, appeared to be impossible when the Ukrainian Supreme Soviet voted on 27 June to postpone discussion of the draft treaty until after 15 September 1991.[43] Moreover, Leonid Kravchuk, the chairman of the Ukrainian Supreme Soviet, argued that Ukraine wanted the new union to be a confederation. Eventually, Gorbachev and Yeltsin decided not to wait for Ukraine, and it was arranged so that the RSFSR would sign the treaty on 20 August with the other republics, with Ukraine, it was hoped, following suit by early October. The negotiated treaty would have devolved considerable powers to the republics, but the process was cut short on 19 August 1991. The USSR Vice President, Gennadi Yanayev, acting as President at the head of an eight-man 'State committee for the State of Emergency' in the USSR, seized power. Yanayev himself had no independent power base and could not be considered to have been the moving force behind this coup that ousted Gorbachev.[44] The driving force was not an individual. It was the military-industrial complex, the network of interests represented by the armed forces and the defence industry, which was traditionally defended by the 'Secret Police'. The disintegration of the Soviet State precipitated by Gorbachev's liberalization reforms and the attempts to move towards a market economy instituted by Gorbachev and furthered by Yeltsin struck directly at the interests of this complex which, until Gorbachev's rise to power, had enjoyed priority access to scarce resources.[45] The real powers on the Emergency Committee were the USSR Defence Minister, Dmitrii Yazev, the USSR KGB Chairman Vladimir Kryuchkov, and the USSR Minister of Internal Affairs, Boris Pugo, who was also a major general in the KGB. Another key figure was the USSR Prime Minister Valentin Pavlov. The majority of the ringleaders of the coup were predominantly elderly and unpopular with the Soviet people. They were possibly blinded by their own extreme conservatism and they may, for this reason, have misjudged public opinion.

It is generally believed that the abortive coup of August 1991 was timed to prevent the signing of the Union Treaty and prevent the new formula from being put to the political test. This small group of Party, police, and military officials who tried to seize power in August also aimed to preserve the Soviet State. By 1991, however, there was very little to preserve and there was hardly anyone powerful and popular enough in the Union to reverse the flow of events. The cumulative effects of *glasnost* had undermined the key institutions that might have halted the process of political disintegration by the large-scale use of violence. As a result of Yeltsin's courageous public stand against the coup leaders and the republics' reluctance to support them, it became clear that the coup would fail. Indeed, it lasted just three days and on 21 August it crumbled. Yeltsin's stand earned him enormous public support. On 22 August 1991, the day Gorbachev returned to Moscow from Crimea where he had been detained during the coup, he had effectively lost power as had all the central institutions that he had created. He tried to continue as President of the USSR, but it was Yeltsin who had become the pre-eminent leader in the country. The Baltic republics moved swiftly to complete the process that they had begun in 1990. So did Georgia which had declared itself sovereign in April 1990. Moldavia, Armenia, and most importantly, Ukraine and Belarus indicated their desire to follow suit.[46] Yeltsin acted to ban organized Communist Party activity in the Soviet armed forces, the KGB and the police within the territory of the RSFSR. That evening (22 August), the offices of the CPSU Central Committee in Moscow were sealed, as were the headquarters of the Communist Party organizations in Moscow, Leningrad and a number of republican capitals. In Uzbekistan, however, the renamed Communist Party remained firmly in power. On 24 August, Gorbachev announced his decision to resign as the Party leader. He also ordered the nationalization of Communist Party property, called for the dissolution of the CPSU Central Committee, and banned Party cells in the armed forces, the KGB, and the police throughout the territory of the USSR.[47] On 5 September 1991, the Soviet Union virtually ceased to exist as a federal state. The decisions adopted on the same day by the USSR Congress of People's Deputies formally recognized the current political realities in the Soviet Union, whereby the centre had lost almost all its credibility as a result of the abortive August coup. The devolution of state power to the republics was formally recognized by this Congress. Thus the allegedly voluntary Union of fifteen Soviet republics had imploded.[48] Following this, the Russian government under the leadership of Yeltsin began an inconspicuous takeover of Central Soviet institutions.

After the coup when power passed into the hands of the republics, the republics had an ambivalent attitude to signing a new Union Treaty. On the one hand, they felt a need, to remain in a political union with other Union republics. On the other, they wanted to become masters in their own house and not be bound by any laws or regulations that did not suit them. Yeltsin reiterated the immediate need for a new Union Treaty, and fresh negotiations resumed under the nominal leadership of the USSR President Gorbachev, but they now had a completely different character. Instead of trying to create a new, democratic federal state, republican negotiations now concentrated on finding ways to prevent the immediate and catastrophic collapse of what remained of the unified Soviet economy.[49] After intensive negotiations an agreement was finally signed on 18 October 1991 by only ten of the republics who committed their signatures to what became known as the 'common economic space'.[50] At this point Gorbachev was still hopeful that he could save the Soviet Union by creating a new form of confederation — a voluntary association of independent sovereign states coordinated by a limited central authority. In fact, political union was not possible any longer, as each republican government established itself as a sovereign entity and simply ignored or bypassed the Federal Supreme Soviet. Indeed the RSFSR breached the economic agreement almost immediately, embarking on its own economic reforms without consultation with other member states. Therefore, progress on the various subsidiary agreements necessary to make the economic treaty work was delayed.

In the immediate aftermath of the coup, Yeltsin's insistence on a new Union Treaty led to more negotiations. On 14 November 1991, the RSFSR, Belarus, and five of the six Muslim republics approved in principle the revised draft, which granted still more powers to the republics; and an initializing ceremony was planned for 25 November. However, the ceremony had to be cancelled at the last minute after Yeltsin objected to Gorbachev's insistence that the new Union should be a 'confederative state' rather than a confederation. The republican leaders decided that the draft should be submitted to their parliaments, where it would undoubtedly have run into serious opposition.[51] However, the developments that followed the Ukrainian referendum and the overwhelming vote for independence in Ukraine on 1 December 1991, marked the end of any attempts by Gorbachev or any one else to keep some sort of federation or confederation together. Hence, without Ukraine, the second most powerful republic in the Union, political union would have been unlikely. Yeltsin met with the elected president of Ukraine, Kravchuk, and the chairman of the Supreme Soviet in Belarus, Stanislav Shushkevich, in Minsk on 8 December 1991 and there they reached an agreement on creating a new Commonwealth of Independent States (CIS). The three republics also signed a declaration on the coordination of economic policy, the agreement on the creation of the CIS, and an accompanying declaration that stated that negotiations on a new Union Treaty had reached a dead end and that the USSR actually ceased to exist as a subject of International Law and as a geopolitical reality.[52] The parliaments of the three Slavic republics ratified the agreement and denounced the 1922 treaty that had created the Soviet Union. The Central Asian republics showed signs of wanting to join the CIS, and the armed forces also seemed to be siding with Yeltsin. Even at this late stage Gorbachev continued to resist these moves but was eventually forced to bow to the inevitable and resigned as President of the USSR on 25 December 1991.

Initially only Kazakstan was to be given the right to be a founder member of the CIS together with the three Slavic republics. But other Central Asian republics were determined not to be treated as second-class citizens. So at a meeting in Alma-Ata (now Almaty) on 21 December, a protocol to the agreement of 8 December in Minsk on the creation of the Commonwealth was adopted, under which Uzbekistan and four other Central Asian republics as well as Armenia, Azerbaijan and Moldavia became founding members. The result was that of the twelve republics that had remained as part of the Soviet Union, only Georgia was not a member. Hence in late December 1991, the disintegration of the mighty 'Empire of the Iron Curtain' ended an extraordinary chapter of history and resulted in the emergence of 15 newly independent states from the Baltic to Central Asia. The three Slavic countries – Russia, Ukraine and Belarus; the three Baltic republics – Estonia, Latvia and Lithuania; the Soviet foothold in the Balkans – Moldavia; in the

Caucasus – Armenia, Georgia and Azerbaijan; and the five Central Asian republics – Kazakstan, Uzbekistan, Kyrgyzstan, Tajikistan and Turkmenistan.

The emergence of the Independent Republic of Uzbekistan
After the creation of the former Uzbek Soviet Socialist republic the then leadership was forced to abandon the cultivation of grain and other food products and concentrate on providing cotton for Russia's textile industry, and thus accept a 'cotton monoculture'. Throughout the decades of Communist rule in Uzbekistan, the key factors in Moscow's policies towards the republic were its desire to dictate policy, control its implementation and control the republic's leadership. It asserted its power to mandate who would serve in which posts and to remove those who no longer served the Centre's needs. Many of these changes and removals were often brutally enforced. During the Stalin era, they took the shape of national purges, summary imprisonment, public trials and executions. The terror and the oppressive character of the Soviet regime were so harsh that they generated tremendous hatred towards the regime in the republic, but at the same time a sense of fear that led people to be silent about what was going on around them. The Kremlin took advantage of this situation to tighten its grip on the staffing of the Party and the state *apparat*, especially at the crucial *oblast* (region) and *raion* (district) levels where policies were implemented. For a while, this provided the Moscow leadership with full control of Party and state activity in Uzbekistan.

The decades after Stalin's death in March 1953, however, witnessed a quiet transfer of power in the republic away from Moscow towards the republic's Party organs. Central control of recruitment was loosened and virtually ended in the later Brezhnev period. Personnel decisions were left to the Party organs at the republican, *oblast* and *raion* levels. This marked the eventual erosion of Moscow's ability to control staffing of the party *apparat*, in Uzbekistan. The local elite took almost full control over recruitment and promotion within the political elite, and asserted its authority in personnel matters in the country. By 1983 large numbers of people had been elevated to the republic-wide bureaucratic elite, whether in the Party, government, economic or cultural institutions. These recruitments and promotions were carried out not in line with who was best suitable for given jobs, but rather who was willing to work in line with the republican Party organs. Hence the cadre policy led to widespread corruption, discrimination and abuse of power by those in the office, as well as unsatisfactory performance at almost every level of the state *apparat*. This subsequently gave way to widespread bribery, embezzlement, padding, thefts and nepotism at the republican, *oblast* and *raion* levels.

With the sudden death of the Uzbek Communist Party Chief Sharef Rashidov in November 1983, after three decades in power, the Moscow leadership discovered just how little control it had over Party and state activity in Uzbekistan.[53] In response to the scandals, Moscow initiated in early 1984 a series of measures designed to reassert its authority in personnel matters. It relied on traditional authoritarian methods, operating through the Party command system, but corruption was entrenched even there. As a result of more disclosures during 1984–6, the Uzbek Communists were accused of incompetence and unreliability at all levels of the hierarchy in the republic, and many individuals were charged with criminal behaviour against the Soviet state. This was not confined to the indigenous elements; Russians holding several key positions, supposedly to protect Moscow's interests in the republic, were also found guilty. A former Russian incumbent of the Second Secretaryship, the traditional proconsular post which was intended to protect the Kremlin's interests in Uzbekistan, was placed under arrest in 1986. Another Russian who was charged with corruption was a former deputy Chairman of the republican Council of Ministers.[54] In his speech to the Moscow Communist Party Congress of 1986, Gorbachev declared that the leadership had been taken by surprise with regard to the shortcomings in Uzbekistan, which he said had not 'occurred all at once', but were the 'accumulations of years', and he called for a thorough investigation. Thus the anti-corruption purges, which had been running for two years, were stepped up and in early 1986 they penetrated deep into lower levels of the Party and government departments. Until 1986, some 750 persons in leadership positions had been replaced. In 1986 alone, 158 leaders were expelled from the Party and more than 2,000 received denunciations.[55] By 1988 the number of persons guilty of crimes against the state was conceivably in the tens of thousands at every level of the state authorities, including collective farms and law-enforcement institutions. The lawlessness and abuse of power ran so deep that corrupt cadres ended up being replaced by other corrupt colleagues, or those ousted resurfaced in other responsible posts. This practice continued despite sharp condemnation at the 1986 Party Congress. In July 1987 a decree passed by the Central Committee in Moscow again condemned the corruption, but this too failed to put a stop to it. The cadre campaign at the regional and district levels provoked a storm of resistance. At the republican level the political elite concealed the true grounds for dismissal through 'face-saving announcements' that those ousted were being transferred to other positions. A further failure was Moscow's policy of the 'inter-republican exchange of cadres' to help prevent the illicit cooperation of Russians and other outsiders in the native networks, and supposedly guaranteeing the loyalty of the republican officials. The officials who were sent to Uzbekistan to replace the disgraced locals were removed for 'negative reasons' just months after their appointments.

In its efforts to defeat the Uzbek elites, Moscow tried to win grassroots support in Uzbekistan. The masses had been encouraged to use *glasnost* and *perestroika* to criticize officials and unmask their shortcomings and misdeeds in the name of 'democratization'. In addition to this the slogan of 'electability', which had been introduced by Gorbachev, seemed to arouse some anti-elite feeling in the republic. People used the occasion to express their anger towards the political elite and its corrupt managers. Letters and telegrams were sent to Moscow when they perceived something to be wrong. Workers began to disobey their directors and managers, and the central authority in Tashkent came under immense pressure. Local leaders who remained in office were harassed and humiliated in the media by Moscow. At this point, Moscow's efforts to use the Uzbek masses to pressure the elites from below began to backfire. The political elite in the republic successfully enlisted the country's cultural figures (e.g. writers, artists, scholars and scientists), to link the leadership with the masses in rallying national opinion to oppose Moscow's policies and directives. The elite in the republic fought back against Moscow's attempts to turn the masses against them. These cultural figures appealed to the nationalist feelings of the Uzbek public to persuade them that the purges were also aimed at them and not merely at the officials involved. The very autonomy and integrity of their republic was under threat. Many articles began to appear in the Uzbek media full of resentment towards Moscow, claiming that much of the criticism of their country in Moscow newspapers was unjustified and an insult to Uzbek honour at all levels of society. There was also an outcry against the term 'the Uzbek affair', which had been coined by Moscow officials and newspaper writers as a euphemism for corruption. Uzbeks noted indignantly that the rewards of corruption had ended up not in Uzbekistan but in Moscow. As a result, the wounded feelings of all Uzbeks helped to produce a national consensus of resistance to Moscow; a consensus that won.

The poet Muhammad Salih expressed in an Uzbek newspaper Uzbek bitterness at the Kremlin's anti-corruption and cadre campaign:

> Let's say if a journalist from the central press wants to write about the crime of false accounting, then he naturally picks Uzbekistan and doubtless the 'padder' Rashidov as the example. At the same time, that journalist well knows that in order to 'give false account' for millions of tons of cotton in secret from the Politburo it takes not just Rashidov but two people... They were taking money not just in Tashkent but in the Kremlin... In Uzbekistan nine million people were living out their days below the poverty level. Before we could talk about this, we had to prove that those nine million people were not all thieves... In the process of exposing criminals, thousands of guilty and innocent were thrown into jail.[56]

Consequently, 'the Uzbek affair' alienated Uzbekistan from the Central Soviet authorities, and both Uzbek Communists and dissidents considered that their republic had been unfairly singled out for investigation. The first USSR Congress of People's Deputies in the spring of 1989 was a turning point. Uzbek officials spoke out publicly, levelling forthright criticism at the Centre. The deputies from the Uzbekistan Supreme Soviet voiced criticism of policies towards the republic, focusing on regional economic, health and environmental problems. In the end, the Moscow leadership tried, though largely failed, to regain control of cadre policy in Uzbekistan. It may well be true that Uzbekistan, like other Central Asian republics, lagged behind others in challenging the Kremlin's authority during the *perestroika* period. However, the leadership of the native elite in the republic had, since the early 1970s, been seeking ways to combine underlying loyalty to the Soviet system with the advancement of national ambitions. The goals, strategy and tactics of the elite became the leading force of Uzbek nationalism throughout *perestroika*. Gorbachev's reform policies in Uzbekistan largely lacked firmness and direction in the face of resistance in the republic. They failed to effect a general restructuring of the Uzbek party and government apparatus by political means. The reforms were addressed more to the style of work than to the fundamental criterion of recruitment. The reforms of the electoral system weakened not only the Centre's grip, but also that of the republican establishment. This increased national power in society, threatening not only Moscow's control, but also that of the Uzbek elite in the late 1980s. Nevertheless Gorbachev, in the wake of dangerous and dramatic riots in Fergana in June 1989, found the opportunity to reject Rafik Nishanov's policies, and replaced him with someone uncontaminated by previous attachments. Nishanov's successor as Uzbek Communist Party First Secretary was Islom Karimov, an outsider to the Party *nomenclatura* throughout most of his previous career. He had never been a member of the republican Party's Politburo nor had he held a position in the central Secretariat. Following the failure of the Moscow coup almost two years after his appointment as the leader of the Uzbek Republic, Karimov asked the republic's parliament to approve a declaration of State Independence on 31 August 1991. A presidential election was held in late 1991 in which Karimov was elected as the first President of independent Uzbekistan with the votes of 86 per cent of the people.

Post-Soviet Uzbekistan
After the failure of the Moscow coup in August 1991, Islom Karimov was accused by his opponents in Uzbekistan of having supported the Coup Committee. Although he may have felt some sympathy with their proclaimed intention to restore order in society, the reality, from the Uzbek point of view, was that Karimov had just returned from a visit to India when he was faced with the first declaration of the emergency committee. He was confused and not well informed. Thus, after a period of hesitation, he expressed his opposition to it and, anxious not to let his opponents seize the initiative, Karimov declared Uzbekistan's political independence. The Karimov government then began taking steps to consolidate its power over the republic. Karimov resigned from the CPSU on 23 August 1991, and on 26 August the Ministry of Internal Affairs and the KGB were both nationalized and legally subordinated to the Uzbekistan leadership. The Uzbek Communist Party was nationalized

on 30 August, and the Uzbek Party itself changed its name, though not its structure or personnel, to become officially the People's Democratic Party of Uzbekistan.

Uzbekistan's initial steps as an independent state have been uncertain. During pre-coup discussions and negotiations over the form of a renewed Union, the Uzbek leader had argued for a state structure that would allow Uzbekistan the maximum possible freedom of action at home but with the minimum disruption of the Union's economic ties. President Karimov favoured the structure of a confederation with aspects of a federation. Declaring Uzbekistan's sovereignty was meant to express the leadership's desire to escape from Moscow's interference in Uzbekistan's internal affairs. Full independence for Uzbekistan was seen as a realistic possibility only by a small number of nationalists. The dissolution of the USSR was an unexpected event for which the Uzbeks were unprepared. However, Uzbekistan's declaration of independence soon involved a more serious desire to assert itself as a state in its own right, and to distance itself from the interference of the central Soviet authority. Uzbeks understood that they had to seriously consider taking over the affairs of their own country, and working towards what they called a 'new future, a new generation'. On 16 November 1993, Uzbekistan introduced the new transitional currency, the *Sum coupon*, and announced that roubles would no longer be legal tender after December. On 1 July 1994 the final national currency, the *Sum*, was put into circulation. Karimov put forward his policies for social, political and economic reforms – what he called Uzbek model of progress – having previously considered various other models of development for Uzbekistan. According to Karimov, the Uzbek model builds on an indigenous tradition and foresees gradual and steady progress based on 'oriental tradition' (see chapters 3 and 4).

In mid-January 1992 there were student demonstrations at Tashkent University, apparently triggered by price liberalization, which lasted for several days. The students were protesting at poor living conditions in their hostels, but student leaders also raised slogans of the *Birlik* (Unity) and *Erk* (Freedom) opposition parties. All of these revolts were harshly put down. Following this, Uzbek opposition leaders were publicly beaten up, oppressed or simply disappeared. The government initially paid little attention to the idea of a pluralist democracy for Uzbekistan. The leadership made it clear by saying several times that it was working for tomorrow without rejecting yesterday and it was willing to pay any price for the sake of stability, security and peace in the country. Until June 1992 the Uzbek opposition movement *Birlik*, Uzbekistan's largest nationalist legal political party, hoped that despite the government's hostility towards the opposition forces, it would be allowed to register as a political party. As fighting between various ethnic and political forces had worsened in Tajikistan, Uzbekistan similarly had experienced ethnic clashes in the Fergana Valley – in 1989 – and smaller outbreaks in 1990. Karimov exploited this to justify repressing the opposition, which he insisted was merely a front for Muslim extremist groups that aspired to overthrow the existing system in Uzbekistan and set up an Islamic state. Although *Birlik* and *Erk* both stood for a non-Islamic secular democratic state, a degree of Uzbek nationalism and opposition to corruption, neither had a coherent platform on social, political and economic reform. *Birlik* leaders rejected Karimov's claim that they were a front for Muslim extremism, stating that he was crying wolf to fool the West into tolerating his personal authoritarianism. The rhetoric on both sides was intemperate, yet each had some grounds for its argument. Uzbekistan's Islamic Renaissance Party, which has never been legalized, was immediately banned in 1990. Its leader, Abdulla Utaev, disappeared in December 1992, reportedly taken away by the security forces, and he has never been heard of since. A number of small Islamic groups sprang up in Uzbekistan, but they were kept under close scrutiny. In mid-June, *Birlik*'s chairman, Abdurrahim Pulatov, was harassed and assaulted, the group's office was shut down by the authorities, and the *Birlik* newspaper was proscribed. Some of its members were fired from their jobs. A few days after the seizure of the *Birlik* activists, the Uzbek parliament voted to revoke *Birlik*'s registration, thereby effectively banning the largest opposition organization. *Erk* suffered less in the first wave of repression, though its leader, Mohammad Salih, a deputy to the Supreme Soviet, was forced to resign his seat. As *Birlik* had been banned, Salih's group was experiencing a rise in popularity.

After the crackdown on the major opposition groups in 1992, a re-registration requirement for all the political parties was introduced in 1993 and the only remaining political party, the *Erk* Democratic Party, was stripped of its registration. The persecution of the Uzbek opposition continued throughout 1993. Even the Uzbek Vice President, Shukrulla Mirsaidov, was not immune from prosecution. In January he faced criminal charges, believed to have been fabricated by the government to disable a potentially powerful rival. By mid-1993 some of the opposition leaders had been exiled, some had been imprisoned, and others disappeared. With the new regulation, all independent media were also denied registration and the state media was brought under strict control. The aim was to stop further 'trouble makers' struggling for power at a time when the country needed unity to find a way of overcoming the severe economic dislocation.

In 1994 President Karimov sought to deal with the ever-worsening economic situation and falling living standards. The crisis was a result of the collapse of the Soviet-era supply systems for raw materials and manufactured goods, and it affected all parts of the Commonwealth. The leadership tried to maintain and strengthen existing trade and economic links with the former Soviet states while actively seeking to establish new ties with the rest of the world. The Uzbek leadership was quick to establish trade ties outside the CIS, but could not prevent severe shocks to the standards of living in the country. To make sure that the reform process went ahead smoothly and without any interference, President Karimov announced in September 1994 that the old parliament would be replaced by a new one after elections in December of that year. The elections were designed to strengthen the leadership and bring some sort of legitimacy to the parliament. The Supreme Soviet met for the last time on 22 September and was replaced by a smaller legislative body. The parliamentary elections were held on 25 December 1994 with two further rounds of voting on 8 and 22 January 1995. Following the elections a national government was formed. The Uzbek national government consisted of a Council of Ministers, headed by the Prime Minister Abdulkhasim Mutalov, nominated by President Karimov. In practice, the President exercised total control and appointed *hokims* (regional governors). Rustam Akhmedov became defence Minister; Abdulaziz Khamilov became Foreign Minister, the Finance Ministry was headed by Bakhtoyor Khamidov; the Interior Ministry was headed by Zakijon Almatov, and Justice Ministry was given to Mukhed Bobir Malikov.

The domestic political scene in 1995 was dominated by the government's attempts to control its opponents, but in late 1995 there were signs of opposition activity in the country. Aware of its authoritarian image, the government began a discreet dialogue with the exiled opposition *Birlik* party in the United States after the general election, ostensibly to introduce a more liberal stance on political parties. For some, however, this was an attempt by Karimov to mollify the United States and exploit opposition divisions, but no concrete results were achieved. Thereafter, the authorities resumed their tough line with the opposition. In late December, President Karimov tried to reshape his domestic and foreign policy, after replacing his Prime Minister Abdulkhasim Mutalov with Uthkir Sultanov, previously the Minister of Foreign Economic Relations. In 1996 Karimov continued with his economic reforms, was actively involved with improving his country's image abroad, and became a champion of peace in the region. He held several meetings with the Tajik opposition leader, Sayid Abdullah Nuri, and his representatives during 1995–6, though Karimov was known as a supporter of the Rahmanov government in Dushanbe. The aim of these talks was to try to find a common ground for peace talks to continue.

On 7 May President Karimov announced a reorganization of local broadcasting, which transformed the State Television and Radio Broadcasting Company of Uzbekistan into the Television and Radio Company of Uzbekistan or Uztelradio. Uztelradio was transferred into a government-controlled private company responsible to the Council of Ministers. Uztelradio was exempt from taxes until 2000 and thereafter expected to finance itself. Although the reorganization was ostensibly to provide objective, reliable and diverse information and to tackle news and current affairs in a constructive manner, the real motive was to abolish the old Soviet structure of broadcasting. Little has changed in the content. The state has complete control over all media outlets, including print and broadcasting. Uztelradio's mission is also to promote love for and loyalty to the homeland, as well as free enterprise in a socially oriented market economy.

On the eve of the fifth anniversary of state independence day, President Karimov announced an amnesty. Of the 85 prisoners released, only five were political prisoners, three of whom were from the secular anti-Karimov opposition. The Uzbek authorities also allowed two international human rights organizations, Human Rights Watch/Helsinki and the Open Society Institute, to open offices in Tashkent in September of the same year.

President Karimov gave an unusual speech to the Uzbek Parliament on 29 August 1996. He stated that he wanted a press with Western standards, the protection of civil rights and active opposition parties. He complained that the press was not being critical at all, that the opposition parties had not been active enough, and that he wanted to ensure that Uzbekistan meets international human rights standards. Uzbek journalists, however, do not believe that the President really means it. They face an impossible dilemma. They have been ordered to be free, but everything they write must be passed by the Centre. If they continue their praise of the President the risks are eradicated, but if they stop they could cause a far worse disaster. In these confusing times, most of them are more cautious than ever. On the human rights issue, there are many laws that either weaken or restrict human rights in the country. On the political parties, a new law passed by parliament on 26 December, which came into force on 7 January 1997, still restricts political parties' activities. To give the impression that he is a politically neutral head of state, President Karimov resigned from the ruling People's Democratic Party on 15 June 1996. Although the PDP is still very much the President's party, it does not wield significant influence. President Karimov has gradually bypassed party structures, shifting power to government agencies headed by personal allies and his own presidential staff. Karimov's position in Uzbek politics is extremely strong and he is certainly a popular political figure in Uzbekistan today. His political career, however, depends on his policies of economic reform. If the reforms are successful and people's living standards improve, he will be the dominant political figure in his country for a long time. If the economic transition takes longer than expected, his power may be undermined and he could face rebellious challenges. As far as the democratic reforms are concerned, the old 'iron curtain' has been replaced by a new 'glass curtain'.

The Uzbek government has also taken a serious political risk by putting the entire opposition in the same basket as 'fundamentalists', 'extremists' and 'nationalists'. Authoritarian rule could elicit more powerful radicalism and extremism. The government's policy of suppressing all dissent is counterproductive and will simply end up creating more militant oppositions that the authorities already claim to be fighting. In December 1997 when four traffic policemen were murdered in the Fergana Valley during a gang warfare it was blamed on Islamists groups, in particular the Wahhabis, and a wave of arrests of Muslims followed in the region in 1998. During this crackdown, a large group of over one thousand men, women and children also fled the region and began moving into Tajikistan. On 16 February 1999 six large car bombs exploded in Tashkent within the space of a few minutes. These narrowly missed President Karimov, killed sixteen people and injured one hundred and fifty more – a virtually unprecedented act of violence. It is not clear whether the bombs were an attempt to assassinate President Karimov, as was officially claimed, or a more general attack on the government. The officials were quick to blame Islamic militants. In 1998 the government mounted a crackdown on alleged Islamic terrorists, who were accused of killing several police officers in the Fergana Valley and at show trials many were sentenced to long prison terms. But the Islamic militants are not the only ones who might seek retribution against the present government in the country. Karimov, in early February 1999, said Uzbekistan would withdraw from the CIS Collective Security treaty, a pillar of Russian influence in Central Asia. He accused Russia of using the treaty to further its own ambitions. Neighbouring Tajikistan was shaken by an armed rebellion and attempted coup in early November 1998. Tajikistan accused the Uzbek government of supporting the rebels when a former Tajik army officer, Colonel Mahmud Khudoberdiyev, led a force of some one thousand men into northern Tajikistan from a base in Uzbekistan. Other possible culprits include rival factions within the regime. In the past two years President Karimov has sacked most of the thirteen regional governors and several ministers. In November 1998 Karimov sacked his first deputy prime minister and began a purge of high-ranking officials for corruption and mismanagement. Whatever the reason behind the Tashkent bombings in February 1999, they were used to justify further repression of the government opponents. The government's response was heavy-handed tactics of mass but indiscriminate arrests. Thousands of people were arrested throughout the country and have gone through interrogations, many were persecuted by the security forces. Suspects apprehended in Kazakstan, Kyrgyzstan, Tajikistan, Russia, Ukraine and Turkey were extradited to Uzbekistan for trial. Between June and July 1999, 22 people were convicted of involvement, with six receiving death sentences. The internal situation has been complicated further by the appearance of an Uzbek armed Islamic group in the neighbouring Kyrgyzstan, in August 1999. The six hundred armed Islamist gunmen, most of whom were Uzbek political exiles belonging to the Islamic Movement of Uzbekistan (IMU) headed by Tohir Yoldashev, were lead by Juma Namangani, a wanted criminal in Uzbekistan who is accused of killing the four policemen in late 1997. Tohir Yoldashev is former head of *Lashkari Islami,* (Troops of Islam), an informal Islamic group in the Fergana Valley, which emerged in early 1990s as a non-violent organization. The militants captured several villages in Batken and Chon-Alai regions, took a number of hostages including one general, one colonel, and four Japanese geologists who were working at a gold-mining site in the area. They demanded to be allowed to cross into Uzbekistan. The hostage crisis lasted for almost two months and was finally over after indirect negotiations. One of the Kyrgyz hostages had been killed by the IMU, but all the other surviving hostages were released. During the two months of intermittent fighting between the IMU and the Kyrgyz forces, with assistance from the Uzbek air force, scores of Uzbek Islamists were killed, including Abdulvali Yoldashev, the brother of Tohir Yoldashev; a dozen Kyrgyz troops and a number of Kyrgyz civilians were also killed. The remaining gunmen of the IMU withdrew to Afghanistan under Kyrgyz and Tajik government surveillance. In early November, just weeks after the end of the crisis in Batken and the Chon-Alai regions, an unidentified group of gunmen crossed into Uzbekistan from Kyrgyzstan and attacked a police post close to Yangiabad. The attack was probably the work of the IMU – designed to show that it is still able to attack Uzbekistan. The IMU has little chance of ousting the Karimov administration by force but it could create considerable problems in border areas by hit-and-run attacks. It could also complicate Uzbekistan's relations with its Central Asian neighbours at a time when Uzbekistan needs to build good relations and maintain close cooperation with these states. In addition, the IMU can exploit the current economic difficulties and the widespread problem of corruption in Uzbekistan and so cause social unrest.

On 5 and 9 December 1999 new parliamentary and local elections were held in the republic, followed by the presidential election on 9 January 2000. As expected, Islom Karimov was re-elected president with 92 per cent of the vote. The only candidate alternative to Karimov, Abdulhafiz Jalolo, who received only 4 per cent of the vote, has later admitted himself that he had also voted for Karimov, thus making his opposition to Karimov a joke. Following the elections on 11 February 2000, the new parliament approved the new Uzbek cabinet named by the president. Utkir Sultanov retained his post as prime minister, while new ministers of justice (Abdusamat Palvan-Zade) and energy (Valery Otayev) were named and the post of defence minister remained vacant until 14 Februrary, when it was filled by the appointment of Lieutenant General Yurii Agzamov. The total number of cabinet ministers was cut from 37 to 34, but the majority of ministers retained their posts. This is not because they were efficient, but because of a lack of qualified candidates to replace them. The success and the failure of the new cabinet, and indeed, the new parliament, however, will undoubtedly be determined by the course of further reforms and the resultant changes in society.

The Karakalpak Autonomous Republic
The Karakalpak Autonomous Republic was first created as an autonomous region within Kazakstan on 16 February 1925. On 20 March 1932 it was upgraded to the Karakalpak Soviet Socialist Autonomous Republic, and from 1930–6 it remained, with the same status, within the Russian Soviet Federal Socialist Republic. On 5 December 1936, the Karakalpak Autonomous Republic was transferred to the Uzbek Soviet Socialist Republic. Karakalpakistan is situated in the north-western end of the republic of Uzbekistan. It has 15 districts, 12 cities, 16 towns and 107 villages. Karakalpakistan declared its sovereignty on 14 December 1990. On 14 December 1992 at the regional parliament's eleventh session the flag was approved and on the 9 April 1993 at the twelfth session, the constitution and emblem were approved. On the 4 December at the fourteenth session of the regional parliament, the national anthem was also adopted. According to the constitution the sovereign republic of Karakalpakistan is part of the republic of Uzbekistan and the security and integrity of Karakalpakistan is protected by the republic of Uzbekistan. The laws of the republic of Uzbekistan are binding in the territory of Karakalpakistan. The economy of the autonomous republic is dominated by agriculture, mainly the cultivation of cotton and wheat. The life of the people, however, is deteriorating as a result of the environmental problems caused by the decline of the Aral Sea.

The ethnic origin of the Uzbeks
The Uzbeks have established a commanding position in the politics of Central Asia. The most populous of the CIS's various Muslim nationalities, they are increasingly asserting control over their own state. Over a period of many centuries their ancestors conquered the region, from the

Eurasian steppes to the North. The majority settled in the regions where the warmer southern climate reigned and mixed with the people living in the region. Ethnically, the Uzbeks of today are descendants of various Turk tribes that had begun moving to Maverannahr between the fifth and tenth centuries AD. They intermingled with the original inhabitants, predominantly the Tajiks of Persian stock, and a conglomerate of Turkic-Mongol (*Ozbegs(k)-Uzbeks*) tribes that had migrated to the region with Muhammad Shaybani Khan around 1500 AD. Even today, a large number of Uzbeks are bilingual, speaking both their own language, which is related to the Turkish language, and Tajik, a Persian language of the Indo-European family, which differs little from the Farsi of Iran. This book accepts that as a 'nationality' in the modern sense, the Uzbeks are a product of the early Soviet period, being shaped by the federal institutions of the Soviet System under Stalin and his successors. But it also argues that *Uzbek*, as an *ethnic* identity, was formed in the fifteenth century. The term '*Uzbek*' goes back to the middle ages. It was the name of the Golden Horde Khan, Ghiyath ad-Din Muhammad Ozbeg (1312–42). According to the Khivan Khan Abul Ghazi Bahadur (1642–63), 'after the conversion of the Golden Horde to Islam by Uzbek Khan, the entire Golden Horde Khanate of Chinggis Khan's Empire was, thereafter, called the Uzbek Khanate'.[57] This name designated a combined group identity (a supratribal name). Originally the name *Uzbek* as a group identity had more of a 'politico-historical' than an ethnic meaning. Judging from the fact that they had 92 clanic names, 'pure Uzbeks' were composed of the most diverse branches of the Turkic and Mongolic tribes. Abu-l Khayr Khan (1428–68), was a descendent of Batu's brother, Shayban, a grandson of Ghiyath ad-Din Muhammad Ozbeg (Uzbek) Khan, and was a paramount chieftain of the Shaybanid *Ulus*-subjects; who were already called *Ozbegs(k)*. He succeeded in uniting all the nomadic tribes between the Ural river, the Syrdarya, Mugholistan and Tobol, and formed a new state which, he called Ozbekiston, meaning 'land of Ozbeks'. It has not yet been clear by whom and exactly when this people were called *Ozbeg(k)s* (Uzbeks), but it is most likely that this name was adopted during the Ozbek Khan's rule during 1312–42.

Geoffrey Wheeler, however, argues that the Uzbeks belong to the Caucasoid group being originally nomadic, round-headed, of medium height, and having dark hair and eyes. He goes further and suggests that Mongoloid features can also be found among the Uzbeks of northern

Khorezm and of Fergana. They are the largest Turkic group in the Soviet Union (now CIS) and the largest in the world after the Turks of Turkey. They were also called Sarts by the Russians, which, broadly speaking, meant a town dweller.[58] Bartold and Gavin Hambly lend support to this view.[59] Coates and Coates, state that the Uzbeks are a continuation of 'Turk and Mongol tribes who in the fifteenth century constituted a section of the Golden Horde, speaking Turkic language and those who took their name from the Golden Horde Khan-Uzbek.'[60] On the other hand, Edward A. Allworth argues that Tatar tribesmen made up that first conglomeration of people called *Uzbeks*.[61]

Of particular note is the research of A. Zeki Velidi Togan (1890–1970). A professor of history for over half a century, he taught at several universities in Turkey. He was also a principal leader of the Turkestan National Liberation Movement in Central Asia (1916–30), which is known as the Basmachi Movement by the Russians. A Bashkurt-Turk, Togan's first book was entitled *Türk ve Tatar Tarihi* (*Turk and Tatar History*), Kazan, 1911. He then studied in Austria and Germany for his PhD and, as a result of his investigations and research on the origins of *Özbeks* (*Uzbeks*) and *Kazaks*, his second book *Türkili Türkistan ve Yakin Tarihi* (*Fatherland Turkestan and its Near History*) was first published in Istanbul in 1948, though it had been completed in 1928. The second edition of this book was published in 1981. According to Togan the *Ozbeks* (Uzbeks) of today living in *Transoxiana* and *Khorezm* (Uzbekistan), comprise the dominant group known under the rubric name of '*Tatar*' in the *Jochi Ulus*. He also accepts that the original Uzbeks were '*Tatars*', but goes further and gives a very detailed account of the origin of the 'Uzbek-Tatar' concept. Togan's analysis and documentation, which is rarely available in the West, is as follows: Abu-l Khayr Khan, who took the 'Tura and Bashkurt' regions from the other branch of the *Shibagan* descendants of western Siberian Khan Mahmudek, was previously governing these territories. Abu-l Khayr Khan later seized the lower reaches of Syrdarya and Khorezm in 1431. He pursued a policy of basing the governance of the state upon the southern and northern agricultural and settled regions of the *Jochi Ulus*. During the sixteenth century, a large portion of the Uzbeks made the transition to village and agricultural life in the Zaravshan basin and in Khorezm. They perhaps belonged to the elements arriving from the Syrdarya and Tura regions where they had already adapted themselves to this lifestyle.[62] On the tribal composition, Togan states that the Uzbeks are referred to as '*doksan iki boylu Ozbek*' (Uzbek with 92 tribes) in all historical documents written on Uzbeks. Among the Uzbeks, there is a 'genealogy' naming their 92 tribes. There are slight discrepancies between the sixteenth and seventeenth centuries and later manuscripts of the genealogy. He maintains that, undoubtedly, the genealogy lists of those 92 tribes refer to those at the time of the Golden Horde, meaning prior to the separation of this Horde into *Mangit*, *Nogay* and *Kazak*. The 92 tribes listed by Togan, are as follows:

> Min, Yüz, Qirq, Üngeçit, Calayir, Saray, On, Qonrat, Alçin, Nayman, Argin, Qipçaq, Çiçak, Qalmaq, Uyrat, Qarlik, Turgavut, Burlaq, Buslaq, Çimerçin, Qatagan, Kileçi, Kinegeş, Böyrek, Qiyat, Bozay, Qatay (Khitay), Qanli, Özce, Buluci(?), Topçi(?), Upulaçi, Culun, Cit, Cuyut, Salcavut, Bayavut, Otarçi, Arlat, Kireyit, Unqut, Mangit, Qangit, Oymavut, Qaçat, Merkit, Borqut, Quralas, Qarlap, Ilaci, Gülegen(?), Qisliq, Oglan, Küdey, Türkmen, Dürmen, Tabin, Tama, Meçet, Kirderi, Ramadan, Mumun, Aday, Tuqsaba, Qirgiz, Uyruci, Coyrat, Bozaci, Oysun, Cora, Bataş, Qoysun, Suldiz, Tumay, Tatar, Tilev, Qayan, Sirin, Kürlevüt, Çilekes, Uygur, Yabu (Yabaqu), Agir (Agiran), Buzan, Buzaq, Müyten, Macar, Qocaliq, Çoran, Çürcüt, Barin (Behrin), Mongul, Nöküs (Nukus).[63]

Thirty-three of these tribal names belong to the *Mongols*, and the others to the renowned Turk tribes of the *Jochi Ulus*. Not mentioned above are the *Barlas* and *Kavçin*, which lived in Transoxiana (modern Uzbekistan) prior to the arrival of these Uzbek tribes. Among these 92 tribes, however, only 45 make up the Uzbeks of today.

According to Togan, the sub-divisions of these tribes before Soviet rule were as follows:

(1) The *Kongrat* tribe: this has five oymaks.[64] (a) *Qancagli* consists of fourteen aris: Orus, Qara-Qursak, Çölik, Quyan, Quldavli, Miltek, Kür-Tugi, Gele, Top-Qara, Qara-Boz, Nogay, Bilgelik, Döstlik; (b) *Oyinli*, which consists of nine aris: Aq-Tana, Qara, Çuran, Türkmen, Qavuk, Beş-Bala, Qarakalpak, Qocay, Khoca-Bece; (c) *Qostamgali* which also consists of nine aris: Kül-Abi, Barmaq, Kücer-Khun, Köl-Çuburgan, Qarakalpak, Qostamgali, Seferbiz, Dilberi, Caçaqli; (d) *Oqtamgali*, which consists of seven aris: Tartuglu, Ağamayli, Işiqali, Qazancili, Üyükli, Bükeçli, Qaygali; and (e) *Qir*, which is made up of five aris: Güzli, Küsevli, Ters, Baliqli, Quba.

(2) The *Nayman* tribe, which consists of three oymaks: Qoştamgali, Uvaqtamgali and Sadir.
(3) The *Kineges* tribe, which has five oymaks: Qayrasali, Taraqli, Açamagli, Çikhut, Abaqli.
(4) The *Mangit* tribe, which has three oymaks: Toq-Mangit, Aq-Mangit, Qara-Mangit.
(5) The *Tuyaqli* tribe
(6) The *Müyten* tribe
(7) The *Saray* tribe
(8) The *Barin* tribe
(9) The *Khitay* tribe
(10) The *Qipçaq* tribe
(11) The *Min* tribe
(12) The *Üc Uruğ* tribe
(13) The *Burgut* tribe
(14) The *Arlat* tribe
(15) The *Qanli* tribe
(16) The *Qirq, Yüz* and *Min* tribes.
(17) The *Bataş* tribe
(18) The *Qarakalpak* tribe, which consists of five oymaks: Qara-Qayli, Qara-Singir, Oymavut, Istek, Açamayli.[65]

With regard to the Uzbek tribes in Afghanistan, Togan states that 'we are only in possession of a table prepared at the beginning of the nineteenth century by the Indian historian Mir Izzetullah, which consists of eleven tribes living in Sibirgan, Sayyad, Sencayrek, Kunduz, in the vicinity of Balkh, Eskemis of Badakshan and in Narin'. The Uzbek tribes living in Tajikistan were the *Laqay, Marqa Kiçi Yüz* and *Qarliq*.

According to the new history books in use by the secondary school and university students in Uzbekistan, the Uzbeks along with the Tajiks are the original inhabitants of Central Asia, whose ancestors came and lived there during ancient times. The history of the Uzbeks has close connections with the Sogdiana, Khorezm, Fergana and other developed centres of civilization in the region. Even though the name 'Uzbek' came from *Dasht-i Qipchaq* in the fourteenth century, the Uzbeks within the Sogdia-Khorezm civilization lived with Tajiks throughout centuries as Turkic-speaking people. The new history states that three main ethnic elements form today's Uzbeks:

(1) Turkic-speaking peoples who settled in the regions close to Central Asia, who moved to Maverannahr around the end of 1000 BC and settled in the Fergana Valley (almost 52.7 per cent), Tashkent, Khorezm and around the Zheravshan regions. These inhabitants are called 'Sarts'.
(2) Various Turkic tribes and mixed Turkic-Mongol tribes that began moving into Maverannahr a long time before Shaybani Uzbeks and continued to do so until the fifteenth and sixteenth centuries. These people are called 'Turks' in ethnographic literature.
(3) The *Dasht-i Qipchak* tribes that moved to Maverannahr with Muhammad Shaybani Khan during the fifteenth and sixteenth centuries. It is rather interesting to note that the official history calls these tribes *Küchmanci Uzbeklar* (migrant Uzbeks).[66]

The Uzbek media stressed well-known figures throughout Uzbekistan's history, such as Abu Ali Ibn Sina (Avicenna), Al Khorezmi, Amir Temur (Timurlane), Ulugbeg, Mir Alisher Navoi, Al-Bukhari and Babor. The television, radio and the press referred to these figures as the fathers of Uzbek People. The aim was to create a strong Uzbek nationhood combined with a sense of Islamic and Turkic linkages. Whatever the case, today there is a strong sense of Uzbek identity and an identification with Uzbekistan (Uzbek Nationhood) with a linkage to Islam and its cultural history. This patriotic love of *Vatan Uzbekistan* (Homeland Uzbekistan) is penetrating the vast majority of the young generation in Uzbekistan.

NOTES

1. Geoffrey Wheeler, *The Modern History of Soviet Central Asia* (London: Weidenfeld & Nicolson, 1964), pp. 180–8, 190–8. See also Diloram Ibrahimova, *The Islamization of Central Asia: A Case Study of Uzbekistan* (Leicester: Islamic foundation, 1993); G. Wheeler, *The Peoples of Soviet Central Asia: A Background Book* (London: Bodley Head, 1966), pp. 10–40, 100–11; G. Hambly, *Central Asia* (Weidenfeld & Nicolson, 1969), pp. 63–85.
2. Interview with Professor A. E. Ergashev, Sustainable Development Advisor UNDP, Uzbekistan on 11 September 1996. An interesting discussion of the environmental problem in Central Asia can be found in Keith Martin, 'Central Asia's Forgotten Tragedy', *RFE/RL Research Report*, 3:30, 29 July 1994, pp. 35–48.

3 Interview with Professor A. E. Ergashev, on 11 September 1996.
4 Ibid.
5 For further discussion of the ecological problems in the Aral Sea basin, see 'The Aral in Crisis', *Aral Sea Basin Monitor: A Gazette for Sustainable Development* (Tashkent: EC-ICAS and the Aral Sea Basin Capacity Development Project (ASBCD)) Issue 2, Spring 1996.
6 Ibid. p. 5.
7 Ibid. pp. 6–8.
8 Ibid. pp. 9–10.
9 For a further discussion of the conference held on 18–20 September 1995, see *International Conference on Sustainable Development of the Aral Sea Basin: Final Report*, prepared jointly by UNDP and Inter-state Council on the Problems of the Aral Sea (ICAS), September 1995.
10 Several interviews regarding the status and role of Uzbek women in the republic were conducted with the representatives of the various women's rights organizations in July–September, 1996 in Tashkent. These included the Women's Committee (on 20 August 1996); the Women's Resource Centre (25 July 1996); the Centre for Young Women (20 August, 5 September 1996); and the Business Women's Association (25 July 1996). An excellent account of the status and role of Uzbek women in pre- and post-Soviet society in the republic can be found in Deniz Kandiyoti, 'Women and Social policy' in Keith Griffin, (ed.), *Social Policy and Economic Transformation in Uzbekistan* (Geneva: International Labour Office, April 1996), pp. 129–48.
11 Deniz Kandiyoti, 'Women and Social Policy' in Griffin, op. cit., p. 146.
12 Faizulla Boyinazov, *Urta Asiayaning Antik Davri, (the Ancient Period of Central Asia)* (Tashkent: 1991), pp. 5–100. See also Uzbekiston Respublikasi Fanlar Akademiyasi, *Uzbekistan Xalqlari Tarikhi I, (The History of the People of Uzbekistan)* (Tashkent: Fan Nashriyati, 1993), pp. 3–61; Hambly, op. cit. 1969, pp. 1–62.
13 Uzbekiston Respublikasi Fanlar Akademiyasi, op. cit., pp. 62–114; Hambly, op. cit., pp. 49–63; Wheeler, op. cit., pp. 1–101.
14 Hambly, op. cit., pp. 58–103.
15 Ibid.
16 Ibid. pp. 127–39.
17 Ibid.
18 Ibid. op. cit., pp. 114–19.
19 Ibid.
20 Ibid. op. cit., pp. 118–26.
21 Ibid.
22 Ibid. pp. 139–62.
23 Ibid. pp. 149–62; see also Buriboyi Ahmedov, *Amir Temur* (Tashkent: 1995), pp. 3–329; Buriboyi Ahmedov, *Sohibkhron Temur, (The Great Temur)* (Tashkent: Fanlar Akademiyasi, 1996), pp. 3–41; *Temur Tuzuklari, (The Rules of Temur)* (Tashkent: 1996), pp. 3–81. Uzbekiston Respublikasi Fanlar Akademiyasi, op. cit., pp. 149–177; Uzbekiston Respublikasi Fanlar Akademiyasi, *Uzbekistan Xalqlari Tarikhi II* (Tashkent: 1993), pp. 4–25, 25–98.
24 For a detailed discussion of Amir Temur's life and his conquests see Ahmedov op. cit., 1995 and Ahmedov, op. cit., 1996.

25 Hambly, op. cit., pp. 163–74; Wheeler, op. cit., 1964, pp. 1–30; Zeki Velidi Togan, *Türkili Türkistan ve Yakin Tarihi, (Fatherland Turkestan and its Near History)* 2nd edn (Istanbul: Enderun, 1981), pp. 23–42.
26 Togan, op. cit., pp. 23–42.
27 Hambly, op. cit., pp. 163–74.
28 Hambly, op. cit., pp. 174–87. Wheeler, op. cit., 1964, pp. 48–116.
29 Uzbekistan Respublikasi Fanlar Akademiyasi, *Uzbekistan Xalqlari Tarikhi II* (Tashkent: 1993), pp. 98–245; Hambly, op. cit., 1969, pp. 187–226; Wheeler, op. cit., 1964, pp. 48–116.
30 Uzbekistan Respublikasi Fanlar Akademiyasi, op. cit., vol. II, pp. 130–245.
31 Hambly, op. cit., pp. 187–226. See also George N. Curzon, *Russia in Central Asia in 1889 and the Anglo-Russian Question* (London: Frank Cass & Co. Ltd, 1967), pp. 326–414; Uzbekistan Respublikasi Fanlar Akademiyasi, op. cit., vol. II, pp. 93–8.
32 This subject was discussed with several Uzbek and Russian historians in Uzbekistan during the summer of 1996. For an interesting discussion of the local divisions and their disagreements with the Bolsheviks in Moscow in the wake of the 'national delimitation' process and the creation of Uzbek Soviet Socialist Republic in 1924, see Donald S. Carlisle, 'Soviet Uzbekistan: State and Nation in Historical Perspective' in Beatrice F. Manz (ed.), *Central Asia in Historical Perspective* (Westview Press, 1994), pp. 103–22; Carlisle 'Power and politics in Soviet Uzbekistan: From Stalin to Gorbachev' in William Fierman (ed.), *Soviet Central Asia: The Failed Transformation* (Boulder: Westview Press, 1991), pp. 105–20.
33 For a further discussion of the events that led to the dissolution of the Soviet Union, see Alexander Dallin and Gail W. Lapidus (eds), *The Soviet System in Crisis; A Reader of Western and Soviet Views* (Boulder: Westview Press, 1991; 1st edn), pp. 3–36, 97–111, 116–27, 176–203. For another excellent discussion of this issue see Rachel Walker, *Six Years that Shook the World; Perestroika, the Impossible Project* (Manchester: Manchester University Press), 1993, pp. 73–220.
34 Stephen White, *Gorbachev and After* (Cambridge: Cambridge University Press, 1991), p. 17; Goldman Marshall, *What Went Wrong with Perestroika?* (New York: Norton, 1991), pp. 82–3.
35 Walker, op. cit., 1993, pp. 77–86; Marshall, op. cit., 1991, pp. 15–30. See also Dallin and Lapidus, op. cit., pp. 3–36.
36 Juan Linz and Alfred Stephan, 'Political identities and electoral sequences', *Daedalus*, 121, 2, (1992), pp. 123–39., Walker, op. cit., 1993, pp. 86–87.
37 Alexander Motyl, 'Totalitarian collapse, imperial disintegration and the rise of the Soviet West: implications for the West' in Michael Mandelbaum (ed.), *The Rise of Nations in the Soviet Union: American Foreign Policy and the Disintegration of the USSR* (New York: Council on Foreign Relations Press, c1991), p. 45.
38 For further discussion of this see Walker, op. cit., 1993, pp. 89–94; Motyl, op. cit., p. 45.
39 Karen Dawisha and Bruce Parrott, *Russia and the New States of Eurasia: The Politics of Upheaval* (USA: Cambridge University Press, 1994), p. 19.
40 Ann Sheehy, 'Commonwealth Emerges From a Disintegrating USSR', *Report on the USSR*, RFE/RL Research Institute, 1:1, 3 January 1992, pp. 5–6.
41 Alexander Rahr, 'Is Gorbachev Finished?', *Report on the USSR,* RFE/RL Research Institute, 3:51/51 (December 1991), pp. 1–3.

42 Ann Sheehy, 'The Union Treaty: A Further setback', RFE/RL Research Institute, 3:49 (December 1991), pp. 1–4.
43 Steve Crawshaw, *Goodbye to the USSR: The Collapse of Soviet Power* (London: Bloomsbury, 1992), pp. 160–182. For a further discussion of the events before, during and after the military coup in Moscow, see Martin Sixsmith, *Moscow Coup: The Death of the Soviet System* (London: Simon & Schuster, 1991). See also Walker, op. cit., pp. 222–44.
44 For a further discussion of this, see Crawshaw, op. cit., pp. 185–203.
45 Sheehy, op. cit. (3 January 1992), p. 8.
46 Walker, op. cit., p. 186.
47 Elizabeth Teague and Vera Tolz, 'CPSU, Report on the USSR', RFE/RL Research Institute, 3:47, 22 November 1991, pp. 1–5. See also Walker, op. cit., p. 186.
48 Ann Sheehy, 'Commonwealth of Independent States: An Uneasy Compromise', RFE/RL Research Institute, 1:2, 10 January 1992, pp. 1–4.
49 Sheehy, op. cit., 3 January 1992, pp. 2–7.
50 Ibid.
51 Rahr, op. cit., p. 3.
52 Sheehy, op.cit., 10 January 1992, pp. 7–8.
53 For a detailed discussion of the Uzbek authorities' ability to take control away from Moscow of staffing and promotion in the Party organs; their assertion of control over their state activities; and the scandals that brought home to the Moscow leadership the disturbing truth of the Kremlin's failure in reasserting its control over Party organs and state activity in former Soviet Uzbekistan, see Donald S. Carlisle, in Fierman, op. cit., pp. 105–20; James Critchlow, 'Prelude to Independence: How the Uzbek Party Apparatus Broke Moscow's Grip on Elite Recruitment' in Fierman, op. cit., 1991, pp. 131–53; James Critchlow, 'Further Repercussions of the "Uzbek Affair",' *Report on the USSR*, 2:18, 1990, pp. 20–22. For further discussions of political corruption in the republic during the Soviet era, see Sheehy, 'Major Anti-Corruption Drive in Uzbekistan', *Radio Liberty Research Bulletin*, RL 324/84, 30 August 1984, pp. 1–17.
54 A former Russian incumbent of the Second Secretaryship, the traditional proconsular post which was intended to protect the Kremlin's interests in Uzbekistan, was placed under arrest in 1986. Another Russian who was charged with corruption was a former deputy Chairman of the republican Council of Ministers. This information was obtained during an interview with an independent journalist, Mirhan M. Nazmutdinov, in Tashkent in July–August 1996. See also Critchlow, in Fierman, op. cit., p. 135.
55 See, for example, Critchlow, in Fierman, op. cit., pp. 136–46.
56 *Ozbekiston Adabiyoti va Sanaati*, 15 December 1989, pp. 4–5. See also Critchlow, in Fierman, op. cit., p. 149.
57 See also Togan, op. cit., 1981, pp. 29–41, and E. Allworth, *The Modern Uzbeks: From the Fourteenth Century to the Present: A Cultural History* (Stamford: Hoover Institution Press, 1990), pp. 32–33. For further discussion of this see V. V. Bartold, *Four Studies on the History of Central Asia,* I (Leiden: 1956) and II (Leiden: 1958); Hambly, op. cit., 1969, pp. 140–42; James Critchlow, *Nationalism in Uzbekistan: A Soviet Republic's Road to Sovereignty* (Boulder: Westview Press, 1991), pp. 3–15. Two interesting discussions of this subject are Isa Jabbarov, *Uzbek Khalki Ethnografiyasi, (The Ethnography of the Uzbek People)* (Tashkent:

Uzbekiston, 1994); and Usmon Turan, *Turkiy Khalkar Mafkurasi,(The Ideology of Turkic People)* (Tashkent: Cholpan Nashriyoti, 1995).
58 Wheeler, op. cit., 1966, pp. 9–24.
59 See V. V. Bartold, *Four Studies on the History of Central Asia*, I (Leiden: 1956 and II, 1958); Hambly, op. cit., 1969, pp. 140–2.
60 W. P. and Zelda K. Coates, *Soviets in Central Asia* (London: Lawrence and Wishart Ltd., 1951), p. 30.
61 Allworth, op. cit., Chapter 3.
62 Togan, op. cit., pp. 31–2.
63 Ibid. pp. 41–3.
64 '*Uruk*'–'*Oymak*'–'*Aris*'–'*Soy*'–'*Tire*'–'*Ara*'. These Turkish terms define the nomenclature applied to the sub-divisions from the tribal confederation down to the smallest unit. '*Uruk*' is composed of '*Oymaks*', which are made up of '*Aris*', which are in turn a composition of '*Soy*'.
65 Togan, op. cit., pp. 42–3.
66 Isa Jabbarov, *Uzbek Khalki Ethnografiyasi* (Tashkent: Uzbekiston, 1994), pp. 26–149. See also Uzbekistan Respublikasi Fanlar Akadamiyasi, op. cit., pp. 3–25; and Usmon Turan, *Turkiy Khalklar Mafkurasi* (Tashkent: Cholpan Nashriyoti, 1995).

2

Social Transformation: Past, Present and Future

The land that today is known as Uzbekistan has itself undergone substantial change. It has historically been a place of encounter between peoples of different races and cultures. Many mighty empires and dynasties were formed and destroyed there and its boundaries have consequently been redrawn many times. There have always been mass population movements as people were replaced, displaced, expelled or assimilated. These movements and migrations of people, and three thousand years of conquests, have produced a high level of civilization in the region. New conquerors were continually destroying the civilizations that existed before them and then restoring afterwards the artifacts of ancient cultures. Even today, it is possible to admire magnificent architecture and art of medieval age in the cities of Khiva, Samarkand, Bukhara, Khokand and Tashkent. These towns are virtually museums, which are alive but silent witnesses of the old civilization.

Russia's invasions of the East (Siberia) and South (Caucasus) were completed by its invasion of Central Asia in the late nineteenth century. All these empires had an impact on the people's lives, but none have so profoundly changed the social character of the nomadic tribes in the region as the October Revolution of 1917, which brought to a close the formation period of the modern Central Asian societies. However, if we are to pinpoint one decisive moment in the history of Uzbeks before the October Revolution, it must be the period of Mongol rule in the thirteenth and fourteenth centuries. Here we see a striking extent of the evolution of systems of government, society and legitimation that remained in force for centuries until the Russian invasion. The other important feature of Mongol rule was that Uzbeks took their name from one of the Khans of Golden Horde – the *Ulus* (state) of Batu, an empire of 'Turko-Mongol'[1] people who comprised the nomadic tribes of the steppes. We describe the tribes in or around Mongolia and northern

China, who marched to Central Asia in the early twelfth century, as 'Turko-Mongol' since they amalgamated and it is by no means clear in all cases which were Turkish and which were Mongol. Even this would mean no more than that they spoke Turkish or Mongolian respectively. In any case the tribes intermarried freely, probably with the exception of the Tatars. These 'Turko-Mongol' tribes later intermingled with predominantly more Turkish tribes of the Qipchaq plains, during Batu's, and especially Berke's reign. We will name the tribes of the Golden Horde from Berke's reign onwards as 'Turko-Mongolic', because the Mongol tribes adopted the local culture and Turkish became their language. We will name the Turkish tribes of the Golden Horde of this time, and those in the south of the Syrdaria, who also mixed with Persians, as 'Turkic' meaning that, to a large extent, they intermingled with the Mongol and non-Mongol elements. There have also been intermarriages between these tribes.

The nomads

In ancient times the nomads were the enemies of China, the only settled Asian civilization that they had contact with. These nomadic people with their flocks and herds moved from place to place along the outskirts of the Gobi Desert; though they were often driven back into the desert, they could be neither destroyed nor subjugated. When their mounted hordes were scattered, the various nomadic tribes would gradually gather together in their flight westwards. This ever-growing human mass would descend on the civilized states in their path, establishing short-lived dominions upon the ruins, or, when they were repelled, assailed that state and moved further on, inciting new tribes to war. Out of the forests of the north and from the surrounding mountains, they moved into the vacated areas of Mongolia and Central Asia searching for pasturelands and eager for booty. They rapidly refilled the places from which others had been expelled, ever on the watch for the first signs of weakness in their settled neighbours. Meanwhile they engaged in unceasing petty wars among themselves for grazing grounds, livestock, and the pitiful possessions of the nomads. This remained the situation for century after century; during a thousand years the names and the races changed, but it was always the same picture.[2]

At the eastern end of the Mongolian homeland was the vast belt of the steppe grassland that stretched as far west as the Hungarian plain. To the north was the impenetrable Siberian forest. To the south was the Gobi Desert and beyond that China. The steppe is treeless pasture, not suitable for agriculture, but ideally suited for the pasturing of flocks and herds. The nomads relied above all on sheep and horses. Sheep provided skins for clothing and wool for the manufacture of felt tents – often called *Gers* (*Yurts* in the west), which were the nomad's homes – mutton, milk and cheese for food, and dung for fuel. Horses were the principal means of transport, both of men and goods, and were essential for hunting, which was a major source of food. They were also used in warfare. Their milk, when fermented, provided the staple alcoholic drink, *Qimiz*. Other integral parts of the steppe economy were camels and oxen, which were used to pull carts.

The nomadic tribes also migrated seasonally, typically from summer pastures on the plain to winter pastures in sheltered valleys. These migrations moved along well-trodden routes from one customary pasture to another. Disputes often arose because better pasturelands were often claimed by others. The distances travelled on these seasonal migrations could vary according to circumstances, ranging from the very long to the very short. The nomads had to satisfy some of their needs through trade with the settled societies to the south, among which were the Tatars and the Uighurs. The nomads needed grain but they also traded in 'luxuries' such as tea and textiles. Most importantly the nomads required metals with which to make their weapons. The settled civilizations also found uses for the nomad's own products. The relationship between the steppe and the sown land (modern Uzbekistan) was not one of constant hostility. In times of peace, however uneasy, it was more a relationship of mutual dependence, although the settled communities' products were more essential to the nomad's needs than anything from the steppe was to the settled communities.

Around the sixth and the seventh centuries AD the nomads of the steppe came into contact with a second settled civilization, as a result of the creation of the formidable empire of the Turks. This was exclusively a steppe empire that united almost all the nomadic tribes from Mongolia to the Caspian Sea. It was during, and after, this empire that the nomadic Turkish tribes began settling south of the Amu Darya river where they were introduced first to the Sasanian culture and later to the inhabitants of the sown land. These were people of Persian stock, who were the forerunners of the Tajiks. From the sixth century onwards, until Chinggis

Khan's invasion of Central Asia, more and more nomadic Turkish tribes moved south. Yet many other tribes, mostly Turkish, remained in the north and retained their nomadic lifestyle. Thus from ancient times until the Turkish empire, little had changed in the nomadic life of those who remained on the steppe, though more tribes were engaged in trading. This continued until the march of Chinggis Khan into Central Asia in the early twelfth century.

This latter period also saw a trend towards the desegregation of large tribes into smaller units, thereby numerically expanding the ruling elite, the steppe aristocracy. The precise time and reason for this is not clear, but a division in function had emerged between those engaged in breeding sheep and cattle, and those in horse-breeding and trade, not to mention the fierce struggle between the clan leaders. Whatever the real motive behind this development, throughout the twelfth century a new pattern of social relationships had emerged, a variety of nomadic feudalism. This provided the social and military basis for Chinggis Khan's conquests, but it was also strengthened in turn by him and his descendants. For instance, there was the *Qurultai* or assembly of princes and chieftains. Society was divided into classes with a military aristocracy immediately beneath the ruler and his family, and with serfdom and slavery at the base of a well-defined social pyramid. The nomadic aristocracy was elevated above the rest of the community by its wealth in livestock. It was bound together by intimate ties of birth and marriage as well as by the unique perspective and heroic code of morality of a warrior caste. The *Yasa*, the law of Chinggis Khan, was not a code of mutual obligations or rights, but a collection of mandatory inductions to be obeyed without question by his subjects and successors alike. In theory there was no limitation to the exercise of unrestrained tyranny by the ruler, but in practice tyranny might be curbed by custom and the strength of clan feeling which cut across gradations in the social hierarchy. It was further tempered by the fear of revolt.[3]

The last major nomadic invasion of Central Asia was that of the Mongols under Chinggis Khan, who united all the Turkic and Mongolic tribes around the Gobi Desert and marched into Central Asia in the early thirteenth century. Their first appearance in the region brought destruction and devastation, though later they gradually assimilated with the local population, adopting their language and culture. After Chinggis Khan the agricultural centres of Asia and Europe became provinces of a world empire ruled from Mongolia. The Mongols had united the steppe and settled lands into one political unit and had created a uniform class over both. However, pastoralism and agriculture continued to comprise separate economic systems. The western part of the Mongol empire known as the Golden Horde, developed under Batu in accordance with Chinggis Khan's principles as a wholly nomadic realm. The only result of its contact with the two Asiatic civilizations, the Chinese and the Islamic, was that it received all the advantages that the steppe dwellers expected from settled populations.

By the time of Berke's rule, the Turko-Mongol tribes of the Golden Horde gradually blended in with the original inhabitants of the Dasht-i Qipchaq, predominantly Turkish tribes, and the 'Turkish' language began to evolve as a lingua franca. Islam, the bane of the Ilkhans, had since Berke's time been the dominant religion, a civilizing influence for the Golden Horde. Muslim architects developed Berke's New Sarai into a splendid city full of palaces, mosques and baths – a town of marble and porphyry equipped with all the luxuries of the day. There established a remarkable urban civilization in which the dominant cultural influences appeared to have been Egyptian and Syrian, rather then Persian.[4] This stemmed from the foreign policy pursued by Berke and his immediate successors. A political alliance with the Mamluks enriched the cultural life of the Golden Horde, bringing artists, craftsmen, scholars and theologians from Egypt to centres such as Sarai and New Sarai. It also marked the end of that phase of Mongol expansion which took for granted the Chinggiskhanid family unity as the basis for world conquest. Simultaneously, with the products of the two great Asiatic civilizations, the wares of the West found their way to the Volga. From the south, Italian merchants travelled to the Horde, while from the north, by way of Novograd and Nijni-Novgorod, Hansa goods came to the Volga. Yet despite being served by all these civilizations, the Khans were nevertheless able to preserve the ancient customs of their people, and remained nomadic.

The boundary between the steppe and settled worlds reappeared in Central Asia with the rise of a new Turko-Mongolian conqueror, Amir Temur, in the Chagatai Khanate. He subjugated most of the steppe, but he and his successors consolidated their power only over settled regions. Chagatai Khanate remained under Temurid control until the end of the fifteenth century when it fell to the Ozbeks (Uzbeks).

With the re-emergence of the boundary came sharper and more lasting divisions among the Turko-Mongolic ruling classes of the former Mongol Empire. This period also saw the development of more specific identities, many holding ethnic names that survive today. The process of differentiation was chiefly a political one, centred around the creation of tribal confederations and loyalty to individual leaders, most of whom descended from Chinggis Khan. It was also confined to the issue of nomad-sedentary relations. Some Turko-Mongolic groups, that were semi-settled, such as the Uzbeks, moved nearer to the settled regions to exploit the wealth of the agricultural populations. Others such as the Kazaks and Kyrgyzy chose to remain in the steppe and continued with their nomadic life.[5]

In 1501 the Uzbeks, led by Abu-l Khayr's grandson, Shaybani Khan, overthrew the fragile Temurid dynasty in Maverannahr and seized the fertile land that belonged to this dynasty. The Uzbek Khans strengthened the Chinggis tradition in the region, but they soon came to promote a 'Perso-Islamic' culture when Muslims and other new arrivals who were eager for cultural prestige intermingled with the local population. Within Central Asia, the semi-settled, semi-nomadic Uzbeks controlled a sedentary population. The society that developed in this period was a mixture of Turko-Mongolic and Persian. The ruling class spoke Turkic, but the high culture it nurtured was almost exclusively Persian, produced by an elite of the subject population comprising Iranians, now called Tajiks and Turks. Although many Uzbeks who moved to the region with Shaybani Khan eventually became sedentary, the politically active class preserved their identity by maintaining their tribal affiliations. This secured them a place within the ruling stratum. The administration was also mixed, many high military and court offices being held by Uzbeks, while the civil and financial administration remained in the hands of the Persian-speaking bureaucracy.[6]

It was thus the achievement of the Shaybanids to make Maverannahr the permanent home for the Uzbeks. However, the simultaneous rise of the Safavid dynasty in Iran and the firm hold that the Indian Temurids (especially Babor, 1483–1530, founder of the Mongol dynasty in India), retained on the region south of the Hindu Kush, prevented even the greatest Shaybanid rule from re-enacting Temur's conquests. Instead a balance of power emerged between these three dynasties. The Uzbek state was decentralized, and the chiefs of Uzbek tribes used the frequent dynastic struggles to enhance their power, sometimes becoming 'kingmakers'. Tribal leaders or junior members of the dynasty acted as local rulers whose level of autonomy depended on the personality and power of the ruling khan. Even within the smaller regions of the empire, power was not highly centralized, nor was it wielded entirely by the dynasty. Uzbek rule was more of a superstructure, resting on top of a subject population with its own organization. Among the settled population the elite classes of the cities held a position of considerable strength. Much of the city governance lay in the hands of religious men, major landowners and merchants, who maintained their power through family and patronage networks. These served as a link between the local population and the Turko-Mongolic ruling class.[7]

By the end of the sixteenth century there was a gradual decline in the economy and the development of education stagnated in the region. There were several reasons for this: Firstly, there were persistent quarrels between the Kazaks who retained the traditional nomadic style of life through to the period of the Russian conquest, and the inhabitants of the oasis-cities, Uzbeks and Tajiks. Secondly, there was a steady decline in the trans-continental caravan trade which had always underlain the prosperity of the oasis-cities of Central Asia. This followed from the discovery of the sea-route between Europe and the Far East. Maverannahr, the centre of the 'Great Silk Road' had been the principal meeting place of the commerce and civilizations of China, India, the Middle East and Europe. As a consequence of these discoveries, the old trade routes declined in importance, precipitating the economic decline of the region. The gradual demise of the caravan traffic meant an enormous loss of wealth for those Uzbek rulers whose main source of income had been the taxes charged on goods passing through their territories. Thirdly, despite economic decline, new forms of production were not sought. Instead orientation to agricultural development was preserved as well as old feudal forms of land ownership which had become obsolete. Fourthly, as a result of the destruction of the main trade route, the Uzbek empire was isolated from newly developing markets. Feudal-despotic forms of political power became more dominant. The growth of the dervish order (*silsileh*), which had flourished well enough during the Chagatai and Temurid periods, found the Uzbek regimes peculiarly well-disposed towards them. The members of this order inspired huge veneration among almost all classes of the population, whether nomads or oasis-dwellers. In both city and countryside, Sufi *shaykhs* (dervishes) controlled large holdings including charitable endowments and commanded considerable followings among the population, to whom they offered protection and social services. Dervishes then began deriving their support from the most disruptive and 'barbarous' elements in the societies of southern and northern Syrdarya. Even among the educated classes of the urban centres there began an excessive concentration on the study of theology at the expense of other disciplines. In the seventeenth century, the dervishes represented Islam at the level of the lowest common dominator.[8] They became the dogmatic clergy and important powers in the society. The relationship between the clergy and the local rulers in certain areas provided a solid base for independence and enabled those areas to develop as separate power centres. Economic backwardness, illiteracy, military-political weakness, disunity and civil strife all continued unabated, setting the scene for the break-up of the Uzbek empire into three separate dynasties in the mid-eighteenth century. Although the state formations (Khanates) of this time were dominated by particular tribal groupings, their subjects included representatives of many different origins and thus, from a modern outlook, they were multi-ethnic states.

The Khanate of Khokand was ruled by the Uzbek Ming tribe in the east, the Khanate of Bukhara by the Mangits in the centre stretching to the south-east including modern Tajikistan, and the Khanate of Khiva by the Qungrats in the north-west. Towards the end of the eighteenth century, extensive tracts in the region began to show signs of recovery and the three regimes strived with varying degrees of success to impose a greater degree of administrative centralization than had formerly existed in the area. It became possible to undertake the construction of useful public works, in particular in the Fergana Valley under the Khanate of Khokand. Irrigation projects were initiated, a considerable amount of public building was undertaken in traditional styles and craftsmanship of some quality survived. Commercial activity was undertaken and modest prosperity ensued. However, socially, politically and economically the regimes were weak and remained so until Russian rule. Under such circumstances it is hardly surprising that Muslim Central Asia contributed so little to Islamic civilization under Uzbek rule. The only real exception was the emergence of the Chagatai Turkish language and literature which had developed rapidly as a language of polite learning during the Temurid period and which blossomed under the patronage of Sultan Husayin Bayqara of Herat and Mir Alisher Navoi, the greatest Chagatai poets. By the late fifteenth century, it had become a mature vehicle for literary expression and complemented Persian, although it failed to replace the latter as the language of the cultural elite. Chagatai poetry was warmly patronized, and written by a number of Shaybanid rulers, including Muhammad Shaybani himself and Ubaydullah. It was also under Shaybani and his descendants that the Uzbeks of the steppe settled down in various districts of the oases of Maverannahr and began to work on land and engage in farming. They intermingled with the Iranians (Tajiks) and other native populations, largely Turkish, to form a single mass of, to a large extent, settled town dwellers – the Uzbek nation of today.

The transformation under Russian rule
As soon as Central Asia came under Russian rule, the problem of organizing the conquered territories arose. From the invasion to 1898, the status of Central Asia underwent many changes. The equivocation of the Russian government over the question of organizing Central Asia stemmed above all from a profound ignorance of the region. It misunderstood the aspirations of the conquered people, and constantly had to try to readjust its policies to realities as it was progressively made aware of them.[9] The real changes however, even after 1898, were in territorial organization. The result of the new organization was the creation of a greater Turkistan Guberniia composed of five regions: Syrdarya, Fergana, Samarkand, Semirechie, and Transcaspia, with Tashkent becoming the capital of both the Guberniia and Syrdarya. Bukhara and Khiva retained the status of protectorates. This territorial organization survived until the 1917 revolution.

The structures employed replicated the system of territorial organization in effect throughout Russia, but all power in the region was wielded by the military. The authorities allowed the existing local judicial institutions, and the political institutions, of the villages to continue, but they intervened to confirm the election or designation of judges, who were placed under the control of low ranking Tsarist officials. For any affair involving neither Russian subjects nor interests, and not falling within remits that might interest the Russian administration, judgements were rendered according to traditional standards. Legislation and administration at the local level remained in local hands, and for all practical purposes, in the control of the traditional authorities. The political organization of the region was based on the principle of managing the population without interfering in its affairs, thus rendering the machinery of colonial domination progressively lighter and less costly.[10] In the regions where thickly populated oasis land possessed an ancient civilization, rural colonization was more difficult, so such areas remained relatively protected. In the field of education, a few Russian schools opened but they had little impact on the population. As non-Russians, the local people were exempt from military service, and there was generally little incentive to mix them with the Russian population even temporarily.

The settlers did not arrive in the area until the beginning of the twentieth century. Despite the small numbers involved, the scarcity of good land created conflicts between Russians and the local people. What profoundly altered the economic, social and cultural life of the region was the construction of a railway system. This changed the country, allowing the development of a textile industry and leading to the arrival of many Russian workers who gave a new character to the urban life of the Guberniia. Purely Russian towns sprang up along the railway route in present-day Uzbekistan. The old cities of the region rapidly took on the character of 'colonial' cities comprising a modern 'European' quarter, populated exclusively by Russians existing side by side with the old native city. The main changes, however, were in the economic sphere. The production of cotton and the land reforms were furnished for the needs of the Russian textile industry, the territory of present-day Uzbekistan becoming Russia's principal supplier of cotton. Large tracts of irrigated land were turned into cotton plantations as Russia sought to turn the territory into a source of raw materials and cheap labour. In the process, a new class of middlemen and landowners emerged. The working people of the region came under the double yoke of exploitation, by the local rich on the one hand and by Russian capitalists and officials on the other. For all practical purposes, the only permanent proletariat of this region by 1905 was essentially Russian. In order to prevent the penetration of revolutionary ideas among the native people, the government systematically prevented the development of a local proletariat, favouring instead the Russian proletariat who, to local eyes, appeared like a privileged class.[11]

In the second half of the nineteenth century new movements arose in the Muslim world, mostly pan-Islamic or pan-Turkic, although this period also witnessed the beginnings of narrower linguistic nationalisms. These centred in the Ottoman Empire and many were strongly influenced by European ideas, though they reached this region comparatively late. This was also the era of pan-Slavism, of 'orthodoxy and nationalism'; one in which the Tatars of the Volga and the Crimea suffered considerable discrimination.[12] The pan-Turkic movement began among the Tatars of the Russian Empire, and gained wider publicity in 1905. The major concern of the new reformists of the Russian Empire was education. Through their introduction of a new system, known as 'Jadidism', they promoted ideas of unity among Turks and Muslims of the Russian Empire. In Central Asia, it was largely through the agency of the Tatars that the Jadid movement spread to the east, but it received mixed responses. The most receptive to nationalistic ideas were the Kazak intellectuals, some of whom were Russian educated. They lived under direct Russian rule and saw their lands disappear under Russian colonization. Resentment proved a fertile breeding ground for nationalistic feelings. In Uzbekistan the spread of the Jadid reformist movement was rather slow, even though the early pan-Islamic ideas had achieved some acceptance. In the areas where the Russians ruled directly, officials left religious educational institutions intact. Throughout all this area the conservative *ulema* (educated class) remained the preponderant force in education until the Russian revolution. In Khiva and Bukhara, rulers and *ulema* maintained a hostile attitude to Jadid activities. Nonetheless, Jadidism gave birth to the demand for national self-determination by the local people, endowing them with a modern education and bringing in its wake fresh political ideas. In the cultural sphere it brought new attitudes, a modernization of past practices, and the adaptation of Islam to modern conditions.

However Russia in general, like other imperialist powers, used the region entirely for its own benefit and sought to crush every manifestation of native culture and independence. Russian penetration broke up the old order and to some extent paved the way for further progress, putting an end to the constant feudal wars between the various khans and amirs that were devastating the land and ruining lives of the people.

The transformation of Uzbekistan under the Soviet Union
After Tsarist Russia had incorporated the area of Uzbekistan into its empire in the 1860s, it permitted the area a significant degree of political

and cultural autonomy. This was to change after the Russian revolution as the new Soviet regime set about transforming Central Asia. The first important reform came with the creation of 'proto'-nation-states. The construction of these new 'nation-states' was followed by a comprehensive campaign to modernize, and at the same time, 'Sovietize', the region. The key mobilizing factors in Uzbekistan became secularization, collectivization, industrialization and intensive education.

A massive literacy campaign for children and adults was undertaken immediately after the creation of the new Uzbek republic. This would serve two basic aims: firstly, it would produce a more efficient workforce, and secondly, it would help to politicize the population and thereby integrate people into the Soviet system. The government introduced free and compulsory primary and secondary education, and provided textbooks for all children, as well as for adults. The system began with a limited primary curriculum which was gradually increased to an eight-year, then a ten-year and finally an eleven-year programme of study. The government also initiated an extensive programme of teaching and training to raise levels of adult literacy. Thousands of special literacy schools were established all over the country; many factories were workshops for reading and writing. The campaign to raise literacy levels showed some success despite being hampered by a severe lack of resources, and the substitution of the Latin script for the Arabic and later the Cyrillic for the Latin. In the early Soviet period, average literacy rates were 2–3 per cent, but by the late 1970s, it was estimated at over 90 per cent for the younger generation. Today it is virtually 100 per cent. An official history, literature and national language (Uzbek) were created.[13]

Efforts were also made to draw the local population into the party organization, the central and regional administration, and the legal apparatus. Women were given equal rights with men in law, in education and in the workplace. They were encouraged to seek paid employment outside the home and take an active part in the socio-political life of the community.

The formation of collective farms and the development of irrigation, together with the establishment of new industries, also changed the face of the country. Collectivization brought fundamental changes both to the organization of labour and to work skills. Traditional forms of farming, manufacture and trade were eradicated in order to make way for modern methods and large-scale communal projects organized by the state. The changes were undertaken in accordance with the First and Second Five-Year Plans (1928–32) and (1933–7) with dramatic results, particularly in the cultivation of cotton. By 1948 some 98.8 per cent of Uzbek peasant households were conjoined in collective farms. Cotton planting and cultivation were mechanized and the land was harrowed by machines. Electric power production started while new thermal power stations and hydroelectric plants were built in the major cities.[14]

Under Soviet rule, the appearance of Uzbek cities, towns, *kishlaks* and *auls* (villages) underwent enormous changes. Most areas were electrified and had water mains, streets were planned and paved and a system of straight main arteries was developed with squares and parks. These roads were lined with modern buildings, theatres, cinemas, social clubs, higher educational establishments and industrial enterprises. Medical centres and hospitals were built with special attention being paid to maternal and infant welfare; crèches and kindergartens were provided for young children. New communication and transport networks were developed. This infrastructure provided the Uzbek people with a framework to eliminate not only economic, but cultural backwardness.

However, alongside the efforts to establish new norms and values, and bring about a modern society, a concerted campaign was undertaken to remove every visible vestige of the pre-Soviet culture. Inevitably, the main target was Islam. Until the early 1920s, Islam was treated with an uneasy tolerance, but thereafter, with minor variations in tactics, the official attitude for the next five decades would be one of unrelenting hostility. The social and organizational infrastructure of Islam was destroyed. The religious schools, colleges, charitable endowments (*Waqf*), law courts and titles were abolished. The great majority of mosques were closed and most of the religious leaders were either executed, imprisoned, forced to flee abroad, or coopted into the service of the Soviet regime. Little attention was devoted to the creation of manufacturing industry and so Uzbekistan became highly dependent on inter-republic trade. The process of social transformation was hastened by the purges of the 1930s. Although the purges did not eliminate all potential sources of opposition, they created a climate of mass terror that resulted in self-censorship, and which in turn produced what can only be termed defensive 'amnesia'.[15] Many people with whom I discussed this subject in various parts of Uzbekistan, stated that the terror and the oppressive character of the regime was so harsh that it created tremendous hatred towards the regime but at the same time a sense of fear that led people to be silent about what was going on around them. Only family networks and clan relationships – one of the few features of pre-Soviet society to survive – provided a degree of protection against the arbitrary excesses of the system. This provided some counterbalance to the enormous changes that were taking place in the public domain. These networks became a safety valve, enabling such high levels of social transformation to take place, while providing some degree of stability.

The educational system transmitted Soviet ideology. Other aspects of the modernization campaign were similarly activated by ideological concerns. The creation of an official 'national' (Uzbek) language, literature and history were certainly not purely academic exercises, but were rather part of an attempt to shape the intellectual response to Uzbek society. The primary goals were two-fold: to instil a sense of 'national' identity on the one hand, and to ensure that this remained subordinate to an overriding Soviet identity on the other. The change of script kept the Uzbek people ignorant of their history and culture and made them rely heavily on what was printed in Russian. The Communist Party and its ideology became the only guiding force of the society in all spheres, whether cultural economic, political or educational. Uzbekistan suffered in full measure from the shortcomings of the Soviet system. Patchy development followed from inefficiency and inadequate technical maintenance. Catastrophic environmental problems followed from environmentally destructive technologies and unsustainable and excessive use of the irrigation system and natural resources. There was also a lack of familiarity with international institutions and modern international financial management. Even so, it was under Soviet rule that Uzbekistan progressed from a purely agricultural to an agricultural-industrial society. In essence, Soviet policies transformed Uzbekistan from a traditional society to a modern one.

The post-Soviet transformation
The collapse of the Soviet system took with it the ideological framework within which modern Uzbek society had functioned: the Soviet national constructs including administrative identities, history, language and territorial boundaries. The responsibility for planning and implementing

developmental policies shifted from the Centre to the newly independent republic, but there were no ready alternatives to adopt. The socio-economic bases of the 'tribal-states' of the pre-Tsarist period had been so thoroughly destroyed that there could be no return to them. Supra-national bonds, be they pan-Turkic, pan-Islamic or pan-Iranian, had little emotional significance for the vast majority of the people. A new orientation, one that could inspire a sense of national pride and confidence was required. The state, using many of the same mechanisms of the Soviet period, took the initiative in shaping a new ideology fit for an independent Uzbekistan.

The sudden transformation from what was, in effect, colonial status to that of *de jure* independence, brought to the fore an intense sense of insecurity in Uzbekistan. This concerned questions about the role of the individual and the state, and the role of Uzbekistan in regional and international affairs. Which path for further development would be the best? What should future political institutions look like? What should guide future changes, reforms and reorganizations? What should be the conceptual framework of internal and foreign policy? The new ideology of national independence would provide the answers.

By definition, a coherent set of doctrines constitutes an ideology. Ideologies are belief systems that help to structure people's view of the world. Martin Seliger defines an ideology as 'a set of ideas by which men posit, explain and justify the ends and means of organized social action, irrespective of whether such action aims to preserve, amend, uproot or rebuild a given social order'.[16] Ideologies thus provide the intellectual prism through which policy makers observe reality. Messages and cues from the external environment are given meaning, or interpreted within the categories, predictions, and definitions provided by doctrines comprising the ideology. Soviet policy makers interpreted a foreign civil war as a manifestation of a class struggle; they saw conflicts among 'capitalist' states as a fight between their ruling classes over markets; and they regarded any recession in a free market economy as evidence of Marx's predictions regarding the laws of economic development. Also, ideologies prescribe for policy makers both national roles and images of the future state of the world. They establish the long-range goals of a state's external behaviour, to be promoted through diplomacy, propaganda, revolution or force. Third, they serve as rationalizations and justifications for the choice of more specific foreign policy decisions. Finally, ideologies posit moral and ethical systems that can prescribe the 'correct' attitudes and evaluative criteria for one's own actions and those of others. Communism is distinguished from other ideologies primarily because it claims to be an objective and scientific ideology and moral system, rather than merely the preferred ideology of particular leaders. Communist theoreticians maintain that Marxism–Leninism is all powerful because it is correct, and, since only Marxists–Leninists are 'armed with the truth', only they have a legitimate claim to power in the world. Since they are on the side of history, they maintain that all other doctrines or economic systems are retrograde. 'Good' people are those who swim with the current of history, building communism and fighting imperialism and fascism, whereas 'bad' people (or states) are those that resist history by clinging to doomed economic systems and the colonies they produce. Any technique used to fight capitalism or imperialism is, *ipso facto*, moral and justified. Ironically, it was these same moral directives that has created a situation in which the Marxists' constraints ceased to exist. All these elements of the Marxist doctrine are now out of fashion in the republic and have been replaced by a new Uzbek national ideology by the same people who had championed building socialism and fostering a sense of socialist internationalism for so long. Many of the elements that were until recently condemned as evil – Western social, political and economic systems or Western popular culture – have suddenly became acceptable to the same people.

The Uzbek ideology of national independence
When the communist regime's values lost their relevance, an ideological vacuum emerged, raising the need for a new doctrine. The first years of independence saw the initial search for a new ideological framework, which in its character and essence would be adequate to the historical process. At the same time, chaos and the lack of a clearly defined ideology threatened the integrity and internal situation of the republic. The Director of the Philosophy and Law Institute, Abdulkhafis Jamolov, noted:

> Our public consciousness is suffering deep and radical changes. Those definitions, views and notions which seemed yesterday absolutely infallible, today all collapsed. There appears a spiritual emptiness, and the values collapse leaves the people in confusion. We

should carefully think over and elaborate the future ideology, which would best meet the national psychological spirit of Uzbekistan's people and which would meet the requirements of the political situation. We also should bear in our minds that any mistake in elaboration of this concept may lead to unrecoverable consequences.[17]

Indeed the break-up of the Soviet Union discredited the ideology on which it was built. For more than seventy years, communism had been the source of political legitimacy and power and had provided the guidelines for economic, social, and political action. Yet socialist development failed to raise living standards of the Soviet peoples to the level of those in the advanced industrial societies. The demise of the communist ideology left a large ideological and conceptual vacuum in the post-Soviet Uzbek republic.

A totalitarian past left Uzbekistan with a command-administrative system, a one-sidedly developed economy and obsolete state management methods. The government of Uzbekistan undertook reform policies in order to overcome these problems and determine the direction of its internal and external relations. President Islom Karimov, in his well-known five principles of the transitional period, pointed out that: 'The necessities of national culture and spiritual revival, socio-economic and political renovation of the state structure, sovereignty and independence strengthening have brought us to the national independence ideology.' This was regarded as the missing component that would harmoniously fit into the general reformation concept. President Karimov added that this ideology, 'with all its criteria, shape and conditions basing on the national spirit, language, customs, ancient traditions of our people, should in the future install in our minds belief, mercy, tolerance, fairness and the great thirst for knowledge.'[18]

Ikrom Utbosarov states that, this ideology, 'based on the power and might of our state and adherence to the universal values, must bring up in our people's minds a constant aspiration to take a deserving and equal position among the leading states of the world community. It must provide the achievement of our greatest aim – independence strengthening and moving forward.'[19]

Seventy years of communist rule, however, left a legacy of mistrust between the government and the people, as well as a political culture characterized by authoritarianism, intolerance, mistrust and clientism.

The political culture that existed before the Soviet rule in the region, though non-totalitarian and much less repressive than communism, was also 'paternalistic' and built upon the preponderant power of an authoritarian figure. Moreover, recent developments have so far also produced a negative impression of the republic. The old nomenclatural system and censorship continue to retain their primary importance. The symbols and ideas presented from a weak, top-down ideology hardly resonate with the majority of people in any meaningful way. Under these conditions, it is difficult to see how all the above-stated virtues will be able to produce such a society.

The national independence ideology and the general problem of elaborating a new ideology was discussed in newspapers and magazines and there were several books devoted to the issue. The People's Democratic Party of Uzbekistan (PDP) played a leading role in giving an impetus to these discussions. A programme document of the PDP on the ideology of national independence was adopted. Despite the fact that different people use different terms to describe the ideology, e.g. the ideology of national independence, national ideology, the ideology of national progress etc., all of them agree that the new ideology espouses an aspiration to independence, national cultural revival, political and economic renewal, and a strengthening of patriotic spirit. For instance the PDP defines the new ideology as follows:

> Our ideology is to concentrate in itself first of all vitally important ideas such as independence, freedom, social equality, labour exalting, love to the native land and humanism that were the dreams of our people during centuries . . . It is based on universal values, rich spiritual legacy of our ancestors, progressive trends and customs, history, language, culture, beliefs, religions of all the nations that live in our mother land.[20]

The PDP Central Council Secretary Akmal Saidov claims this ideology is the unity of the following elements: (1) strengthening of the feeling of independence in the people's consciousness; (2) maintenance of Uzbek national ideology; (3) patriotism towards multinational Uzbekistan; (4) family supremacy in the society; and (5) laws, order and discipline observance.[21] S. Djuraev and A. Taksonov identify the following structural elements of the national independence ideology: ideology of national revival; ideology of culture and upbringing; ideology of market relations.

The ideology of national independence ties together these elements and provides the basis for them.[22]

The national ideology performs two basic functions, sociocultural and political. The sociocultural function includes strengthening the feeling of patriotism and independence; national culture, traditions and customs revival; nation consolidation; and the establishment of the new types of social relations. The political function involves the restructuring of political institutions; the establishment of a new political system corresponding to the spirit of the national ideology; and protection and strengthening of the sovereignty and independence of the republic. In reality these two functions are indivisible.

Sociocultural function
The value system of the Soviet period did not destroy the national culture but it did change it in many ways, adding components of Soviet culture. Moreover, one must remember that the Uzbek nation existed as part of an integral multinational system and had extensive links with the other nations, so different values 'exchanged'. It is with these contacts and value exchanges that many Uzbek intellectuals were more concerned. They argued that it was the system of values that restricted the development of the national culture. Patriotism and the spirit of independence in Uzbekistan were totally suppressed. Therefore, the aim of the national ideology in this sphere would be the development and fixation in the people's consciousness of these feelings and convictions that were formerly lacking and not encouraged. President Karimov said 'We must start with the spiritual revival of the society, with the moral awakening of the people.'[23] This means that spiritual sources are based on the culture of the Uzbek nation which is a product of centuries-long development and is handed to Uzbek people from generation to generation. Spiritual and material sources provide people's conceptual and cognitive frameworks. In other words, people's world outlook, their actions and the motivations for their actions are to a large extent shaped by this framework.

The sociocultural function has a huge task to promote new social relations corresponding to market laws; to mould the modern labour and industrial culture; to nurture genuine patriots who love their motherland and believe it has a great future; to create and fix firmly the spirit of independence in the people's consciousness; and to revive the national culture.[24] These constitute the internal power of the state and its people. The major task for Uzbekistan's political elite is the welfare of the state. The fruits of the sociocultural function are one of the crucial assets of this power. The most important function of the national independence ideology is to implant in people's minds a national(ist) consciousness in the shortest possible time. This is the substance that links all the structural elements of the national ideology and becomes the life source for them. This substance is central to the structure of the national ideology. Since patriotism and the spirit of independence were not encouraged during the Soviet period they now take a prioritized character.

So the aim of the sociocultural function is a national cultural revival which will provide a spiritual framework of a great durability and stability that can withstand both internal and external pressures. At the present time this huge task of defining and developing the idea of independence and patriotic feelings is of outstanding importance in Uzbekistan. With time this 'substance' will gradually lose its patriotic character and will take its place in the general structure of the national culture, national ideology, and national security. In other words it will become 'transparent'. This, at least, is what would happen in theory. In practice, the ideology that has replaced communism in the republic can be best described as secular authoritarianism with a dose of free market philosophy. Uzbek leadership, like all other Central Asian leaders, has concluded that, under the present conditions in Uzbekistan, a period of authoritarian rule is a necessary stage in the transition from communist totalitarianism to liberal democracy'.[25] Moreover, the authoritarian character of the regime and the lack of any genuine debate have so far prevented a broad-based consensus on the ideological underpinning of Uzbek society. It is likely that once the current leadership departs, the debate will rekindle.

Political function
The old political system in Uzbekistan lies in ruins; building a new one will require enormous effort. New political institutions must be established. At present, the state is more concerned with strengthening its independence by a variety of means including its foreign policy doctrine. These tasks are to be fulfilled by the political function of the ideology of national independence: constructing political institutions;

building a new political system that would reflect the spirit of the national ideology; and protecting and strengthening the sovereignty and independence of the Uzbek republic.

According to this ideology, each state structure is the product and manifestation of the nation's self-spirit and the level of its consciousness. The nation must feel that the state structure corresponds to its laws and its consciousness. This is why the Uzbek political elite is more concerned with directing people's world outlook. The Soviet style of state building has been rejected today. It is now claimed that this system was forced on the Uzbek people, but it did not work because it did not correspond to the moral and spiritual values of the people. This would explain the huge discrepancy between what was presented and what actually existed, and why such a state did not have a future from the very beginning. President Karimov states that:

> 70–80 years are only a moment in the nation's history. We have a historical chance when building our state to come back to our historical sources, to adopt and develop every best thing which is presented in our rich historical past. The state that we build must be based on the mentality of our people . . . one should take into consideration the fact that there are no ready recipes, ready models of state building. Despite the comprehensive processes of economic and spiritual integration there were not and have not been structurally identical states. Each state is unique. The state that we build must be based on the mentality of our people. That is why borrowing different institutions and establishments from the other states and the efforts to adopt them in the alien soil never give the expected result'.[26]

Nationalism and its philosophical underpinnings are compelling for the Uzbek leadership, which seeks to justify its post-Soviet existence by the discourse of national sovereignty.[27] This also fits well with the Uzbek intelligentsia's attempts to define and popularize the concept of national identity. The modern Uzbek republic, with all its borders and institutions, is a product of the former Soviet system from which the political elite learnt how to influence public opinion to legitimize the post-Soviet rule in Uzbekistan.

The political function of the national ideology of Uzbekistan is to create a conceptual scheme for internal and foreign policy, to give it the right direction and to correct it during the process in accordance with the established purposes. Internal policy implies state building, a new political system, and establishing new political institutions by reforming the old which would harmoniously fit the structure of the national culture and correspond to the national spirit. This factor of correspondence and compatibility is of great importance to the regime. Therefore, the social, political and, to a large extent, economic transformation of Uzbekistan will be dictated by the Uzbek national ideology. The effects of this are already evident. Although the post-Soviet leadership is taking a more gradualist path – reintroducing pre-Russian traditions without destroying everything created during the period of Russian and Soviet rule – it seems that they are committed to act in line with this ideology. Where Soviet policy attempted to eradicate national identity and national consciousness, President Karimov has made it the defining feature of the republic. Where Soviet policy attempted to relegate the Uzbek language to second-class status relative to Russian, the new leadership has reinstated Uzbek as the official language. Where Uzbek history was destroyed during the Soviet period, it is now being 'recreated'. The Russian language street signs, and Russian names of squares and parks have almost disappeared. The statues of early rulers and other symbols of Central Asia's own proud history have replaced Lenin and Marx. Communism and Russian culture alike are out of fashion. 'Uzbekization', or 'Uzbekistanization', continues to replace 'Sovietization' ('Russification').

Nation building in Uzbekistan
The Soviet project of linking identity to national territory has certainly had as lasting an impression on the Uzbeks as it has done on the other people of Central Asian states. The future of Uzbekistan appears to be dominated by the political implications of this national identity. Once the Soviet Union disintegrated, the Uzbek elite was left to its own devices, and it tried to justify its existence in the language of nationalism. This partly stemmed from a simmering anti-Russian sentiment even though the Soviet experiment created the general structure of the contemporary Uzbek national community. The Uzbek elite finds this a fitting frame of reference in the current global scale which is stimulative to attempts at glorifying the Uzbek nation by that state. The Uzbek nation is presented as eternal, and the elite presents itself as the sole supporter of this eternal community, seeking to justify its claim to power.

It is apparent that the officially sanctioned process of Uzbek national revivalism took its roots from the gross falsification of official history of the Soviet period, strengthened by an unmistakably designed nationalist interpretation of the post-Soviet era history and historical events. Official history-writing in the Soviet period and that of the post-Soviet period tends to obscure the origins of the Uzbek national community in order to claim antiquity. The new regime presents the Uzbek nation as one stretching back to the mists of time. Eternity, in this sense, belongs to Uzbeks and by extension to the champions of the Uzbek state. To distance himself from the old nomenclatural system and to strengthen his public image as a defender of the Uzbek nation, President Karimov has sponsored the revival of Uzbek cultural landmarks, one of which is the Uzbek language.

The constitutional recognition of Uzbek as the official language was aimed at de-Russifying the state. In the Soviet period Russian had become the dominant language in decision-making organs. Despite repeated Soviet promises to uphold the native languages of the local populations of the Union, the native language of Uzbekistan was practically pushed out of the top divisions of party and state hierarchies. While Russian dominated in all the government departments, Uzbek was used only for popular consumption and the implementation of the Communist Party's decisions. The domination of Russian fuelled Uzbek aspirations for the restoration of national pride. The Uzbek intelligentsia saw the official installment of Uzbek as a vital element in the Uzbekization of the state and crucial to the consolidation of the Uzbek identity. Article 4 of the new constitution confirms the reinstatement of Uzbek as the official language of the state. A presidential decree on 24 August 1995 replaced the Russian Cyrillic alphabet with a new Uzbek Latin alphabet of 29 characters, which was introduced in the 1996–7 academic year from the first years of primary schooling in the country. There is a terminology committee attached to the Cabinet of Ministers to facilitate the transition from Russian to Uzbek in administrative and scientific fields. It has sanctioned the removal of all non-native place names, such as towns, streets, underground stations, parks and so on.

The regime in Uzbekistan also identifies the historic personalities of Maverannahr as the forebearers of Uzbek identity. According to the present regime, Uzbek national pride is rooted in the great military, scientific and cultural exploits of such men as Amir Temur, his grandson

Ulughbek and Mir Alisher Navoi. In December 1994 President Karimov decreed the grand celebration of the 660th anniversary of Amir Temur's birth. The celebrations reached their climax in October 1996, in Tashkent, Shahrisabz (Temur's birth place) and Samarkand (the capital of his empire), turning into a festival that lasted for about a week. The state film industry produced a film, and the state theatre produced a play on Amir Temur. A number of monuments were erected in Tashkent, Shahrisabz and Samarkand. A large museum based on the theme of Amer Temur was opened in the capital near Amir Temur Square (formerly Revolutionary Square). Amir Temur is referred to as '*babomiz buyuk Temur*' (our father the great Temur) in the history books and this is also expressed by the president in his speeches in the media and in public. Temur's monument and his tomb in Samarkand have been refurbished and Bibi Khatun's (his most beloved wife) monument was also refurbished. Amir Temur is also taught about in the public schools and universities, where he is depicted as a great statesmen and a hero of Uzbek people, although he actually fought against the Uzbeks and defeated their Khan Tuqtamush in 1395. In September 1996, by a presidential decree, the post office issued stamps featuring Temur and at the same time the Central Bank of Uzbekistan celebrated his birthday by minting gold-plated *Sum* coins with his likeness. A big statue of Amir Temur riding on a horse was built in Tashkent, in the centre point of the square that used to be the revolution square.

Temur's grandson, Muhammed Ulughbek (1394–1449) provides the state with equally ample material for representing a glorious Uzbek past. The 600th anniversary of Ulughbek's birth was celebrated in Tashkent, Bukhara, Nukus, Shahrisabz and Samarkand in October 1994.[28] In September 1994 the Uzbek government organized the 675th anniversary of Bahoad-Din Naqshband's birth; he is the founder of the hitherto scorned sufi *tariqat of Nakshbandi*. Tashkent became the venue for a seminar on Imam Ismail Muhammad al-Bukhari's theological writings. Al-Bukhari lived between AD 810 and 870, and his collection of *hadith*, known as *as-Sahih*, remains the most respected book after the Qur'an among Hanafi Sunni Muslims,[29] who lived long before Uzbeks moved to the region.

The old Soviet state medals of bravery for commitment to the motherland (signifying the Soviet Union) were replaced by new Uzbek state medals. In April 1994 the Uzbek leadership introduced its own medals of *Mustakilik* (Independence), *Dostlik* (Friendship), *Shukrat* (Honour) and *Jasarat* (Bravery) for commitment to the *Vatan* (Homeland), signifying the Uzbek State.[30] In the fifth year of independence, President Karimov conferred the *Dostlik*, *Shukrat* and *Jasarat* medals to over 190 people, including *hokims* (local governors), Uzbek and foreign diplomats, the UN representative in Tashkent, military personnel, writers and farmers.

The concept of *Vatan*, with commitment to the Uzbek state, is emphasized at every opportunity to strengthen patriotism. Whether it is a meeting, a gathering or a conference, the authorities find occasion to remind the public that it is their *Vatan* that should benefit first and foremost. The new version of *mahalla* (neighbourhood), the foundation of *Saghlam evlot ucun* (for a healthy generation) the *Kamolat* (the Youth) and the official *Novruz* (spring festival) celebration as the beginning of a new season, are all meant to strengthen nationhood and cultivate patriotism throughout Uzbekistan. Patriotism is also connected to Islam. One can see writings on streets, even in the countryside, recalling: '*Vatani sevmok imandandir*' (loving one's homeland is a commitment to one's faith). President Karimov has given overriding importance in particular to the *Manaviyat va Marifat* (Spirituality and Enlightenment) organization. During his meeting with a representative of the organization, broadcast on Uzbekistan's TV2 on 20 August 1996, Karimov stated that it provides 'high spiritual values in society, national ideology and education of young people in a spirit of respect for the Uzbek rich cultural heritage and historical traditions and in the spirit of love for the *Vatan* and devotion to the ideals of independence'. In other words it is designed to encourage patriotism with aspects of Uzbek nationalism. Indeed, the transition from communism to nationalism is developing fairly smoothly. The old Soviet Voluntary Society for Cooperation with the Army, Air Force and Navy (known by its Russian initials as the DOSAAF) has been transformed into the *Vatanperver* (Patriotic) organization. It provides assistance to the defence sector of Uzbekistan. The principal goal remains the same, but the direction of patriotic education has changed: to help in the country's defence; to train young people for work and to develop combat and other technical kinds of sport. It held its first congress on 23 August 1996.

The authorities have been developing several mechanisms to encourage the development of national identity in Uzbekistan, hoping to create social cohesion in times of economic crisis and provide a stabilizing force. The campaign seems to have had significant success in some major urban centres, though the extent to which the people in rural areas receive this promoted idea remains open to question. These people are more preoccupied with the appalling economic conditions.

Responding to his opponents who accused him of being a product of the communist nomenclatural system, and in an effort to improve his public image as a defender of the Uzbek nation, President Karimov has actively sponsored the revival of Islam as an Uzbek cultural landmark. This would appear to show that the past seventy years of Soviet rule in Central Asia have proved false the Marxist–Leninist tenet that 'religion is the opiate of the masses'. Every effort made by a host of atheists attempting to erase religion from the people's minds has failed.

Islam in Uzbekistan

Islam, and the formation of social organizations on its basis, has had enormous political importance for the independent Uzbekistan, though in an ambivalent way. On one side the government had to symbolize the close ties between the national culture and religion through the 'rebirth of Uzbekistan'. President Islam Karimov wanted to present himself as the champion of this rebirth, but on the other side he has had to confront the Islamic tradition in his country. He could, however, through affirming Islam, emphasize the time-change and so distance Uzbekistan from the Soviet past.

For 'Soviet Islam' Uzbekistan was of exemplary importance. Tashkent was the biggest seat of the four spiritual heads of Muslims in the Soviet Union and the director of these was the Mufti of Tashkent. He was the highest representative of state-controlled 'official Islam'. In Uzbekistan this sector, in comparison with the other Central Asian republics, was the most educated. For example, the only two Islamic universities in the Soviet Union were here. Uzbekistan was also an important centre of non-official 'parallel' or 'shadow' Islam. The liberalization of the religious sphere was followed by the new building of mosques and the foundation of new Islamic education centres, and also saw the convergence of 'official' and 'non-official' Islam. The government supported this process and tried to put itself at its head.

On the other hand, the government in Tashkent is focusing on the opposite, destabilizing the elements of 'Islamic rebirth'. It has declared 'ethnic and religious extremism' the main enemies of the state and tends to label all movements or perceive them as potentially 'dangerous extremists'. There is also an ambivalence between the fear that the government could be a threat to religiously motivated political movements in Central Asia, and its desire to take advantage of this for its own political goals, especially for legitimizing its authoritarian rule.

Thus, it appears that what is problematic for the state is not the religious content of Islam but rather its expression as a social and political catalyst. Islam is not only tolerated in Uzbekistan; it is an essential part of the government. At the same time, however, Islamic movements not under government control are repressed. The government is intolerant of anything that is less than explicitly loyal to state-run Islam, fearing that independent movements may lead to the rise of extremist opposition to their rule. The Uzbekistan branch of the Islamic Renaissance Party was banned in 1992 and, in the same year, its leader, Abdulla Utaev disappeared. He was reportedly taken away by security forces in December 1992 and since then he has not been heard from. There were rumours in Tashkent that he was held by the NSS (SNB, formerly KGB) and is still being held in one of the cells in the basement of the NSS building. Human Rights Watch/Helsinki has requested information about whether he was held by the government, and the Ministry of Foreign Internal Affairs promised to look into it, but the request for information remains unanswered. Khokim Satimov, the leader of the informal Islamic community action group *Adolat* (Justice), was arrested in 1993. Suspect religious groups are kept under close surveillance by the security services. Some of the activists have been given long prison sentences. District governors who in the past often turned a blind eye to the activities of Muslim leaders are now held personally responsible for their conduct. The newly-formed Committee for Religious Affairs, attached to the Cabinet of Ministers, has been given sweeping powers which it can use effectively to destroy the independence of religious institutions. Mufti Muhammad Sodiq, once the embodiment of optimism, was finally ousted from office in the spring of 1993. The official reason was corruption in the higher levels of the religious administration, but this was also the authorities' usual way of removing opponents and enabling someone more loyal to be appointed.

The government in Tashkent also felt alarmed, especially as a result of the developments in Tajikistan where, since 1991, Islamic movements have entered into a coalition with the secular national democratic forces and formed a strong opposition power against the old political elite. Though the conflict that was occurring in the neighbouring country was too complex and local for its ideological and political faultiness to be defined, the basis for an anti-regime coalition between 'Islam' and 'democracy' also existed in Uzbekistan. The Tajik civil war of 1992 was interpreted in the Uzbek and Russian media as an onslaught by religious extremists who had to be defeated. The developments in Tajikistan were, in fact, of high concern in political and security terms for Uzbekistan.

Some 90 per cent of the total population of Uzbekistan consists of Sunni Muslims of the Hanafi school. During the first years of Soviet rule, despite numerous tactical twists and turns, there was a guarded toleration of Muslim customs and sensitivities. By 1927, however, the Soviet regime was sufficiently entrenched to abandon this policy of goodwill. With the introduction of modernization and secularization measures, the Soviet approach became the use of mass terror, exercised through arbitrary arrests, long terms of imprisonment and summary executions. All the religious foundations were destroyed. This affected all faiths equally. In the case of Islam, public manifestations of faith, such as the 'five pillars of Islam' – (1) the declaration of faith (*shahada*); (2) prayer five times a day (*salah*); (3) alms (*zakat*); (4) fasting during the month of Ramadan (*sawm*); and (5) performing the pilgrimage to the holy city of Mecca (*hajj*) – were strictly prohibited and punished. The mere possession of a book in the Arabic script was a sufficient pretext for capital punishment. Large numbers of religious functionaries died in the purges and many were sent to Siberian prison camps or fled abroad. From 1927 to 1929 some 20,000 mosques were either destroyed or turned into stock houses and hospitals. This campaign of fear was accompanied by relentless anti-religious atheistic propaganda, disseminated through all the channels of mass communication, and underpinned by the system of compulsory state education. Further coercion was extended through the Communist Party and its subsidiary organs and the state-controlled social and professional associations – even those who attempted to greet each other in an Islamic way could not become members of the Communist Party. The consequence of this multifaceted onslaught was that, within a generation or two, Islam had almost ceased to function as a living religion in Uzbekistan. In the pre-Soviet period, society as a whole operated within an Islamic framework and it was this contextual environment that was destroyed during the Soviet regime. What survived, however, was a fragmentary system of rituals of religious content that remained in people's consciousness. This had developed itself outside of the state's control and existed purely within the family core with its own educational institutions and communication structures. These remained the constituent elements of the region's cultural and historical identity that each generation owed to the foregoing. What has returned today in public life is, however, the mobilized version of what survived underground. The Sufi order, despite its earlier contribution to the spread of Islam, is no longer a dedicated major force capable of leading resistance to infidel rule. Its functional role has been reduced to a merely symbolic link with tradition.

In the 1970s the re-Islamicization of society began in Uzbekistan with the emergence of a revivalist movement in the Fergana Valley. The Soviet press referred to its followers as *Wahhabis* implying that they were backed by foreign sponsorship, presumably from Saudi Arabia. This movement, which advocated a return to the teachings of Islam, was a rather spontaneous grassroots revival with no external links. Its inspiration drew from an ascetic sect that was active in the region at the beginning of the century. Some experts on Islamic movements in Uzbekistan have stated that the religious activists in Uzbekistan did not have any contact with corresponding groups from abroad before 1990, but they introduced their followers to the classics of the Islamic teachings of the twentieth century: Hassan Al-Banna (Egypt, 1906–49), Abu-l-Ala'Mawdudi (India/Pakistan, 1903–79) and Sayyid Qutb (Egypt, 1906–66). Some however admitted that the movement in Fergana was affected by Muslims in Afghanistan via Tajikistan by the mid-1970s, but how effective this was in practical terms is an open question.[31] Another strong impetus for the revival of this movement was a more conciliatory approach to tolerance towards religion throughout the Soviet Union. By the late 1970s the Islamic groups in the Fergana Valley became strongly influenced by the Islamic groups in Afghanistan through Tajikistan. The Afghan government's failure to stop this motivating influence on the development of Islamic movements in Central Asia brought the military occupation of the Soviet Union in Afghanistan. The occupation did not only fail to stop the Islamic influence in the Fergana Valley but actually increased the Islamic sentiment throughout Uzbekistan with the unexpected rise of the Afghan *Mucaheddins*' resistance against the Soviet Union, which was later to play an important role in the collapse of the Union. This further intensified the Islamic sentiment throughout Central Asia. Indeed, this disturbed the Soviet nomenclatural in Moscow so much that on 24 November 1986 the new Communist Party General Secretary, Mikhail Gorbachev, gave a speech on the religious question in Tashkent in which he demanded a 'determined and uncompromising fight against all religious manifestations, a strengthening of mass clearing up and of atheism propaganda'.[32] Soon afterwards the same Gorbachev made the liberalization of religious politics possible in the Soviet Union, first covering the Russian-Orthodox Church but later affecting other religious communities. Islam had previously been blamed for impeding social and economic progress, but from 1989 onwards the reintroduction of Islamic values was provided by a sudden shift in government policy. The Muslim Board for Central Asia and Kazakstan became more active in the daily life of Muslims and the Mufti Muhammed Sadyk, the new head of the official Board, received substantial support from the authorities and acquired a prominent role in public affairs. He made several concessions to the Muslim community. More mosques were opened, restrictions concerning the pilgrimage to Mecca were relaxed and the provision of religious literature increased. There appeared to be a genuine sense of satisfaction that the validity of the region's culture had been recognized and was finally being given proper respect. This process accelerated after the break-up of the Soviet Union and the political elite moved swiftly to promote Islam as the basis of the new state ideology. Public opinion was mobilized through articles in the press, the pronouncements of leading public figures in the media and in public gatherings, emphasizing the need for a return to Islamic ethics. President Karimov took his Oath of Office on both the Qur'an and the Constitution to underline this point. The following year he performed the pilgrimage to Mecca. In May 1993, at the twelfth session of the Supreme Soviet of Uzbekistan, he emphasized the positive role that 'official Islam' played in society and the important work that imams had done in the name of peace, friendship and spiritual cleanliness. During Ramadan it is now quite acceptable to admit to observing the Fast.

The formal re-Islamicization of Uzbekistan was accompanied by a campaign to propagate the faith. Establishing a network of mosques has been a priority. In Uzbekistan until the late 1970s there were hardly any mosques open for worship. In 1989, however, there were about 270, and by late 1996 the number of mosques had soared to over 5,000. Schools and voluntary bodies run courses to teach the Arabic script and give instruction in reading the Qur'an. Opportunities for more advanced Muslim education are provided by *Madrassah* and Islamic centres that are mushrooming in Uzbekistan. The courses are open to female and male students. Much of the finance for these institutions comes from charitable contributions from individuals, local communities and the district authorities. There is also a significant input of human and material resources from Muslims abroad, both from governments and private foundations. There are nineteen schools from a *Naqshbandi* religious sect from Turkey known as *Fetullah Hoca's group*, teaching religion as well as sciences according to the official line. The schools of this group are located in Tashkent, Samarkand, Khorezm, Nukus, Bukhara, Fergana, Namangan, Andijan, Termiz, Khokand and Angren.

By 1993 the only unified Islamic administration for Central Asia, the Muslim Board that existed under the Soviet regime, had been dismantled and all five republics established separate nationally-based Muslim organs. The primary function of the post-Soviet body is to serve the interest of its government in Uzbekistan, as is the case in the other Central Asian republics. The religious body is formally separated from the state and its leader is chosen by the Islamic body, though in practice the President has a big role in the selection or dismissal of the religious leader, the Mufti. The separation of the religious body from the state is purely a Soviet tradition in Uzbekistan. It is not free to pursue independent policies to promote pan-Islamic or even regional-Islamic solidarity. The current phase of Islamic revivalism in Uzbekistan incorporates the traditional Central Asian features, mainly those of Bukhara, Samarkand, Khokand and Khorezm, but exogenous influences often prove to be powerful. Muslim missionaries from abroad, representing a variety of orthodox and unorthodox sects, are introducing new, more 'correct' interpretations of Islam. The activities of some of these missionaries have created deep rifts in society. It is not surprising to find mutually hostile Muslim factions each with their own mosque in some parts of Uzbekistan. There is also a revival of interest in Sufism, but its influence is not very strong. The majority of Muslim missionaries were expelled from Uzbekistan in 1998, and the activities of independent local Muslim groups have been minimized and kept under close surveillance. There are also large numbers of Christian missionaries in the country, mainly led by Americans, but with members from European and Latin American countries. As it is not legal for any missionaries to register in Uzbekistan, the Christian missionaries have registered under the name of several non-governmental charity organizations, some of which have set up three American libraries in the republic. Although the Christian missionaries are mainly concerned with the Christian community, they have also targeted a considerable number of young male and female Muslim students at the University, and even students from secondary schools. Some Muslim students have claimed that they were taken to Christian camps in the USA while they were in the country through an exchange programme. Some Christian missionaries organize summer camps to teach English to secondary school children in Uzbekistan, but the main aim is to acquaint the Muslim students with Christian values. Other missionaries are organizing seminars and house meetings for the University students to 'practice' English for the same purpose.

Islam in Uzbekistan has, in general, rarely taken an extremist character. It has rather shown a considerable capacity for adaptation and accommodation. There is undoubtedly a stronger sense of Islamic identity in the Fergana Valley, but there is also a growing sense of Islamic identity among younger men and women in the Tashkent, Khorezm, Kashkadarya and Surkhandarya regions. This is not only as a result of independent Islamic movements in the region, but also because Islam has become a key element in the state and nation building process. The Islamic movements – the *IRP*, *Adolat* which does not appear to differ significantly from *IRP*, *Wahhabi*, *Laskari Islami* (Troops of Islam) and *Hizbi-ut-Tahrir* (Party of Liberation) – are still active, but because of government repression they are all underground so it is difficult to judge their strength, nor it is easy to give a clear and complete picture of the social and cultural changes that are now in progress. Our overall prediction is that in Uzbekistan Islamic activism will increase, particularly among young people who live through social uncertainty and who have religious education. Islamic 'awakening' movements will proliferate with increased social and economic problems, especially in regions with high portions of middle and lower class people, but it is unlikely that religion will become a political factor in the near future. However, the continuation of the authoritarian, repressive nature of the present regime means there is little opportunity for a genuinely free and open debate on policy issues. Those who disagree publicly with government policies are regarded as subversives or even rebels. The government's heavy-handed tactics, and, to a large extent, indiscriminate crackdown on independent Islamic groups in 1998 for alleged anti-government activities, have already radicalized many of them and driven many into opposition abroad. The Islamic Movement of Uzbekistan declared a 'holy war' against the Uzbek government and captured several villages in southern Kyrgyzstan taking several hostages. This crisis lasted for almost two months, resulting in many deaths and undermining the stability of the country. In time, the deepening economic crisis, which is causing a large part of the population to feel marginalized and betrayed, could also capture the Islamic high ground, and opposition groups could try to use Islam as a vehicle through which to voice their anger and frustration. To try to find ways to accommodate or integrate some of the Islamists and/or opposition groups into the political system might be as much in the interest of the region as it is in the interest of Uzbekistan. Uncompromising and intolerant attitudes on the part of the authorities, and the lack of a constructive political dialogue, will create more fertile ground for extremist activities in the region and more armed rebels for the government to deal with.

The most disruptive threat to the regime is likely to come from the Islamist movement, though this is not a coherent political force and is divided between various groups. These range from the extremist hardline to a more moderate faction, some of whom are willing to work with the regime. Being well aware of the potential problems, President Karimov invited a respected Uzbek religious leader, Mufti Muhammad Yusuf Muhammad Sodiq, to return home from exile in May 1999. After years in exile, Mufti Sodiq, the former head of the official Muslim Board of Central Asia, who many still consider the most influential religious leader in Uzbekistan, returned to Tashkent on the eve of the presidential election on 9 January 2000. In this explosive environment, if he wishes and/or is allowed to pursue an independent mediation, Muhammad Sodiq has the potential to play an important role as a mediator between the government and the independent Islamic groups, and to reduce the threat of the spread of instability and strife from Afghanistan and Tajikistan into Uzbekistan.

Ethnic minorities and inter-ethnic relations in Uzbekistan
In Central Asia, there are several different social groups, which by virtue of their history, culture, economic status, geographic location, gender, race or other such distinguishing features, would be defined as 'minorities' in relation to a dominant 'majority'.[33] This book, however, is concerned only with groups of minorities living in Uzbekistan; that is, ethnic groups or, in Soviet terms, 'nationalities' which are domiciled in a state in which they are ethnically different from the titular group (e.g. Koreans or Russians in Uzbekistan).

Uzbekistan, at the time of its creation as a Soviet Socialist Republic was a multi-ethnic state. The ethnic diversity was, however, greatly increased in the period 1925–52. Initially, hundreds of thousands of immigrants, mostly from the Slav republics, were moved there. They included party activists, administrators, military, security and law enforcement personnel, professional and skilled technicians. There were also political exiles. During the Second World War there was another wave of immigration, most of these people being placed in the industrial enterprises that were relocated from the endangered western republics to Uzbekistan. Considerable numbers of orphaned and homeless children from these republics were also sent there; some of them were adopted by local families and the remainder were placed in state orphanages. The larger group of the next migration, however, were the 'punished peoples', entire populations who were accused of treason against the Soviet state. Over half a million of the three million people exiled to Central Asia in the period 1936–52 were sent to Uzbekistan under the 'special settlement regime'. These included Koreans from the Maritime province; Meskhetian Turks from Georgia; Tatars from the Crimea and Kazan; Chechens and Ossetins from the Caucasus; Jews from Ukraine, Belarus and the Russian Federation; Germans from the Volga; Pontic Greeks from the Black Sea region and several others.[34] There was a huge loss of life and an immense amount of suffering during and immediately after the deportations.

Ethnic minorities

According to the 1989 Soviet Census (so far the latest official one), there were 100 ethnic groups listed in Uzbekistan. The main historical and cultural divide between ethnic minority groups in the republic, was, and still is, the 'immigrant' and the 'indigenous' communities. The immigrants include voluntary migrants, mainly of Slav origin, who were drawn from different social backgrounds, and the deported peoples, who had been transported *en masse*. Although most small groups have been assimilated, the deported people, to a large extent, retained their original social structures. This was, in addition to their different customs and languages, reinforced by the stigma of their alleged treachery which remained with them long after they had been rehabilitated, and which put a distance between them and the local population.

Until 1989, of the 100 ethnic groups that were listed in the 'national' census in Uzbekistan, 21 groups were represented by under 100 persons; 37 groups were in the 100–1,000 range; and 17 were in the 1,000–10,000 range. There were 13 groups over 10,000–100,000 and in the 100,000–1,000,000 range there were 10 groups. The two groups beyond 1 million were Uzbeks as the largest titular group, and Russians as the second largest minority group. According to the 1989 census, the national structure of the republic is as shown in Table 2.1.

Uzbekistan is the third most populated republic in the CIS, after Russia and Ukraine. By May 2000 its population had reached 24.5 million. The native population has increased continuously for many years, while the number of European nationalities has declined. As well as a great difference in the birth rate of the native and European populations, there has also been a migration of Europeans for economic and social reasons. For example, while Russians and Ukrainians respectively comprised 13.5 per cent and 1.1 per cent of the population in 1959, by 1989 this had declined to 8.3 per cent and 0.8 per cent respectively. According to the Goskomstat (the State Statistical Committee), whereas the population of the former USSR increased less than two-fold from 1897 to 1991, the figure for Uzbekistan was almost five-and-a-half-fold. What is most interesting about the 1989 population statistics is that Table 2.1 shows an excellent example of social engineering by the old Soviet state, as many numbers follow each other in an almost numerical order. It also shows that the numbers in several ethnic groups

TABLE 2.1
The national structure of Uzbekistan

Ethnic group	Number of residents	Ethnic group	Population
Uzbeks	14,142,475	Kalmyks	517
Russians	1,653,478	Northern nationals	495
Tajiks	933,560	Balkarts	488
Kazaks	808,227	Ingush	474
Tatars	467,829	Komi	472
Karakalpaks	411,878	Tabasarans	457
Crimean Tatars	188,772	Karachayits	329
Koreans	183,140	Khakas	288
Kyrgyzy	174,907	Shorts	283
Ukrainians	153,197	Cubans	253
Turkmens	121,578	Tats	242
Turks (Meskhetian)	106,302	Vietnamese	233
Jews (Ashkenazian)	65,493	Hungarians	211
Armenians	50,537	Cherkess	211
Azerbaijani	44,410	Georgian Jews	210
Germans	39,809	Karelians	194
Uighurs	35,762	Altayits	191
Bashkirs	34,771	Gagauzs	190
Belorussians	29,427	Assyrians	186
Central Asian Jews	28,369	Yakuts	183
Persians	24,779	Finns	181
Gypsies	16,397	Crimeans	173
Mordva	11,914	Permian Komi	171
Greeks	10,453	Rumanians	158
Chuvashis	10,074	Adigeyits	139
Moldavians	5,955	Abkhazis	129
Ossetins	5,823	Agulys	128
Georgians	4,704	Mongolian – Khalkhas	119
Lezgins	3,071	Italians	104
Polish	3,007	Czechs	94
Mari	2,964	Nogays	91
Lakts	2,807	Abazys	79
Arabs	2,805	Tuvas	73
Udmurts	2,466	Karaites	55
Bolgars	2,166	Spanish	54
Dargins	2,030	Rutults	53
Kurds	1,839	Udins	46
Afghans	1,655	Slovaks	42
Lithuanians	1,628	Austrians	34
Dungans	1,353	Ijorts	29
Latvians	1,131	Serbs	26
Chechens	1,006	Sakhurs	24
Kabardins	907	Beluchis	20
Estonians	854	Dutch	19
Chinese	816	Japanese	19
Avarians	767	Albanians	16
Indian or Pakistanis	756	Croats	14
Kumikis	713	French	3
Buryats	635	English	2
Mountain Jews	617	Yakuli	1

Note: Whole population = 19,810,077. Source: Statistics regarding the numbers of ethnic minorities who lived in Uzbekistan until 1989 and results of the 1989 population census taken from the *Goskomstat* (the State Committee for Forecasting and Statistics), Tashkent. Results of the Soviet population census of 1989 were also published in *Vestnik Statistiki*, Moscow: Financyi Statistika, no. 11, 1990. But only 97 ethnic groups are listed.

are overstated, while others are not shown at all. During my interviews with several ethnic minority representatives, I was told that for those Central Asian indigenous populations who considered Russian as their first language, their nationality was given as Russian in the census while a large number of Tajiks and many Kyrgyzy were counted as Uzbeks. Almost half of the Uighur population was not counted at all. Nonetheless it is the only official population data for recent years that exists. However, there have recently been enormous changes in the population of Uzbekistan. The demise of Soviet rule and of its tight system of population control have led to the breakdown of the existing population registration system not only in Uzbekistan, but all over the CIS. As a result, the current official data tends to underestimate the true scale of migratory movements in and out of the republic. The break-up of the Union and the formation of the independent states constituted a turning point in the migration processes taking place within the CIS. The break-up of the Union also led to the opening up of the former Soviet borders, and migrants started emigrating to non-CIS countries in growing numbers. In Uzbekistan, these emigrations retained a strong ethnic character and mainly consisted of Jews emigrating to Israel and the USA, Germans moving to Germany, and Russians and Ukrainians moving to their homelands. As a result of the deteriorating economic situation, there has also been a rapid increase in the emigration of highly skilled scientists; the ensuing 'brain drain' is becoming a serious concern not only for Uzbekistan, but for all the CIS countries. Starting from the late 1980s, Uzbekistan witnessed a significant increase in emigration to other Soviet republics. Overall between 1989 and 1997 around one million people emigrated from Uzbekistan and over 350,000 people immigrated. The Russian Federation and Ukraine have continued to be the main countries of destination for emigrants from Uzbekistan. In the period between 1989 and 1997 a very large proportion of the Russian population has left for the Russian Federation while over 90,000 Ukrainians have also left Uzbekistan.

A very good account of the emigration and migration of the CIS countries is in the International Organization for Migration's *CIS Migration Report 1996*, published in 1997. According to the Report, however, the overall emigration from Uzbekistan during 1989–96 was 862,292, while independent sources in Uzbekistan put the figure for the same period at around 1.2 million people. Although this figure could well be too high, the real figure is believed to be around 1 million people.

The Report also puts the number of Russian emigrants between 1990 and 1996 from Uzbekistan at 364,800 (p. 141). The Russian embassy in Tashkent put the numbers for the same period at 600,000, while during my interview the Representatives of the Russian Cultural Centre in Tashkent stated the figure of 450,000 people.

These are by no means the final and objective statistics. The official and unofficial statistics in Uzbekistan vary enormously. It is quite hard to obtain objective data on the subject at present. Until there is an independent official census conducted in Uzbekistan it is hard to state the exact number of emigrants and immigrants. However the statistics given on the current ethnic composition of the republic are the results of a careful study of the numbers obtained from Uzbek officials, from representatives of ethnic minority groups, and from independent bodies, though they may be of uneven quality and quantity. The changes in the main ethnic groups in Uzbekistan since the 1989 population census are presented in Table 2.2.

TABLE 2.2
The changes in the main ethnic groups

Main ethnic groups	% of total in 1989	% of total in 2000*
Uzbeks	71.4	76.0
Russians	8.3	3.4
Tajiks	4.7	8.0
Kazaks	4.1	5.0
Tatars	3.3	2.0
Karakalpak	2.1	2.2
Kyrgyz	0.9	1.5
Koreans	0.9	1.0
Ukrainians	0.8	0.2
Others	3.5	0.7

Note:
*Estimates. The Tatar Documentary and Information Centre, Tashkent

Russians
Until the break-up of the Soviet Union, Russians formed the largest single minority in the republic. The Russians in Uzbekistan came in different stages. The first group consisted of those who settled during the Tsarist

period. Today, the descendants of these families are the third or fourth generations and, in general, they are more accustomed to local conditions and have a strong sense of belonging to the region. They have also in most cases been accepted by the local population as an integral part of the community. The second group was the settlers who arrived during the first decades of the Soviet period. The vast majority of these were government officials, policy-making and law-enforcing personnel. They too, to a large extent, have a strong sense of belonging to the region. The third group was the immigrants who were neither interested in, nor have shown any understanding of, the local culture and way of life, but who led more self-contained lives. This group of Russians came to Uzbekistan circa 1941. During the Second World War a huge number of Russians were evacuated along with industrial, academic and cultural enterprises. Over a million were moved to Uzbekistan alone. After the war many returned to their original bases but a large number preferred to stay, mainly attracted by the quality of life as well as by the professional opportunities offered in the republic. By 1959 there were over a million Russians in Uzbekistan and the last significant wave of immigrants was those who arrived in Tashkent in 1968 to help rebuild the city after the devastation caused by the 1966 earthquake. Throughout the entire period of migration to Uzbekistan, the Russians settled in urban areas where, along with other non-indigenous groups, they developed a specific Euro-Asian cosmopolitan subculture.

In the 1960s and 1970s, the proportion of Russians in the population of Uzbekistan began to decrease year by year. This was due mainly to the higher birth-rate of the indigenous population. At its high point the Russians comprised 13.5 per cent in 1959 but this fell to 10.8 per cent by 1979. In the 1980s, their numbers also began to decline in absolute terms, caused by their emigration from the republic. The main reasons for the emigration of this period were increased competition for employment and housing, and a rise in poverty in the region in comparison to the western part of the Union. After the dissolution of the Soviet Union, however, the exodus of Russians from the republic increased dramatically. From 1989 to 1996 the number of Russians decreased by more than half; overall, between 1989 and 1997 over 800,000 are believed to have left. There were several factors causing the exodus of Russians from Uzbekistan during this period. The Russians were in theory a minority group in the country during the Soviet period, but in practice they dominated culturally and politically. Suddenly, and unexpectedly, they became the real minority. During the same period they also held about 70 per cent of the key positions throughout the country. After the break-up of the Union this have been reversed in favour of Uzbeks. The native Uzbek language shifted from being a second language to becoming the first. Russian lost its status within society, though it is still the medium of communication in public affairs. The Russians did not like this at all. The second factor was that the opposition parties of *Birlik*, and later *Erk*, had initially taken a rather nationalist and extremist stance causing fear among the Slavs. A third reason was economic. In November 1993, there was pressure on the official exchange rate of Russian roubles and later there was the introduction of the Uzbek national currency. Many Russians panicked, fearing they might lose their money. The fourth factor was political. The Russian Federation government introduced a new national law on citizenship to eliminate the so-called article number 18 of the constitution of the old Soviet Union. According to this, all Russian Embassies were given rights to grant Russians outside the Russian Federation citizenship without any bureaucratic procedures. Those who had held Red Soviet passports for four months were to be granted citizenship without any documents other than two pictures. The deadline for this was stated as 5 February 1995. This also raised panic among the Russians and long queues appeared around the embassy. In an interview at the Russian Embassy in Tashkent, I was told that those Russians who left Uzbekistan via the embassy numbered only 10,000 people. The vast majority did not even bother to come to the embassy; they simply got on the trains and left for Russia. The embassy officials, however, admitted that it was a mistake to give such a short deadline, as this contributed to the exodus of Russians. Initially the Russian Federation also wanted to take their nationals back from the 'hostile' environment, but by late 1995 the government in Moscow realized that it was beneficial to keep Russians in Uzbekistan for future cooperation. The National Cultural Association of Russians in Tashkent is also working for this cause. The fifth factor was the introduction of national passports by the Uzbek government in December 1994. The government encouraged citizens of the old Soviet Union to obtain Uzbek passports, but dual nationality was ruled out. Many

Russians opted for Russian citizenship. Finally there was fear of Islamic extremism caused mainly by the Afghan and Tajik conflicts.

The emigration of Russians from Uzbekistan during 1992–4 caused serious concern for the Uzbek government as many of them were highly qualified specialists and skilled professionals who made an important contribution to the social and economic life of the country. The Uzbek leadership tried to reassure the Russian community that the prospects for them were not bleak by upholding the principle of equal rights and freedoms for all citizens, regardless of ethnic origin. They also adopted a gradualist approach to the introduction of Uzbek as the only language of communication in public affairs. Russian cultural rights were, to a large extent, preserved. A cultural centre dedicated to the protection and furtherance of Russian culture was officially opened in May 1992, and still operates in the country. There was an increase in the number of Orthodox churches and hardly any reduction in the number of schools in which Russian was the main language of instruction. Russian also continued to be widely used in higher education and research institutes. However, problems remained. Today the vast majority of these schools no longer teach Russian history, geography, literature or culture. To get into the University or research institutes one has to know the Uzbek language first, as this is a requirement to pass the University entrance exams. Russian language newspapers continue to be published in Uzbekistan, but they are all controlled by the government. No independent Russian newspapers are allowed to be published in the country. There has been a large increase in Uzbek language broadcasts, with the only official Russian TV channel ORT's broadcast being reduced to only four hours a day. Although there does not seem to be explicit discrimination against Russians in Uzbekistan, it does exist covertly, e.g. in the workplace. There is also a fear among many Russians that an increase in Uzbek nationalism might take on a xenophobic character.

Today some 60 per cent of the remaining Russians live in Tashkent. Others live in centres such as Bekabad, Chirchik, Almalik, Navoi, Zarafshan, Uchguduk, Bukhara, Samarkand, Gulistan and Fergana. Uzbeks are reasserting their national identity and this entails a degree of cultural reorientation from the Russians. Learning the Uzbek language is a problem for many of them. Throughout their history in Central Asia, Russians have always ignored the native languages. With the introduction of the Cyrillic alphabet during the Soviet period, Russian became the only influential language of communication in public affairs. This further isolated the native languages in these societies. Russians now find it difficult to accept that they have to learn a language that their ancestors always ignored. During the 1996–7 academic year, the Uzbek government introduced an Uzbek version of the Latin alphabet, starting from the first year of the primary school onwards, which will gradually replace the Cyrillic alphabet and to a large extent the Russian language. Those Russian families who are prepared to remain in Uzbekistan have realized that their children at least will need to learn the local language, and thus many of them have enrolled their children in these schools. However, 30 per cent of the remaining Russians are considering leaving Uzbekistan, especially the young generation, who want to find jobs in the Slav republics, while many pensioners are also willing to emigrate, but do not have the means to travel.

Tajiks

The Tajiks, who trace their origins in the southern regions of Uzbekistan back at least 6,000 years, form the largest single ethnic minority group in the republic today. They officially amount to one million, just less than 5 per cent of the total population, although according to Tajik official statistics they comprise as much as 20 per cent. Unofficial figures from both sides, however, put the figure at around two million people, or just above 8 per cent. The officials in Uzbekistan still tend to give the Soviet statistics of 1989 for the number of Tajiks living in their country. The Tajik officials at the Tajik embassy in Tashkent, during an interview I conducted with them, put the figures as high as 20 per cent. During my interview with the Tajik Cultural Centre representatives in Tashkent in August 1996, the figure stated was 2 million people. The Tajik students and various other people (Tajiks and Uzbeks) to whom I spoke in different parts of Uzbekistan, gave figures more or less the same as those given by the Cultural Centre.

The majority of the Tajiks live in and around the traditionally Persian-speaking cities of Bukhara and Samarkand, but they are also located in Surkhandarya, Kashkadarya, Namangan and Tashkent. Most are fluent in both Uzbek and Tajik. In general, there does not seem to be much discrimination against Tajiks in Uzbekistan. There is a great deal of intermarriage between Uzbeks and Tajiks. Most Uzbeks and Tajiks consider themselves as 'one people speaking two different languages'.

In the wake of the break-up of the Soviet Union, there were increasing ethnic tensions in the region, as most ethnic groups were trying to reassert their identity. A Samarkand Tajik Cultural Movement was established demanding more cultural and spiritual rights, and it has even sought to unite some parts of Uzbekistan with Tajikistan, much to the concern of some Uzbek officials. Such a wish has been expressed by several Tajik informants in Samarkand and Namangan. The result of such efforts was further pressure from several local officials on the Tajiks of Samarkand and Bukhara to identify themselves as Uzbek. Eventually, the Tajik Samarkand Movement was banned in 1992 and its leaders were repressed. Tajik broadcasts have been discontinued. The Tajik department at the Samarkand State University encountered numerous problems as have Tajik sociocultural groups in Bukhara. Since then, however, the Uzbek government has made some effort to resolve existing problems. A National Association of Tajik Culture, dedicated to the protection and furtherance of Persian culture, was opened in 1994. By 1997 over 240 Tajik schools had been opened in the republic where about 130,000 students study. Tajik broadcasts on local TV and radio were restarted in 1995. There was also an increase in local Tajik newspapers in Samarkand and Bukhara. Although the situation has now improved and specifically 'Tajik' ethnic-based problems are unlikely to exist in the republic at the present time, three factors could rekindle the 'Tajik' problem in Uzbekistan. Firstly, there is economic hardship, which is causing large part of the population to feel marginalized and betrayed. Secondly, the more the nationalist wing of the leadership pushes for an Uzbek national identity, the more Tajik groups will look to ways of differentiating themselves from the Uzbeks. Finally, ethnic-based problems could be triggered by the policies or aspirations of the government in Dushanbe. Relations between the Tajiks and Uzbek authorities remain uncomfortable.

Kazaks
According to the Soviet statistics of 1989, there were over 800,000 Kazaks in Uzbekistan. Unofficial estimates in late 1996 put the figure at 1.2 million, although the official Kazak estimates state 1.5 million.[35] The majority of the Kazaks of Uzbekistan live in the Tashkent region, bordering

Kazakstan. In the seventeenth century after the sedentarization of the nomads, many Kazaks settled there. When the borders between Uzbekistan and Kazakstan were redrawn in the 1950s, the Uzbek boundary was expanded further bringing even more Kazaks into Uzbekistan. During the Soviet period these Kazaks, although living in Uzbekistan, considered themselves as citizens of the USSR. After the break-up of the Union, they found themselves as Uzbek citizens. They sought to adopt dual nationality but neither Kazakstan nor Uzbekistan permitted this. Officially there are no problems between Uzbeks and Kazaks in Uzbekistan, yet although there have not been any open clashes between them, many Kazaks feel that they are being discriminated against and seen as an 'inferior' class of people. This has led to resentment and frustration in some Kazak circles, though it is generally muted and privately voiced. This might not lead to an ethnic conflict between Uzbeks and Kazaks but, nonetheless, it indicates distrust between them. After all, Uzbek officials have taken some measures to improve the relations between the two communities. A National Association of Kazak Culture, dedicated to the protection and furtherance of Kazak culture, was officially opened in 1992. Education facilities have increased since then and several primary and secondary schools for Kazaks have opened, their number increasing to 627 by late 1997.

Tatars
Today there are two groups of Tatars in Uzbekistan, their combined populations amounting to 610,000. The Crimean Tatars, according to the 1989 Soviet census, numbered 188,772, though by 1998 there were only 110,000. The Volga Tatars totalled 467,829, in 1989; by 1998, this had risen to 500,000.[36]

The Crimean Tatars are descendants of the Crimean Khanate of Haci Giray Khan, founded in 1441 after the disintegration of the Golden Horde, and of the Anatolian Turks who began to settle in the Crimea during the sixteenth century. The Giray dynasty ruled over Crimea without interruption until 8 April 1783, when it was officially annexed by Russia. Hundreds of thousands of Crimean Tatars fled their homeland in waves of massive emigrations. The population of Crimea, estimated at around 5 million during the height of the Crimean Khanate rule, had fallen to 300,000 on the eve of the Bolshevik revolution. By the end of the nineteenth century, there was an emergence of Crimean

Tatar national consciousness, launched by Ismail Bey Gaspirali. This resulted in the *Jadid* movement, which had a strong pan-Turkic and pan-Islamic orientation influenced by similar movements in the Ottoman Empire. On 28 November 1917 an independent Crimea was established by Numan Celebi Cihan, but it survived for only six months. In October 1921, Soviet rule was finally established and the Crimean Autonomous Soviet Socialist Republic was created as part of the RSFSR (Russian Soviet Federative Socialist Republic). The years 1921 to 1927, saw the 'golden age' of the Crimean Tatars under the leadership of Veli Ibrahimov. During this time Crimean Tatar nationalism flourished. In 1927, however, Veli Ibrahimov and several of his allies were arrested and executed for being 'bourgeois nationalists'. Thousands of Tatars perished during the deportation of the Kulaks in 1928.

During the Second World War the Crimea was occupied by German forces from 1941–4. Immediately afterwards it was retaken by Soviet forces. On 18 May 1944, the entire Crimean Tatar population was accused of collaboration with the Germans, rounded up, loaded in to cattle wagons and deported to the Urals, Siberia and Central Asia. Hunger, thirst and disease led to deaths: 46 per cent of the total Crimean nation died. The survivors were forced to live in 'special settlement camps'. The Crimean ASSR was officially abolished with a decree on 30 June 1945. On 19 February 1954, Nikita Khruschev transferred the entire Crimean province to the Ukrainian SSR as a special gift to commemorate the 300th anniversary of the Ukrainian-Russian friendship.[37] On 28 April 1956, the Crimean Tatars were officially released from the 'special settlement camps' during Khruschev's de-Stalinization reforms. Though they were only partially 'rehabilitated', this limited freedom was sufficient to give rise to a Crimean Tatar National Movement, the first of its kind in the history of the Soviet Union. The main aim of this socio-political movement was to secure a complete political rehabilitation and the right to return to their homeland. Initially the campaign began with individual letter-writing and telegram-sending to various organs of the Communist Party. This later changed to a petition-sending campaign. During the height of this campaign in 1966, a petition containing 120,000 signatures and 37 volume of documents was sent to the 23rd Party Congress in Moscow. On 5 September 1967, an official decree exonerated the Crimean Tatars from any wrongdoing during the Second World War. Following this, thousands of Crimean

Tatars attempted to return to the Crimea, but they discovered that they were not welcome in their ancestral homeland. Once more, thousands were expelled from Crimea by the local authorities. They had to settle in various parts of Central Asia, the majority remaining in Uzbekistan, and most of those went to the Tashkent and Fergana regions. By 1996, they numbered over 200,000. Although a large number of the Crimean Tatars managed to emigrate to the Crimea, there are still about 110,000 in Uzbekistan. There does not appear to be any discrimination against Crimean Tatars in the republic but they still live with the stigma of the past and are determined to return to Crimea.

The second group of Tatars in Uzbekistan contains four ethnic subgroups. The majority of these are descendants of Volga Tatars, the westernmost of all Turkic 'nationalities' of the former Soviet Union who were descendants of the Kazan Khanate which emerged in the 1440s after the break-up of the Golden Horde. The Khanate remained an independent entity until 1552 when it was annexed and destroyed by the armies of Ivan IV. The most urgent task confronting Ivan after the annexation was the absorption of these new elements into the social fabric. Throughout the centuries, the Russian state pursued a policy of national integration that meant the conversion of millions of Tatars to Christianity, and cultural assimilation. Religious, legal, educational and economic policies were all designed and enforced in a concerted effort to transform the '*inorodtsy*' into better Russian subjects by first making them Christians. Missionary activities represented one of the major channels through which the Russian state exercised religious pressure on its '*inorodtsy*'.[38] *Inorodots* means non-Slavic Eastern peoples of the Russian Empire. Sometimes mild and sometimes forceful approaches were adopted to convert Tatars to Christianity, but neither punitive nor conciliatory measures did much to increase the number of Tatar converts. On the contrary, they increased the discontent of the Tatars, making them more prone to open rebellion. The conversion policies likewise promoted the beginning of an exodus of the Volga Tatars towards the Kazak steppes and Central Asia. Many, finding themselves expelled from the fortress cities, had no other choice. Their best lands were confiscated and distributed among the Russian nobility or given to the monasteries or peasants arriving from central Russia. The forceful measures of converting the Muslim Tatars to Christianity continued until the reign of Catherine II. This reign marked the 'golden age' of the Muslim Tatars as their persecution stopped. Catherine realized that Tatar merchants could facilitate Russian trade with the Muslim Khanates of Central Asia and with the Kazak steppes. Therefore Tatars were allowed to engage in trade and to organize commercial enterprises. As a result, many Tatars moved to the Kazak steppes and some joined the local Tatars of Siberia, where they founded commercial outposts for trade with Central Asia and established new Muslim settlements. They also sent their children to the famous Bukhara Madrassah to receive higher education. This time probably marked the beginning of the Tatars' emigration period to Uzbekistan. The emigration of these people increased further after the conquest of Central Asia by the Russians in the late nineteenth century. The non-Crimean Tatars of Uzbekistan are the descendants of those Volga Tatars who had emigrated to the Kazak steppes and Siberia during the reign of Catherine II, and who later moved south to engage in trade and study in Bukhara. Today, although they classify themselves as Idil, Ural, Sibir and Asatrakhani Tatars, their sense of belonging to a common Tatar group is stronger. The Uzbek Tatars, unlike many other Muslim Turkic groups in the region, are more modernized and also more Russified. They are also the most highly urbanized of the major Turkic peoples. Many of the Tatars in the republic also speak Uzbek, as the majority do not know their native language. They have a near-European level of fertility, and thus have a smaller proportion of children than any other Turkic people. In addition, mixed marriages are widespread. Today the relationship between Tatars and Uzbeks is, in general, reasonably good. The majority of Tatars hold good positions in the country. Over 70 per cent of the Uzbek Tatars are intellectuals, each of whom have at least Master's degrees. There are initiatives from their community to learn and teach their children the Tatar language, history and culture. A National Association dedicated to the furtherance of the Tatar culture was granted official registration in 1992. There is also an independent Tatar Information and Cultural Centre, set up in Tashkent in 1994, dedicated to introducing language courses for native Tatars and establishing links between the Tatars of Uzbekistan and those of the rest of the former Soviet Union.

Karakalpaks
The Karakalpaks people are of predominantly Turkic origin. They have a rather complicated history but it is generally known that by the

sixteenth century they were settled along the lower reaches of the Syrdarya. They then split into two groups. One migrated to a location higher up the Syrdarya, while the other settled in the southern delta of the Amu Darya. In the Karakalpak Autonomous Republic, which has a total population of 1.5 million people, Karakalpaks are almost equal in number to the Uzbeks, comprising 32.9 per cent of the population to the Uzbeks' 32.7 per cent. The remaining parts include Kazaks (26.3 per cent), Turkmens (5 per cent), Russians (less than 1 per cent), Koreans (0.8 per cent), Tatars (0.7 per cent), Ukrainians (0.1 per cent) and Kyrgyzys (0.1 per cent). The population density is 8.1 per person per square kilometre. It is estimated that 60 per cent of the population lives in rural areas. Its capital is Nukus, which has a population of about 185,000. The Karakalpaks as an ethnic group were shaped between the fifteenth and seventeenth centuries. They were composed of diverse branches of the Turkic and Mongolic tribes, who were the conglomerate of the Oghuz, Qipchak, Mangit, Qarakalpak, Nöküs, and Nayman tribes. They also contain some Selchuk and Khorezm elements.

Although they are ethnically close to Kazaks, and culturally proximate to Uzbeks, today the sense of being Karakalpak is stronger. The Karakalpaks, although economically and politically dependent on Uzbekistan, theoretically enjoy their own sovereignty but, in practice, the Karakalpak Autonomous Republic is not very much different from any of the *oblasts*. There are several schools in which Karakalpak is the main language of instruction. There is a university and a Pedagogical Institute in Nukus where some tuition is available in the native language. There are newspapers, books and periodicals published in Karakalpak and there also are cultural facilities in this language, such as radio, television, films and theatres. A National Association of Karakalpak Culture was also opened in 1992 in Tashkent to protect and develop further the Karakalpak culture and to assist about 10,000 Karakalpaks living in and around Tashkent.

Karakalpakistan suffered enormously from the major ecological crisis that resulted from the desiccation of the Aral Sea, which was originally triggered by the huge, but mismanaged irrigation system of the Soviet period. As a result, a large part of the population left the region. Russians and Ukrainians were the first to leave, most of whom had gone by 1995. They were followed by Turkmens and Kazaks who migrated to Turkmenistan and Kazakhstan respectively. The migratory movements of the native people remained at low levels, and took place mostly within the republic. As a whole, between 1989 and 1996 about 440,000 people left the Karakalpak Autonomous region, but about 400,000 people immigrated to the republic.[39] By 1999, Uzbeks, Kazaks, Turkmens and Tatars were the largest ethnic groups in the autonomous republic.

Koreans
The presence of the Korean minority in Uzbekistan is the result of decades of Russo-Soviet and Japanese imperialistic rivalry for control of the Korean Peninsula, dating back 130 years.[40] In 1979 the population of Koreans in Uzbekistan stood at 163,100, while the 1989 All-Union Population Census recorded 183,100 Koreans in Uzbekistan. By 1997, there were 200,000 Koreans in Uzbekistan, of whom 50,000 lived in Tashkent, the remainders residing in other centres such as Samarkand, Bukhara, Khorezm and Karakalpakistan. 30 per cent of the Koreans work in the agricultural sector, 30 per cent in business markets, and about 38 per cent form part of the intellectual community: artists, writers, academics and scientists. About 1–2 per cent of the Koreans are believed to be unemployed. They have, to a large extent, been Russian culture oriented people, and the majority are now Russian speakers. About 20 per cent are Christians, 1–2 per cent are Muslims and the rest are non-religious. Buddhism has almost died out among the Koreans in Uzbekistan. About 70 per cent of them speak Uzbek reasonably well. The relationship between Koreans and Uzbeks is not excellent, but it is good. In general, there does not seem to be any obvious discrimination against Koreans, and no conflict is foreseen between the Koreans and Uzbeks. Today almost all of the Koreans in Uzbekistan, with the exception of the immigrants, are descendants of those who were deported from the Maritime Province.

Russia annexed the Maritime Province in 1860 with the signing of the Treaty of Peking with China. The government of Tsar Alexander II extended its grip on the Pacific coast of the Amur River until 1889. The new conquests, east of the Ussuri River, provided Russia with a strip of the Pacific coasts as far as the Korean border along the Tumen River. Russia emphasized the strategic significance of this territorial gain by the immediate construction of Vladivostok, the role of which was to plant the empire firmly and permanently on the Pacific coast. In 1895, immediately after China was defeated by Japan, both Russia and Japan openly adopted rival ambitions for Korea for imperial reasons. This led to the 1904–5 Russo-Japanese war which ended in humiliating defeat of the Tsarist Empire. Consequently, on 22 August 1910, Korea became a Japanese colony causing thousands of Koreans to flee north into Russian territory. A large number of Koreans, over 30,000, had already migrated northward before 1904. These were mainly farmers or workers attracted by the big construction projects stimulated by Russia's fast expansion in the Maritime Province since 1860. A third wave of Koreans, largely peasants, moved north to escape the famine of 1869. All those who entered the Russian territory by 25 June 1884 received Russian citizenship. Those who came after 1905 were mostly Korean political refugees escaping Japanese occupation. They proposed to fight for the liberation of their country, hoping to obtain political support from the Russian Empire. Russia, however, concealed the same colonial ambitions for Korea as the Japanese. Nevertheless, the Russians represented for the Koreans the best sponsor to evict the Japanese; for the Russians, the Koreans were a potential front army unit for future Russian anti-Japanese policies on behalf of Korea.

From 1905 to 1917 Korean refugees organized themselves and established a Korean community organization, which became a *de facto* movement for Korean liberation. This organization soon became a centre of anti-Japanese activity, posing a problem for the Russian authorities. With the Russo-Japanese treaties and the Convention of 1907, Russia officially recognized Japan's presence in Korea. Although they did not want to prevent Korean armed units from training and crossing the border into northern Korea, Russia eventually had to abide by the Russo-Japanese Treaty of Extradition signed in 1911 and bow to Japanese pressure to put restraints on its Koreans. However, the Tsarist authorities agreed to move many of them northward into Siberia far from the Korean border, rather than sending them back to Korea.

During the October revolution, however, the majority of Koreans sided with the Bolsheviks as they played the anti-imperialist card. The Bolsheviks opened all the prisons in the region and released radical Korean political prisoners. By April 1918, Russian Koreans came together to form the All-Russian Korean Association, which stemmed from their collective fear of a Japanese invasion of the Maritime Province. As a result of this fear, Koreans and the Bolshevik Soviets became natural allies throughout the civil war. After the Bolsheviks re-emerged as the dominant force in the Maritime Province in mid 1919, there began an open struggle for control of the Province between the Japanese and the Bolsheviks, the latter being supported by some well-trained and motivated Korean units. By October 1922 the Japanese had withdrawn back to Korea from the southern segment of the Maritime Province, which then became incorporated into the Russian Soviet Socialist Federal Republic, as part of the USSR. The Koreans witnessed the reinstatement of the pre-1917 *status quo* under the Tsar and the international border remained the same; the Japanese held Korea, while the Russians, in the form of the Bolsheviks, remained the reluctant hosts of militant Koreans, though the latter emerged from the civil war overwhelmingly pro-Communist. After 1922, all Koreans were invited to take full USSR citizenship and expected to adopt Soviet values in line with Lenin's script. Subsequently they should integrate into Soviet society, though only a small number accepted citizenship. On the other hand, as a result of a new wave of Koreans exiled during 1925–6, the proportion of Koreans who refused the offer remained about 60 per cent. The majority of Koreans perceived themselves as temporarily inside the Soviet Union, but hoping to go back soon to an independent Korea. Hence they were against the assimilation policies of the Soviet government.

Those Koreans who had adopted citizenship moved north and westwards for land work, while the majority of those Koreans who refused citizenship remained in the Maritime Province. From 1923 and throughout the early Stalin years, the Koreans in the Province engaged in some political participation, many becoming members of the Communist Party. They enjoyed a fair amount of state-approved cultural life but all requests for a Korean autonomous province within the Soviet Union were rejected. In September 1931 when Japan invaded Manchuria, virtually all Koreans in the Union allied with the Soviet regime. This support was also shown by non-opposition to Stalin's decree of 1932 ordering all Koreans to become citizens of the Soviet Union. There appeared a 'golden era' in the relationship between Moscow and the Korean minority. This, however, did not survive long. With the agreement between Japan and the Soviet Union in early 1935, Moscow complied with Japanese requests to curb all Korean activities in the province. This coincided with the nationwide purges. Koreans were accused of espionage and other charges, including that they had been infiltrated by Japanese agents. Stalin ordered the mass deportation of Koreans to Central Asia to join a large number of Koreans who had migrated there voluntarily in the early years of the Soviet regime. Within three months, entire villages and towns in the Maritime Province were cleared of Koreans. They suffered enormously during the deportation era and a large number died from cold, disease or hunger. By 1937 exiled Koreans arrived in Uzbekistan where they were placed in certain rural areas, with their movement being restricted. Yet the local Uzbeks extended them hospitality, helping them to survive in the face of government brutality. During 1937–9 about 75,000 Koreans arrived in the republic. In 1937, during the purges, 70 per cent of Korean intellectuals were allegedly removed and killed. Stalin thought that there were many Japanese spies among the Koreans who had to be cleared. The peasants were left untouched. After the punitive regime was relaxed in 1954, citizenship was re-offered and most Koreans took up the offer. They were allowed to settle in urban areas, where they attended schools, universities and institutes. They also began to join collective farms where they contributed greatly to the cultivation of cotton and rice. They worked very hard and made good use of whatever facilities were available to them. The post-war generation produced many agricultural specialists, scientists, writers and intellectuals. They were not, however, allowed into the military schools until 1958, with the first group graduating in 1968. The chairman of the Korean cultural centre in Tashkent, a retired colonel Peter Kim, was one of the first Koreans to enrol for the military school.

After the break-up of the Soviet Union, the entire region witnessed the so-called 'epic of the Renaissance', all the 'nationalities' of the old Soviet Union suddenly seeking to rediscover their pasts. Koreans were among these 'nationalities'. For the past seventy years, the national cultures had been forbidden, the only 'national' culture being Soviet culture. The large nations such as the Uzbeks, Kazaks, Tajiks and Turkmens enjoyed limited privileges, but smaller ethnic minorities had no cultural rights at all. In 1993 an International Cultural Centre was established in Uzbekistan dedicated to protecting and supporting the cultural rights of minorities in Uzbekistan. The Korean Cultural Centre was also formed as part of this organization. In 1994 one Korean MP was elected to the Uzbek Parliament (he is also a director of a large factory). Two Korean Chairs, one at the Institute of Oriental Studies, the other at the University of World Languages, were also established for this cause.

Courses in the Korean language are also provided at the University of World Economy and Diplomacy.

The reaction of Koreans to the break-up of the Soviet Union was neutral, but they were enthusiastic about independence for Uzbekistan because it gave them the chance to regain their culture, history and way of life. They have benefited from established governmental and non-governmental links with South Korea. Although the old generation wants to go back to South Korea, the young generation considers Uzbekistan to be their homeland. The Republic of Korea is, in any case, not willing to take them back, as there are major differences in their culture. Instead, they preferred to invest in Uzbekistan to improve their fellow nationals' conditions in Central Asia as well as discovering new markets. In Uzbekistan there is an effort to open more Korean schools and theatres, publish a newspaper in the Korean language, establish more Korean folklore groups and promote national songs and dances among their school children. The Koreans have substituted their short-lived Soviet citizenship with the new Uzbek citizenship but they prefer to live and remain as Koreans. Prospects for them in Uzbekistan are promising. In terms of income and status today, they appear to be the most successful of the minority groups in the republic.

Meskhetian Turks
Meskhetia is a mountainous region situated in south-west Georgia and north-east Turkey.[41] Meskhetian Turks are an ethnically heterogeneous group of Turkish-speaking Muslims who lived in the Meskhetia region of Georgia until 1944. In November of the same year, mainly elderly women and children were deported *en masse* from the region to Central Asia while their menfolk were fighting with the Soviet Army against the Nazis. Stalin wished to clear potentially pro-Turkish inhabitants from the border areas of Georgia. Thus a group numbering around 100,000 was deported to Uzbekistan, of whom more than 20,000 died during the process. The men who were fighting with the Soviet Army were later stripped of their honours and privileges and were also exiled to Uzbekistan. The Meskhetian Turks were subjected to an exceptionally harsh regime even after the deportation. Although this eased in the late 1950s it was not until 1968 that they were officially 'rehabilitated', becoming the last deported people of the Soviet regime to be cleared of

the false charges of treason. By 1989 there were 106,000 Meskhetian Turks in Uzbekistan, the majority of whom lived in the Fergana Valley. They lived with the stigma but worked hard and made good use of the facilities available to them. Within a short period of time they became quite prosperous and many held influential positions in the local administration, while others were making good use of the fertile lands of the Fergana Valley. This brought them into competition with the Uzbeks, who viewed them as rivals. Tension between the two groups had been rising for some time culminating in a brutal gang warfare in May 1989. The rioting and arson that broke out between Uzbeks and Meskhetian Turks in the Fergana Valley lasted for almost two weeks. Over 100 Meskhetians were killed, their houses were burned down and entire villages were destroyed. More than 75,000 of them were airlifted to safety in other parts of Uzbekistan. About 44,000 of the Meskhetian Turks went to Azerbaijan, while others sought refuge in Kazakhstan, Kyrgyzstan and the Russian Federation. After the break-up of the Union about 300 of them attempted to return to Georgia, but there they were met with hostility and treated as intruders. Therefore they began to return to Uzbekistan, while others remained in Azerbaijan and the Russian Federation. By the end of 1996 about 15,000 Meskhetian Turks lived in Uzbekistan, once again stigmatized by the locals. In April 1998, the numbers of the Meskhetian Turks returning to Uzbekistan had increased to 45,000. Some find it difficult to forget the past and are uncertain about their future, while others try to start a new life.

Jews
According to the 1989 Soviet Population Census, there were 94,689 Jews in Uzbekistan. The Jewish community in the republic comprises four different groups. The first group is the Central Asian Jews, who are generally known as 'Bukharan Jews'. They numbered 28,369 people in 1989, and were living in and around Bukhara-Samarkand. Their history goes back at least 2,000 years.[42] They have a very strong sense of belonging to the region. They have always lived side by side with the other indigenous people of the region, the Uzbeks and Tajiks. The Bukharan Jewish community considers itself hardly different from Tajiks or Uzbeks. Its people have suffered neither serious discrimination nor harassment from the Uzbeks or Tajiks. Like the Uzbeks and Tajiks, they are bilingual, speaking Persian and Uzbek, although some still retain a

Judaic language. They had always practised their religion freely until the Soviet regime was firmly established in the region. Their educational, cultural and religious centres were closed during the purges of the 1930s. They remained separate from the later Jewish immigrants and there have been few intermarriages between the immigrant Jews and Central Asian Jews. There have, however, been many intermarriages between Central Asian Jews and Tajiks and Uzbeks. They maintain their customs, though there has been enormous degree of intermixing with other indigenous cultures. In 1992 a National Cultural Association for Jews established by the Israeli government and the Jewish Agency of the Bukharan Jewish community, dedicated to the development of Jewish culture, was granted official registration in Tashkent. There is a cultural and religious revival among the Bukharan Jews, promoted mainly by the government in Jerusalem for those who remained in the region. In the cultural centres in Bukhara and Tashkent, courses in Hebrew are also organized. There has been some emigration of the Bukharan Jews from Uzbekistan, mainly to Israel and the USA, but by late 1996 some 20,000 remained in the republic.[43]

The other groups of Jews that moved to Uzbekistan were European (Ashkenazic) Jews, Mountain Jews and Georgian Jews. By 1989, their numbers were 65,493, 617 and 210 respectively. During midsummer of 1941, and continuing throughout 1942 after the invasion of the Germans, several industrial, academic and cultural enterprises were transplanted to eastern and far eastern parts of the Soviet Union, accompanied by the evacuation of a large number of civilians. About one million Ukrainian and Belarusian Jews in the eastern regions of the republics and around half a million Jews from the western parts of the Russian Federation were evacuated during this period. Around half a million of those who found refuge from the Nazis were moved to Uzbekistan. Jews in the republic were moved to the Samarkand, Khokand, Khiva, Bukhara and Andijan regions, though the majority stayed in the Tashkent region. After the war a large number of them returned to their bases while those who stayed, like other Slavs, remained separate from the indigenous peoples, including the Central Asian Jews. Subsequently they became more oriented to Russian culture and by the 1980s the majority of them were Russian speakers. There were many intermarriages between these Jews and the Slavs. They too, like many other Slavs in Uzbekistan, were highly qualified and skilled professionals. In the 1970s when emigration to Israel became slightly easier for Jews throughout the Soviet Union, the European Jews from Uzbekistan were among the first to leave. By the 1980s, many emigrated either to various parts of the Soviet Union or outside of the Union.

Finally, Mountain Jews are those Jews who immigrated to Uzbekistan during the 1960s from Nagorno Karabakh. Georgian Jews also emigrated to the republic during this time. They too were largely Russified. By late 1999, the total number of Jews in Uzbekistan, both Bukharan and Europeans, amounted to 25,000 people.

Germans
Most of the Germans in Uzbekistan today are descendants of the Volga Germans, whose ancestors were colonists invited from Germany in the late eighteenth and early nineteenth centuries by Catherine the Great and Alexander I to settle on the newly acquired lands in the south of Russia. Following their arrival in Russia in 1763, the Germans flourished and grew in numbers from the original 100,000 settlers to almost 2.5 million on the eve of the First World War.[44] The success of the Germans was due to their well-known endurance and skill as farmers and artisans. They also enjoyed special favours including economic concessions; exemption from military service; and protection of their traditional social, cultural and religious rights. In the last years of the nineteenth century, however, they lost their privileged status during the reforms undertaken by Alexander II. They experienced economic setbacks and growing anti-German prejudices. For a short period after the revolution, the Volga German Autonomous Republic and several autonomous districts were created by the Soviet authority. However, the Second World War signalled an end to this short-lived 'golden era', and destroyed the historic German way of life in the Soviet Union. When Nazi Germany attacked the Soviet Union in 1941, Stalin falsely accused the Soviet Germans of disloyalty and ordered their deportation to the east. Over half a million Soviet Germans were brutally dispatched to Siberia where they were forced into labour camps where most of them died. Their autonomous units were dissolved, their property confiscated and their religious centres closed. The German population of the Crimea, Caucasus and some parts of Ukraine, came under the control of the invading Nazis, but about 100,000 of them were forcibly repatriated to the Soviet Union after the war by the allied forces as part of the

'Operation Keelhaul'.[45] Many were also deported to the camps east of the Urals Mountains.

The Soviet Germans were not released from the camps until 1955, as a gesture to mark the establishment of diplomatic relations between the Soviet Union and post-war Germany, when the then first chancellor of West Germany interceded on the Soviet Germans' behalf. The released Germans were allowed to settle in south-western Siberia and Kazakstan, but were banned from returning to their former homes. They were officially rehabilitated in mid-1964 and exonerated of wartime crimes, but were not allowed to return to their former homes or seek compensation for losses caused during the war. In the late 1950s about 18,000 of the survivors of the camps were settled in Uzbekistan and took up jobs in agriculture and industry. The 1989 Soviet census stated the number of Germans living in Uzbekistan to be 39,809. Most Soviet Germans in Uzbekistan spoke neither German nor Uzbek, but only Russian, having been almost fully Sovietized (Russified). No German cultural behaviour and tradition was left among them. The new generation is more Russian than German. By 1992 their number was estimated to be over 40,000. There has been something of a cultural and religious revival among those who remained. A national Cultural Association was granted official registration in 1992. A Protestant Church in Uzbekistan, which was closed by Stalin, was returned to the Germans by the Uzbek government in 1993. There is also a German Society operating in Uzbekistan. There was an effort by the governments of both Uzbekistan and Germany to encourage Germans to stay there hoping that they will facilitate commerce and cooperation between the two countries, but by 1996 the number of Soviet Germans in Uzbekistan had decreased to less than 20,000. The remaining German community also wants to emigrate, either to Russia or Germany. The German officials do not seem to be too concerned about teaching them German but they do seem to be concerned with culture. As one German official in Tashkent put it, there is no sign of German culture, and this will make it impossible to integrate them into German society.

Kyrgyz
The Kyrgyz are indigenous people of the region who speak a language of the Northern Turkic group. In the early 1920s and late 1930s, when the borders between Uzbekistan and Kyrgyzstan were redrawn, some

100,000 Kyrgyz remained within Uzbek boundaries. According to the 1989 Soviet census there were 174,907 in Uzbekistan. Today, about 350,000 Kyrgyz live in Uzbekistan. Of these, some 25,000 live in Tashkent, while the rest live in the rural areas of the Fergana Valley. The Kyrgyzy authorities insist that many of them were registered as Uzbeks during the Soviet period, a view that is rejected by the Uzbek authorities. This issue continues to create tension between Uzbekistan and Kyrgyzstan.[46] A national association of Kyrgyzy culture, dedicated to the protection and furtherance of their culture, was not granted official registration until 1995. Culturally and linguistically the Uzbeks and the Kyrgyz are fairly close to each other, yet one of the worst conflicts in the history of the Soviet Union erupted between these two peoples. In southern Kyrgyzstan, the Uzbeks farm the best land, bringing them into competition with the Kyrgyz. In June 1990, a wave of rioting rapidly escalated into brutal gang warfare between Kyrgyz and Uzbeks over land rights in the fertile Osh valley, leaving about 320 dead. No fighting has occurred since 1991, but some bad feeling still remains. The Kyrgyzy leadership has guaranteed the safety of Uzbeks living in Kyrgyzstan and the Uzbek leadership has maintained strict control over the border dividing the two countries.

Uighurs
The Uighurs are a Muslim Turkic people, whose language belongs to the East Turkic group and so is quite close to Uzbek. They originate from the Ili district of what is now the north-west of China named as the Xinjiang-Uighur Autonomous Province of the People's Republic of China. By tradition the Uighurs are traders and agriculturists. Today, the majority of the 12 million Uighurs live in the Xinjan Autonomous Region. About 350,000 live in Kazakstan and 250,000 reside in Kyrgyzstan.[47] The Uighurs in Uzbekistan, like the majority of those in Kazakstan and Kyrgyzstan, are the descendants of the Uighurs of the former Soviet Union, who had migrated to the region from Xinjiang in the late nineteenth century as the Russian Empire expanded eastwards.

In the South of the Tien Shan lies Kashgaria, the land of the six cities (Alty Shahar), which was populated predominantly by the Uighurs. Whereas Jungaria looked towards Mongolia in the east, Kashgaria tended to have close relations with the Muslim Central Asian Khanates to the west, such as Khiva, Bukhara and, in the nineteenth century, Khokand.

During both the Han and T'ang Dynasties, the Chinese extended their influence into Jungaria and Kashgaria, and both regions also formed part of the Mongol empire. In Ming times these regions remained outside the Chinese empire. The regions, however, were overrun by the Chinese in late 1759, and in 1760 the Manchus created their own administration and ruled the region until the first half of the nineteenth century. Their rule began to decline as the empire itself became caught up in internal upheavals in the mid-nineteenth century. The Muslim people of this region were also stirred by religious movements, creating opposition to the Manchus. The latter were further weakened by the advance of Russian power in Central Asia. Between 1850 and 1860, Russia acquired by treaty the right to trade and reside in Ili and Kashgaria. At the same time Russian posts like Verniy (Almaty) in Semirechie (modern Kazakstan) brought Russian military power south of Lake Balkhas towards Ili. These developments created a state of unrest throughout Chinese Turkistan. By the beginning of 1864 the Chinese had lost control of much of Kashgaria. Russia occupied the Ili Valley in 1871, evidently to maintain peace on their frontier. In the spring of 1877, on the Kashgarian border, Tso Tsung't'ang, defeated the army of Yakup Beg, who had become the undisputed ruler of all the territory south of the Tien Shan range. In December Kashgar was taken and by the beginning of 1878 his kingdom was completely destroyed. There now arose the problem of retrieving Ili from the Russians. For a while it looked as if China would rather go to war with Russia than come to terms over Ili. The crisis was solved by a Chinese minister in London, who, early in 1881, signed a new agreement with the Russians whereby the Chinese regained Ili, but had to pay inflated compensation to the Russians for their occupation costs.[48] From this time onwards, the regained territory of Eastern Turkistan was no longer governed by indirect Manchu rule. It was converted into a new Chinese province and in November 1884 an imperial decree announced the creation of Sinkiang or Xinjiang 'the New Dominion' and the capital was to be at Urumchi.

All these events prompted outward migration of the Uighurs from Xinjiang to former Soviet Central Asia in 1828, but the majority of the Uighurs who migrated to Uzbekistan did so between 1881 and 1884. They were from the part of the Uighur population of the Ili Valley that came under Tsarist rule in 1871. The majority of the Uighurs who moved to Russian territory settled in the Semirechie region and about

21,000 of these Uighurs are estimated to have migrated to the Tashkent and Fergana regions between 1883 and 1884. According to the 1989 Soviet Census, there were 35,762 Uighurs in Uzbekistan, but some Uighurs claimed that this under-represented their true number. According to the Uighur Cultural Centre in Tashkent, there were by the end of 1997 over 75,000 Uighurs in the republic, the majority of whom live in the Tashkent region, with the rest in the Andijan, Fergana and Syrdarya regions. The Uighurs, like many other 'nationalities' of the Soviet Union, had also suffered at the hands of Soviet officials during the purges. A large number of Uighurs were sent to the Siberian labour camps and never returned. There had been a 'cleaning system' put in force by Stalin by which he aimed to destroy the Uighur intellectual community. Thus a large number of Uighur intellectuals simply vanished. Moreover, as a small group of the Soviet 'nationalities', they had been given no cultural rights throughout the Soviet period. The majority of them lost their sense of identity and knowledge of their history and culture. In the wake of the break-up of the Soviet Union, like many other ethnic groups, the Uighurs also sought to reclaim their 'national' identity. With the independence of the Uzbek republic, a National Association dedicated to the development of Uighuri culture was granted official registration in late 1992. There does not appear to be obvious discrimination against the Uighurs in Uzbekistan, and they do seem to have a future in the republic. The relationship between the Uzbeks and the Uighurs appears to be quite good. The majority of the Uighurs in Uzbekistan, like many of those in Kazakstan and Kyrgyzstan, are sympathetic to the aims of the Chinese Uighur nationalists, and cherish dreams of forming a greater Uighur republic of Eastern Turkestan.

Inter-ethnic relations

Throughout the Soviet period, although inter-ethnic relations in Uzbekistan were in general cordial, social boundaries between the immigrants and the titular 'nationality' groups were strongly maintained. Even informal socializing was comparatively low. Mixed marriages were rare, not only between the titular groups and the immigrants, but even between different indigenous groups. According to the Soviet population census of 1970, 93 per cent of all Uzbek families were ethno-homogeneous. The 1989 Soviet population census states that only 4.2 per cent of all Uzbek males had wives from other ethnic minority groups while 3.5 per cent of all Uzbek females had husbands from another ethnic minority, mainly from the indigenous groups. The percentage for Russians is rather different. There is a very high level of inter-ethnic marriages, but there is a predominance of marriages between the European immigrant groups and less with Central Asian indigenous people.[49]

Nevertheless, the regime was successful in providing scope for advancement for a sufficiently wide range of people for there to be a general perception of ethnic equality. There were tensions between the titular peoples and different immigrants, but this remained at a low level. There were instances of discrimination and harassment, but there was no institutionalized racism. Instead there was a notable degree of harmony between the different ethnic groups. Many people suffered horrendously during the purges and the deportation processes, yet there has been little bitterness against the Slavs or any other ethnic group, but rather a feeling of common tragedy shared by all. There remained an anti-Russian feeling among the Uzbeks in late 1980s, but this was provoked largely by the purges of anti-corruption investigations.

By the late 1980s, when the power of the central government was beginning to diminish and economic and environmental conditions were deteriorating, hitherto latent ethnic tensions suddenly exploded into open conflict in the Fergana Valley, between Uzbeks and Meskhetian Turks in spring 1989, and between Uzbeks and Kyrgyzy in 1990, where hundreds of people were murdered. On the eve of the demise of the Soviet Union, ethnic relations in Uzbekistan were quite tense. There appeared expressions of anger and resentment against people, who were now categorized and demonized by group origin, rather than being judged primarily as individuals, as had previously been the case. The sudden and unexpected collapse of the Union changed the relative status of ethnic groups further. Previously, the titular 'nationalities' had been one group among equals. After the break-up of the Soviet Union, 'this underwent an elevation and became expressly, equated with the state. The other "nationalities" suffered a corresponding diminution of status. They were suddenly regarded as being less authentic.'[50]

This unexpected shift was deeply felt, especially among Slavs, who feared that they would be marginalized and treated as second-class citizens. Their anxieties were aggravated by the aggressively xenophobic behaviour of some of the more nationalistically inclined members of the indigenous peoples. There appeared an immense confusion, not only at the public level but also at the governmental level, about how to tackle the exploding ethnic problems. The system that held them together had collapsed. Law and order was also on the verge of collapse. The political elite, however, inherited from the former Soviet regime a single method to solve any sort of unrest in the country, namely the use of force, to which the authorities did not hesitate to resort. The regime continued to be authoritarian. Several cultural movements were banned, political parties that had just began to emerge were also closed down. All opposition movements were repressed, and many of their members were silenced or imprisoned. Some have simply vanished. Today the confusion has, to a great extent, died down. Several national associations dedicated to develop and further the ethnic minorities' cultures were granted official registration. The Uzbek government has, to a great extent, managed to preserve the social accord while introducing new changes. The migration flows from the republic during 1989–92 were largely triggered by the social and political unrest in the region as a whole and later this was exacerbated by the deteriorating economic conditions in the republic. The existing migratory flows are bound to continue, though at a reduced rate. The Russian Federation will probably continue to be the main receiving country. The speed and intensity of this process will depend on the economic and political situation in both the republic and the countries of destination. Ecological migration will also continue to be of great concern, as will illegal transit migration.

In various parts of Uzbekistan, I frequently discussed the question of inter-ethnic tension or conflict with many people from different ethnic backgrounds, but the majority of respondents did not point out any obvious reasons for possible future tension or conflict in the republic. Moreover, the majority of them not only denied the existence of any inter-ethnic tensions but also avoided making any projections. They were more concerned with the deterioration of their economic conditions than about ethnic relations. Chronic inflation, shortages of basic household goods, delays in the payment of wages, growing unemployment and concerns about job prospects have made daily life a struggle. Although the leadership has taken a more cautious approach towards the programme of privatization and the transition to a free market economy, the effects of the free market economic policies are hitting the whole of society hard. People, especially those in the rural areas, dislike the present situation and fear for the future. So long as the economic situation is the overriding issue, it is difficult to provide a full picture of the nature of ethnic relations in Uzbekistan. Nevertheless, the prospects for ethnic minorities in Uzbekistan appear somewhat brighter than they were during the break-up of the Soviet Union. In general, ethnic relations in the republic appear to be quite good and there seems to be social accord throughout the country. The early indications are that inter-ethnic relations will remain relatively harmonious in the future. But this depends on a number of interrelated factors including no serious economic, political or social setbacks and no unexpected events happening to fuel the latent ethnic tensions which undoubtedly still exist. But if there is a conflict in Uzbekistan, it will not be a clash between civilizations, rather it will be a clash within a civilization. To be more precise, potential conflict in the republic is more likely to occur between Central Asian titular nationalities than between the latter and non-titular nationalities. We have already witnessed the conflicts between Uzbeks and Meskhetian Turks, and between Kyrgyz and Uzbeks.

NOTES

1 For a detailed discussion of Turkish tribes see, Togan, op. cit., 1981; R. P. Lindner, *Nomads and Ottomans in Medieval Anatolia,* especially Chapter I, and 'What was a Nomadic Tribe', *Comparative Studies in Society and History,* 24:4, 1982, pp. 689–711. Another excellent discussion is in David Morgan, *The Mongols,* New York: Basil Blackwell, 1986.
2 Two excellent accounts of nomadic life are Michael Prawdin, *The Mongol Empire: Its Rise and Legacy* (George Allen & Unwin Publishers Ltd, 1940); J. J. Saunders, *The History of the Mongol Conquests* (London: Routledge and K. Paul, 1971).
3 V. A. Riasonovsky, *Fundamental Principles of Mongol Law* (Tientsin, 1937, reprinted at the Hague, 1965). See also Morgan, op. cit., for an excellent discussion of the Turkish and Turko-Mongol tribal history, and Hambly, op. cit., pp. 1–18, 86–117.
4 Hambly, op. cit., pp. 118–39.
5 Manz, op. cit., pp. 4–7.
6 Uzbekiston Respublikasi Fanlar Akademiyasi, op. cit., vol. II, pp. 13–25. See also Y. Bregel, 'Turko-Mongol Influences in Central Asia' in Robert Canfield (ed.), *Turko-Persia in Historical Perspective* (Cambridge: Cambridge University Press, 1991), pp. 59–60.
7 Manz, op. cit., pp. 9–11. See also Hambly, op. cit., pp. 163–86.
8 Hambly, op. cit., pp. 169–73. Uzbekiston Respublikasi Fanlar Akademiyasi, op. cit., pp. 16–86.
9 Helene Carrere d'Encausse, 'Systemic Conquest, 1865 to 1884' and 'Organizing and Colonizing the Conquered Territories' in Edward Allworth (ed.), *Central*

Asia: 130 Years of Russian Dominance, A Historical Overview, 3rd edn (Durham: Duke University Press, 1994), chapters 4 and 5. See also Hambly, op. cit., pp. 202–26.
10 Allworth, op. cit., chapters 6–8; Wheeler, op. cit., chapters 4 and 5. See also Seymour Becker, *Russia's Protectorates in Central Asia: Bukhara and Khiva, 1865–1924* (Cambridge, MA: Harvard University Press, 1968), pp. 11–93, and Elizabeth E. Bacon, *Central Asians under Russian Rule: A Study in Culture Change* (Ithaca, New York: Cornell University Press, 1966), pp. 92–115. See also Michael Rywkin, *Moscow's Muslim Challenge: Soviet Central Asia* (Armonk, N.Y.: M.E. Sharpe, 1982), pp. 3–19.
11 A very good discussion of this is in Ian Murray Matley, 'Agricultural Development, 1865 to 1963' and 'Industrialization, 1865 to 1964' in Allworth, op. cit., chapters 11–12. A discussion of this subject is also found in Uzbekiston Respublikasi Fanlar Akademiyasi, op. cit., pp. 150–65.
12 A good discussion of the independent movements affected by Jadids is in Uzbekiston Respublikasi Fanlar Akademiyasi, op. cit., pp. 179–230. See also S.A. Zenkovsky, *Pan-Turkism and Islam in Russia* (Cambridge, MA: Harvard University Press, 1960), and Jacob M. Landau, *The Politics of Pan-Islam: Ideology and Organization* (Oxford: Clarendon, 1984).
13 Bacon, op. cit., pp. 189–201; Coates and Coates, op. cit., pp. 226–281; E. Allworth, *Uzbek Literary Politics* (The Hague: Mouton, 1964), p. 190; D. Azimova, *Youth and the Cultural Revolution in Soviet Central Asian Republics* (Moscow: Nauka, 1988). See also Shirin Akiner's case study of Uzbekistan, in M. Kirkwood (ed.) *Language Planning in the Soviet Union* (London: Macmillan, 1989), pp. 100–22.
14 See Coates and Coates, op. cit., and Bacon, op. cit., pp. 151–88. See also Olaf Caroe, *Soviet Empire: The Turks of Central Asia and Stalinism* (London: Macmillan, 1967), pp. 154–61, 173–214.
15 See also Shirin Akiner, 'Post-Soviet Central Asia: Past is Prologue' in Peter Ferdinand (ed.), *The New Central Asia and its Neighbours* (London: Pinter Publishers, The Royal Institute of International Affairs, 1994), pp. 10–26. A very good account of the 'Sovietization' of Central Asian societies is also in Shirin Akiner, *Central Asia: Conflict or Stability and Development?* (London: Minority Rights Group, 1997).
16 Martin Seliger, *Ideology and Politics* (London: Allen & Unwin, 1976), p. 14. See also Andrew Heywood, *Political Ideologies: an Introduction* (London: Macmillan, 1992).
17 *Vecherniy Tashkent*, 7 March 1993.
18 Islom Karimov, *Uzbekistoning Milli Istiklol Mavkurasi* (*Uzbekistan's National Ideology of Independence*) (Tashkent: Uzbekiston, 1993), p. 89.
19 *Xalq Sozi*, 25 May 1993.
20 Demokraticheskoi Parti Uzbekistana, *Ideologiya Nasionalnoi Nezavisimosti Narodno (The Ideology of National Independence)* (Tashkent: Uzbekiston, 1994), p. 9.
21 *Perspectiva*, 1993, no. 1, 2, 3.
22 *Xalq Sozi*, 9 December 1992.
23 Karimov, op. cit., p. 49.
24 See Demokraticheskoi Parti Uzbekistana, op. cit., p. 18.

25 Hunter, op. cit., pp. 38–9.
26 Islom Karimov, *Rodina Svyashenna Dlya Kajdogo (Motherland is Sacred for Everybody)* (Tashkent: Uzbekiston, 1995), pp. 173–7.
27 An interesting account of Uzbek nationalism can be found in Shahram Akbarzadeh, 'Nation-building in Uzbekistan', *Central Asian Survey*, 15:1, March 1996, pp. 23–31.
28 *Xalq Sozi*, 8 October 1994, p. 1. *Ozbekiston Ovozi*, 13–15 October 1994, pp. 1–2.
29 *Xalq Sozi*, 17 September 1994, pp. 1–2. *Ozbekiston Ovozi*, 19–21 September 1994, pp. 1, 3.
30 *Xalq Sozi*, 13 April 1994, p. 1. *Ozbekiston Ovozi*, 13 April 1994, p. 1.
31 See Abdujabar Abduvakhitov, 'Islamic Revivalism in Uzbekistan' in D.F. Eickelman (ed.), *Russia's Muslim Frontiers: New Directions in Cross-Cultural Analysis* (Bloomington: Indiana University Press, 1993), pp. 81–90.
32 *Pravda Vostoka*, 25 November 1986.
33 See H. Tajfe, *The Psychology of Minorities* (London: Minority Rights Group, 1992) for an interesting discussion of this subject. An excellent discussion of the minorities and minority rights in the newly independent Central Asian States of the former Soviet Union, is also in Akiner, op. cit., 1997. For a detailed analysis of Soviet nationalities policy, its success and collapse, see Ian Bremer, 'Reassessing Soviet Nationalities Theory', and Victor Zaslavsky, 'Success and Collapse: Traditional Soviet Nationality Policy' in Ian Bremmer and Ray Taras (eds.), *Nations and Politics in the Soviet Successor States* (Cambridge: Cambridge University Press, 1993), pp. 3–22, 29–41 respectively.
34 The most detailed account of these is in A. Nekrich, *The Punished Peoples* (New York: Norton, 1978).
35 An interview was conducted at the Kazak Cultural Centre in Tashkent in August 1996, and several official and unofficial interviews were conducted in Kazakstan in May and September 1996.
36 Two interviews, one with the official Tatar Cultural Centre, the other with a non-official Tatar Cultural Centre, were conducted in Tashkent in July and August 1996. Several discussions were also conducted with individual Tatars in Uzbekistan. An excellent work on the Crimean Tatars is A. Wilson, *The Crimean Tatars: A Situation Report* (London: International Alert, 1994). See also *Crimean Tatars: Repatriation and Conflict Prevention* (New York: Open Society Institute, 1996).
37 A detailed discussion of the deportation of the Crimean Tatars is in Mubeyyin Batu Altan, 'A Brief History of the Crimean Tatar National Movement', *The Crimean Review*, special issue (Boston, MA: 1995).
38 For further discussion of this and for an excellent discussion of the Volga Tatars and the annexation of their land by the Russians, see Azade-Ayse Rorlich, *The Volga Tatars: A Profile in National Resilience* (California: Hoover Institution Press, 1986), pp. 37–180.
39 An interview was conducted at the Karakalpak Cultural Centre in Tashkent on 15 September 1996. The figures were taken from this Cultural Centre. Similar figures were also published by the International Organization for Migration. See IMO, op. cit., p. 148.
40 An interview was conducted in Tashkent with the president of the Korean Cultural Centre, Mr Peter Kim, and several other Korean Pensioners in May

and July 1996, where a detailed account of the Korean minority in Uzbekistan was provided. A very good discussion of the Russo-Soviet and Japanese rivalry over Korea and the event that led to the Koreans' deportation to Central Asia is provided by Henry R. Huttenbach, 'The Soviet Koreans', *Central Asian Survey*, 12:1, 1993, pp. 59–69.

41 A National Cultural Association (Turkish Cultural Centre) established in Tashkent, dedicated to assist the Meskhetian Turks and Crimean Tatars, granted official registration 1992.

42 An interview was conducted in Tashkent with a representative of the Jewish Cultural Centre on 10 July 1996. Discussions were held with several members of the Uzbek Jewish community in Bukhara in September 1996.

43 Information obtained from the Israeli Embassy in Tashkent on 1 August 1996 put the remaining numbers of the Jewish community in Uzbekistan at around 15,000–20,000, which included the Jewish immigrants.

44 An interview was given by a German Embassy official in Tashkent on 28 August 1996. I have also held discussions with the representative of the German Cultural Centre in Tashkent in August 1996. Several other discussions also took place with members of the German Community in Tashkent. An excellent update on Soviet Germans is Sidney Heitman, 'The Soviet Germans', *Central Asian Survey*, 12:1, 1993, pp. 71–80. A very good account of the deportation of the Russian/Soviet Germans to the Soviet East is in Ann Sheehy, *The Crimean Tatars and Volga Germans: Soviet Treatment of Two Nationalities*, (London: Minority Rights Group, 1977), pp. 25–8.

45 Sidney Heitman, op. cit., p. 74.

46 Interviews were conducted with the representatives of the Kyrgyzy Cultural Centre in Tashkent on 9 March 1996 and 3 September 1996.

47 An interview was conducted with the chairman of the Uighur Cultural Centre in Tashkent in early June 1996, where several issues regarding Uighur history, culture and their presence in Uzbekistan were discussed. An excellent discussion of the nineteenth-century history of the Uighurs, their culture, immigration and emigration of the Semirechi (modern Kazakstan) Uighurs in the late nineteenth century is in M. N. Kabirov, *Pereselenie Iliiskikh Uigur v Semirechie, (Migration of the Ili Uighurs to Central Asia)* (Alma-Ata: A.N. Kazakhskoi SSR, Izd., 1951).

48 See Hambly, op. cit., pp. 294–313, and Allen S. Whiting and General Sheng Shih-ts'ai, *Sinkiang: Pawn or Pivot?* (USA: Michigan State University Press, 1958), pp. 3–19.

49 A good discussion of inter-ethnic marriages in Uzbekistan during the Soviet period is in Ronald Wixman, 'Ethnic Attitudes and Relations in Modern Uzbek Cities' in Fierman, op. cit., pp. 159–83.

50 See for further discussion, Akiner, op. cit., p. 17.

3

The Transition to Democracy in Uzbekistan

The year of 1991 will, in time, be remembered as the year that the totalitarian empire in the Soviet Union collapsed. More than ten independent sovereign states were established in its wake. Most, however, share the same problems, determined by the pre-Soviet historical development of these countries as well as seventy years encased within the totalitarian Union. They now face similar problems: the transition from a command economy to a market economy with market relations; the formation of a truly democratic society; the construction of civil society; the institutional consolidation of democracy through the creation of a functioning, competent parliament, a multi-party system and free elections.

The history of the twentieth century, particularly towards its close, suggests that the best conditions for the development of civilization are democracy, recognition of all human beings, and recognition of the individual. This rejects the view that individuals are simply a means of progress rather than the beneficiaries of progress. Individual freedom, is the basis on which modern society stands. In order to consolidate this freedom people created democratic institutions as the foundation of the whole political system. The ideas of modern democracy emerged, were implemented and flourished after acceptance of the classical form in western Europe over the last three hundred years. The forms of democratic systems that developed in the course of the development of European civilization have yet to prove their universality and effectiveness: can they be applied to countries that do not belong to the cultural tradition of western Europe? The experience of building democracy in various countries shows that while in theory there are universal democratic values that are applicable everywhere, in practice, a ready-made Western model of democracy has not produced the concepts of equality and freedom in the post-Soviet states to the extent that the theory claims.

The intention of this chapter is to study the political system and the institutions of democracy in Uzbekistan, examining how they have been shaped by historical and cultural factors. In this respect special attention will be given to the basic features of the newly established democratic institutions in Uzbekistan: a) the presidency; b) the new parliament as the basis of the 're-formation' of the political system; c) the multi-party system and political parties; and d) the restructuring of the local government system.

The problem is complicated and requires careful analysis. Among the important issues are the demolition of the old political system, the rejection of the former ideology, the establishment of new relations in the economic, political and spiritual spheres of society, and the formation of a new political system. The present period is witnessing the establishment of democracy and democratic institutions in Uzbekistan. Understanding these processes is the primary task of this book, but the matter is complex.

First of all, there is disagreement among political scientists as to how the problem should be understood. The USSR had no political scientists; political science, insofar as it existed at all, was subsumed under sociology, which in turn was narrowly Marxist–Leninist. Historically these problems in Soviet sociology were understood within the confines of the Marxist–Leninist principles with their classical approach to almost all social phenomena. The belief about a special Soviet democracy as the highest form of democratic development standing much higher than 'Western bourgeois democracy', the unwillingness to see general aspects of humankind in understanding democracy, rejecting the right of existence of the Western liberal democracy, and ignorance of its achievements led Soviet sociology into a *cul-de-sac*. Its comprehension and explanation of democracy and democratic values were out of tune with reality. Therefore, the primary task of Uzbekistan's modern political science is to study and understand the problems of democratic development. It needs new approaches that will shift Uzbekistan away from Marxist dogmas and provide its political system with a sound structure.

Analysing the post-totalitarian development of former USSR countries, we can see, taking into account all the differences and particular features of the transition to democracy, that in almost all the countries there are two basic trends, two approaches to the transition to a market economy and a free democratic society. The first is a rapid, revolutionary transition from the old totalitarian system to a democratic society and from a planned command economy to a market economy. This belief in the possibility of a fast transition from one system to another is based on the idea that there are general, universal methods for regulating society which are applicable and effective in any system, regardless of particular features of historical development and national psychology. One has only to put into operation the elements of a market economy and there will be a market, so the market economy will begin to function. One has only to put into operation democratic institutions, then start the democratic procedures and you can get a democratic society. However, such a view ignores the different experiences, consciousness and views of those living in democratic and totalitarian systems. This gap cannot be overcome with a simple leap, and such an attempt may be suicidal for a society.

The ideas of a strong state and belief in government as the core of social life and autocracy were fundamentally important in the social consciousness of most, if not all republics in the former USSR. The idea of democracy in a modern form in the pre-Soviet societies was rarely developed and cultivated. More than seventy years of Soviet totalitarianism thwarted the development of democracy in the lifestyle and consciousness of the whole society. Today Uzbek politicians need pragmatic and sober approaches to reform of the political system taking into consideration all these historical realities. In this respect I would like to examine the second conception of the transition to democracy and a market economy, that chosen by Uzbekistan. The fundamental aspects of the Uzbek model are: a) sober and realistic consideration of Uzbekistan's current economic and social situation; b) consideration of particular features of historical development, distinctive features of national psychology, mentality and society's traditions while building a democratic society; c) rejection of revolutionary leaps and acceleration of reforms, and instead, a step by step evolutionary approach to reforms; d) retention of civil, and international agreements, and social and economic stability in society as a basic condition for the successful implementation of reforms; e) the principle that the economic and political reforms are being implemented not for their own sake, but for the people and their well-being, and to nurture democracy; f) development of long-lasting and carefully thought out programmes of reformation. Positive results might be expected from a reformation model in which the principal priority is not the pace of reforms, but a long-lasting, strategic purposefulness in encouraging democratic development.

The political, economic and cultural distinctiveness of Uzbekistan's historical development

The first task is to consider the historical conditions and particular features that determined the social development of Uzbek society from the time the first states were formed on the territory of present-day Uzbekistan. Only a comprehension of the economic, political and cultural background and history can enable us to understand the development of democracy in Uzbekistan and determine the primary parameters of the newly emerging socio-political system. This approach helps us to understand how historically developed conditions and forms of farming activities, economic relations, forms of government systems, types of political powers, and their reflection in social psychology influenced the forms of state system and methods of democracy in contemporary Uzbekistan. The examination of the history of Uzbekistan poses a significant problem for researchers: why did democracy not have a chance to form in Uzbekistan? Why did monarchical despotic regimes remain as the basic political entity? One can answer these questions by looking at the forms of economic activities that existed in Uzbekistan.

Beginning from ancient times the basic economy – not only of Uzbekistan, but also of other states of the East and eastern societies – was water-farming. Due to natural geographical conditions (aridity), productive farming in Uzbekistan was possible only on the basis of the artificial irrigation of land. But artificial irrigation, by virtue of its complexity and labour intensity, was impossible without a joint labour force made up of large numbers of people. Therefore, as the basic farming unit was in the rural community, the government united the peasants in a large labour force used to construct artifical irrigation systems. Creation of the water supply system was possible only through this joint effort by peasants under the direction of the government, and in part this determined the special role of government in the societies. The government played the role of chief irrigator and organized irrigational water works. Another distinct feature that determined the nature of Uzbek society's historical development was that the land and water were the property of the government, which under monarchical rule meant they were the property of state rulers. Only the rulers owned the land and water. Only the rulers had the right to sell it, give it away, or rent it out. In this case, rural communities would step forward as collective renters of land and they were obliged to pay taxes and keep the irrigation network in order.

A third distinctive feature is that there was no right of private land ownership, or for people to manage their own land. An obstacle in the way of the establishment of private ownership institutions was the fact that there was no legal basis for individual protection and ownership under despotic monarchical government. No system flourished that would enshrine the political and economic independence of individuals from government. That is why the cities, after becoming the centres of development of trade, craft and economy between the tenth and fifteenth centuries, could not become political bases from which to oppose feudal despots. Nor could they become power cores which would protect the interests of people if these conflicted with those of the government or monarchy. Typical features of communal collective lifestyle also resulted in the impossibility of individual farming activities outside the framework of the community. The collective and constant burden of despotic governments, and the lack of legal protection for individuals, denied the conditions needed for the development of free ownership and politically and economically independent individuals. In other words, there were no citizens in society. This explains why collective norms were dominant in the social consciousness and the authority of community was prevalent. Individuals remained within the framework of their communal or collective origin. The hold of collective norms over the mentality of people is demonstrated by the fact that even in the cities, where collective lifestyle was not determined by economic necessity as in the villages, *mahallas* (neighbourhoods) were formed and continue to exist as city communities today. *Mahallas* exist as a territorial unification of people within the framework of which many social problems, in relation to people or the state, are solved collectively. Gradually, the *mahalla* transformed into an institution of self-governance of citizens, becoming one of the most significant regulators of people's lives at the local level. The *mahalla* had a double function: on one hand it was an important tool for implementing state policy, regulation, and controlling the masses' frame of mind; on the other the *mahalla* community was an intermediate link between the government and individuals, and functioned as a restraining factor.

All of the above-mentioned historical factors should be taken into consideration when examining the policies of contemporary Uzbekistan. It is possible to understand particular features of Uzbekistan's post-totalitarian development if one takes into account these particular factors.

They give us a chance to move away from existing subjective and simplistic approaches to, and evaluations of, democratic development processes emerging in Uzbekistan. This gives us a chance to understand the problems of democracy in Uzbekistan and evaluate our arguments about how a democratic government can be formed in a country that has no democratic heritage. The simple existence of democratic organs and institutions does not necessarily amount to democracy, particularly if there is no social base for democracy; that is, no sanctity of the individual and private property relations. It is true that democracy does not by itself generate private ownership but the latter nevertheless provides a base for it. The power of the government over an individual's rights, and approbation of the government – be it despotic, communist totalitarian or nationalistic – above the law are obstacles to democracy in Uzbekistan.

Basic conditions of the Uzbek model of reform
The experience of the USSR shows that a country based on state control of all areas of social life, be they ideological, economic or political, and the disregard of national differences, could not provide the basis for individual freedom and social development. Instead it created economic, political and spiritual crises, which took hold in the mid-1980s. Attempts by Communist Party leaders to overcome these crises by partial liberalization and reformation of the system – *perestroika* (reconstruction) – simply speeded up the demise of the command administrative system of management and of the monopoly of the Communist Party of the Soviet Union. In its place, new powers emerged in the various republics. In Uzbekistan, the goal of the new authority was not to find ways of redesigning the old system within the framework of the USSR, but to demolish this system. It would be replaced by a new system based on a free market economy, where individualism could flourish. *Perestroika* led to the removal of restraints on the development of national consciousness among the peoples of the USSR. This awakening of national consciousness spawned the creation of national freedom movements in the republics of the old Soviet Union. Such feelings had been suppressed in the Soviet era as the Party tried to foster 'Soviet consciousness'. By the end of the 1980s, disparate movements arose, motivated by various ideological inspirations but with the common goal of destroying the

status quo, and providing in its place human rights and freedoms, democracy and a law-based state. National freedom movements or national fronts, which were launched in almost every republic of the USSR as the system teetered on the brink of collapse, came forward with slogans of democratization, freedom and sovereignty. But in Uzbekistan, this surge did not reach the same level of intensity as it did in Lithuania, Latvia, Estonia, Azerbaijan and Georgia.

By 1991, new movements emerged in Uzbekistan which, despite ideological differences, were united in their pursuit of a common goal: self-determination and the destruction of the status quo. These powers had various objectives. Firstly, government leaders no longer wanted the imposed judgements of Moscow, and sought to share power and influence with the Centre. These attitudes became especially intense in the start of the 1990s when political nomenclatural leaders of the USSR failed to react adequately to radical changes in the political life of the Union. The Centre was weakened and, deprived of support from the masses, was unable to stop a radical decentralization of power and the disintegration of the republics. The political elite of Uzbekistan took advantage of this favourable situation. Secondly, democratic movements in Uzbekistan also moved in this direction but with different long-term goals. They presented themselves as a democratic intelligentsia adopting the slogans of protection and retention of the native cultural landmarks which were under threat of oblivion, and urged the liquidation of single-party rule and the hegemony of communist ideology. They demanded democracy and the formation of a law-based state, but they were not powerful enough. These spontaneous national movements organized themselves and formed a movement in May 1989 called '*Birlik*' ('Unity').

Before the collapse of the USSR in 1991, the leaders of Uzbekistan presented a plan for keeping the structure of the Soviet Union, but claiming wider rights for the republics within it. They advocated reforming the old political and economic systems and an eventual transition to a market economy. The Republic of Uzbekistan was one of the first republics to establish the institution of presidency when, in the spring of 1990, the Supreme Council Parliament of Uzbekistan chose Islom Karimov, the First Secretary of the Communist Party, as President of the republic. A declaration of sovereignty by the republic was adopted. The gradual transformation of the Soviet Union into a new state, spurning centralized government in favour of a union of sovereign states, was interrupted in August 1991 after a *putsch* by hard-line communists who sought to overturn *perestroika*. This destroyed attempts to reform the Union, leading instead to the collapse of the USSR. The Republic of Uzbekistan acquired its independence and started to build a new country. The primary goals of this new republic were proclaimed as: the establishment of a democratic law-based country; a law-based society; the formation of a socially oriented market economy; the provision of citizens' rights and freedoms, and a commitment to a multi-party system. But the fulfilment of this task was complicated by various factors: (1) Uzbek society is a traditional society in many respects, which has strong collectivist and ancestral traditions. (2) There were no traditions of democracy, parliamentarism or multi-party competition before or during the Soviet era. (3) The basis of private ownership that existed in Uzbek society before the revolution of 1917 was destroyed during the years of Communist rule. (4) Traditions of authoritarianism and ideas of strong government, combined with a dependency culture among the majority of the population manifested in a belief that the government should provide most of the needs of society. (5) Government ownership and the planned distributive systems were dominant in the economy. (6) Uzbekistan had a one-sided economy and was used to providing only raw materials for the other republics of the former Union. (7) Uzbekistan was one of the poorest republics and had a low-level per capita income. (8) Uzbekistan is located in a global economic crisis zone and suffered from the Aral Sea environmental catastrophe.

The unfavourable economic situation demanded: (a) evolutionary, gradual reform of the political and economic system; (b) retaining the leading role of the government as the principal initiator of reforms; (c) consideration of the historical values and traditions of Uzbek society; (d) the development of a long lasting, well thought out, strategic reform programme. These became the primary indicators of the 'Uzbek model' of reform.[1]

A parliamentary election in December 1994, which became the first ever 'democratic' election in the history of Uzbekistan on a 'multi-party' basis, was a significant event and certainly a step forward in the sphere of political reform. The parliament, as a realm for independent activity is, however, yet to be recognized. The event which led to this election was, most certainly, the decision of the old parliament to adopt a new constitution for the republic.

Constitution

In most societies, the constitution is the basic legal document that determines the relationship between the people and the state, the form of the government, and the conditions under which to adapt or suspend the basic rights and freedoms. After acquiring its independence, the main aim of legislative activity in Uzbekistan was the acceptance of a new constitution.[2] The constitution itself contains several democratic principles and it is more democratic than the constitutions of some of the so-called democratic states. It remains, however, only a document at the present time (most presidential decrees become law). The electoral system in Uzbekistan is based on proportional representation. The old constitution, adopted in 1978, enshrined the Communist Party as the leading and directive power in society. It consolidated the priority of the state's nationwide ownership as the basis of the economy. After independence, these ideas were fetters on socio-political and economic transformation. On 8 December 1992, the Supreme Council of Uzbekistan adopted a new constitution. The authorities claimed that it had been adopted after a nationwide discussion that established the basic principles of the social system, and that it consolidated the basic freedoms, rights and duties of citizens. An examination of the major newspapers published in Uzbekistan shows that there were virtually no dissenting voices over any of the constitution. This demonstrates that none of the opposing views were given expression in the mass media before the referendum.

The new constitution of 1992 defines Uzbekistan as a sovereign, democratic, secular and presidential republic. All citizens of the Republic of Uzbekistan, regardless of their ethnic origin, constitute the people of Uzbekistan. The constitution declares the people to be the only source of the government, and the state shall express the will of the people and serve their interests. Public life is to develop on the basis of the diversity of political institutions, ideologies and opinions. State bodies and officials shall be accountable to society and the people. Priorities of personal, economic, political and social freedoms and rights of citizens are clearly stated in the constitution. It also devotes itself to participation by the citizen in the political process and is committed to a principle of individualism that is unusual in Central Asia. The Uzbek media itself frequently characterizes democracy in the republic as being based on principles common to all humankind, according to which the ultimate value is the human being – his or her life, freedom, honour and dignity.

The course of development on the domestic policy scene is, however, going in the opposite direction. Political pluralism is associated with destabilization, 'street democracy' or anarchy, and the opposition is oppressed under the guise of 'maintaining stability' in a region threatened by instability.

The system of state authority in the Republic of Uzbekistan is based on the principle of the division of powers between the legislative, executive and judicial authorities. The legislative authority belongs to the parliament (*Oliy Majlis*), the executive authority belongs to the president and the Cabinet of Ministers, and the judicial authority belongs to the courts, led by the Supreme Court. The constitution also determines the territorial administrative system of the republic. According to the constitution, the Republic of Uzbekistan consists of regions, districts, cities, towns, *kishlaks* and *auls* (villages) and the autonomous Republic of Karakalpakistan. It also states that the sovereign Republic of Karakalpakistan is part of the Republic of Uzbekistan and its sovereignty is protected by the Republic of Uzbekistan. The Republic of Karakalpakistan is to have its own constitution, which must be in accordance with the constitution of Uzbekistan. The laws of the Republic of Uzbekistan are binding in the territory of Karakalpakistan. Any alteration of the boundaries of Karakalpakistan must be sanctioned by the *Oliy Majlis* of Uzbekistan, but this may not be done without the consent of Karakalpakistan.

The constitution determines and consolidates the fundamentally new system of state body authorities in regions, districts and cities where *hokims* are the leaders of both local representative bodies and executive authorities. They carry out their tasks on the basis of one factor – that they are not elected but are appointed (or dismissed) by the president. Thus a strong executive authority has been formed and led by the president. The political elite of Uzbekistan claims that the constitution of 1992 is the work of a profound study of the experience of constitutional and democratic processes in countries with developed democracy, but at the same time a reflection of specific Uzbek conditions and traditions.

Taking into consideration all the advantages of the new constitution, especially in comparison to the old one, we should remember that it determines only the general principles of the social system. A constitution, even the most democratic one, cannot provide democracy, freedom and a law-based society solely by itself. It serves only as a compass that points out the goals of social development. But it remains as a document if there is no political or economic freedom for citizens. If the conditions for implementing these freedoms are absent and if the legal and political culture is not sufficiently developed, then the constitution is simply a part of the process of democratic development, even if it is a very significant part. One should neither denigrate nor exaggerate its role. Social development itself will determine only the course of democratic development, and the constitution is just a reference point on this way.

The Presidency of the Republic
The post of President of Uzbekistan was established in March 1990, during the opening session of the first popularly elected parliament in the history of Uzbekistan. According to the constitution the president of the republic is head of state and executive authority, central figure and central unit of the political system. It is impossible to understand the functioning mechanisms of political authority in the republic without comprehension of his role and place in the state authority system. President Karimov has managed to concentrate political decision-making in his own hands while neutralizing potential opponents. Presidential decrees carry the force of law and over 90 per cent of the legislature is composed of members of Karimov's former party, the People's Democratic Party (PDP). At present the only credible threat to Karimov's control over his country's affairs are the economic woes that Uzbekistan, like all the former Soviet republics, is experiencing and possibly his rather authoritarian rule radicalizing the outlawed oppositions further.

Islom Abdughanievich Karimov was born on 30 January 1938 in Samarkand. His father was an office worker. After finishing school he entered the Central Asian Politechnical Institute and graduated as a mechanical engineer. Later he attended the Tashkent Institute of National Economy where he received a doctorate in economics. He is also an Honorary Doctor of a number of foreign universities. Islom Karimov's working career started at the Tashkent Farm Machinery Plant where he worked as an assistant and a technical foreman. A considerable part of his life is linked with the Tashkent Aircraft-Making Plant – a major manufacturer of cargo planes in the former USSR, where Karimov worked as an engineer and leading design engineer. From 1966 on, Karimov worked as a civil servant, initially at the State Planning

Committee of Uzbekistan where he progressed all the way from leading specialist of a department to the first Vice-Chairman of the State Planning Committee (*Gosplan*). In 1983 he was appointed Uzbek Minister of Finance and in 1986 he became the Vice-Chairman of the Council of Ministers – Deputy Head of Government, and simultaneously Chairman of the State Planning Committee. In June 1989 Karimov actually headed the republic after being elected First Secretary of the Uzbekistan Communist Party Central Committee. With the implosion of the USSR, the Uzbek Communist Party transmuted into the People's Democratic Party in November 1991 with an almost new ideology and policy. Karimov was Chairman of the People's Democratic Party until 15 June 1996 when he resigned from it to indicate that he is an independent president of his country.

On 24 March 1990 Karimov was elected president of the republic at the session of the Supreme Council of the Uzbek SSR. On 29 December 1991, he was again elected president of the country with 86 per cent of the vote in the first nationwide presidential election. The president of the republic is elected by direct suffrage for a term of five years, but at its first session in February 1995 the new parliament unanimously voted to hold a nationwide referendum to approve an extension of the President's term of office. On 26 March 1995, 99.6 per cent of the eligible electorate voted to extend Karimov's term in office from 1997 to the year 2000, and as expected, Islom Karimov was re-elected in a presidential election on 9 January 2000 with almost 92 per cent of the vote.

Karimov was nominated by the newly created political party of *Fidokorlar Milliy Demokratik Partiyasi* (Self-Sacrificers' National Democratic Party). The Organization for Security and Cooperation in Europe (OSCE) refused to send observers to monitor the election stating that there was 'no genuine choice' for voters. The government also made little effort to present the polls as being fair. The sole candidate allowed to oppose Karimov was the candidate and First Secretary of the Uzbekistan People's Democratic Party, Abdulhafiz Jalalov. Jalalov himself was a loyal party man, first to the Communist Party and then to its successor, the Uzbekistan *Xalq Demokratik Partiyasi* (the People's Democratic Party). Abdulhafiz Jalalov took only 4 per cent of the vote, and then admitted that he himself had actually voted for President Karimov.

The president appoints and dismisses the prime minister, his deputy prime ministers and other members of administration, the procurator general and his deputies. He is the Chairman of the Cabinet of Ministers and the Supreme Commander-in-Chief. The president appoints diplomats, represents the country and conducts negotiations with the heads of foreign countries, proclaims a state of war, and, if necessary, a state of emergency to restore order in the interests of people's security. He has the right to dissolve the *Oliy Majlis*. He forms the national security and state control services. He presents to the *Oliy Majlis* his nominees for the posts of chairman and members of the Constitutional Court, the Supreme Court and the Higher Economic Court, together with the Chairman of the Board of the Central Bank, and he also appoints and dismisses judges of regional, district and city courts. He appoints and dismisses regional *hokims*. He suspends and repeals any acts passed by the bodies of state administration as well as *hokims*. The constitution thus consolidates the presidential system of the republic, where the president is provided with a strong power. The image of the president is more significant and weighty than the image of parliament and local government institutions in Uzbekistan.

It is generally accepted that a strong presidential authority is required during the time of transition from the old communist system to a democratic system. It is not simple to overcome and fill the tremendous gap that exists in Uzbek society between these two incompatible systems. Democracy in Uzbekistan requires some time to transform and adjust the old establishments so that they are ready to accept new relations, norms and institutions. Quick and unplanned political moves towards a liberal democracy, which is an alien phenomena to a society that has never had a democratic history, might lead to accumulation of social tension. Rejection of the old values and ideologies which have been immutable for generations, could have led to considerable popular opposition. The low level of political culture and the inability of the majority of the people with diverse interests to solve these conflicts via democratic procedures, could have led to the rise of political extremism. In this situation the strong executive authority headed by President Islom Karimov played a very significant role in preventing a social explosion and total anarchy during the first years of independence.

Today, however, we tend to believe that in Uzbekistan the two political issues – a strong executive authority and authoritarian rule

– are inter-related. Favouring a concentration of power in a leader, or in an elite not constitutionally accountable to the people, is one thing, and acting according to the right granted by the people in a democratic manner is another. The question is: where and in what direction is this authority evolving – democracy or dictatorship? It is an open question. Even taking into consideration the reality that social and political consciousness in general is not authoritarian, there is a tendency towards dictatorship. To prevent this, the country needs steady but open implementation of economic reforms; privatization, the creation of conditions for economically strong and independent citizens; the promotion of genuine democratic values; the implementation of ideas of freedom and a law-based state; and the realization of national cultures. Mirroring the dominant role of the government in the history of Uzbekistan, the post-independence government, headed by President Islom Karimov, became the obvious candidate as chief reformer. The example of Uzbekistan, however, illustrates a paradoxical role for the government in the democratization of the society. On one hand it has to introduce democratic values and democratic institutions in the country; on the other, it aims to neutralize, if not eliminate, potential opponents and tends to label those who disagree publicly with government policies as subversive or rebels. It is in this context that democracy in Uzbekistan is poised to develop in the future. Nonetheless, President Karimov appears to be the man who can introduce democratic values in Uzbekistan, though he is limited by the bureaucratic structures formed in the communist era which may not be adapted to the new conditions. He is possibly compelled to overcome the powerful resistance of the bureaucracy. In 1992 a Presidential Council was created and, at present, this Council forms the core of the political leadership and is effectively the 'government' in Uzbekistan.

The Parliament – *Oliy Majlis*
The highest state representative body is the *Oliy Majlis* (the Supreme Assembly) which exercises legislative power. It consists of 250 deputies elected by territorial constituencies for a term of five years. The *Oliy Majlis* is a unicameral parliament. The exclusive powers of the *Oliy Majlis* include: the adoption and amendment of the constitution; approval of the budget of the republic submitted by the Cabinet of Ministers; the

setting of taxes; the adoption of laws; determination of the guidelines of home and foreign policies; determination of the structure and powers of the legislative, executive and judicial branches of the republic of Uzbekistan; election of the Constitutional Court, the Supreme Court and the Higher Arbitration Court of the republic; ratification of the decrees of the President of the republic of Uzbekistan on the appointment and removal of the Prime Minister and the members of the Cabinet of Ministers. Yet, although it has such wide-ranging authority, the *Oliy Majlis* does not at present enjoy the same status in the political system as parliaments in other developed democratic countries. Again, this can be explained mainly by the fact that there are no traditions of parliamentary activity in Uzbekistan.

The entire history of Uzbekistan is largely an uninterrupted chain of absolute monarchies, be it a strong, centralized despot or an economically and politically weak set of feudal territories or monarchies. The power of the monarch was sacred. He could divide power among feudal tribe leaders and their groups and clergy. There has never been an institution through which people choose their own representatives and express their interests, thereby (at least partially) limiting the monarch's absolute power. The system of 'democratic' Soviets that existed in the former USSR only discredited the idea of democracy. Thus, after independence, Uzbekistan had to deal with the problem of establishing a democratic society, and forming a new, competent parliament, without any experience of parliamentarism. The present poor condition of the parliamentary system in the republic is in part the result of past historical development.

The history of developed democratic countries demonstrates the long way the ideas of democracy and the parliamentary system have proceeded until gaining their present form. To develop democracy and a parliamentary system, officials in Uzbekistan first studied and borrowed from their own limited experience, though the first steps in acquiring parliamentary experience have not been completely successful. The transition to parliamentarism in the newly independent states, particularly Russia, has not been easy, as political actors seek to determine the relationship between the various branches of government. The complex process of institution-building has only just started in Uzbekistan. It may be unwise to demand effective and more powerful acts immediately from the newly emerging democratic institutions. If Uzbekistan really is willing to become a respectable member of the international community, sincere steps are required towards democratic reforms. Undoubtedly a strong parliament is one of the cornerstones of democracy, but how much power can be given to a young institution with no experience of democracy is an open question.

Since independence, the composition of a new type of parliamentary system in Uzbekistan has passed through two phases. The first phase was the activity of the Supreme Council of the Republic of Uzbekistan which was elected in December 1989. The majority of deputies in this parliament were elected without any opposition and almost all of them were on the lists of the Communist Party. In spite of this, the Supreme Council adopted the state's 'sovereignty' in 1990 and 'state's independence' in 1991. The deputies played an active part in working out the first constitution of independent Uzbekistan in 1992.[3] The activity of the Supreme Council contributed to the formation of new structures of state authority and institutions. They adopted laws in the sphere of economic reform which generated and regulated the process of an economy based on free market relations. In spite of all this the parliament could not become a strong and independent force in society because the executive authority headed by the president played a very significant role in implementation of reforms. The role of the parliament was restricted to a legislative body providing reform policies with minimum participation in political life and being a symbol of stability and accord in society. Excessive political activity by the parliament at this stage could have led to a power struggle between the executive and the legislature, and could have become a destabilizing factor leading to the Russian scenario of 3 October 1993, when President Yeltsin ordered tanks to fire at the parliament building in Moscow.

The second phase of restructuring the parliamentary system in Uzbekistan consisted of the elections to the new parliament. The parliamentary elections were held on 25 December 1994 with two further rounds of voting on 8 and 22 January 1995. The new 250-member parliament, the *Oliy Majlis*, was elected.[4] These elections proceeded according to the new law adopted on the 'elections to *Oliy Majlis*'. At the last session of the Uzbek Supreme Soviet, a law was passed to hold elections on an 'Uzbek way of multi-party' system. 634 candidates were registered for the 250 vacant seats, including 243 candidates from the People's Democratic Party of Uzbekistan, 141 candidates from the *Vatan Taraqiyoti* (Homeland Progress) Party and 250 candidates from local authority bodies. As a result the following factions were organized in the parliament: 69 of the deputies belong to the PDPU, 14 of the deputies belong to the FPP and 47 of the deputies were drafted to provide the *Adolat* (Justice) Social Democratic Party which was created in February 1995. The rest of the deputies, although remaining as representatives of the local authorities and *hokims*, have close ties with the PDPU. In theory the PDPU had only sixty registered members elected to the parliament, with the remaining nine not being members of the PDPU. But the party had recommended them to their constituents and the vast majority of the MPs selected by the local authorities also have close ties with this party. The ethnic composition of the Uzbek Parliament was as follows: out of the 250 members of the parliament 215 were Uzbeks, 5 Tajiks, 5 Kazaks, 5 Karakalpaks, 9 Russians, 3 Ukrainians, 1 Kyrgyz, 1 Turkmen, 1 Tatar, 1 Armenian, 1 Ossetin, 1 Iranian, 1 Korean and 1 Gagauz.

Elections to the *Oliy Majlis* in December 1994 and the establishment of the new parliament were clearly significant events for the republic. Even if it did not entail competitive multi-partyism, it was nevertheless a step forward on the road to democracy in Uzbekistan. The new parliament works in sessions. Deputies are called several times during a year to work in sessions. Each session lasts several days during which time the deputies examine the amendments put to the parliament, and work out solutions. Their task is also to ratify the decrees of the president, approve the budget and determine the taxes. In reality, the deputies simply approve what has been offered. In the parliament, however, some fifty deputies work on committees on a permanent basis. Most of the deputies also work on state authority bodies. The chairman and speaker of the *Oliy Majlis,* Erkin Khalilov and his vice chairmen were elected as also were the personnel and chairmen of 14 permanent parliamentary committees. In May 1995 the parliament adopted the new Cabinet of Ministers presented by the president. The judges of the Constitutional, Supreme and Higher Arbitration Courts have taken oaths and were confirmed.

The third phase of restructuring the parliamentary system in Uzbekistan consisted of a parliamentary election held on 5 December 1999, with a second round of voting on 19 December. The election for the unicameral 250-seat *Oliy Majlis* in December 1999 differed little from the previous elections. The only difference was that this time two more parties took part in the elections, increasing the number of contesting parties to five. All the political parties which had received permission to contest the 1999 parliamentary elections supported the president, and a number of nominally independent candidates had been carefully checked by provincial governors. No genuine opposition candidates were able to gain registration as candidates to stand for the elections. The first round of the election, on 5 December, filled 184 seats with a 93 per cent turnout. The second round, on 19 December, produced an 87 per cent turnout and filled the remaining seats. 1,240 candidates were registered for the 250 vacant seats, including 247 candidates from People's Democratic Party of Uzbekistan; 133 candidates from Homeland Progress (*Vatan Taraqiyoti*) Party; 222 candidates from *Fidokorlar* (Self-Sacrificers') National Democratic Party; 156 candidates from *Adolat*; 113 candidates from National Revival (*Milli Tiklanish*) Party; 238 candidates from local authority bodies and 131 independent candidates. In order to win in the first round, a candidate needed to secure 50 per cent of the vote in a constituency. If a candidate failed to secure the majority of votes and was not running unopposed, then the two candidates with the highest number of votes went through to a run-off. From the first round of the parliamentary election 98 seats went to the independent candidates, 32 were won by the PDPU, *Fidokorlar* came third with 19, *Adolat* and *Vatan Taraqiyoti* secured 9, and *Milli Tiklanish* took just 6. A further 11 seats went to other independent candidates but in 66 constituencies voting went to the second round. The results from the second round were 12 seats won by independent candidates; 16 to the PDPU; 15 to *Fidokorlar*; 2 to *Adolat*; 11 went to *Vatan Taraqiyoti*; 12 were won by independent candidates nominated by local governments, and 6 seats went to other independent candidates. As a result of the two rounds of voting in Uzbekistan, the following factions were organized in the parliament: 48 of the deputies belong to the PDPU, 34 of the deputies belong to *Fidokorlar*, 20 of the deputies belong to *Vatan Taraqiyoti*, 11 of the deputies belong to *Adolat*, 10 of the deputies belong to *Milli Tiklanish*, 110 of the deputies were elected by the local governments and a further 17 of the deputies are independents. The electoral system provides universal suffrage at the age of 18, while 25 is the required age to be elected as a member of the parliament. MPs can be elected only twice in their lives. The electorate in December 1999 consisted of over twelve million people and each constituency needed 40,000 voters to elect an MP.

Analysing the results of the elections to the *Oliy Majlis* and the results of the parliament's activity in the last phase of restructuring the new parliament, it is evident that the *Oliy Majlis* has not yet reached the stage where it can function freely as one of the highest state authorities. The parliament is still not in a position to compete for influence with the president and the presidential authority. One of the determining factors of the parliament's malaise is the low level of political culture among the population and the backwardness of democratic consciousness. The parliament, like the other institutions of democracy, is currently in no position to become an independent force in the political system. There is no doubt that the restructuring of the parliamentary system has suggested the makings of a political system based on the people's will, but fulfilling its duty to the people is complicated by its being held accountable to those few directly involved in decision-making processes. The lack of a political and legal culture among the majority of the population also largely determined the selection of the members of parliament. On the one hand, the fact that a large number of deputies in the parliament are representatives of local authorities is a positive move. On the other hand, it replicates the previous relationship between voters and deputies, when citizens tried to elect their representatives in local government simply to satisfy their emerging local needs. The only difference is that the previous MPs and institutions supported the obsolete communist ideology. The parliament was a totalitarian body, which was basically directed towards the fulfilment of punitive functions prepared by a few specialists, for example lawyers in the sphere of constitutional legislation, public and private law. Today, there is the presence of businessmen, more specialists among the deputies of the *Oliy Majlis*, and more activity with at least the will to get involved in public life. The key question is whether it is possible to have a parliament with strong powers and at the same time a strong executive body. A weak legislative authority deprived of influence in society fetters social development, and a strong but weakly controlled executive authority is a threat to society. It is therefore important to establish legislative consolidation of distinct systems of interaction between the legislature and the executive authority. The role of the parliament and its influence on the course of social development is of utmost importance for the maintenance of political and social stability.

Functions and features of local authority bodies in Uzbekistan

After independence in 1991, Uzbekistan had to face the problem of establishing a new system of state authority bodies and a way for them to participate and function within the new political environment. Two goals had to be achieved. First, in place of the old Soviet totalitarian state machinery, there had to be a new system of state authority which would be legitimate, democratic and favour the market economy. Second, during the transition period it demanded increasingly the power of the executive-managing authority, and concentrating basic powers in executive bodies, both at the Centre and at regional local levels. The term of office of the Soviet People's Deputies (the regional parliaments) and their leaders (*hokims*) would be five years.

According to the law on the 'state authority bodies' adopted on 2 September 1993, the Soviet People's Deputies are the representatives of state authority in regions, districts and towns. The *hokim* of regions, districts and towns are the highest officials of the state's local authorities and they simultaneously serve as heads of representatives and executive authorities in their respective territories. The *hokim* of the regions and the city of Tashkent are accountable to the President of the Republic of Uzbekistan and to appropriate Soviet People's Deputies. The *hokim* of districts and towns are accountable to regional *hokims* and to appropriate Soviet People's deputies. The *hokims* of regions and the city of Tashkent are appointed and dismissed by the president while the *hokims* of districts, cities and towns are appointed and dismissed by the *hokim* of the appropriate region.

The *hokims* of city districts are appointed and dismissed by the *hokim* of the appropriate city while the *hokims* of towns subordinate to district centres are appointed and dismissed by the *hokim* of the district. The *hokims* of regions, districts, cities and towns exercise their powers in accordance with the principle of one-person management and bear personal responsibility for the decisions and the work of the bodies they lead. The *hokim* makes decisions within his/her vested powers and they are binding on all enterprises, institutions, organizations, associations, officials, and citizens in the relevant territory. In the small settlements, *kishlaks* and *auls* (villages) and in the residential neighbourhoods (*mahallas*) of cities and towns, the residents of the particular *mahallas* decide all local matters at general meetings. These local self-governing bodies elect their chairmen (*aksakal*) and the members of his chamber for a term of two-and-a-half years. The *aksakals* are usually responsible to city districts' *hokims* or *hokims* of towns. The *aksakal's* role as headman in the *mahalla* is important as he becomes a government employee.[5]

The sudden collapse of the USSR and the formation of a new sovereign state precipitated a reduction in the number of executive disciplines at all levels of the government, and led to an increase in lawlessness in the whole society and in state authority bodies in particular. There was a need to establish an institution of *hokims* appointed, but not elected, by higher bodies to which lower bodies are subordinate. This offered a chance to concentrate the efforts of different bodies in one direction, and to discourage rivalry between the different branches of authority bodies. It gave the chance to implement reforms more decisively at the local level, to carry out structural reconstructions, and to provide social guarantees to the most vulnerable members of the communities. The powers of the Soviet People's Deputies and *hokims* are distinguished by the constitution and particular laws. The Soviet People's Deputies' main duties in the regions, districts and towns are to ensure the observance of laws, maintain law and order and ensure the security of citizens. These include: directing economic, social and cultural development within their territories; proposing and implementing the local budget; determining local taxes; and proposing non-budget funds. They also direct the municipal economy; protect the environment; ensure the registration of civil status acts and pass normative acts; ratify the local budget presented by the *hokims* and report on its implementation; and ratify the development programmes of territories. They also approve the *hokims* and deputy *hokims*, and can remove them, as well as hear their activity reports. Finally, they can cancel laws and the decisions of *hokims* and lower Soviets if they violate the legislation of the Republic of Uzbekistan.

The *hokims* organize the enforcement of laws and acts of the *Oliy Majlis*, the decrees of the president and decisions of the higher bodies of the state authority and the appropriate Soviet People's Deputies. They also take measures regarding the observance of social order and the fight against crime; provide the safety of citizens; protect the rights and health of the people in the particular region; ensure the provision of infrastructural and training requirements of economic and social development in the districts, regions and towns; they prepare the regional, district and town's budgets for approval by Soviet People's Deputies and report on its implementation. The *hokims* present decisions on the appointment and removal of deputy *hokims* and heads of structural subdivisions of the executive authority for ratification by the Soviet People's Deputies. They also appoint and remove heads of subdivisions of the *hokimiat's* machinery. They are the representatives of the regions, districts and towns of the republic.

In theory, power is divided between the regional assemblies and the regional governors, enhancing the prospects for democratic reforms in different parts of the country. In practice, however, things are rather different. In the local assemblies, power usually rests in local governors' hands, and this is usually a *hokim* who is not elected by the people but appointed by the president of the country. The establishment of this kind of system of state authority at the regional level, with the concentration of representative and executive authority with *hokims*, may have been acceptable during the first stage of reforms when the retention of independence, implementation of economic reforms and maintenance of stability in society were the main priorities for the regime. This of course does not mean that the first stage of the reforms was a total success. There have certainly been wrongdoings and misuse of power all over the country, but nonetheless, the political elite did manage to hold Uzbekistan together during the difficult period of transition to a market economy and a democratic civil society. The reason why President Karimov wants to appoint regional governors, rather than allow their election by the people of the regions concerned, is probably guided by the fear that during the implementation of the progressive economic reforms there would be pressure for economic independence in different regions. If they achieved this, decision-makers would concentrate on their own regions and ignore the wider picture of the country. The government considered this a dangerous move which might have led to the rise of separatist or segregationist tendencies in particular regions. At the present stage, where the government is trying to implement the second and third stages of the reforms, serious alterations to the system of regional assemblies became necessary. As instruments for the realization of the reforms, they may be effective during one stage but ineffective and even harmful under other conditions if one does not take measures to improve the structure and mechanisms of state authority. This analysis of the local authorities has shown that the problem of a weak legislative authority in Uzbekistan exists, not only at the level of local representative state authority bodies, but also at the highest legislative level, the parliament of the republic. The parliament is as weak before the president as the local assemblies are before the *hokims*. All these signs of obvious weaknesses of the legislative authority and the underdeveloped mechanisms of interaction between the executive and legislative bodies may well be a result of the absence of reliable and effective mechanisms and the absence of any control on the activity of executive authorities by the legislature or a representative authority.

Party system and political parties in Uzbekistan
In the countries where regimes are based on the principles of democracy, it is difficult to imagine conducting politics without parties. There are various ways of defining 'party' and a simple definition can neither solve the problem nor satisfactorily capture the distinction between parties and other institutions. Nevertheless the definition of 'party' proposed by Alan Ware has some value. He defines the political party as an institution that (a) seeks influence in a state, often by attempting to occupy positions in government, and (b) usually consists of more than a single interest in the society and so to some degree attempts to 'aggregate interests'.[6] As far as the structure of political parties is concerned, Maurice Duverger separates two aspects of party structures, the organization and membership. With respect to organization, he distinguishes four kinds of what he terms 'basic elements'. The first two consists of the cell, found in conventional communist parties, and the militia, found in fascist parties. The other two are the caucus and the branch. As there are no fascist parties in Uzbekistan the militia cell is unimportant for the purpose of this study. Although the old Communist Party of Uzbekistan has renamed itself as the People's Democratic Party of Uzbekistan we need to look at the conventional Communist Party's cell to see if this party has really changed. The caucus and the branch are of great interest as new parties have been formed and the old Communist Party has transmuted. Duverger defines the caucus as a closed group consisting of a small number of members who do not try to increase their numbers, while the branch 'is extensive . . . tries to enrol members, to multiply their number, and to increase its total strength'.[7] With respect to membership, Duverger makes a further distinction between cadre and mass parties, this distinction being in regard to their structures. Cadre parties are

groupings of 'notabilities for the preparation of elections, conducting campaigns and maintaining contact with the candidates'.[8] Mass parties actively seek dues – paying members so that they can spread the cost of election campaigning more widely. Duverger then argues that the 'distinction between cadre parties and mass parties coincides with differences arising out of the various kinds of party organization. Cadre parties correspond to the caucus parties, decentralized and weakly knit; mass parties to parties based on branches, more centralized and more firmly knit'.[9]

The parties' activities, however, are largely allowed to function within the limits of the type of party system. Sartori has put forward two criteria for a party to be counted as part of the party system. According to Sartori, if a party meets neither of these it should not be counted as part of the party system. The two criteria are coalition potential and blackmail potential. In the first case, the party must be needed, on at least some occasions, for a feasible coalition that can control government; and in the second case, the party's existence affects the tactics of those parties that do have coalition potential.[10] The first condition may be applicable to those systems in which governments are usually formed on a coalitional basis. In this case the 'coalition potential' criterion is required to separate the small parties that are never needed to join a coalition government from those that are. In the absence of the second criterion there would be a number of countries where some parties could never secure anything like enough votes to form a government, yet there would be no doubt that, despite their lack of coalition potential, the small parties could exert a major influence on the competitive and cooperative strategies of the other parties. As party systems involve both competition and cooperation between the different parties in that system, naturally party systems vary. Alan Ware has stated that there are four main ways in which party systems differ from one another. They are: (a) the extent to which parties penetrate society; (b) the ideologies of the parties; (c) the stance of the parties towards the legitimacy of the regime; and (d) the number of parties in the system.[11] In this light, an attempt will be made to provide an analysis of the political parties and party system of the Republic of Uzbekistan. As a contemporary state, Uzbekistan asserts that it has committed itself to universal democratic principles and a multi-party political system. Thus, the government of Uzbekistan introduced a new law on political parties, which came into force on 26 December 1996.

Uzbekistan has published its draft law on political parties for public discussion in the main newspapers.[12] The law on political parties came into force on 26 December 1996 when it was passed by parliament, and the text of the law 'on political parties' was published on 7 and 9 January 1997 in Uzbekistan's major daily newspapers. I have translated this law into English from the Uzbek text published in *Ozbekiston Ovozi*. The law differs from the draft law in only a few aspects. The signatures of 5,000 members are now required to apply for registration; the bill suggested 3,000. Under the law, party funds must not be used for purposes other than those specified in the party statutes, whereas the draft law had said parties could use their funds for charitable ends even if these were not mentioned in their statutes. Finally, the final version of the law omitted a paragraph which the draft law added under the final article, 17, stipulating that representatives of the Justice Ministry had the right to attend party events and examine their records. The new Uzbek political party system provides for multi-partyism, but at the same time it holds the prospective parties in check.

According to the law, political parties in Uzbekistan operate according to the constitution, the law on political parties, and any other laws adopted by the parliament or presidential decrees. Parties based on ethnic or religious lines, and parties advocating war or the subversion of the constitutional order, are prohibited. Citizens can become members of only one party at a time and parties must not discriminate either against or in favour of their members. The promotion of party members should be based only on their abilities, qualifications and qualities. The president, as the representative of the citizens, reserves the right to suspend or revoke anyone's membership of a political party. Military and law-enforcement personnel, members of the judiciary, foreigners and stateless persons are debarred from party membership. Prospective parties with a list of a committee of fifty people who will be responsible for the establishment of the political party, must submit full details of the party and of 5,000 members spread over eight of Uzbekistan's 14 regional-level administrative territories, along with constituent documents and registration fee, to the Justice Ministry which will decide whether to register them or not. The application must be made within seven days of the formation of the party. The Justice Ministry will reject the application of any party if the documents contradict the constitution or legislation, or if a previous party or a social or political movement was registered with an analogous name, though the party can appeal within one month. In this case the party has to resubmit its application according to changes required by the Justice Ministry who must complete the registration procedures within two months. The Supreme Court has the right to suspend registered parties for up to six months and eventually ban them if they persist in violating legislation.

Parties can take part in elections, publish their own newspapers, form parliamentary and local assembly groups and have the right to parliamentary interpolation. Party funding must be transparent, and parties are banned from using foreign bank accounts and accepting donations from state, foreign, religious or anonymous sources. The state may subsidize parties taking part in elections. Under the law, party funds must not be used for purposes other than those specified in the party statutes. The Justice Ministry reserves the right to monitor political parties to see whether they are acting constitutionally and within the remit of existing legislation.

The history of attempts to form a multi-party system in Uzbekistan goes back to the pre-revolution era and during the period from 1917–24. The Russian Tsar Nikolay signed a document on 17 October 1905 which liberalized the polity, creating a parliament – the Duma – and permitting the formation of political parties. Then several parties of a liberal-democratic leaning were formed in Russia, such as the 'Octoberians',[13] the Party of Constitutional Democracy, the Russian Social-Democratic Workers' Party, the Party of Socialists-Revolutionists, and several other smaller parties. These parties also became active in the territory of Turkestan, the general-gubernatorial administrative region of present-day Central Asia, that was then under Russian rule. They participated in the elections of the first State Duma, but, after the latter's dispersal by the Tsar in 1906 when he introduced harsh new regulations on participation in elections, the people of Turkestan general-gubernatorial region were stripped of the right to participate in the elections. Ostensibly the reason was that the people had a low level of political culture and so were not ready for elections. As a result, the activity of Russian parties in Turkestan was virtually stopped, and until the revolution in 1917 they did not influence Turkestan society much, local movements taking over instead. The organizations and movements created by the local Turkestan intelligentsia, the *Jadids* who were the representatives of Turkestan's educated strata and the Turkestan bourgeoisie, had more influence on the indigenous population and played a significant role in social life. They did not form their own political party but they became active in developing education among the local population based on European experience and formed new-method schools for the local population. They also attempted to publish national newspapers and magazines, and created conditions under which the young generation was able to receive a university education in the countries of western Europe, particularly in Germany. They expressed a loyal attitude towards the Russian Tsar's authority but at the same time managed to establish a basis for the rise of national awakening which later became a national freedom movement after the revolution of 1917. In the territory of Bukhara Emirate and Khiva Khanate, which were vassals of the Russian Empire, the pre-revolutionary feudal-despotic regimes were still dominant and free political activity was limited.

After the revolution of February 1917, which resulted in the overthrow of the monarchy and established a 'democratic republic' in Russia, various political parties and movements began active operations in Turkestan. The parties *'Shuroi Islamia'* (Islamic Council) and *'Shuroi Ulammo'* (Council of Intelligentsia/learned people) were formed in this period. These two parties were allies on many issues and expressed the interests of the national bourgeoisie, the clergy and the intelligentsia. Their basic demand was the granting of autonomy to Turkestan within the framework of Russia and these parties were at the head of national freedom movements in Turkestan. After the October revolution of 1917, when the Bolsheviks came to power, the Turkestan land was proclaimed as the Turkestan Autonomous Soviet Socialistic Republic. Analysis of the activity of this Autonomous Turkestan Republic headed by Bolsheviks shows that it was fully military-politically and economically dependent on Russia and implemented decisions dictated by Moscow. In other words, the autonomy and sovereignty of Turkestan was largely mythical. In February 1918 the representatives of *'Shuroi Islamia'* and *'Shuroi Ulammo'* and other national movements meeting in the Khokand region proclaimed the establishment of a Turkestan Autonomous Republic with its centre in Khokand city. However, by the spring of 1918, the Turkestan autonomous region had been liquidated by armed Communists. Armed national freedom struggles soon spread across the whole territory of Turkestan and the rallying slogan of this movement became a 'struggle against Communism and a demand for independence'. This movement was finally defeated in the mid-1920s by the joint efforts of Turkestan and Russian Communists. During the course of this struggle Communist authority liquidated all the national political parties and movements in the region. Most of the organizers of these movements were killed, some of them were exiled and others were compelled to cooperate with the Communists. Almost all of the movements were eliminated in the course of Stalin's repression in 1930s. So, by the mid-1920s, Communist hegemony had been established.

The role of the Communist Party was seen as helping to bring about the demise of the capitalist state. Communism was distinguished from other ideologies primarily by its claim to be an objective and scientific ideology and moral system, rather than merely the preferred ideology of particular leaders. Communist theoreticians maintained that Marxism–Leninism was all powerful because it was correct, and since only Marxist–Leninists were 'armed with the truth', only they had a legitimate claim to power in the world. History was 'on their side', and they maintained that all other doctrines and economic systems were retrograde. Good people were those who swam with the current of history, building communism and fighting imperialism and fascism, whereas bad people (or states) were those who resisted history by clinging to doomed economic systems and their colonies. Capitalism was immoral according to the evaluative criteria of Marxist doctrines, as it was a barrier to human progress. Any technique used to fight capitalism or imperialism was *ipso facto* moral and justified because it was in accord with the laws of historical development. Messages and cues from the external environment were given meaning, or interpreted, within the categories, predictions and definitions provided by doctrines comprising the ideology. Soviet policy makers interpreted a foreign civil war as a manifestation of the class struggle; they saw conflicts among 'capitalist' states as a fight between their ruling classes over markets and they regarded any recession in a free market economy as evidence of Marx's predictions regarding the laws of economic development. Foreign policy actions were justified as being consistent with the general values inherent in communist ideology. Membership of the Communist Party in Uzbekistan was restricted to those who had close connection with Communist Party officials and to those who were keen to preserve and spread the communist ideology. There was a Communist Party Academy in Tashkent and almost all of the party officials who were to be appointed to the government's key departments were trained there. In Uzbekistan, people who failed to greet one another in a Communist way were expelled from the Party organs. The monopoly of the Communist Party in power continued until the mid-1980s and the beginning of *perestroika,* after which the party's power began to disintegrate.

As a result of *perestroika* in the late-1980s, the government in Uzbekistan had to face a variety of political challengers and opposition parties. The two most publicized opposition groups were the umbrella movement *Birlik* (Unity) and the party *Erk* (Freedom).[14] At the peak of its influence in 1989, *Birlik* was the strongest independent political movement in not only Uzbekistan, but also Central Asia generally. The opposition parties in Uzbekistan began their activities from the end of 1988, somewhat later than in the Baltic Republics or Russia. The national movement *Birlik* was the first opposition organization in Uzbekistan. The founders of *Birlik* were Uzbek writers and scientists who demanded that the Uzbek language be accorded the status of state language; the solving of ecological problems; liquidation of cotton monoculture in agriculture; and the pursuit of an agenda of further democratization of Communist-dominated politics. *Birlik* from the very beginning of its activity strived to build a modern and democratic state. Its demands were of nationalist origin and gradually the organization became a *de facto* national movement with the idea of a national reawakening of Uzbeks. An initiative group established itself as a strong movement on 11 November 1988, comprising, among others, Abdurakhim and Abdumannop Pulatov, the academician Bekh Toshmukhamedov and the writer Usman Azim. The founding conference of the *Birlik* movement was held on 28 May 1989. During this period the movement turned into a powerful social force consisting of tens of thousands of people. The Uzbek language was proclaimed as a state language after several meetings of the movement. *Birlik* also demanded the suspension of service in the Soviet Army outside of Uzbekistan by Uzbek youth. The growing influence of the movement in society, and its attempts to gain political power, prompted active opposition from the Uzbek authorities. The increasing confrontation between the leaders of the movement and the leaders of the republic precipitated the departure of many loyal members of the movement, headed by Muhammad Solih. This move was mainly triggered by personal clashes and differences over how to continue their resistance against the Karimov government. They formed the *Erk* Democratic Party, the first general congress of which was held on 27 April 1990. On 5 September 1991, the party was registered and this gave it a chance to participate in the first presidential elections. Its chairman, Muhammad Solih, became the opposition candidate to Islom Karimov in the first alternative, presidential elections in Central Asia where he received 12.4 per cent of the vote. *Birlik,* meanwhile, was gradually transformed from an amorphous political unit into a political party. The party was formally announced at a conference held on 17 June 1990 and was named the Democratic Party of Uzbekistan. On 27 October 1991 a second meeting saw it renamed as the *Birlik* Party. After Uzbekistan's declaration of independence in 1991 the hostility between the leaders of the republic and the opposition leaders began to escalate. The leaders of the opposition accused President Islom Karimov of authoritarianism. The *Erk* Party supported the idea of granting private ownership of land, and the implementation of a fast liberalization of the economy based on the Polish model. But the leaders of Uzbekistan developed and implemented a different course of reforms, the basis of which was gradual, evolutionary reform of the economy, and the rejection of any speedy liberalization of prices or private land ownership. They argued that private land ownership could lead to a lack of irrigation lands, the dissatisfaction of peasants and eventually a social explosion in the rural areas. Though the leaders of both the republic and the opposition wanted to build a democratic, modern, law-based state with a commitment to form a market economy, they differed over tactics, leading to a conflict that reached its climax at the start of 1993. Some of the leaders of the opposition were forced to abandon their activities and leave the country for choosing a non-parliamentary struggle for power. In March 1993 the Cabinet of Ministers passed decisions according to which all the political movements had to re-register at the Ministry of Justice. *Birlik* and *Erk* were denied re-registration and had to stop their activity in Uzbekistan. The newspaper of the *Erk* party was also proscribed. The government also undercut *Birlik's* and *Erk's* attractiveness by manipulating the groups' platforms and exploiting statements by the opposition to fan fear of ethnic violence among Uzbekistan's population, at a time when tension was high in the country and the two groups were using nationalistic slogans.

Some other minor political groups also existed in Uzbekistan. Many of these small parties were formed by disaffected members of the major groups, especially of *Birlik*. The two other strong parties were

Adolat (Justice) and the Islamic Renaissance Party (IRP), both religious-based groups. But these two were never allowed to operate freely and were banned as soon as they appeared around 1992. In contemporary Uzbekistan, thus, the first stage of attempts to establish a multi-party system was over.

Essentially, the secular opposition could not develop a constructive and realistic programme of reforms based on a consideration of those particular features and conditions that characterized economic, political and social traditions and the mentality of Uzbek society. They were poorly organized, did not have a clear agenda for the future of the republic and were possibly rather naive. The actions and slogans of most of these groups, especially their premature demands for the priority of the rights of Uzbek people, and their proclamation of ideas of national rebirth, alienated non-Uzbek ethnic groups in Uzbekistan. They posed a threat to already damaged inter-ethnic relations. Nonetheless, they were the first political opponents to emerge after 74 years of totalitarian rule, during which time the Communist Party oppressed anyone disagreeing publicly with its own policies and ideology. Moreover, they operated in a society without a political history of free democratic opposition. On the other hand, the state authorities did not have experience of engaging in civilized dialogue with opponents, but instead had traditionally relied on smashing them. In the end, the state authority headed by the leaders of the republic turned out to be more dynamic and more flexible in the process of implementing the reforms. It was able to seize the oppositions' slogans and their agenda regarding sovereignty, independence, democratization and national renaissance. Most importantly, it could execute them more successfully. The opposition could not adjust to these new conditions, and so was wiped out.

The year 1995 marked a new stage of multi-partyism in Uzbekistan. The previous stage, commencing from 1991, was characterized by the existence of three parties and one political movement until 1993. They were the People's Democratic Party of Uzbekistan, *Vatan Taraqiyoti* (Homeland Progress), *Erk* Democratic Party and the *Birlik* movement. After the *Erk* Democratic Party and the *Birlik* movement had been completely banned by late-1993, only two parties were left to function in the country. One was the old Communist Party, which had changed its name to the People's Democratic Party of Uzbekistan, and the other was the *Vatan Taraqiyoti* Party. The People's Democratic Party of Uzbekistan, which can be characterized as the ruling party, was headed by President Karimov until June 1996. *Vatan Taraqiyoti* announced itself as a party of 'constructive opposition'. Hence a two-party political system emerged. In the first half of 1995, however, two new parties and a political movement were created. The two parties were *Adolat* (Justice) Social Democratic Party (not to be confused with the banned Islamic movement *Adolat*), and *Milli Tiklanish* (The National Rebirth) Democratic Party. The political group was the *Xalq Birligi* (People's Unity) Movement. In December 1998 *Fidokorlar Milliy Demokratik Partiyasi* (Self-Sacrificers' National Democratic Party) was set up as a new party. Currently, the largest, strongest and best-organized party in Uzbekistan is the *Uzbekiston Xalq Demokratik Partiyasi* (the People's Democratic Party of Uzbekistan, the PDPU).

Uzbekiston Xalq Demokratik Partiyasi

The old Communist Party of Uzbekistan held its 22nd congress in 1990 and there the delegates accepted a slightly different charter for the party which stressed the value of sovereignty for Uzbekistan.[15] After the failed August military coup in Moscow and the unresolved negotiations over the new Union with Gorbachev, which finally ended with the dissolution of the Soviet Union, the party held its 23rd general congress on 1 November 1991. There it adopted a rather different charter, departing from the old Communist values and opting for independence for the republic. One party official claimed that, during the 22nd congress:

> we came to the conclusion that there was a need to be closer to the people, to understand their feelings, thoughts, customs, religions and traditions and that all these should have been protected. The old Communist Party was above the people and did not even attempt to take any of these into account. There was the communist ideology and everybody had to obey it whether they liked it or not. Any ideology staying far away from its people is bound to fail – the collapse of the Soviet Union proved this. So with the 22nd congress a new ideology was adopted which brought us close to our people, and with the 23rd congress taking all of this into account, we adopted policies based on the universal values of human rights, the market economy and 'Oriental Democracy'.

The PDPU may not be a completely different political party from the former Communist Party, either in its membership or in its administrative infrastructure, but it has shown signs of change. It has jettisoned the old Communist ideology. It has played an important role in the transfer of power from the Party to the state. It also contributed to the introduction of the principles of a market economy and privatization, recognizes the rights of minorities living in Uzbekistan and advocates a state based on the principles of law. The PDPU has a general congress which meets every five years, shortly before general elections, a central Party Council of 150 people and an Executive Committee made up of twelve. President Islom Karimov was the chairman of the party until 15 June 1996. After his resignation from the party the chairmanship was abolished. The Secretary of the Central Council of PDPU is a doctor of philosophical sciences, Professor Abdulkhafis Jalolov. On 1 November 1991 the party had about 351,000 members of whom 80,000 were not members of the Communist Party. By the end of 1998 membership had reached 500,000. In theory, anyone who has reached the age of eighteen can become a member of the party, though, in practice, the party executive council determines the membership. Members have to pay one per cent of their salaries every month. Members who have financial and health problems are temporarily exempted and the wealthy members are encouraged to contribute more. 81 per cent of its members are Uzbeks, the remainder being Tajiks (4 per cent), Kazaks (4.5 per cent), Russians (3 per cent), Karakalpaks (3 per cent), Tatars (1.3 per cent) Kyrgyz (0.8 per cent), Ukrainians (0.3 per cent) and others (1 per cent). Just over 25 per cent of the total membership is female. The party has its central office in Tashkent and 13,365 offices all over Uzbekistan. The PDPU took over all the properties of the old Communist Party of Uzbekistan and oversees its press network. The official party organ is *Ozbekiston Ovozi (Voice of Uzbekistan)*, an Uzbek newspaper which is published three times a week. A Russian version of *Voice of Uzbekistan* is published once a week and a journal, *Mulakat*, is published in Uzbek once a month. It focuses on social, political and economic issues. The new party programme and the charter have been renewed and published in 1995. The party was able to retain the Communist Party's full arsenal of management skills, intellectual potential, and the middle and high echelon party members. Moreover, in spite of some of its members leaving the party during 1991–2, it was later able to attract large numbers of business people, and a considerable number of active, sincere youths who are now the core of the party.

Imposing firm discipline and enjoying a strong material and informational base, the party far-sightedly emphasized the activity of local structures, especially *mahallas*. Involvement in the everyday concerns of citizens provided the legitimacy for the PDPU's existence. The party has a strong influence on society as a result of Islom Karimov's leadership, which encouraged the leaders of the PDPU to identify their programme and documents, with the strategy and tactical tasks of the president. The party supports the formation of a social market economy, the formation of a legal, democratic country, and evolutionary methods of reformation. It also supports equal rights for the different nationalities in Uzbekistan, in order to maintain national accord in society. This has given it support not only from Uzbeks, but also from other ethnic groups, especially Russians. In this connection the programme of the party contains a proposition about the national revival of Uzbekistan which undoubtedly attracts the support of Uzbek people. Thus, the PDPU strives to become a nationwide party which expresses the interests of the whole society. The party was an elite-based cadre party until June 1996 since almost all the policies were shaped by President Islom Karimov. After his resignation from the party, power has been transferred to the Executive Committee. The party is now a hybrid of an elite and a membership party, though the activists have little direct influence over party policy. The control over the nomination of MPs is vested both in local constituencies, in which members vote, and the party Central Executive Committee. Party policy is made by party elites. The party is also an example of a party with a mass base, but power does not reside even formally with that base. The party neither relies on membership fees to fund party activities, nor does it recognize that party members have certain rights to influence at least some party affairs. It is more like a social democratic conservative party which has nationalist aspirations but at the same time tries to present itself as a bulwark for inter-ethnic harmony in the republic. The most serious defect of this party is that it seems to speak only to itself. It shows no desire to engage with other parties and movements which have similar programmes and aims, but rather treats them and their leaders as opponents, for example the *Vatan Taraqiyoti*.

Vatan Taraqiyoti Partiyasi
The *Vatan Taraqiyoti* Party[16] (The Homeland Progress Party) held its

first general congress in May 1992, and on 10 July of the same year it officially registered as an 'opposition' political party. The first chairman of the party, Anvar Yuldashev, was one of the founders of the *Birlik* movement. Since 1998 its chairman has been Ahtam Tursunov. The party has a central advisory council of 37 people and four party secretaries. Its organizational structure consists of a central council, regional and district committees, and political clubs. On 4 July 1996 it set up a business club to attract more businessmen and women. The new programme and charter of the party was adopted during the meeting of the second general congress on 9 September 1993, and by August 1996 it had about 35,000 members. The party committee tends to choose its members from among business people, students, tradesmen and women and intellectuals. The minimum age for membership is nineteen and almost 95 per cent of the members are said to be Uzbeks, though there seem to be members from other ethnic groups, e.g. Russians, Kazaks, Tajiks, Turkmen and Jews. Just 8 per cent of the members are women. Prospective members have to apply in writing. Members are required to pay one per cent of their monthly salaries to the party. It claims to be the party of business people. The party also has an MP in the president's council. It has a weekly newspaper which is published in Uzbek and about 10,000 issues of which are published and sold every week. At the time of its formation, the party proclaimed itself a party of the intelligentsia, entrepreneurs and youth, but since then it has failed to express or realize the interests of these groups. In the party newspaper *Vatan* there are almost no articles about the problems, lives of or any events relating to these groups of people. There is no analysis of changes in society, almost no articles about the political reform process or problems facing political parties, and there is hardly any analysis of the course of the economic reforms. The economic publications are mainly about the activities of this or that enterprise without revealing the problems facing the development of entrepreneurship. This newspaper is devoted mainly to questions of culture, art, history, speeches of the president and official documents. According to its programme, the party, like the PDPU, advocates liberal democracy, rights and freedoms of the citizens, and the gradual development of a liberal market economy. It is, however, poorly organized, weak, unable to deal with social issues, and fails to cooperate with other parties and movements. The absence of a strong leader hinders its ability to compete with the PDPU. It also finds it difficult to consolidate and widen its influence in society, or strengthen itself financially.

Adolat Sosial Demokratik Partiyasi

The *Adolat Sosial Demokratik* Party (ASDP) was formed on 8 February 1995.[17] The party leader is a well-known journalist, Anvar Djurabaev, and the chairman of the party is Turghunpulat Obidobic Daminov. The party consists of a council of 49 people, an executive body of eleven people and six secretaries. It has established a central office in Tashkent, one in Karakalpakistan and in addition to these there are 12 main regional offices and 147 district-based offices. All over the country there are 1,021 offices in total. It has just over 30,000 members and the vast majority are said to be teachers and lecturers. Those who agree with the party ideology and the programme can become members. The minimum age for membership is nineteen and members must pay at least one per cent of their monthly salaries towards their membership. The poor and pensioners are not required to pay a membership fee. It has almost 30 per cent female members. It has a newspaper, *Adolat*, which is in Uzbek; 10,000 issues are published and sold weekly. According to the programme the ASDP advocates a political system based on universal social democratic principles; a care for the poor and people with low income and a state based on the principles of law are essential. It rejects communist ideology, but has an interest in international socialism. It aims to help the government of Uzbekistan to strengthen its sovereignty and independence. It supports an economic policy based on a gradual transition to a socially oriented market economy where the government should have more say and supports the implementation of a strong social policy and retention of the state's position in the economy with equality of different forms of ownership. It strives to become a champion of social democratic ideas in society, but as most of these ideas are implemented by the People's Democratic Party of Uzbekistan, the party is not yet ready to compete with the PDPU, nor indeed with any others. It is poorly organized, weak, and unable to deal with social issues. In particular, the absence of a strong leader hinders its ability to compete with the PDPU. It also finds it difficult, like *Vatan Taraqiyoti* and the *Milli Tiklanish Democratik Partiyasi*, to consolidate and widen its influence in the society, or strengthen itself financially.

Milli Tiklanish Demokratik Partiyasi

The *Milli Tiklanish Demokratik* party was created in April 1995 and held its first general congress on 3 June. Its founder is a scientist, Aziz Kayumov.[18] It has a central executive body of over fifty people and one central office in Tashkent, with 14 regional offices. It has about 74 offices all over Uzbekistan, and 10,000 members, most of whom are scientists and artists. The leader of the party is Ibrahim Gofurov. The membership requirement age is over eighteen and prospective members have to apply in writing. It has about 15 per cent female members. According to the programme and charter of the party, its main aims are to work for national progress, to strengthen and maintain the country's independence, and to assist the president in every way to implement social, economic, and political reforms, step by step without any rush, throughout the transition period. It also advocates a democratic law-based state founded on the principles of the market economy, and the revival of the spiritual and cultural traditions of the Uzbek people. The party has a weekly newspaper, *Milli Tiklanish*, 6,000 issues of which are published in Uzbek. It has a faction in the parliament consisting of ten MPs. Despite being dominated by scientists and artists, the party potentially represents the views of many more Uzbeks with regard to national reawakening. However, it has not yet been able to tap into this well of potential support.

Xalq Birligi Xarakoti (People's Unity Movement)

The *Xalq Birligi Xarakoti*[19] was created on 27 May 1995. The initiators of the movement were a group of public figures who were the representatives of various ethnic groups and who were the official leaders of these groups' cultural centres in the country. This movement was planned to be a public movement supporting the introduction of the economic reform policies of President Karimov and helping in their implementation by holding in check ethnic tensions. It is a united body of different nationalities who advocate national accord and the equal development of all people in Uzbekistan. Turabek Dalimov was elected as chairman of its central council in 1995. The programme and charter of the movement was approved and it has a weekly newspaper, *Xalq Birligi*. The leader of the movement is now Rasulov Karim Rasulovich. The movement does not have a permanent official membership, though collective membership is allowed and this makes it difficult to determine its size. The movement represents the 23 officially created cultural centres of the ethnic minorities. The main aim of the movement is to help to preserve social stability while assisting ethnic minorities, especially those who want to live according to their culture and traditions and to have those traditions preserved within Uzbek society.

Fidokorlar Milliy Democratik Partiyasi

The *Fidokorlar Milliy* Democratic Party (FMDP) was formed on 28 December 1998 in Tashkent. The party leader is Erkin Norbutaev. The party, at the time of its creation, consisted of a council of 37 people, an executive body of 12 people and four party secretaries. It has established a central office in Tashkent, one in Karakalpakistan and, in addition to these, there are 12 main regional offices and 202 district-based offices. Across the country there are 2,000 offices in total. It has just over 14,000 members and the vast majority are said to be young people. It has 30 per cent female members. The party has a newspaper, *Fidokor*, which is in Uzbek and is published three times a week; 60,000 issues are published weekly. According to the programme, the FMDP advocates a political system based on the principals of liberal democracy and supports an economic policy based on open and free market principles. Although this party is still too young to compete with the PDPU, it seems to be in a better state than the *Vatan Taraqiyoti*, the *Adolat* and the *Milli Tiklanish*. The party managed to send 34 deputies to the *Oliy Majlis* after the December elections of 1999. It also nominated Karimov for presidential elections. One party official informed the author in early April 2000 that President Karimov was very much interested in the party's charter and programme which is why he wanted to be nominated by the FMDP. The FMDP, however, on 14 April 2000 held a joint general congress with the *Vatan Taraqiyoti* in Tashkent and the delegates adopted a resolution to merge the two parties. The new united party adopted the name *Fidokorlar*, and now has an estimated 60,000 combined members and a total of 54 deputies in the parliament, making it the second largest parliamentary faction. Its leader remains Erkin Norbutaev and a working group was set up to draft the party's new programme and statutes.

Conclusion

The analysis of the party system in Uzbekistan has shown that at the present stage there is only one political party that can still influence social life and the reformation process. The PDPU enjoys its dominant role as successor to the old Communist Party and, given that it was the only party in the country for the last 74 years, the PDPU enjoys clear advantages over other political parties. The main weakness of the PDPU is that it strives to become a nationwide party, expressing the interests of all existing and emerging strata and groups in society without acknowledging the conflicting views and interests of these groups. The party structures have also been bypassed by the president and its power has shifted to the government agencies headed by his personal allies and staff. Thus, the dominant role of the government at all levels of the country's transformation has obviated the role of other parties as a channel of information between the citizens and the state. The president conveys his messages to the public directly rather than through parties. It is, therefore, important to note that at the present stage the remaining political parties have not shown themselves, in terms of programme, ideology or leadership, as opposition parties in the real sense. Most analysts believe that they hardly differ from one another and are 'government-friendly' parties which have been created on the president's initiative for two main reasons. First, to assist the government throughout the transition period to implement the economic reforms at home, and second, to respond to critics who accused the president of not allowing opposition parties be formed. The parties do not have any appropriate party ideology in terms of a unified system of views on the political, economic and spiritual development of society and they hardly have any distinctive organizational structures. All the parties except the PDPU have failed to gain support in the rural areas; indeed, many rural people are not even aware of their existence. They are parties basically of the metropolitan and provincial intelligentsia. They are mainly parties organized by groups of people holding similar views. The nature of the formation of the party system in Uzbekistan is based on the fact that parties are formed from above while the normal process of formation of parties is via initiatives from below. Therefore possibly all the defects of the present party activity is the result of this artificial 'growth' of parties. The present-day party system in Uzbekistan can be characterized only as a system with one dominant party, the PDPU, and a host of others imitating the main party. The process of forming new parties is certainly not over; new parties may emerge as a result of splits that already exist within all the parties or as a result of more parties being formed from above. Only the course of events will show how viable they are and what place they will take in the spectrum of political parties in contemporary Uzbekistan. The course of further reforms and the resultant changes in society will undoubtedly have a decisive influence on the development of the multi-party system. It is also important to note that the multi-party system exists as an institution of democracy like all other institutions established or reformed in the republic, and only the process of democratic reforms will fill it with a content that will complete the organization and structure. The course of reforms, democratic transformation and changes in the economy will lead to the emergence of new interest and power groups. Each will strive to increase its role in society and this may well form the basis for the emergence and existence of new opposition forces with the priorities of national ideas, national accord and regional stability.

NOTES

1 Islom Karimov, *Uzbekistan: Along the Road of Deepening Economic Reform* (Tashkent: Uzbekiston, 1995). See also Karimov, *Our Road – The Road to Independent State and Progress* (Tashkent, 1994); Karimov, *Uzbekistan: The Road of Independence and Progress* (Tashkent: Uzbekiston, 1992); Karimov, *Uzbekistan: A Country with a Great Future* (Tashkent: Uzbekiston, 1992); E. Akhmedov and E. Saidaminova, *Uzbekiston Respublikasi: Kiskacha Malumotnoma* (*Uzbekiston Reference Book*) (Tashkent: Uzbekiston, 1995).
2 *Uzbekiston Respublikasining Konstitutsiyasi (Constitution of the Republic of Uzbekistan)* (Tashkent: Uzbekiston, 1992).
3 *Official Bulletin of the Supreme Council of the Republic of Uzbekistan*, 1992, nos. 1 and 6. 1993, no. 9 and 1994, no. 1. See also *Uzbekiston Respublikasining Sailov Tughrisidagi Konunlari (The Election Laws of the Republic of Uzbekistan)* (Tashkent: Uzbekiston, 1994).
4 See also K. Buronov and V. Kolyeova, *Birinci Chakirik Uzbekiston Respublikasi Oliy Majlisining Deputatlari, (The First Term Parliamentary Deputies of the Republic of Uzbekistan)* (Tashkent: Uzbekiston, 1995).
5 See also Shuhrat Jalilov, *Davlot Khokimiyati Makhalliy Organlari Islokhoti: Tajriba va Muammolar* (Tashkent: Uzbekiston, 1994); *Makhalla Yangilanish Davrida (Mahalla in the Revival Period)* (Tashkent: Mekhnat Nashriyoti, 1995); Savkat Mirolimov, *Makhalla Mekhri (The Affection of Mahalla)* (Tashkent: Navruz, 1994); Islom Karimov, *Buyuk Maksad Yolidan Ogishmailik (On the Way*

to the Great Goal) (Tashkent: Uzbekiston, 1993) and *Uzbekistoning Siyosi-Ictimayi va Iktisodiy Istikbolining Asosiy Tamoyillari (The Main Principles of Political-social and Economic Revival of Uzbekistan)* (Tashkent: Uzbekiston, 1995).

6 Alan Ware, *Political Parties and Party Systems* (Oxford: Oxford University Press, 1996), pp. 1–13, 63–212. See also Alan Ware (ed.), *Political Parties: Electoral Change and Structural Responses* (Oxford: Basil Blackwell, 1987), pp. 5–23.

7 Maurice Duverger, *Political Parties* (Cambridge: Cambridge University Press, 1954), pp. 17–35.

8 Ibid. pp. 63–6.

9 Ibid. p. 67.

10 See also Giovanni Sartori, *Parties and Party Systems* (Cambridge: Cambridge University Press, 1976), pp. 121–3; Ware, op. cit., 1996, pp. 148–9.

11 Ware, op. cit., 1996, pp. 148–9.

12 *Narodnoya Slovo,* 19 September 1996, *Xalq Sozi,* 19 September 1996 and *Ozbekiston Ovozi,* 21 September 1996.

13 The information was gained during my interviews with the political party representatives in Tashkent in the spring and summer of 1996, and after discussing the issue with various scholars and historians in the region throughout my stay in the region for over a year.

14 An interview was conducted in Tashkent on 20 September 1996 with one of the founders of *Birlik,* Abdomanov Poulatov. The issue was also discussed in detail with other party officials as well as with scholars of political science in Tashkent. See also *Programma Demokraticheskoi Partyi Erk* (Tashkent, 1991).

15 Interview with party officials at the Tashkent Central Office of the People's Democratic Party of Uzbekistan on 16 April 1996. See also *Uzbekiston Xalq Demokratik Partiyasining Dasturi* (Tashkent, 1992 and 1995). *Uzbekiston Xalq Demokratik Partiyasining Milliy Istiklal Mafkurasi* (Tashkent, 1994). See Akmal Saidov, 'Mustakilik Komusi, Tashkent, 1993', *Ozbekiston Ovozi,* 30 January 1996.

16 Interview with party officials at the Tashkent Central Office of *Vatan Taraqiyoti Party* on 4 March 1996. See also *Uzbekiston Vatan Taraqiyoti Partiyasining Nizomi va Dasturi* (Tashkent, 1994) and *Vatan,* 30 May 1996.

17 Interview with party officials at the Tashkent Central Office of *Adolat Sosial Demokratik Partiyasi,* on 11 April 1996. See also *Uzbekiston Adolat Sosial Demokratik Partiyasining Dasturi* (Tashkent, 1995) and *Adolat,* 22 February and 24 August 1995 and 2 March 1996.

18 Interview with party officials at the Tashkent journalist's compound on 1 May 1996. See also *Milli Tiklanish,* nos. 1, 10 June 1995 and 2, 4 June 1996.

19 Interview with some party officials and members, 21 June and 3 July, 27 July and 21 August 1996 in Tashkent. See also, *Uzbekiston 'Xalq Birligi' Hkarakatining Nizomi va Dasturi* (Tashkent, 1995) and Abdulhkafiz Jalolov, 'Kuch Xalq Bilan Birgalikda, (Power is being with the Public)' in *Mulokot* (Spring 1995).

4

The Economic Transformation

Uzbekistan is blessed with an abundance of natural resources. There are large reserves of petroleum, natural gas and coal, and there is considerable potential for hydroelectric power. The republic was a leading centre of the natural gas industry in the former Soviet Union with an estimated output of 41 billion cubic metres in 1990. Petroleum output stood at 2.8 million tons in the same year. Substantial deposits of gold made Uzbekistan the second largest producer of gold in the Soviet Union and the seventh largest producer in the world. There are also substantial deposits of silver, copper, lead, zinc, wolframite and tungsten. State participation in production was extensive, with about 80 per cent of the labour force employed in the public sector. The structure of production was dominated by agricultural and industrial output. The fertile Fergana Valley and the water resources of the two main rivers formed the basis of a sizeable agriculture sector. Agriculture represented over 40 per cent of net material product (NMP) and 30 per cent of employment. The country was the world's fourth largest producer of cotton. Cotton crops accounted for about 40 per cent of the gross value of agricultural production and it was grown both on collective and state farms. Almost all cultivated land was irrigated and the rapid increase in agricultural production was attained through an expansion of irrigated areas in recent decades. In the wake of the break-up of the Soviet Union, about 4.2 million hectares were irrigated from 170,000 kilometres of canals. Other important products included grain, vegetables, fruit and silk cocoons. Industrial production was based mainly on the processing of agricultural raw materials, accounting for 30 per cent of NMP and 18 per cent of employment. Local processing accounted for only 12 per cent of raw cotton output, 20 per cent of sheepskins, and 60 per cent of silk cocoons. The industrial sector included the manufacture of machinery directly or indirectly linked to agriculture, e.g. cotton harvesters and textile machinery, chemicals (mostly fertilizers) etc. It also included metallurgy and aircraft. The Chkalov aircraft factory is a huge state-owned production enterprise and the only aircraft factory in Central Asia. It was founded in Moscow in 1932 and moved to Tashkent in 1941 as part of the Soviet Union's massive industrial evacuation during the Second World War. The factory produced parts for twelve different aircraft such as the AN-8, AN-12, AN-22, AN-70, IL-14, IL-114 and other Russian cargo planes. However, production has slumped dramatically since the break-up of the Soviet Union. The management still tries to maintain broken channels with former customers and suppliers from the countries of the former Soviet Union. The factory is still capable of diverse production, but much more needs to be done to modernize the technology, which may well be beyond the republic's means.

Trade has been an important feature of the country's economy. In 1991, exports to other states of the former Soviet Union accounted for 31 per cent of gross domestic product (GDP), while exports to countries outside the territory of the old Union accounted for only 4 per cent of GDP.[1] Similarly, inter-republic imports comprised 30 per cent of GDP and foreign imports 6 per cent. Since each republic of the old Union specialized in particular outputs, there is a very high degree of interdependence and commodity concentration in trade. In the case of Uzbekistan, trade with the other former Soviet republics accounted for 84 per cent of the country's exports and imports. The major exports were cotton, agricultural produce and raw materials. The main imports were food grains, industrial inputs, chemicals and oil products.

Studies for an economic reform process in the Soviet Union did not encourage much hope of sustaining a unified economic reform package beyond mid-1990. Two events played a crucial role in the development of this process. The first was relatively open elections at the local and republican level of government, a first in the history of the Soviet Union, which were held in March 1990. A year later the Union legislature elections were held. Although Communists gained a majority of seats in many institutions, republican legislatures ended up with considerably more reformists than in the Union Supreme Soviet. The second crucial event was the growing fractures in institutional ideology which meant that officials who were more committed to reform began conceiving their policies and programmes in a republican rather than a Union context. Consequently, although the original intent of republican level legislatures was not to destroy the Union, the political structures in which they were now operating conflicted with the responsibilities of the Union government to retain its power instruments for the very purpose of undertaking reforms. Thus the emergence of dual, and thereupon multiple, 'tracks' of reform was inevitable. By September 1990, these led to the emergence of two competing programs of economic reform in the Soviet Union: the Ryzhkov Plan, named after the then Union Prime Minister, Nikolai Ryzhkov, and the Shatalin Plan, after the academician Stanislav Shatalin. In general, the Shatalin Plan was a challenge by the Russian leadership to the Union authorities' claim to be the supreme authorities on economic reform. The Ryzhkov Plan, which was formulated shortly thereafter, was the Union's response to this challenge. The Shatalin Plan called for the republics to have greater freedom in decision making and the undertaking of more radical reforms, especially privatization and price liberalization. It also sought to assign primary taxing authority to the republics and called for funding the Union budget from shares of the republics' budgets. The Ryzhkov Plan, on the other hand, advocated a slower pace of reform and did not cede significant powers to the republics.[2]

The presidential guidelines that were issued in late 1990 attempted to find a consensus between these two plans, but the consensus was limited to a few generalized goals and they failed to specify a timetable for achieving those goals. The guidelines gave the republics significant freedom to set the pace of reform and formulate fiscal policy. They did not, however, specify how or whether policy actions by the republics could be limited if such actions were to threaten the Union reform programme. At the same time, the economic situation in 1990 had been marked by strikes, inter-ethnic conflict, the collapse of the Union-wide market in the face of trade barriers created by the republics, and the collapse of the system of state orders. The role of the party *apparat* as the core mechanism of informal coordination and management in the planned economy began to weaken. All these factors disrupted the existing economic links further and thus the traditional economic structure began to fall apart. Output declined for the first time in the peace-time history of the Soviet Union. Accordingly, with the break-up of the Soviet Union, Uzbekistan inherited a completely disrupted economic and financial system. Like all the other republics of the former Soviet Union, Uzbekistan faced difficulties such as: production inefficiencies, the breakdown of inter-republican trade and the payments mechanism; highly monopolistic market structures; falling output and distorted price and incentive systems; huge budget deficits as a result of the termination of the Union's highest budgetary transfer from Moscow; and hyperinflation. Moreover, world prices for Uzbekistan's two major commodities, cotton and gold, were also falling.

Initial macroeconomic performance after the break-up of the Soviet Union

The economic sphere under the Tsarist administration had seen some industrial developments that were not very significant though there was a substantial expansion in the agricultural sector, mainly due to the introduction of higher-yielding technologies in the cultivation of cotton. In later years this enabled the republic to become a principal supplier of raw materials to the Russian textile industry. The structure of the Uzbek economy was closely integrated with the investment and production system of the Union throughout the Soviet period. Hence all production patterns were designed to meet the needs of the whole Union. As a sub-unit of the Soviet command economy, production in Uzbekistan was planned under the direction of the central authorities in Moscow. The Union-wide state-order system was used to ensure that production targets for specific goods were met, and the central planners decided the strategic productive role of the republic. This determined the evolution of the economic structure in the country, while providing the republic with a budgetary transfer from the centre. This system continued until the break-up of the Soviet Union.

After the break-up of the Union, the Uzbek economy went into recession. Central budgetary transfers equivalent to more than 19 per cent of its gross domestic product, which financed a large part of government expenditure, were lost. Prices of imported petroleum products rose, and trade and payment arrangements with other countries comprising the CIS were disrupted. GDP declined by about 15 per cent between 1990 and 1993, yet this was significantly less than the 40 per cent suffered by other former Soviet countries. A number of factors meant Uzbekistan's economic performance was relatively better than that of other countries of the former Soviet Union. Its economic activity was concentrated more in the fields of agriculture and energy. It was less reliant on the Soviet trading system and more able to sell locally produced commodities such as cotton and precious metals to countries outside the region for foreign currency. Also, the Uzbek leadership was slower than other CIS countries in liberalizing its economy and removing state orders and subsidies.

Agricultural output declined at an annual compound rate of less than one per cent while the share of total employment in agriculture increased. Inflation has been a serious problem in the republic, rising from 169 per cent in 1991 to 787 per cent in 1992 and 915 per cent in 1993. Real incomes rose by an average of 3.2 per cent in 1989 and 1990 but fell dramatically in 1992 and continued to fall in subsequent years.[3] Following this severe erosion of real wages, the government frequently adjusted the minimum wage and the wages of employees of budgetary organizations to reduce the impact of price increases. Average nominal wages rose by 957 per cent in 1992, a rise in real terms of 170 per cent. Average wage increases reached 1404 per cent in 1993, while retail prices increased by 1,312 per cent.[4] To prevent further dramatic falls in real incomes, the government maintained a strong social protection system. Domestic credit to enterprises increased enormously, interest rates remained highly negative in real terms and the budgetary deficit rose to 12.5 per cent of GDP in 1992 and about 12 per cent in 1993. The fiscal deficit was due mainly to the continuance of the government's wide-ranging budgetary transfers to both enterprises and consumers, which were generating inflationary pressures throughout the economy, as well as the fall in production. These subsidies amounted to 9 per cent of GDP, largely for bread and flour, sugar and vegetable oil. Residential gas, heating, electricity and public transportation were also heavily subsidized.

Employment is concentrated in three broad sectors: agriculture, industry and construction, and government services. In 1993, these sectors accounted for 32, 27, and 25 per cent respectively of formal employment.[5] The decline in the number of persons officially employed in Uzbekistan has been small, relative to that experienced elsewhere in the former Soviet Union. The number of people who were registered as unemployed increased from 1441 in mid-1992 to 14,400 in September 1993, while the number of those officially unemployed fell to 13,300 by the end of 1993. The actual number of unemployed, however, is probably considerably higher, partly because statistics provided by government officials did not account for hidden unemployment.[6]

The large fiscal deficits were generating excessive demand in the economy and fuelling inflation. At the same time, as Uzbekistan was part of the rouble zone, the falling value of the rouble against major currencies and inflation in Russia intensified similar pressures in the republic, where it was inhibiting its ability to combat inflation because of its lack of control over monetary policy. Another factor was the immediate effects of certain economic reform measures in Russia,[7] and within the republic, such as the partial price liberalization in 1992 and the reduction of subsidies to enterprises in late-1993. High rates of inflation also meant a steady fall in the level of real wages. The combination of these factors led to a sharp decrease in living standards, especially in the rural areas of the country.

From rouble zone to national currency
Following the break-up of the Soviet Union as a political unit, Uzbekistan has considered having its own national currency some time in the future, but the leadership preferred maintaining the policy of the common currency among the former Soviet states or between itself and Russia. The republic lacked adequate reserves in other major currencies or in gold that would be necessary to back up its national currency. All of the republic's gold had been shipped to Russia and the republic has no knowledge as to how much was actually produced. Moreover, its trade continued to be with Russia and other states of the former Union. A common currency based on the rouble made eminent sense, at least until the country could become more integrated within the global economy and could replace the existing ties with new economic and trade relations with other countries outside the CIS.

Therefore, the Central Bank of Uzbekistan sent delegates to the Central Bank of Russia (CBR) to implement monetary policy decisions. Under the arrangements, the Uzbek government prepared monthly monetary demand forecasts and submitted them to Moscow. This provided Uzbekistan with sufficient cash resources on an interest-free basis to finance the projected level of activity. Then, in July 1993, the CBR acted to divide the rouble zone and introduced a 'new rouble' for use only in Russia, while leaving the old rouble as the national currency of the other members of the rouble zone. The new rouble further aggravated payment and settlement problems within the rouble zone, which was already 'grid-locked' by the unwillingness of parties to extend credit in a rapidly depreciating currency.[8] Following this Russia proposed the creation of a new rouble zone with a stable currency, which became the 'new rouble' displaying the Russian flag and printed only in Russian. The new rouble zone proposal set very stringent conditions for accession that were beyond the capacity of Uzbekistan. New member states were required to coordinate closely their budgetary, financial, and monetary policies. The conditions also required the country to make large deposits in the CBR. Despite these difficulties, on 7 September 1993 Uzbekistan agreed to monetary union. However, because of the terms on which Russia would supply new roubles to the system, the government of Uzbekistan decided to leave the newly created rouble zone in November 1993 and introduce an interim currency.[9] The terms included harsh requirements and a short deadline (the end of 1993) for creating a fundamentally restructured rouble zone. Thus, it was Russia's economic and monetary policies, undertaken unilaterally and without prior consultation, that forced Uzbekistan to adopt its own national currency so quickly. On 15 November 1993, the *Sum* coupon was introduced in the republic to replace the old rouble as a new medium of exchange. After the government announced the introduction of the new currency, many shops closed towards the end of the week preceding the currency reform and did not reopen for the rest of November. For three weeks food could be bought at the market, but most non-food items could not be purchased in the republic. The *Sum* coupons were first issued to pensioners and students. A few days later a third of employees' wages were paid in *Sum* coupons and the remainder was in bank deposits. 10,000 and 5,000 rouble notes were declared void and people were allowed to deposit the void notes only in bank accounts, to be used for transfers but not to obtain cash. Since transfers could be used only to pay taxes and utility bills, which were low, the accounts were practically frozen. The voiding of rouble banknotes was gradually extended to include small denominations. Bank accounts containing over 200,000 roubles were considered to contain illegal income and were thereby frozen for six months without interest, while the account holders were required to prove that their bank balances were obtained legally. Even if the account holders proved that their money was legally earned, in a high inflationary situation they lost much of the value of their money. The *Sum* coupon was officially on a par with the rouble but, despite government efforts to maintain an unrealistic official exchange rate, it depreciated rapidly on the free market and inflation accelerated in the first months of 1994. The coupons were replaced on 1 July 1994 by a permanent currency

– the *Sum* – at a rate of 1,000:1 and the government slowly started to shift away from its expansionary fiscal and monetary policy. Accordingly, the 1994 overall budget deficit fell to below four per cent. The improvement in the fiscal year's position was largely due to the government's decision to eliminate the enterprise sector's access to special budgetary transfers and, to a lesser extent, to cut direct budgetary consumer subsidies. Inflation, which had persisted at a monthly rate of around 22 per cent in the first half of 1994, also fell sharply by the end of the year. This partly reflected seasonal factors and a good harvest.[10]

Towards a national economic model of reform

In the 1990s, the dominant theory on the implementation of successful economic reform and acceleration of the pace of development has been the neo-liberal agenda of mass privatization and marketization. Advocates argue that these twin processes more logically distribute resources within a given economy and, by enhancing competition, eliminate waste and other inefficiencies. The overall result will be raised levels of GNP and improved living conditions for the majority of people. In short, the advocates of this theory believe that the gains in the overall economy will, in time 'trickle down'. The idea of trickle-down rests on the notion that the key to reducing poverty is economic growth. The benefits of this growth percolate down to the poor through an increase in agricultural productivity, increased access to institutional credit and rising wage rates in the rural and urban labour markets. Central to this concept is the theory of economic development with unlimited supplies of labour.[11] In fact, in many developing economies there exist unlimited supplies of labour where the population is so large relative to capital and natural resources that there are large sectors of the economy where the marginal productivity of labour is negligible, zero or even negative. Fifty years of development experience, however, has shown that the process of trickle-down often does not take place and even when it does, it fails to eradicate inequalities.

A highly centralized and statist economy such as the former Soviet economy, dependent on state subsidies, protected from competition, and shackled by a large and inefficient bureaucracy, was a sure obstacle against the efficient use of resources and a brake on economic development. Such an economy would not give itself easily to serial alterations of course when called for by external or internal developments.[12] The free market measures were expected to bring speedy reform, increased levels of production and improved living standards in the republics of the former Soviet Union. In reality, they resulted in collapsing economic reform programs, economic decline and worsening living standards. Mass privatization has not revived the economies of the region. Moreover, without appropriate preparation and the creation of effective mechanisms of support for enterprises, the process aggravated the economic crisis and drove many enterprises to the brink of bankruptcy. It increased unemployment and intensified stratification of the population by income and social status. Privatization not only brought misery for the majority of working people, but also became the subject of corrupt and criminal bargaining behind closed doors. The advice that such measures be implemented immediately in an economy lacking adequate legal, financial, technical (including managerial) and physical infrastructure and enough sources of internal as well as external capital, was a serious mistake. In the global economy international capital plays a significant role for the economies of developing countries, but total dependence on the continued flow of external capital for economic progress and prosperity also creates serious difficulties. The priorities of international capital and those countries in need often do not match. International capital is unreliable and often includes conditions that may be politically, or otherwise, unacceptable. International capital is always supplied to countries where there are better rates of return with lesser risks. The idea that privatization alone can resolve the problems of social and economic inequality is not tenable. A country with a free market economy, perfectly sound macroeconomic indicators and good rates of economic growth, may also have a poor income distribution system and large pockets of poverty. Even among the industrialized countries, recent privatization has widened rather than narrowed, socio-economic inequalities. This theory not only fails adequately to address questions concerning social activity, living conditions, and spiritual and moral values, but also ignores the fact that economic issues cannot be separated from their social, cultural, and political contexts. Cultural peculiarities and attitudes seriously influence different societies' economic behaviour and the way they respond to changes in economic signals. Changes in how a given economy functions are not politically neutral either, since they affect the interests of different regions of a country and various fragments of its society.

As a newly independent republic, Uzbekistan has been limited in its efforts to implement market-oriented reforms. There are several reasons for this. Firstly, the inflexible centralized system of the Soviet economy caused a far greater level of economic damage than in any other country with a large public sector. For decades the economic patterns of the republic had been developed to serve the requirements of the Centre. Secondly, because of the old reliance on subsidies from Moscow for investment needs, the republic lacked a domestic capital base. Thirdly, a culture of traditional entrepreneurship in the republic has partly survived, but the contemporary culture of commerce is different from that of the traditional mercantile culture. Fourthly, the state-owned industrial and agricultural production units were also the fundamental suppliers of social services. Fifthly, the population had been divided, mostly along ethnic lines and into rural and urban sectors. The urban inhabitants were Slavic, mainly Russian and Russified indigenous peoples, who were better educated and skilled, and worked in industries with much higher wages and greater access privileges. The rural population, by contrast, consisted overwhelmingly of indigenous people working in agriculture earning lower wages. This situation, along with factors such as social tensions and ethnic conflicts in the region, led the Uzbek leadership to adopt a very cautious approach to economic reform. They wanted to avoid social unrest while examining various approaches and economic models for the transition to a market economy in Uzbekistan. The Soviet era economic development left the republic burdened by many problems and since independence these problems have accelerated the county's economic decline and complicated the task of economic reform. A new long-term strategy of national development was needed, one which would correspond to the country's fundamental economic, social and cultural characteristics. After examining several models of economic development, the Uzbek leadership rejected the radical way of changing the old system and economic relations formed during previous decades, and accordingly refused to introduce the 'shock therapy option' which was attempted by some other countries of the former Soviet Union.[13] The leadership believed that effective market economics could be established through a painless, gradual step-by-step transformation of the old economic relations. Therefore, in order to minimize possible social, economic and political upheavals and to protect people's livelihoods and well-being during the transition period, Uzbekistan chose a path separate from other CIS countries in its shift away from a centrally planned command economy to a multi-sectoral market economy.

The Uzbek model for building a market economy is based on principles formulated by President Islom Karimov in the initial reform period. The model consists of the following main principles: (1) The economy should prevail over politics and all necessary conditions be created to develop entrepreneurship. (2) The state should be the main instigator of reform throughout the transition period and should initiate the process of reform in the interests of the nation. It should identify priorities of economic progress, elaborate and consistently implement a policy of radical transformation in the economy, the social sphere and the political life of the country. (3) To achieve tangible results in the economic transformation, the entire process of renewal and progress should be founded on adjusted and practically applicable laws. (4) A strong social policy should be implemented, one that takes into account the demographic situation and the existing living standards of the people. (5) The establishment of new economic market relations should be introduced without past 'revolutionary leaps', but with careful consideration, stage by stage.[14]

After the break-up of the Soviet Union, Uzbekistan became the only Central Asian State where the leadership succeeded in preparing a relatively complex and long-term strategy of national development, which corresponded to its fundamental economic, social and moral values. This model, in an epoch of standardized approaches and universal prescriptions for economic growth, might appear to be original. However, in the opinion of many analysts, it recalls the active and decisive role that the state has played in overcoming backwardness and creating full-blown capitalism, a method persuasively demonstrated by the countries of east and south-east Asia.[15] One might even say that the Uzbek economic model replicates the so-called 'Ryzhkov variant' for transition to a market economy. This model is also similar to that found in South Korea and Taiwan. The distinctive element in all these models of development, which became so widespread in south-east and east Asia, is the combination of strict authoritarian rule, the gradual implementation of reforms, and a relatively good economic performance. Nonetheless the Uzbek model of economic development deserves credit for its success in the initial stage of the economic transformation and for the improvements achieved in microeconomic stability in a short period of time. However, it may still be too early to draw final conclusions about the merits and drawbacks of this model since it has been applied for only a few years.

The economic reform process

Uzbekistan's initial approach to economic reform was rather cautious and designed in a step-by-step manner. The government's programme for reform was initiated in two stages; as it has enacted new legislation, created new institutions and implemented structural changes to underpin the process, stage one was undertaken in 1992 and completed by the end of 1994. It concentrated on residential housing, small-scale privatization, retail shops, trade and service enterprises.

Privatization of residential housing was the initial stage. In 1992–3, over 1.2 million state-owned dwellings, comprising 95 per cent of the state housing stock, were privatized.[16] The majority of these dwellings were handed over to the occupants either on favourable terms or for free. War veterans, teachers, medical personnel, scientists and creative intelligentsia became the owners of their houses free of charge. Most urban housing consists of formerly publicly owned apartments located in high-rise buildings. Most rural housing, however, exists in the form of private, individual family dwellings built out of mud or other traditional materials. In the republic today, 90 per cent of all families own their houses or apartments, 7 per cent live in housing owned by construction cooperatives or enterprises, 2 per cent rent privately, and 1 per cent live in hostels. Privatized houses can be freely bought and sold, but as the housing market is not yet well developed, mortgage credit facilities do not exist and real estate and conveyancing professionals are scarce. Therefore, housing transactions are relatively informal, and markets are typically organized in bazaars. Most houses are put on the market by emigrating families. The sale price of housing in 1999 was still quite high, averaging about $8,000 for an apartment in Tashkent. This price is about 10–12 times the average annual income in Tashkent. The problem of homelessness does not exist in the country and for the immediate future, the supply of housing is keeping pace with demand to a greater extent than in other parts of the CIS,[17] though in the cities housing production has not kept pace with population growth. After the demise of the Soviet Union, urban housing construction virtually ceased, while urbanization has increased.

The privatization of small state enterprises was, in theory, supposed to promote a private sector in the country (a small enterprise is in general, defined as having up to 45 employees; a medium enterprise is one that employs up to 500 people; and large enterprises employ over 500 people; other criteria for such clarification purposes are the value of fixed assets and of physical output). In practice, this raised several problems. Substantial institutional and regulatory barriers discouraged the emergence of competitive markets. Bureaucratic interventions and obstacles continued to impede access to credit, land, utilities, permits and licenses. Thus, only a few small-scale enterprises were offered for sale to the public through auctions. Almost all of the privatization of small-scale enterprises was through direct transfer. The authorities simply left most small enterprises either to the staff or sold them at below market prices. Some would argue that assets accumulated in the name of the entire population were simply given away, in whole or in part, to a small minority of the population who happened to have a job in the relevant enterprise, leading to an arbitrary and unfair distribution of capital assets.[18] There are certainly grounds for this contention but it could be countered that the government had little room for manoeuvre. After all, there had been a high level of poverty, increasingly worsening economic conditions and living standards, the inheritance of a highly complex form of bureaucratic administrative-command system and the break-up of decades-old economic links and channels of the whole Union, all accompanied by increasing social tensions. However, during this stage almost 600 medium-scale and 400 large-scale state enterprises were privatized in closed stock form (a closed company is one for which shares are reserved for the state or employees; an open company is one for which shares can be offered for sale to the general public). The problem is that the shares of these enterprises were allocated only to the managers and the government with the latter keeping the majority of shares. The government retained ownership making 'privatization' a misnomer. Thus, privatization in the first stage in these sectors of the economy did not lead to significant gains in efficiency and growth.

However, in comparison with the industrial sector, there have been remarkable achievements in the reform process of the rural economy during the first stage, where the government designed a method of reforming the rural economy. Agriculture provides the main source of income for more than half of the Uzbek population. Therefore, the sustainability of agricultural production was one of the main objectives of Uzbekistan during the initial years of the transition from a command economy to a multi-structural economy. During this time, per capita GDP remained fairly stable compared to other countries of the CIS, and agricultural production contributed to this stability. In the past Uzbekistan specialized in cotton production, which dominated the republic's agricultural sector, thereby creating a 'cotton monoculture'. As a result of this, more than 80 per cent of total grains products, more than half of meat and milk products, and many other foodstuffs had to be imported.[19] Cotton production was characterized by low yields, high input use and spoilage, and large distortions caused by price controls, the state order system and input subsidies. After independence, the government initially kept the state order system intact. This was important for cotton, because the high implicit tax on farmers through state orders was used to finance large consumer subsidies, especially on energy. But in 1993–4 a number of important changes were initiated in the agricultural sector.

At the time of independence the republic's agriculture was organized into *kolkhozy* (collective farms) and *savkhozy* (state farms) with a very small proportion of the total sown land allocated to workers as personal plots.[20] The principal difference between these two forms of ownership was that a *savkhozy* was a state enterprise whose workers were employed at fixed wages. By contrast, a *kolkhozy* paid its workers from its own residual earnings. The trend before independence was towards an increase in the proportion of *savkhozy*, because state ownership was considered 'ownership by the entire population', in contrast to the cooperative ownership of the *kolkhozy*. By the end of 1994, however, almost all the *savkhozy* were abolished and transformed into collective enterprises and *kolkhozy* became entirely new agricultural units. All the existing *kolkhozy* and *savkhozy* were transformed into associations of cooperatives of individual peasant farmers. In a relatively short time span the republic abolished 1,066 out of the 1,137 existing state farms and transformed them into 530 collective farms, about 350 cooperatives and more than 100 leasehold enterprises. This provided the conditions for creating a multi-structured agrarian economy. Accordingly, the distribution of total sown land between different forms of farming units has also changed. In 1990 the percentage of sown land allocated to the *kolkhozy* and cooperatives increased from 34.9 per cent to 47 per cent in 1993 and 75.3 per cent by the end of 1994. The percentage of sown land allocated to *savkhozy* decreased from 58.7 per cent in 1990 to 39 per cent in 1993 and decreased further to only 1.0 per cent in 1994. There was also an increase in land allocated to individual farmers. This stood at 0.1 per cent in 1990, but increased to 0.6 per cent in 1993 and 2.1 per cent in 1994. Other forms of ownership increased from 6.3 per cent in 1990 to 12.9 per cent in 1993 and 21.6 per cent in 1994.[21]

The second important change in Uzbekistan's agriculture reform policy was the move towards individual farming. The amount of land distributed to personal plots for workers in *kolkhozy* and other forms of agricultural organization increased significantly. Total land under personal plots is estimated to have increased from 110,000 hectares before independence to 630,000 hectares in 1994. Of this, crop land amounted to 362,840 hectares.[23] In most places the limit on the land allotted to personal households and private plots was raised from 0.1 hectares to 0.25 hectares per household. This kept unemployment to a minimum among the rural population, which had grown acutely since 1989, and also helped to raise the efficiency of production. Private farming has increased in two ways. One is by an increased amount of sown land owned by individual farmers; the other is that the *kolkhozy* has entered into contract with individual *kolkhozniks* (*kolkhoz* members) under which production is managed and organized by individual farmers while the *kolkhoz* provides certain services and inputs and receives a share of revenues. Apart from these, 1,516 livestock farms have also been transferred to their personnel's ownership to raise the efficiency of production. Those livestock farms of agricultural enterprises not specializing in livestock product are to be sold to private owners. As a result the structure of agricultural production has changed considerably with the introduction of the new forms of ownership. Thus, a new *dekhan* (individual peasants and farmers) farming sector has emerged in the republic. The majority of the reformed *kolkhozy* and *savkhozy* have recently transformed themselves into associations of cooperatives of peasants and farmers' households. The cooperatives are formed along the lines of the former brigades. In general each cooperative is a group more in the sense of having historically belonged to the same brigade and *kolkhoz* than in the sense of farming cooperatively. The distribution of land was based on the number of able-bodied workers per household. A household with an average number of workers received a minimum of about 1.5 hectares of land. Households with more productive workers or more productive resources received more land. The contract is initially signed for ten years, giving farmers the right to long-term leasehold tenure of the assigned land along with the right to inherit by one's children provided that the land is properly used. Land cannot be sold or exchanged. The association receives from each household an amount between 10–20 per cent of its income as payment for the use of the land. For grain and cotton it is usually payment in money, but for other products, the form of payment can vary. It can be in the form of an agreed cash payment or the sale to the association of an agreed amount of product at an agreed price (usually at a price below the market price) or a combination of these. The number of *dekhan* farms in 1994 increased 1.9 times over and by early 1995 the number had reached 25,000. Among these, more than 10,000 farms specialize in the production of livestock products. The total area of land under crops cultivated by *dekhan* farms increased 2.7 times over in 1994 compared to 1993. Production of potatoes, vegetables and melon crops expanded 3.3 times, milk 2.1 times and eggs 1.3 times. The non-state sector has consolidated its position in the countryside. In 1991 the share of the state sector comprised 37 per cent of the overall volume of agricultural production and that of the non-state sector, 63 per cent. In early 1995 the non-state sector accounted for 95 per cent of all agricultural production. 70 per cent of the overall quantity of livestock, and 50 per cent of sheep and goats is concentrated in personal holdings. The share of these holdings in the overall volume of agricultural production has increased from 30–44 per cent. They produce over 76 per cent of milk, 70 per cent of meat, 56 per cent of potatoes, 63 per cent of vegetables and 60 per cent of fruit in the republic.[23]

There has also been considerable change in the structure of land under cultivation in favour of grain crops and a consequent reduction of cotton plantations as part of the economic reforms implemented in Uzbekistan. Accordingly, 2.7 million tonnes of grain were produced in 1994, 44 per cent more than in 1991. To ensure further increases in the production of grain and wheat crops, the area of land under grain crops is to be increased up to 147,000 hectares, including up to 970,000 hectares of irrigated land on account of the further improvement of land under crops and land released from cotton and feed crops. The policy of shifting relative incentives against cotton in favour of grain and wheat crops reflected the government's concern about the country's dependence on the import of these essential commodity products. But there is also a risk in substituting the import of grain at the cost of reducing the export of cotton, one of the republic's most important export products. Self-sufficiency in grain can be achieved by improving productivity and profitability, through investment in the development of seed and technology.

Aware of the deficiencies during the first stage, President Islom Karimov initiated in mid-1994 the second stage of the economic reform programme with new measures designed to deepen economic reform. The aim was to expand privatization and introduce increased competition and openness in the transfer processes. The second stage of the decentralization programme was accompanied by some forty pieces of legislation and administrative acts.[24] On one hand, the second stage focused on the privatization of state property and the formation of a multi-sectoral socially oriented market economy in which competition was encouraged. On the other hand, the leadership concentrated on assessing the merits and demerits of what had been achieved in the course of the first stage and examined the effects on growth, efficiency and equity. Attempts have also been made to encourage the further improvement of taxation, financial and monetary policies and to liberalize external economic activities, overcome the recession, ensure macroeconomic stabilization and increase output by stimulating domestic production activities and reducing inflation, thus ensuring self-sufficiency in some key sectors, such as fuel, energy and grain. The state would maintain the ownership of several large enterprises, but they would become more autonomous. Studies are to be carried out into how to improve the efficiency, flexibility and competitiveness of these enterprises. The process of conversion and privatization would continue in the sphere of transport, including buses, taxis and other vehicles. Efforts were made to privatize tourist complexes in the cities of Bukhara, Samarkand, Khiva and Tashkent through tender sale or converting them into joint-stock companies and setting up joint ventures with foreign partners. The centre of the privatization process was to be shifted from the sectoral republican level to the regional level. The status and responsibilities of the regional bodies has been enhanced and they will have more freedom to implement the conversion and privatization processes. The process of transforming large and medium enterprises into open joint-stock companies was the main focus of privatization during the second stage and closed joint-stock companies that have already been established were to be transformed into open joint-stock companies. In the rural areas favourable conditions were to be created to expand the organizations of private farming and encourage the participation of foreign investors in agricultural production. The government also sought to sell plots of land to the trade and public services enterprises which are being, or have already been, privatized. It hoped to sell plots to build offices, small enterprises, shops and public services.

As domestic output has been one of the most important policy issues for the government of Uzbekistan, more assistance is given to those enterprises aiming to manufacture goods for the population and for export. Irrespective of their form of ownership, they are given priority in terms of having access to investment, raw materials and credit resources, but the full convertibility of the national currency depends on the availability of sufficient foreign exchange reserves. In late-1995, the republic's national currency was *de facto* freely convertible for current transactions. Resident and non-resident enterprises and individuals could purchase and sell foreign exchange at the official auction through authorized banks. However, because of the increased pressures on the balance of payments in 1996, restrictions were imposed on access to foreign exchange in the second half of the year, increasing the demand for a foreign exchange market. Thus, in early 1997, the government established a new multiple currency practice system of foreign exchange. The exchange rate is set by the authorities according to commercial bank rates. In addition, the administration of the numerous trade restrictions was tightened to protect domestic producers from external competition. As a result, the illegal black market for foreign exchange gained in importance and the spread between the black market exchange rate and the official rate widened from about 100 per cent in 1997 to more than 400 per cent by the end of 1999. In response to this the government, in May 2000, re-unified the official exchange rate and the commercial rate once again allowing resident and non-resident enterprises and individuals purchase and sell foreign exchange at the official auction through authorized banks. The effect of this is yet to materialize. There are currently two different currency exchange practices in the republic – an official foreign exchange at commercial rate and an unofficial black market rate. The exchange rate gap between the official exchange transactions and the 'free-market' remains high. The foreign exchange at the black market rate in early 2000 was about 700 *Sums* to $1.00 compared to the official rate of 219 *Sums*.

Macroeconomic progress since independence

Since independence Uzbekistan has attempted to pursue its own path of economic reform and sought to minimize the resulting social costs. The Uzbek government has adopted programmes of macroeconomic stabilization and structural reform designed to contain the decline in output, reduce inflation and the fiscal deficit and improve the balance of payments. The decline in aggregate output has been arrested and real GDP grew by 4.4 per cent in 1998 and continued in 1999 (see Table 4.1), led by a strong performance in the services sector and a recovery in industry.

TABLE 4.1
Real GDP growth (%)

1991	1992	1993	1994	1995	1996	1997*	1998**	1999**
-0.5	-11.1	-2.3	-4.2	-0.9	1.6	2.5	4.4	4.4

Notes:
*IMF, *Republic of Uzbekistan: Recent Economic Developments*, Staff Country Report no. 00/36 (2000)
**Centre for Economic Research, Tashkent
Source: Ministry of Macroeconomics and Statistics.

Industrial production, which accounted for about 17 per cent of GDP, grew by 1.6 per cent in real terms during 1996 after a cumulative decline of 32 per cent in 1991–5. The growth was particularly strong in the machine building, metal processing, metallurgy, chemical and wood processing subsectors. This was a result of the government's policy of shifting the structure of the economy in a more industrialized direction. The government has invested substantially in industry and has allocated considerable resources to the metal processing, metallurgy and chemical subsectors (see Table 4.2). The decline in production in some subsectors has been offset by growth in others, reflecting the government's policy of shifting the structure of the economy towards industry. The government considers foreign direct investment, particularly through joint ventures, to be essential in achieving rapid industrialization. A number of large-scale foreign direct investment projects started operation in 1996 and this resulted in a substantial increase in production of the automobile industry and a sharp increase in the production of television sets and video recorders as a joint venture operation with a South Korean company, the UzDaewoo. Production growth in metallurgy and timber and wood processing was also strong. However, the production of a number of consumer goods, including textiles, rugs and carpets and vegetable oils declined. The recovery in the industrial sector continued into 1998, but in the first quarter of 1999 there was a slight slowdown in industrial output which rose by only 4.7 per cent compared to the first quarter of 1998, which involved a 6.4 per cent increase.

TABLE 4.2
Uzbekistan industrial production, 1992–8
(percentage change over the previous year)

Industrial sector	1992	1993	1994	1995	1996	1997*	1998*
Electricity	-6.7	-1.8	-3.6	0.3	1.0	1.3	1.4
Fuel	-3.0	11.9	2.4	-0.2	0.4	1.4	1.7
Metallurgy	-14.5	-1.2	-10.7	-0.7	19.5	14.6	25.5
Chemicals and petroleum	-26.1	-11.4	-22.3	12.6	15.1	-6.6	1.0
Machine building and metal production	0.2	7.9	10.3	19.7	40.1	91.5	44.7
Timber and wood processing	-3.5	13.3	1.5	9.7	21.9	-0.7	-0.4
Light industry	5.2	4.2	7.9	-1.9	6.4	8.4	8.4
Food	-12.1	7.4	3.5	1.3	15.0	17.5	11.9
Others	–	–	-2.2	-6.1	-34.4	14.9	5.8
Total	-6.2	4.1	1.0	0.2	6.0	6.5	

Note:
*Centre for Economic Research, Tashkent

Source: IMF, *Republic of Uzbekistan: Recent Economic Developments*, Staff Country Report no. 97/98 (1997).

The government's policy of pursuing energy self-sufficiency continued throughout 1996. Substantial further investment in this sector took place with foreign participation and domestic budgetary support, leading to the discovery of two new oil fields in Bukhara and Fergana. Production of electricity and coal declined slightly in 1996 (see Table 4.3). The decline in electricity production was mainly due to lower exports to neighbouring states which had experienced payment difficulties. The decline in the production of coal reflected the substitution of gas for coal in household use, but production of crude oil and natural gas rose significantly in 1996. Although growth rates were small compared with 1995, the increase in production continued. From 1995 onwards, Uzbekistan has been able to meet its domestic energy demand. Crude oil production increased from 7.58 million tons to 9.70 million tons while output of natural gas increased from 48.6 billion cubic metres to 55 billion cubic meters.[25] The small rate of increase in the production of natural gas in 1996 was due to the neighbouring countries' importing difficulties.

TABLE 4.3
Production of selected energy products

Energy product	1991	1992	1993	1994	1995	1996	1997	1998
Electricity (billion kWh)	54.2	50.9	49.1	47.8	47.4	45.4	46.0	45.9
Coal (tons)	5,948.0	4,681.0	3,807.0	3,845.0	3,054.0	2,837.0	2,946.0	2,952.0
Natural gas (billion cubic meters)	41.9	42.8	45.0	47.2	48.6	49.0	52.1	54.8
Oil and condensed gas (tons)	2,831.4	3,292.6	3,943.6	5,516.7	7,586.2	7,621.5	8,086.0	9,703.0

Sources: Ministry of Macroeconomics and Statistics; IMF, *Republic of Uzbekistan: Recent Economic Developments*, Staff Country Report no. 00/36 (2000); Centre for Economic Research, Tashkent.

Inflation was significantly reduced from almost 1,300 per cent in 1994 to 64 per cent in 1996 as the government pursued a tight monetary policy and maintained a prudent fiscal policy. But it rose again in the last quarter of 1996 with the government easing both fiscal and monetary policy (see Table 4.4). Inflation was reduced to a more modest level in 1998 as the government tightened control over credit and money supply. As a result of the government's measures to raise revenues and rationalize public expenditure, the fiscal deficit was reduced from above 18 per cent of GDP in 1992 to 2.4 per cent of GDP in 1997 (the IMF's estimate for the consolidated state budget deficit in 1996 was 7.3 per cent of GDP, because it includes the 20 billion *Sums* which was provided by the government to the agriculture sector as loans in late 1996, in the net lending category, hence the IMF's estimate differs from that of government).[26] The republic successfully introduced its own currency in 1994 and international reserves were gradually built up amounting to nearly five months of imports by the end of 1998.

TABLE 4.4
Inflation (year-end) and budget deficit

	1991	1992	1993	1994	1995	1996	1997	1998
Inflation	169	910	885	1281	117	64	27.6	25.9
Budget deficit	-2.6	-18.5	-10.4	-6.1	-4.1	-3.3	-2.4	-2.1

Sources: Data for inflation 1991–5 taken from the IMF, the World Bank and EBRD; data for 1996–8 from the Uzbek Ministry of Macroeconomics and Statistics; budget deficit data from (1991–6) the Asian Development Bank, *Country Economic Review: Uzbekistan* (1997); 1997 and 1998 from IMF, *Republic of Uzbekistan: Recent Economic Developments*, Staff Country Report no. 97/98 (1997).

The recovery in the economy in 1996 was achieved partly by sound domestic investments (see Table 4.5). The rate of domestic investments as a proportion of GDP grew significantly from less than 6 per cent in 1994 to around 21 per cent in 1995. Government investment remained strong in 1996, but non-government investment was low and as a result the overall domestic investment rate dropped to 10 per cent of GDP in 1998. To keep the investment-saving gap within manageable limits and maintain sustainable growth, investment has to be financed by growing national savings. In the republic the gross national savings rate as a proportion of GDP grew from 8 per cent in 1994 to 20 per cent in 1995, but fell back to 15 per cent in 1997 and back further to 9.9 per cent in 1998. This reflected a rise in overall consumption, which increased as a share of GDP from 80 per cent in 1995 to 90 per cent in 1998. Non-government consumption increased because real wages increased and domestic supply conditions improved with more and better imported goods. An increase in government consumption was due mainly to the provision of a large amount of credit to the agriculture sector in late-1996. Thus the national savings rate fell more sharply than the domestic investment rate and a resource gap equivalent to about 8 per cent of GDP emerged in the same year.[27]

TABLE 4.5
Savings, investment, consumption and wages
(as percentage of GDP)

	1992	1993	1994	1995	1996	1997	1998
Consumption	93.3	105.4	92.2	79.6	91.8	85.1	90.1
Non-government	53.2	54.1	62.5	47.1	57.4	60.2	62.4
Government	40.1	51.3	29.7	32.5	34.4	24.9	27.7
Domestic Investment	13.1	3.0	5.7	20.9	16.1	18.9	10.2
Non-government	9.5	0.8	2.1	14.8	9.0	11.5	2.1
Government	3.6	2.2	3.6	6.1	7.1	7.4	8.1
Savings	13.1	3.0	5.7	20.9	16.1	18.9	10.2
National saving	6.7	-5.4	7.8	20.4	8.2	14.9	9.9
Non-government	15.3	9.9	8.3	18.4	8.4	9.8	5.2
Government	-8.6	-15.3	-0.5	2.0	-0.2	5.2	4.7
Saving–Investment balance							
Non-government	5.7	9.1	6.2	3.5	-0.6	1.7	3.1
Government	-12.2	-17.5	-4.1	4.1	-7.3	2.2	-6.6
Resource gap	6.4	8.4	-2.1	0.5	7.9	0.5	-3.5
Wages							
Nominal average wage (end of period; *Sums* per month)	2.3	28.7	305.0	1,073.0	2,166.0	3,697.2	5,414.0
Nominal minimum wage (end of period; *Sums* per month)	1.0	9.0	70.0	175.0	416.0	675.0	925.0

Sources: Ministry of Macroeconomics and Statistics; Ministry of Labour; Asian Development Bank, *Country Economic Review: Uzbekistan* (1997); IMF, *Republic of Uzbekistan: Recent Economic Developments*, Staff Country Report nos. 97/98 (1997) and 00/36 (2000).

Although Uzbekistan had several economic achievements to its credit, it had to confront two economic shocks in 1996. First there was a supply shock because of the poorer than expected cotton and grain harvests. Second, the republic was subjected to a terms-of-trade shock as the world price of cotton, its principal export commodity, fell sharply and the import price of wheat rose. Thus external trade and payments came under pressure in the last quarter of 1996. The current account deficit rose sharply from 0.5 per cent of GDP in 1995 to about 8 per cent in 1996. In response to these shocks, the government relaxed its fiscal and monetary policy stance in 1996 by extending large credits to agriculture through the Central Bank to prepare for the 1997 planting season. In addition to this, the government imposed restrictions on foreign trade and exchange to protect international reserves in order to ease pressure on the balance of payments. However, these actions were in breach of the programme targets under the Standby Arrangements (SBA) signed with the International Monetary Fund (IMF) in December 1995. This resulted in the IMF suspending the disbursements under the SBA in December 1996. Since then the IMF has held negotiations with the government, but a mutually satisfactory programme has yet to be concluded.

The budget deficit in 1996 was almost entirely financed by national resources including credit from the Central Bank of Uzbekistan (CBU). In the first quarter of 1997, the government proceeded with a cautious fiscal policy stance and the consolidated state budget deficit was maintained at about 3 per cent of GDP (at present the state budget comprises the national budget and the budgets of 14 local authorities, i.e. the budgets of 12 *oblasts*, the Autonomous Republic of Karakalpakistan and the city of Tashkent). Total government revenues amounted to 18.8 million roubles (30.4 per cent of GDP) in 1991. The government implemented a major reform of the tax system in early January 1992 and revenue increased to about 139.8 million roubles (31.3 per cent of GDP) in 1992. Turnover and sales taxes were abolished, while a value-added tax (VAT) and excise taxes were introduced. The standard, single VAT was introduced in 1992 at a rating level of 30 per cent and this was steadily reduced to 17 per cent in 1996. In 1997, the standard rate rose again to 18 per cent on most goods, and a lower rate of 10 per cent was introduced on four basic food products: flour, bread, meat and dairy products. However, from 1 January 1998, the VAT rate was again increased to 20 per cent on all goods and services imported into Uzbekistan and collected by customs officials. Technological equipment imported into Uzbekistan is exempt from the VAT if the equipment is used for investment. The basic food product rate rose from 10 to 15 per cent. The enterprise profit tax was replaced by an enterprise income tax. The authorities also adopted a cash management system to control expenditure. In this system, expenditures were authorized only up to an amount equal to revenues received in each month and priority was given to wages, subsidies, transfers and imports of food, medicines and other strategic goods. VAT and cotton-marketing activity were the two largest sources of revenue, providing 30 per cent and 22 per cent of total revenue, respectively. However, the country was only at the initial stage of its tax reform process and naturally it not only raised several problems but also made the administration of taxes more difficult. The VAT did not allow an exemption for small enterprises nor it did cover wholesale and retail trade or most services. It was levied on the import price exclusive of custom tariffs. Thus only small amounts were raised by other taxes introduced with the January 1992 tax reform. Taxes on international trade, comprising customs duties, yielded revenues amounting to only 1.1 per cent of GDP in 1992.[28] As part of the 1993 budget law, several changes were introduced to the tax code in January 1993, so that total revenues amounted to 1603.8 billion roubles, comprising 36 per cent of GDP. In 1994, however, revenues fell to 28.3 per cent of GDP, due to the introduction of the new national currency. The following year, revenues amounted to 105 billion *Sums*, and in 1996 they totalled 192 billion, 34.2 per cent of GDP. This was 0.4 per cent less than in 1995 and followed largely from a decline in non-tax revenue receipts. Tax revenues, on the other hand, increased from 28 per cent of GDP in 1995 to over 50 per cent in 1998. State revenues amounted to 440.1 billion *Sums* (32.4 per cent of GDP). The main sources of government revenues were the income and profit tax, VAT and excise taxes. Revenue collection from these taxes improved significantly in comparison with 1995. While part of the improvement in tax revenue collection undeniably aided economic recovery, the government's efforts to coordinate revenues also played an important role.

During the first nine months of 1992, the government maintained a strict cash management system. Under this, budgetary expenditures on wages, grants, social benefits, food and service subsidies, and medicines were given priority over investment in industry, subsidies to enterprises, and maintenance and development of infrastructure. Although the fiscal stance was eased during the last quarter of the year, the total budgetary expenditure for the year as a whole decreased from 53 per cent of GDP in 1991 to 43 per cent in 1992 (see Table 4.6).[29] To achieve this, however, capital, operations and maintenance expenditures were either limited or postponed, and direct transfers to enterprises and organizations financed through the state budget were replaced with credits from the banking system. In 1993, the government's attempts to meet both its budget deficit target of 5 per cent of GDP and its objective of maintaining real incomes among the population became increasingly difficult due to inflation and rising import costs. To maintain living standards, the government continued with the constant adjustment of both wages and

TABLE 4.6
Summary of public finance

	1991	1992	1993	1994	1995	1996	1997	1998
Government revenues								
In millions of Sums	30	140	1,836	18,936	104,813	191,551	293,676	440,140
As a percentage of GDP								
Total revenue and grants	48.8	31.3	36.0	29.2	34.6	34.2	30.1	32.4
Total expenditure and net lending	53.1	43.4	53.6	33.3	38.1	39.8	32.5	35.9
Composition of government revenues								
Taxes on incomes and profits	9.0	7.9	10.3	8.7	11.5	13.5	11.2	10.2
VAT	n/a	8.6	9.3	5.0	5.8	6.4	7.5	9.8
Excises	n/a	8.7	5.7	7.3	8.4	10.1	6.0	6.1
Cotton	n/a	6.6	4.8	4.9	4.4	2.2	0.6	0
As a percentage of total government revenue								
Tax on incomes and profits	18.0	25.2	28.4	26.8	33.0	39.0	45.0	51.0
VAT	n/a	27.4	25.7	15.3	16.0	19.0	30.0	31.0
Excises	n/a	27.7	15.7	22.7	24.0	30.0	15.0	20.0
Cotton	n/a	20.7	15.7	16.9	12.4	6.2	0	0
Total expenditure and net lending								
In millions of Sums	32	194	2,730	21,620	115,318	222,941	317,350	488,297
As a percentage of GDP	53.1	43.4	53.6	33.3	38.1	39.8	32.5	35.9
Composition of government expenditures and net lending								
As a percentage of GDP								
National economy	9.6	4.6	2.7	2.4	4.3	4.7	4.1	4.0
Education	8.6	10.1	9.3	8.3	7.4	7.4	7.1	7.9
Health and sport	4.4	4.6	4.1	3.5	3.6	3.7	3.3	3.3
Other current expenditure [a]	4.7	5.0	7.7	6.9	11.6	8.1	5.6	6.6
Capital expenditure (investments)	6.0	2.7	2.2	3.5	6.1	7.1	7.4	7.0
Others [b]	0.5	0.6	1.0	0.9	1.0	1.1	0.8	0.8
Net Lending	n/a	n/a	14.8	n/a	0.5	3.6	0	1.2
As a percentage of total expenditure								
National economy	18.7	10.8	5.1	7.3	11.3	11.8	13.0	19.5
Education	16.8	23.1	17.4	25.4	19.4	18.5	22.5	38.5
Health and sport	8.5	10.8	7.6	10.4	9.3	9.2	10.4	16.1
Other current expenditure [a]	9.2	9.8	14.3	20.7	33.6	23.6	17.7	32.2
Capital expenditure (investments)	11.7	8.6	4.1	10.3	16.1	17.9	23.4	34.1
Others [b]	0.9	1.5	1.8	2.6	2.5	2.7	2.5	3.9

Notes:
a Covers mainly spending on defence, and public order and safety.
b Covers mainly state administration.

Sources: Ministry of Finance; Asian Development Bank, *Country Economic Review: Uzbekistan* (1996 and 1997); IMF, *Republic of Uzbekistan: Recent Economic Developments*, Staff Country Report nos. 97/98 (1997) and 00/36 (2000).

controlled prices throughout 1993. New taxes were introduced in conjunction with the 1993 budget, though expenditure increased. Total budgetary expenditure for the year was over 53 per cent of GDP. In 1995, total budgetary expenditures were around 115 billion *Sums*, (about 38 per cent of GDP), and in 1996 they amounted to 203 billion *Sums*, (36.2 per cent of GDP). In 1998, total budgetary expenditures increased further, amounting to 472.2 billion *Sums*, (34.8 per cent of GDP). The government allocated major expenditures for the operation and maintenance of the economy, education, health and capital investment. There was a concerted effort during 1996 to cut public spending and keep government expenditures within the bounds of the programme. The effort focused on two main issues – cutting spending on the operation and maintenance of the economy, which included substantial water and electricity subsidies; and reducing 'other current expenditures'. This mainly covers spending on defence, public order and safety, and state administration. The government also made every effort to maintain the state welfare system for the most vulnerable segments of the population. Despite serious resource restrictions, capital expenditure and expenditures for social services were protected. These were clear priority categories in the budgets until 1998. The government viewed the completion of some public sector investment projects, including joint ventures, as essential for economic recovery, and therefore allocated budgetary resources for capital investment. As a result, public capital expenditures as a share of GDP rose from 6 per cent in 1995 to 7.0 per cent in 1998. More than half of government revenues were from indirect taxation. VAT made up 31 per cent of the total revenues. Education, health and culture accounted for over one third of total expenditure.

Official statistics on government expenditures in 1996 exclude about 20 billion *Sums* which was provided as loans to the agricultural sector. After the disappointing cotton and grain harvests of 1996, farms faced major financial problems. Responding to this, in the last quarter of 1996 the government borrowed money from the CBU and extended loans to the agricultural sector to help prepare for the 1997 planting season, an advance that will be recovered against deliveries of produce. Therefore, the government did not consider it to be an expenditure item in the official statistics in the budget. Nevertheless, the provision of such loans through CBU financing contributed to an increase in the money supply and an upturn in inflation in late 1996, breaching the government's SBA agreement on money supply and inflation programme targets with the IMF.

The republic's economy also faced serious balance-of-payments difficulties during 1992–3, but this mainly resulted from collapse of external trade and payments from the former Soviet Union. Since then the Uzbek government has taken significant steps to improve the situation. By 1994 a remarkable surplus was achieved on the current account (see Table 4.7). The position remained relatively comfortable in 1995 with only a small current account deficit. The external trade and payments situation, however, came under pressure in 1996, causing the current account deficit to rise sharply from $50 million (0.5 per cent of GDP) in 1995, to $1.1 billion (7.9 per cent of GDP) in 1996. The decline in the current account resulted mainly from the rising deficit in merchandise trade, amounting to $931 million in 1996.[30] This large trade account deficit can best be explained by three main factors. Firstly, despite an increase in the volume of cotton exports, the export value of cotton in 1996 declined by 3 per cent due to a sharp fall in the world price of cotton (the World Bank reported that the world price of cotton fell by 17 per cent from $2,128 per ton in 1995 to $1,773 per ton in 1996).[31] Uzbekistan was hoping to obtain self-sufficiency in grain production in 1996, but due to the unfavourable climatic conditions less than the forecasted amount was harvested. The expected amount was about 4.1 million tons, but the actual quantity harvested was 2.7 million tons. Therefore, Uzbekistan had to import a large amount of wheat even though the import price of wheat rose on average from $186 per ton in 1995 to $251 per ton in 1996. Because cotton accounts for over half of the republic's total export receipts, declining export earnings from cotton stagnated exports at their 1995 level, though a further decrease in export earnings was offset by growing gold exports, most of which resulted from an increase in volume. Secondly, imports of foodstuffs increased rapidly due to a lower than expected domestic grain harvest and a rising import price of wheat.[32] Domestic consumptive demand for grain is estimated to be about 4.1 million tons. In 1996 only 2.7 million tons were produced and about 1.4 million tons were imported. Thirdly, due to the increased capital investment of joint ventures and huge construction projects such as the Bukhara and Fergana oil refineries, imports of machinery surged by over 30 per cent. Exports continued to decline in 1997 and 1998 by 4.4 per cent and 20 per cent respectively, mainly mirroring the decline in raw material prices and weak demand in export markets. In the first quarter of 1999, however, exports of cotton, chemicals and food products had recovered slightly. Cotton still continues to be the backbone of Uzbek exports with a share of over 40 per cent, though the government aims to increase the share of industrial goods. The development of the energy sector has made Uzbekistan a net exporter of energy products. The energy sector accounted for about 8 per cent of the overall exports. The government strictly regulates imports through access to foreign exchange markets and therefore there is a downward trend in the value of imports.

TABLE 4.7
Balance of payments (in millions of US dollars)

Title	1991	1992	1993	1994	1995	1996	1997	1998
Current account	7,225	-237	-429	118	-50	-1,075	-584	-39
Merchandise trade balance	668	-235	-379	213	208	-931	-72	171
Exports	11,829	1,424	2,877	2,940	3,806	3,781	3,695	2,888
Cotton fibre	6,353	861	1,172	1,508	1,798	1,748	1,390	1,198
Gold	–	–	559	375	611	906	738	277
Other	5,476	563	1,146	1,057	1,396	1,201	1,280	1,090
Imports	11,141	1,659	3,256	2,727	3,597	4,712	4523.0	3288.7
Foodstuffs	–	716	625	861	687	1,391	678.0	644.0
Energy products	239	315	658	674	59	50	23.0	16.0
Machinery	–	–	–	–	1,279	1,391	1,868.0	1,352.0
Other	–	628	1,973	1,192	1,572	1,558	1,091.0	903.0
Current account balance (as a percentage of GDP)	20.5	-11.8	-8.4	2.1	-0.5	-7.9	-4.0	-0.3

Sources: IMF, *Republic of Uzbekistan: Recent Economic Developments*, Staff Country Report nos. 97/98 (1997) and 00/36 (2000); TACIS, *Uzbekistan Economic Trends Quarterly, First Quarter 1999*; Centre for Economic Research, Tashkent.

The progress in trade liberalization continued apace in 1996, though there were some trade restrictions, such as the introduction of additional tariffs on imports of some consumer goods and raw materials and a requirement for 'ex-ante' registration of import contracts in mid-1996. A large part of international trade, including gold and cotton exports, wheat and grain imports, continued to take place through the official channels during 1998 and 1999. In early 1996 the maximum rate, excluding cars, was lowered to 40 per cent, the total number of goods subject to import tariffs was decreased, the number of tariff bands reduced, and the average rate was lowered as more goods were concentrated in the lower bands. In late-1996 the maximum rate was lowered again, from 40 to 30 per cent, but tariffs were extended to a large number of commodities that were not subject to import taxes before, and existing duties were also raised for other groups of imports.[33] In addition to these, a one per cent tariff replaced the zero tariff where applicable.

After the break-up of the USSR, there were serious disruptions in the trade and payments system of Uzbekistan. Since independence, the republic has attempted to diversify its trade away from the countries of the former Soviet Union, to the rest of the world. After recording a surplus each year during 1993–5, the republic's trade balance with its traditional partners recorded a deficit of over 2 per cent of GDP in 1996 (see Table 4.8). However, trade with non-former Soviet partners increased sharply in US dollar terms by 35 per cent in 1996 and comprised over 70 per cent of total trade.[34] Trade with the states of the former Soviet bloc fell from 30 per cent of total trade to 25 per cent in the same year. In terms of the composition of exports, raw materials and processed industrial products, including cotton fibre, constituted over 70 per cent of total exports to non-traditional partners. The value of cotton exports to these countries rose by 14 per cent; 92 per cent of total cotton exports went to these countries in 1996, compared with 78 per cent in 1995. Imports of machinery and equipment, and of foodstuffs, increased by over 80 per cent in 1996 and continued to represent the vast majority of imports in 1998. The share of exports to traditional partners rose to 40 per cent in 1998. But the largest portion of trade continues to be conducted with the countries of the European Union, South Korea, the Russian Federation, Switzerland, Kazakstan, the United States, Turkey and China as a result of project-related investments and maintenance facilities. Although progress continued to be made in liberalizing the foreign trade system in the first half of 1996, government interventions increased in October 1996 in response to the growing current account deficit in an attempt to preserve international reserves. Such interventions included the introduction of a system that required 'ex-ante' registration of all import contracts. In addition, a new licensing requirement for exports of seven product categories was introduced. The categories were non-ferrous and ferrous metals, precious metals, crude oil and related products, cotton fibres, military products, gems, and radioactive metals. Licences were also needed for the import of medicines, poisons, narcotics, pesticides, military products, precious metals, gems, and radioactive materials.

TABLE 4.8
Foreign trade (in millions of US dollars, and in percentages)

	1992	1993	1994	1995	1996	1997	1998
Total Trade							
Exports	1,424	2,877	2,940	3,806	3,781˙	3,695	2,888
Imports	1,659	3,256	2,727	3,597	4,712˙	4,523	3,288.7
Exports to industrial countries	97	504	622	709	817	1,319.0	1,281.3
Imports from industrial countries	212	440	711	764	1,476	1,452.7	1,188.2
Exports to developing countries	65	132	1,221	1,748	1,833	1,382.3	1,214.4
Imports from developing countries	88	373	1,248	2,018	3,287	1,425.5	961.1
Exports to Europe	42	87	1,041	1,529	1,457	2,199.6	2,009.7
Imports from Europe	44	302	1,156	1,611	2,556	1,070.4	1,057.5
Exports to the Middle East	–	1	2	2	–	49.2	65.2
Imports from the Middle East	–	5	4	11	26	396.6	264.3
Exports to Western hemisphere	–	6	41	102	159	40.1	70.4
Imports from Western hemisphere	–	–	–	6	2	375.1	280.2
Exports to Asia	22	39	137	114	216	412.4	350.4
Imports from Asia	43	66	88	390	695	1,036.1	547.3
Exports (percentages)							
To industrial countries	59.9	79.2	33.8	28.9	30.8	45.8	44.5
To developing countries	40.1	20.8	66.2	71.1	69.2	48.0	42.2
Europe	26.1	13.7	56.5	62.3	55.0	76.4	69.8
Middle East	0.1	0.1	0.1	0.1	1.8	1.7	2.3
Western Hemisphere	–	0.9	2.2	4.2	8.0	1.4	2.2
Asia	13.9	6.1	7.4	4.6	8.2	14.3	12.2
Imports from							
Industrial countries	70.7	54.1	36.3	27.5	31.0	50.5	41.3
Developing countries	29.3	45.9	63.7	72.5	69.0	49.5	33.4
Europe	14.8	37.2	59.0	57.9	53.7	37.2	36.8
Middle East	–	0.6	0.2	0.4	0.5	13.8	9.2
Western hemisphere	–	–	–	0.2	15.8	12.2	8.8
Asia	14.4	8.2	4.5	14.0	18.7	36.0	19.0

Sources: *IMF Directory of Trade Statistics Yearbook, 1997*; IMF, *Republic of Uzbekistan: Recent Economic Developments*, Staff Country Report nos. 97/98 (1997) and 00/36 (2000).

In the area of structural reform, Uzbekistan continued its gradual policy of developing a competitive market economy as the principal determinant of sustained growth. The country has good long-term potential for growth due to its extensive natural resources and a relatively high level of human capital. To utilize this strong potential, the authorities need to continue the process of structural adjustment to encourage private investment and to develop free and competitive markets. Since independence, the republic has made progress in a number of important areas. Prices of consumer goods were liberalized. State-owned small enterprises were privatized and the services sector was opened up to private initiatives, resulting in rapid expansion of private businesses in the service sector in 1996. Prices of oil and oil products were brought closer to world market levels, but the state orders system still partially remains in place for grain and cotton. Finally, a large reform agenda needs to be completed to promote rapid and sustainable economic growth.

Economic recovery also contributed to the growth of employment. The decline in the number of people formally employed has been small relative to that experienced in other parts of the former Soviet Union. The small decrease in the number of people employed in the industrial, agricultural, trade and government services sectors during 1991–3 largely reflected the lack of restructuring in these sectors. The number of people who were registered as unemployed increased from 1,441 in July 1992 to 14,400 in September 1993, though the actual number of unemployed was considered to be higher.[35] According to the official statistics, the total population of the country stood at 24.3 million people in late-1998 while the work force in 1998 was about 8.8 million. The official data however, include substantial hidden unemployment in the state-owned enterprises and in the rural areas, as enterprises and collective farms often retain surplus employees to avoid massive layoffs. Officially, registered unemployment remained low in 1996, at about 0.4 per cent, rising in 1998 to 0.5 per cent of the 'economically active population'.[36] The Ministry of Labour estimated that as many as one million persons were unemployed, especially in the rural areas. Many of these earned incomes from informal sector activities. Wage differences among sectors widened substantially in 1996 and continued in 1998 and 1999. Average wages in the public sector increased more rapidly in the financial, information and computer services and industry sectors than in the agricultural, education and health care sectors. The average wage in the agriculture sector was 42 per cent of that in the financial sector in 1995, falling to 30 per cent in 1996.[37] Growing wage differentials have led qualified personnel in the education, health and science sectors to move to other sectors, and often to private enterprises and joint ventures. In 1996, wages in the public sector increased sharply in real terms. Minimum and average wages fell by about 70 per cent and 40 per cent in real terms respectively during 1994–5. These were readjusted in 1996 and increased by 55 per cent and 31 per cent respectively, thereby raising the monthly minimum wage from 250 *Sums* at the beginning of the year to 600 *Sums* in December. While the real average wage in 1996 was already above its 1991 level, the real minimum wage in 1996 was only about half of its 1991 level. The minimum wage was further increased to 925 *Sums* per month and public sector wages were raised by almost 68 per cent in 1998. The readjustment of wages in 1998 increased real average wages further, thereby imposing an additional burden on the state's budget.

TABLE 4.9
Wages and employment, 1992–8*

	1992	1993	1994	1995	1996	1997	1998
Total population ('000s)	21,360	21,853	22,282	22,690	23,136	23,724	24,312
Working age population ('000s)	10,463	10,707	10,963	11,222	11,477	11,824	12,176
Employment ('000s*) of which:	8,271	8,259	8,150	8,449	8,558	8,680	8,800
Industry	1,147	1,167	1,067	1,087	1,107	1,109	1,114
Agriculture and forestry	2,225	2,238	2,180	2,095	2,115	3,515	3,467
Transport and communication	367	348	218	235	239	360	362
Construction	598	561	520	528	539	550	573
Trade and public catering	452	456	565	705	710	715	717
Other services	1,939	1,909	1,996	2,009	2,053	2,074	2,577
Official number of unemployed ('000s)	–	29.0	29.4	31.0	33.8	35.4	40.1
Official unemployment rate (%)	–	0.3	0.4	0.4	0.4	0.4	0.5
Monthly minimum wage (in *Sums*)	1.0	9.3	69.6	175.0	417.0	675.0	925.0
Real monthly minimum wage (index 1991=100)	83.4	121.2	72.3	35.4	54.9	40.0	68.0
Monthly minimum wage in US dollars**	4.8	8.7	10.7	5.7	10.0	10.0	9.8
Monthly average wage in *Sums*	2.3	28.7	305.0	1,072.5	2,166.0	3,697.2	5,414.0
Real monthly average wage (index 1991=100)	78.1	154.2	116.7	94.6	124.2	69.0	72.0
Monthly average wage in US dollars**	10.9	26.4	38.0	35.0	53.9	55.7	57.1

Notes:
* Data includes only the public sector, (budgetary organizations and state-owned enterprises).
** At the official exchange rate.

Sources: Ministry of Macroeconomics and Statistics; IMF, *Republic of Uzbekistan: Recent Economic Developments*, Staff Country Report nos. 97/98 (1997) and 00/36 (2000); Centre for Economic Research, Tashkent.

Sectoral development

The agricultural and industrial sectors have traditionally been of great importance to the economy of the country. In the late-1980s, the share of NMP accounted for by agriculture rose from around 34 per cent in 1987 to over 40 per cent in 1990 due to good crop years and annual rises in livestock and poultry production in 1988–90 (see Table 4.10).[38] These gains, however, were not maintained in 1992 as agricultural production decreased by about 7 per cent in real terms. Agricultural production improved slightly in 1993, owing to the improved cotton crop and the increased efforts of the Uzbek government to raise production of fruit and vegetables through the transfer of small plots of land to private individuals and farms. Agricultural NMP in 1993 declined by only 1.1 per cent in real terms in comparison with a fall of about 7 per cent in 1992. The fall in industrial output in the late 1980s and early 1990s was, however, concentrated in the machinery, metallurgy, and chemical sectors. Industrial production declined by almost 13 per cent in 1992 and it further declined by about 8 per cent in 1993. The construction sector has also declined in relative importance in recent years, but the services sector has grown, while the transportation and communication sector, as a percentage of total output, remained relatively stable.

TABLE 4.10
Sectoral share of NMP (as a percentage of total)

Title	1991	1992	1993	1994	1995	1996*	1997*	1998*
Agriculture	45.0	41.2	30.8	41.3	34.8	32.6	34.4	35.7
Industry	29.7	32.6	29.0	21.5	20.7	18.0	16.0	15.0
Construction	12.3	11.3	11.7	9.1	9.6	10.2	8.6	8.6
Transport and communication	3.9	6.0	7.1	8.0	7.0	7.0	7.0	6.4
Services**	6.1	6.8	6.6	10.4	9.3	26.4	29.4	28.4

Notes:
*Centre for Economic Research, Tashkent.
**Includes trade and catering, and government sector.
Sources: Ministry of Macroeconomics and Statistics; World Bank.

Agriculture

The agricultural sector, which has been dominated by cotton production, plays a pivotal role in the overall economy. In the past the country's agricultural sector was characterized by low yields, high input use and spoilage, and large distortions caused by price controls, the state orders system and input subsidies.[39] There are five main agricultural regions: Surkhandarya, the Fergana Valley, Samarkand, Syrdarya and Bukhara. The sector accounted for about 30 per cent of GDP, about 60 per cent of total exports and 40 per cent of employment in 1996. Agriculture is still the backbone of the Uzbek economy accounting for about 36 per cent of GDP, about 60 per cent of total export and 45 per cent of employment. It also contributes substantially to the development of trade services and the food processing industry. Uzbekistan has developed an important domestic fertilizer industry based on its domestic natural gas resources. Although livestock products are of significance, agriculture is predominantly based on crops and is entirely irrigated. From 1960 until the early 1980s, land under irrigation and cultivation increased from 2.3 million hectares to 4.2 million hectares. However, technology was not improved during this period and output growth declined in the second half of the 1980s as investment was curtailed and water resources and agricultural land were overexploited. The country's two main water sources, the Amu Darya and Syrdarya Rivers, were diverted to inefficient irrigation systems, and inadequate water pricing resulted in considerable environmental damage to the region, including the desiccation of the Aral Sea.

The agricultural sector specialized in the production of cotton for export to other countries of the former Soviet Union until 1991. It was also among the largest producers of fruit and vegetables in the former USSR. In contrast, during the Soviet era, food crops were not cultivated to a great extent in the republic. Grain and livestock products were imported from Russia, Ukraine and Kazakhstan. Uzbekistan produced only 25 per cent of its domestic grain needs, the rest being imported along with sugar, meat, poultry, cooking oil, fruit and vegetables. The impact of the break-up of the USSR on traditional economic linkages, including disruptions in trade and payments arrangements and adverse movements in the terms of trade, resulted in a cumulative decline in real sectoral output by 11 per cent during 1991–5, though real output recovered by 2.3 per cent in 1995.[40] However, the Uzbek government managed to establish alternative and more advantageous markets for cotton exports to improve the balance of payments position, while simultaneously seeking to reduce the sector's 'cotton-monoculture' production structure by emphasizing a shift towards grain production.

In addition, domestic production of high-quality fertilizers provided the agriculture sector with almost 70 per cent of its nitric fertilizer requirements and about 50 per cent of its phosphorus fertilizer requirements. These developments shielded the sector from the severe output and income contractions experienced in neighbouring countries such as Kazakstan and Kyrgyzstan.

In 1995 the level of cotton production remained similar to that of 1994 (see Table 4.11). However, the production of grain, principally wheat, rose by 57 per cent and food imports, as a percentage of total imports, declined sharply from about 33 per cent in 1994 to 18 per cent in 1995.[41] The total cropped area in the same year exceeded 4 million hectares; cotton accounted for 46.2 per cent of that area and nearly 50 per cent of crop production; grain accounted for 47.6 per cent of the area and almost 37 per cent of crop production. Fruit and vegetables accounted for only 6 per cent of the total cropped area, but they accounted for 15 per cent of total crop production. In 1990 grain production was 1.9 million tons and the area under grain was 1 million hectares. By 1995, grain (excluding rice) increased to 2.7 million tons while the area under grain decreased. The sharp growth in grain production was achieved mainly by reducing land under cotton. As a result cotton output fell from 5 million tons in 1990 to 3.4 million tons in 1996. Rapid and sustainable agricultural growth, however, was restricted by sectoral inefficiencies. Cotton yields declined from 2.7 tons per hectare in 1991 to 2.2 tons in 1996 and 2.09 in 1998 per hectare. Grain yields at 1.9 tons per hectare in 1996 were low by international standards. Agricultural output experienced a severe contraction of about 7 per cent in 1996. The main causes of this were bad weather conditions, deteriorating irrigation facilities, and shortages of fuel, spare parts, fertilizers and pesticides. Due to the decline in the sector, the share of agriculture in GDP decreased from 28 per cent in 1995 to 23 per cent in 1996. Production of cotton fell by about 15 per cent from an average of 4 million tons during 1993–5. Horticulture was also adversely affected by bad weather conditions in 1996 and as a result, the production of fruit and vegetables fell by 9 per cent and 3 per cent, respectively. By contrast, grain production grew from 3.5 million tons in 1996 to 3.7 million tons in 1997, largely due to an increase in the total area under grain. Agricultural production increased by 5.8 per cent in 1997 and again slowed to 4 per cent in 1998. The total sown area was 4.14 and 4.03 million hectares in 1997 and 1998 respectively. The sown area of cotton made up over 1.5 million hectares, and grain made up over 1.6 million hectares. The increase in grain production reflects the government's policy of diversifying agricultural production away from cotton to gain self-sufficiency. The area planted with grain made up 38 per cent of the total cultivated areas in 1998 representing a 22 per cent increase since 1995, and the average yield of wheat per hectare was 2.58 tons representing an increase by 81 per cent compared to 1994. The total grain output in 1998 was over the government's target of 4 million tons.

TABLE 4.11
Production of main agricultural products ('000s of tons)

Title	1991	1992	1993	1994	1995	1996	1997	1998
Cotton	4,645.8	4,128.3	4,234.5	3,937.8	3,978.0	3,350.1	3,641	3,236
Grain (in total)	1,908.2	2,257.2	2,142.4	2,466.9	3,215.3	3,549.2	3,788	4,148
of which:								
Wheat and Barley	973.0	1,333.4	1,176.0	1,675.0	2,680.4	2,948.1	3,073	3,556
Rice	514.9	538.9	544.6	498.3	327.6	445.2	394	373
Potatoes	351.2	365.3	472.4	567.1	439.9	490.0	686	692
Vegetables	3,348.0	3,494.3	3,038.7	2,975.3	2,724.7	2,481.0	2,348	2,403
Fruit	516.0	701.5	560.1	555.1	602.3	584.9	546	543
Milk	3,331.4	3,679.2	3,764.0	3,733.4	3,665.4	3,309.3	3,406	3,495
Meat	800.2	777.0	814.1	827.2	852.9	854.3	461	472
Eggs (millions)	2,347.0	1,897.7	1,787.8	1,573.6	1,251.8	1,056.9	1,075	1,165
Wool	25.3	27.4	26.6	24.9	19.5	14.9	15	15
Sheepskin (unit)	1,475.8	1,603.8	1,617.1	1,540.2	1,392.9	1,370.0	1,411	803
Silk cocoons	33.8	33.2	29.6	22.9	23.7	21.7	21	20

Sources: Ministry of Macroeconomics and Statistics; IMF, *Republic of Uzbekistan: Recent Economic Developments*, Staff Country Report nos. 97/98 (1997) and 00/36 (2000); TACIS, *Uzbek Economic Trends*, *First Quarter* (1999).

The quality and quantity of the stock of agricultural equipment were not consistent with changes in the structure of production and area cultivated, even as new forms of production were being created. A three to four-fold reduction in the annual availability of equipment resulted in delayed agricultural activity, leading to a decline in agricultural yields as well as increased labour costs. The government's current objective is to improve the performance of the sector through stricter enforcement of administrative directives, introduction of higher yielding technology, and the gradual improvement of producers' incentives. Accordingly a programme of production was recently undertaken in pursuit of these objectives. In response to the relatively poor harvest in 1996, a number of administrators at the *oblast, rayon* and farm levels were replaced. New technology for the production of cotton under plastic sheeting was introduced on 13 per cent of the cotton area in 1997.[42] A programme was developed to supply modern technology through joint ventures with companies from the United Kingdom, Germany, the United States and Israel. The modern equipment is intended to increase yields moderately, and to shorten the vegetative period for cotton. The programme will enable domestic production by the year 2003 to meet demand for universal tractors, cultivators, sowing and oil-cultivating equipment, as well as fodder-picking and cotton-picking machinery.

The government retained a system of planned production targets for wheat and cotton, combined with state orders for their marketing, storage, processing and distribution. Other products are formally free of mandatory orders for production or marketing. The production of cotton for 1997 was 3,641 million tons and grain was 3,788 million tons, this constituting the aggregate production plan that was allocated at the regional and district levels. Based on the regional level plan, local officials encouraged farm enterprises to enter into contracts with procurement organs for the total quantity of wheat and cotton corresponding to the planned yields on the planned areas. The production plan at the territorial level was thus translated into contractual commitments for delivery at the farm level, requiring farms to deliver the entire amount of their planned cotton production. Contractual commitments for grain were in general, less than planned production, since some grain was retained for use on the farm. Of the total contractual commitment, a portion was designated as the state order quantity. In 1996, the state order proportion of total targeted output was 60 per cent of total cotton production and 50 per cent of total grain production. The procurement targets were further reduced to 25 per cent of total grain production in 1996 and for cotton the procurement targets have been reduced to 40 per cent in the same year. Producers of cotton were required to deliver the full contracted amount, not just the state order quantity. (According to Article 3 of Decree No. 295 of the Cabinet of Ministers dated 22 August 1996, producers of cotton are required to do so.) Those who fulfilled the targets for procurement were paid a higher price for 60 per cent of their delivery. Those who did not fulfil procurement contracts received the state order price, which was 12,500 *Sums* per ton of raw cotton in 1996 for all of their delivery. In 1996, aggregate production of cotton fell 15 per cent short of actual production in 1995, and 16 per cent short of planned production for 1996. Therefore, many producers did not meet their farm level production plans, and could not receive prices higher than the state order price. As a result, over 60 per cent of the 1996 crop was sold at the procurement price of 12,500 *Sums* per ton of raw cotton. Those who were able to receive the higher price marketed their above plan cotton directly through the state processing company *Uzkhlobkopromzbet* in 1996. This monopoly collects all cotton and processes it in 135 state-owned ginning mills. Although the prices of cotton and grain were increased substantially in 1994–6 and converged towards world market prices, the producer price for grain under the state orders system was raised to 50 per cent of the equivalent world market price in 1995. A similar price rise was initiated for cotton under the state orders system, but despite several price adjustments, the real prices of both cotton and grain continued to remain below their respective export and import parity prices at the farm gate. This is largely because of the presence of a few monopsonists. The presence of large vertically integrated associations specializing in the procurement and marketing of these two important agricultural products precludes competition for farm products at the farm level and keeps producer prices depressed substantially below the prices that would prevail under competitive market conditions. Grain producers were, however, required to sell 1.95 million tons, about 50 per cent of planned production for 3.9 million tons in 1996. The state order price was set at 4,800 *Sums* per ton and the producers sold 1.9 million tons of grain to the state, about 70 per cent of actual production and most of this was probably at the state order price. To stimulate agricultural producers, the government adopted a programme for further economic reforms in the agricultural sector in March 1998. The long-term policy goals commencing in 2001 are to increase gradually the importance of private farms and to encourage competitive agricultural production.

Industry
Industry, including mining and energy, accounted for over 30 per cent of NMP in the republic in the late 1980s, corresponding to over 25 per cent of GDP in 1991. Employment in this sector accounted for almost 25 per cent of total employment. In 1990, heavy industry, including electricity, machine building, metallurgy, fuel, chemicals and

paper, accounted for over 40 per cent of total industrial output, while light industry, mainly textiles, provided about 39 per cent. Before the break-up of the Soviet Union, industrial activity was relatively dynamic. Annual output grew on average by 3 per cent in the second half of the 1980s. The industrial structure comprised about 2,000 enterprises employing over 900,000 workers. Light industry accounted for the largest number of enterprises and employed almost an equivalent number of workers as that employed in heavy industry. The industrial sector of Uzbekistan was integrated into the centralized production system of the former Soviet Union. Almost 75 per cent of inputs were obtained from the other Soviet republics and about 60 per cent of industrial output was shipped to other parts of the former Soviet Union.[43] The establishment of industries' assets during the Soviet period was guided by their strategic importance in the system of the Union, rather than by supply and demand criteria or productive capacity. The structure and organization of this sector under the Soviet system inhibited competition, and undermined efficiency in the production and distribution of goods. Production was organized in line with the state orders system where prices of outputs and inputs were extensively regulated. Many enterprises combined in vertically structured groups of associations or amalgamations, responsible to the various branches of the former Ministries which controlled all subsector activities and dominated markets and local transport and distribution networks. This highly centralized system had an adverse impact on the sector following the sudden and unexpected collapse of the economic ties established over the previous decades. During 1991–5 there was a sharp decrease of over 20 per cent in industrial output due mainly to shortages and higher prices of inputs from other countries of the former Soviet Union. There was also a sharp decline in demand from the former Soviet republics for final products. Faced with increasing difficulty in securing inputs and hardening budget constraints, many enterprises simply stopped producing and tried to reduce their inventories. However, the deterioration in output in Uzbekistan was less severe than in neighbouring countries. The mining subsector remained largely under government control. Planning, exploration and production were guided by the State Committee on Geology and Mineral Resources. Private initiative was confined to the participation of joint ventures in mining. Gold production is the country's second largest export earner, accounting for about 15 per cent of export earnings. The annual production of gold has been estimated at about 60–70 tons (see Table 4.12) and most of it is mined at the giant Muruntau gold mine in Navoi province.[44] Gold exports have been a steady source of hard currency earnings, contributing to the country's stable balance of payments position. Gold production in Uzbekistan is internationally competitive and has therefore attracted foreign interest in joint ventures. This subsector also produces significant amounts of silver and copper. Production of copper has averaged over 80,000 tons a year. Most of the copper ore is obtained from two mines and is processed at a concentrator at Almalyk. There is also a growing energy sector, stimulated by the policy of import substitution. The rest of industry is largely concerned with making agricultural machinery and there is some agricultural processing.

TABLE 4.12
Production of main industrial products (in '000 tons)

	1991	1992	1993	1994	1995	1996	1997	1998
Gold*	–	64.5	66.6	64.4	63.6	71.0	82.0	n/a
Cars	–	–	–	0.082	0.300	25,358	64,908	54,456
Television Sets	–	–	16,378	51,795	64,893	139,590	268,450	192,468
Video-recorders	–	–	6,505	23,924	25,280	100,025	140,567	50,096

Note:
*Ministry of Macroeconomics and Statistics; IMF, *Republic of Uzbekistan: Recent Economic Developments*, Staff Country Report no. 00/36 (2000).

Source: IEU *Uzbekistan Country Report*, 1st quarter 1998 and 4th quarter 1999.

The most significant natural energy resources are natural gas and oil, and coal production which has decreased from 3 million tons in 1995 to about 2.5 million tons in 1997, due mainly to the substitution of gas for coal in household use. Two-thirds of the primary energy supply is provided by natural gas. Uzbekistan was the third largest producer of natural gas in the former Soviet Union, after the Russian Federation and Turkmenistan. It is now the major resource in domestic energy production. In 1997 natural gas production accounted for over 80 per cent of domestically produced energy supplies, with an output of over 50 billion cubic metres, surpassing even Turkmenistan. Production expanded by over 20 per cent during 1991–7.[45] Proven natural gas reserves have continued to increase and in 1996 they were estimated at over 2 trillion cubic metres. However, due to domestic demand for gas and the large availability of natural gas in Turkmenistan, the country's exports of gas have fallen considerably. Net exports decreased from over 10 billion cubic metres in 1990 to under 5 billion cubic metres in 1996. The largest volume of exports went to Kazakstan, followed by the Kyrgyz republic and Tajikistan. The Karakalpak autonomous republic and the Khorezm region of Uzbekistan used to obtain gas from Turkmenistan and an equivalent quantity was sold by Uzbekistan to Kazakstan. In 1993, a new pipeline was constructed to transmit gas directly to Karakalpakistan. The republic's two most important natural gasfields are the giant Shurtam gasfield, which currently produces about 20 billion cubic metres of gas, and the Moberek gasfield, which processes about 30 billion cubic metres of gas. All oil and gas production operations connected with prospecting, exploitation, processing and distribution of oil and gas were merged into one agency, *Uzbekneftegas*, with a workforce staff of over 85,000. This agency is headed by a deputy prime minister and reports directly to the Cabinet of Ministers.[46] Its chairman, K. Khakkulov, is responsible for monitoring the fuel and energy complex. Oil and gas exploration activities have remained under the jurisdiction of the State Committee on Geology. The distribution of natural gas within the country is handled by *OBLGAS* under the auspices of the Ministry of Housing and Utilities. An association, the *UZTRANGAS*, operates the uniform gas supply system and sets transportation charges and transit fees. The agency, *Uzbekcoal (UGOL)*, is responsible for the coal subsector and has a workforce of about 30,000. It is responsible for coal production and related activities through a number of enterprises that together constitute *UGOL*. The government of Uzbekistan continued to pursue a policy of energy self-sufficiency in 1996. Production of petroleum products and natural gas increased significantly during that year. With foreign participation and domestic budgetary support, substantial further investment in the sector took place, particularly relating to the Bukhara oil refinery which started operating in 1997. The total production of oil in 1991 was only 2.8 million tons, but production since independence has increased, rising to 7.9 million tons in 1997. Production expanded further with the discovery of two new oilfields: the Minbulak field in the Fergana Valley and the Kokdumalak oil and gas condensate field in Bukhara province near the border with Turkmenistan. The total production of oil rose to 8.1 million tons in 1999. With these developments the republic is expected to increase its exports of gas from 5 million cubic metres, to over 10 million cubic metres, and the country is expected to be exporting about one million tons of oil by the end of 2000.

The republic also plays a strategic role in the electricity trade of Central Asia. Uzbekistan generated over 47 million kilowatt hours of electricity in 1995. Electricity production decreased to 45.9 millions of kilowatt hours in 1998, due mainly to payment difficulties in neighbouring countries importing electricity from Uzbekistan. Of the 47 million kilowatt hours produced in 1995, 74 per cent was generated from natural gas, 15 per cent from hydroelectric power and about 6 per cent each from fuel and coal. The regional generator is located in Tashkent and its electricity generation capacity expanded by over 66 per cent during the last decade. But the economy is also highly energy intensive – the republic is the fourth largest consumer of energy among the CIS republics. The country has been using 35 to 50 per cent more energy than might be expected in comparison to other countries with similar per capita income.[47] The low price of energy does not seem to provide incentives for efficient energy use, such as the use of energy-efficient appliances or energy-efficient industrial processes. The potential for boosting oil and gas production in the country is significant. Large oil and gas condensate fields have been discovered, but substantial investment is required to exploit them. The full development of the discovered fields is beyond available domestic technology and resources, and so attracting foreign investment into the oil and gas sectors has become a priority. Foreign investment is also important in the rehabilitation of old fields and refineries. The financial situation in the power subsector is also deteriorating due to the increase in the cost of inputs and inadequate tariffs. Electricity demand is set to decline over the next few years both in the neighbouring countries and in Uzbekistan as the restructuring of their economies proceeds. To prevent a financial crisis and a systemic breakdown, the authorities needs to address tariff increases at once and the republic should also pursue opportunities to export electricity to other countries.

Transport and communication
Seven organizations, each with ministerial status, are responsible for the transport and communications sectors in Uzbekistan.[48] The republic has a well-developed transport system built during the Soviet era. Cities are well laid out with tree-lined boulevards. Traffic density is low even in the

capital Tashkent. There is an extensive urban transportation infrastructure with 30 kilometres of metro, 288 kilometres of tramlines and 632 kilometres of trolley bus and bus routes. About 16,000 buses, 450 trolley buses, 424 trams, 149 metro cars and over 6,000 taxis provide public transportation in Tashkent. Many rural communities are quite remote from other populated areas and so depend on road connections. The total length of motor roads in Uzbekistan is about 83,000 kilometres, including 43,000 kilometres of national roads. The remainder come under the responsibility of provincial authorities and enterprises. In addition to national roads, there is 3,656 kilometres of railway lines. Rail transport comprises over 60 per cent of all freight movement and almost 20 per cent of passenger travel by public means. The following organizations are in charge of various sectors: *Uzavtoyul* is in charge of public roads and highways; *Uzbekistan Temir Yullari* is responsible for railways; *Uzavtotrans* controls the numerous entities involved in road transport; Uzbekistan Airways is in charge of civil aviation, including airlines, airports and air traffic control; *Tashgorpastrans* is responsible for urban transport facilities in Tashkent; the Ministry of Communications is in charge of telecommunications, postal services, and national broadcasting and finally *Uzbektranstroi* is a government-owned contractor which constructs transport infrastructure. The country's air routes connect Tashkent with many regional centres and CIS countries. There are currently 18 international routes serving Tashkent, including direct flights to London, Frankfurt, Istanbul, New Delhi and Seoul. Uzbekistan is a member of the International Civil Aviation Organization (ICAO). The communication system in the republic reflects the different priorities of the Soviet period; inadequate investment, obsolete equipment, and low quality service are still prevalent today. The country has just over 1.4 million telephone lines with a telephone density of 6.7 lines per 100 inhabitants. This rate is extremely low compared to International Union standards. For example, the equivalent rate in Germany is 44.8, in France it is 52.3, in the United Kingdom it is 45.1 and even in Turkey it is 16.2 lines per 100 inhabitants. At present in Uzbekistan less than half of urban households, and less than one-tenth of rural households, have a telephone.[49]

Although the road and railway infrastructure is reasonably well developed, it has become outmoded for present and anticipated requirements. The majority of national roads are not in a good condition. Road maintenance has been undertaken infrequently. Today a lack of capital funds makes maintenance increasingly difficult to accomplish, despite the increase in the number of automobiles. Much of the transport stock, including buses, coaches, trucks, railway locomotives and wagons, is technologically outdated and inappropriate for serving the more demanding requirements. Airports and passenger services do not meet ICAO standards. Air traffic control utilizes obsolete electronic equipment which also fails to meet international standards. Levels of noise and radiation caused by radio equipment exceed normal levels by more than ten times during landing and take-off. Air buses that were used for international flights have been replaced with more modern ones but there are still no plans to improve the conditions of internal flights.

The material and technical base for telecommunications in Uzbekistan lags thirty years behind developed countries. It is characterized by inadequate and underdeveloped communications equipment, networks and services. There is a lack of up-to-date high-speed networks for data transfer, and too much obsolete equipment. The country also maintains an obsolete analogue system, which provides no more than 15 types of service, at a time when developed countries utilize digital systems that provide up to 180 various types of services.[50] The government continued to focus on improving the telecommunications sector during 1998 with the assistance of several major telecommunication firms. Some progress was made in upgrading existing networks and installing new technology, but this work has so far covered the Tashkent area only. Better quality telecommunications and transformation infrastructure will improve international trade and the domestic economy and help Uzbekistan become a key link in the growing trade between Asia and Europe. Only the development of an efficient and reliable transport and communications sector will enable this to happen.

Construction, trade and services
The construction sector in Uzbekistan has experienced a severe decline in activity in recent years, contracting by 42 per cent in real terms during 1992 and by an estimated 6 per cent in 1993. Much of the decrease in construction activity accounts for about one-quarter of all construction work and has been concentrated on construction of housing, small enterprises and shops, and private farm facilities. Growth in the trading and services sector has been particularly strong since mid-1996, as the private sector began responding to domestic and external trade

liberalization and the privatization of retail shops. Increased activity took place in domestic wholesale and retail trading, restaurants and bars, consulting, auditing and legal services. In the republic, an average of twenty retail enterprises occupying a total of 1,351 square metres of sale space serve over 10,000 people. The urban averages of these indicators are 27 enterprises and 1,963 square metres, while rural averages are at about 16 enterprises covering 963 square metres.[51] The regional distribution of labour, ecological conditions and demographic trends have influenced the character of the service industry in many regions. For example, the economic structure and development of the Fergana Valley increased incomes in the region and stimulated the growth of the service industry. The per capita rate of trade and services is higher in regions like Tashkent, which possess higher rates of employment in industry and construction. The lowest rate of provision of services is in the autonomous region of Karakalpakistan, which has a low population density, a weak economic structure, and ecological problems arising from the desiccation of the Aral Sea.

The underdevelopment of the service industry diminishes labour productivity and leisure time. The consumer market in the Soviet era was characterized by fixed prices, restricted goods and black market trade. Long lines for scarce commodities were a common sight in cities, while in rural centres the choice of goods was extremely narrow. As Uzbekistan specialized in cotton production, the republic had to import over 40 per cent of all consumer goods and experienced shortages in almost one-third of all essential goods. Consequently, people in rural areas experienced the lowest level of retail services. Although over 60 per cent of the country's population lived in rural areas, less than 40 per cent of all products were available in rural communities. The economic reforms, price liberalization and privatization of the commercial and service industries have expanded the selection of goods and increased their availability. The commercial network has been extended considerably in many cities through private construction. In the country's major cities, stores contain more products and the colourful and vibrant bazaars enrich the architectural landscape, selling a wide variety of food products, traditional crafts made by local artisans, and many consumer goods. However, the expansion of commerce, particularly in the large provinces and major cities, has prompted a decline in specialization, and many of the newer and smaller enterprises do not have the capacity to sell modern commercial and technological products. Contrary to some expectations, the expansion of commerce has increased rather than decreased monopolization in different forms.

The fall in production in some subsectors has been offset by rises in others, reflecting the government's policy of shifting the structure of the economy in a more industrialized direction. Substantial government-led investment has taken place in the energy sector and a number of large-scale foreign direct investment projects have commenced operation, though vigorous domestic private sector development is yet to emerge. By the end of 1997 there were over 3,000 registered joint ventures involving Uzbek partners and firms from more than eighty countries. The major joint ventures include UzDaewoo of South Korea which is engaged in car manufacturing, telecommunications, electronic home appliances, textile spinning and weaving mills. The total amount of its investment in Uzbekistan, by the end of 1997, stood at $1.7 billion.[52] Another big joint venture is the Zarafshan-Newmont and Angreen Gold Mining projects with the USA. The state-owned Navoi Mining and Metallurgical Kombinat held a 57 per cent stake in Amantaytau Goldfields. Another 35 per cent was held by UK company, Lonrho, with 8 per cent held by the International Finance corporation. Finally, UzBAT, the British American-Uzbekistan Tobacco company, has invested over $230 million which has been assigned to reconstruct and modernize the tobacco industry in Uzbekistan.

Poverty and social protection

Most researchers who have dealt with the economic transitional countries of the former Soviet Union consider poverty to be a new phenomena in these former socialist states. They perceive poverty as stemming from the difficulties of the transitional period and from the disruption of links that bound together the members of the former USSR. While this theory may be correct for some countries, it fails to explain poverty not only in Uzbekistan but also in other Central Asian republics. In reality, socialism failed to create a society in which people in the Union enjoyed equal incomes and standards of living nor it did sufficiently achieve income equality during the course of the whole Soviet period. In the wake of the break-up of the Soviet Union, the Gini coefficient was 0.234 in Russia, and 0.285 in Uzbekistan. A noticeable differentiation of income also existed between families with European origin and of those indigenous people. In Uzbekistan only 20 per cent of the European families had low incomes, compared to over 54 per cent of the indigenous families.[53] The ineffectiveness of socialist economics fostered 'equality in poverty'. Although one could argue that the majority of the population belonged to the middle strata according to their income level, many people lived in poverty while others enjoyed opulent prosperity. Under Soviet rule, ideological dogma impeded the recognition of poverty in the USSR. Budget analyses of households were conducted by the government but information was available only to a few officials and the available official statistics tried to cover up the real situation. In fact, when Uzbekistan was part of the Soviet Union, a significant part of the rural population was receiving incomes less than the minimum wage. The acknowledgement of poverty in the former Soviet Union became possible only in the late 1980s. In general people who received an income less than the minimum wage were considered to be poor. In Uzbekistan about 45 per cent of the population fell into this category.[54] These consisted primarily of rural inhabitants and members of groups such as pensioners, orphans, widows, lone parents (usually female-headed households) and disabled people. Over the course of *perestroika* high inflation contributed to an increase in the number of relatively poor people. By 1991, about 75 per cent of the total population was living in relative poverty. In the transition period, the problem of poverty became more of a burden since other groups were suddenly confronted with low incomes. Some of these groups once had medium and high levels of income, including doctors, teachers, scientists, government officials, and employees of enterprises, and are now facing financial difficulties associated with structural adjustments.

Since independence, the Uzbek government has undertaken a number of measures to lessen the impact of social costs deriving from the transition process. It has ensured that all citizens continue to have access to health care services and education. Since 1992 all inhabitants have gained ownership of their formerly state-owned flats and houses, which were sold for nominal sums or handed over free of charge. Many families received plots of lands for their personal use. The government has remained committed to creating job opportunities, especially in the rural areas, and maintaining social services as well as social protection for vulnerable groups. Various benefits, transfers and allowances from the state budget have been provided for low income families. The Employment Fund pays unemployment benefits for six months to people officially registered unemployed or those undergoing retraining. In 1994 new forms of targeted social assistance for families with low income, single pensioners and the disabled were introduced. The traditional community associations, *mahallas*, are used to identify needy households and to determine an appropriate level of benefits. As there is no reliable system of monitoring household income and expenditure patterns, this arrangement seems to be useful at present. Allowances currently include a childbirth lump-sum grant, maternity allowances, child benefits up to 16 years of age to cover part of the expenses of child rearing, and material assistance to low income families. Families receive fixed lump-sum grants equal to two minimum salaries for the birth of a child. Since 1995 mothers also receive money for child care which has increased to 925 *Sums* per month, and the term of coverage has been lengthened from 18 months to two years. Child benefit is paid to all families regardless of the parents' income. The maximum allowances available for families with five–six children consists of 175 per cent of the official minimum wage. Family allowance, which is about one and a half times the minimum salary for three months, does soften differences in per capita income between small and large families. However, the amounts are insufficient to bridge the gap completely and most poor families received it only once in 1996. Although the government has attempted to minimize the social cost of the transition to a market economy, living standards still remain low and poverty was still believed to be high in 1999. The Ministry of Labour estimated that, in 1999, 24 per cent of the total population were living below the official poverty line, the monthly minimum wage of 925 *Sums* or about $6 at the official exchange rate. Independent sources put this figure as high as 35 per cent of the country's total population.

Conclusion

For decades the economy of Uzbekistan was integrated into the overall Soviet command system and its pattern of economic development was determined by the needs and requirements of the Centre. Accordingly Uzbekistan was forced to forsake the growing of grain and other food products and accept a cotton monoculture to provide raw materials for the Soviet textile industry. However, if the cotton monoculture was built on colonial exploitation by Moscow, it nonetheless enabled the republic to become one of the world's largest producers and second top exporter of this important commodity. But, the republic has had to contend with difficult economic conditions affecting all major sectors since its independence in 1991. Real gross domestic product plunged by 18 per cent between 1990 and 1995. Real per capita GDP also fell sharply during the same period while inflation and fiscal deficits rose dramatically. In response to the economic difficulties, the government undertook programmes of macroeconomic stabilization and structural reform to arrest the economic decline and protect its people from bearing the full brunt of the recession. It demonstrated its ability to generate important flows of income from Uzbekistan's large stock of natural resources and to diversify quickly the country's exports to non-traditional markets as there had been severe disruptions in traditional trade markets with the break-up of the USSR. The economy started to recover in 1996 and real GDP grew by 2.5 per cent in 1997, and a further increase of 4.4 per cent achieved in 1999. Inflation was cut from a staggering 1,300 per cent in 1994 to a relatively modest 26 per cent in 1998, while the balance of payments position improved enormously. The fiscal deficit was reduced substantially as a result of government measures to raise revenues and rationalize public expenditures. The republic successfully introduced its national currency, the *Sum*, in 1994 and international reserves have been accumulated.

While Uzbekistan has several economic achievements to its credit, there are still serious challenges to overcome. Projections of its medium-term economic prospects are still difficult to make as the government and the IMF have yet to agree a clear-cut medium-term macroeconomic programme. In the face of the economic shocks suffered in 1996, the priorities of the government have focused on issues concerning short-term economic management, though there are indications that the leadership wishes to deepen the process of structural reform. A stable macroeconomic environment is crucial to draw in financial support from international aid organizations, elicit foreign investment and encourage domestic private investment, which will promote the growth of productivity, employment and incomes. The republic has made some progress in moving towards macroeconomic stabilization, but the stabilization process remains fragile. The government has taken some initial steps to establish a modern and effective banking system, but the financial sector remains weak. Many banks have limited experience in dealing with commercial operations. Banking regulations, supervision, and the management and performance of the banking system remains poor. The national currency is still weak and moves towards the full convertibility of the currency will probably be delayed further. Following the restrictions imposed on foreign currency transactions, a curb market has emerged for illegal foreign currency transactions, and this market rate has depreciated more rapidly than the official exchange rate. The gap between the official exchange rate and the 'free' market rose to about 400 per cent in the early 2000. Local and foreign firms continue to have problems gaining access to hard currency. However, large-scale foreign direct investors and foreign firms working solely with full foreign capital are given privileged access to hard currency.

The government's reform and privatization efforts are providing new opportunities for private sector participation in a variety of sectors. The privatization of small enterprises is now largely complete and the privatization of large state-owned enterprises is in progress. A number of large-scale foreign direct investment projects started operation in 1996, but a vigorous domestic private sector is yet to emerge. The majority of joint-stock companies and restructured enterprises in the industrial and agricultural sectors are weak and their production, in terms of output targets, exports and employment, is still very much determined by the various government ministries. In November 1998, the authorities announced that foreign investors would be allowed to own 100 per cent of some enterprises and majority shares in others such as Tashkent Local Telephone, Tashkent International Telephone, Andijon Cable and minority shares in enterprises that included Almalyk Mining, Tashkent Airport and the National Bank for Foreign Economic Activity. Despite the openness to foreign participation, direct investment from abroad has been slow to materialize due to the concerns about the business environment in the country. The country's external debt as a share of GDP has also increased from 18 per cent in 1998 to about 25 per cent by the end of September 1999.

In the agricultural sector, farms owe substantial debts to their suppliers and employees. Farmers are not provided with enough security of land tenure to create incentives for investing in land. There is already a large number of unemployed people in both rural and urban areas and this is poised to increase further as the government continues with the structural changes necessary for ensuring broad-based economic growth and an improvement in the overall business climate. Current efforts to initiate agricultural reforms are not adequately complemented by the institutional reforms. This has caused serious problems in production and has distorted the normal functioning of the economy. Many agricultural sectors are now run by associations, corporations and other organizations, but, the old command system of management remains in force in many agricultural entities. Government ministries, as well as some newly established associations and businesses, are yet to abandon the former command-management methods completely, with deleterious consequences for economic activity and the efficient operation of business. The number of middle-men and 'private tax collectors' involved in business activity has also increased.

Despite government efforts to improve people's living standards and frequent readjustments to wages, living standards for the majority remain low. The average salary can secure only the most basic needs of workers and their families. In most cases, a family earning an average salary cannot afford to take a vacation or visit relatives living in more remote states in the CIS. The financial difficulties confronting many local enterprises delay the payment of employees for several months. Many important fields such as health care and education face serious financial difficulties. Many medical facilities are located in unsuitable buildings with obsolete hospital equipment and a shortage of medicine. The construction of schools, hospitals, kindergartens and nursery schools is subject to long delays. Low salaries have forced many of the most qualified specialists to leave their jobs. In the field of social security the government has continued to protect the most vulnerable groups of the population. Although there is a genuine desire to provide social assistance to people in need, institutional mismanagement has hampered the achievement of this objective. There are three ministries directly involved with the development and implementation of social assistance benefits, and the *mahallas* as local self-managing bodies have the responsibility for determining which people suffer from absolute poverty. If there is not going to be a single agency with much better-trained staff, there must be better coordination among the agencies administering the benefits. Many individuals in need of social protection do not always find it easy to ask for it from the *mahalls* or the *Aksakal*, the head of the *mahalla* committee, who may occasionally be prejudiced when assessing the individual's entitlements to particular benefits.

NOTES

1. International Monetary Fund, *Uzbekistan Country Economic Review* (Washington, D.C.: IMF, 1992). See also Michael Kaser and Santosh Mehrotra, *The Central Asian Economies After Independence* (London: The Royal Institute of International Affairs, 1992).
2. Excellent background information on the chronology of events that led to the disintegration of the former Soviet Union's economy is in World Bank, *Country Study: Russian Economic Reform* (1992) especially Chapter 1, and *Uzbekistan: An Agenda for Economic Reform* (1993), pp. 1–9.
3. *Uzbekistan Human Development Report* (UNDP, 1995), p. 12.
4. International Monetary Fund, *Economic Review: Uzbekistan* (Washington, D.C.: IMF, 1994), p. 10, and Memorandum of the President of the International Bank for Reconstruction and Development to the Executive Directors on a Country Assistance Strategy of the World Bank Group for the Republic of Uzbekistan, 1995, p. 2.
5. IMF, op. cit., 1994, p. 10.
6. Information was obtained during my discussions with the IMF's representative in Tashkent in July 1996.
7. See also Shireen T. Hunter, *Central Asia Since Independence (The Washington Papers/168)*. (Washington, D.C.: The Center for Strategic and International Studies, 1996), pp. 73–4.
8. Information was obtained during my discussions with several local economists at the University of World Economy and Diplomacy and at Tashkent State University in 1996.
9. See also Hunter, op. cit., pp. 73–5.
10. Information was obtained during my discussions with local and non-local experts at the World Bank Office of Uzbekistan in Tashkent, August–September 1996.
11. See A. Lewis, *Economic Development with Unlimited Supplies of Labor* vol. 20 (New York: The Manchester School, 1954), pp. 139–91.
12. For a further discussion, see Hunter, op. cit., 1996, pp. 75–9.
13. See Islom Karimov, *Building The Future: Uzbekistan – Own Model for Transition to a Market Economy* (Tashkent: Uzbekiston, 1993).
14. Karimov, *Uzbekistan: Along the Road of Deepening Economic Reform* (Tashkent: Uzbekiston, 1995), pp. 9–11.
15. For a further discussion, see Alice H. Amsden, J. Kochanowicz and Lance Taylor, *The Market Meets Its Match: Restructuring the Economies of Eastern Europe* (Cambridge: Cambridge University Press, 1994). See also Stanislav Zhukov, 'Economic Development in the States of Central Asia' in Boris Rumer (ed.), *Central Asia: Dilemmas of Political and Economic Development* (Armonk, N.Y.: M.E. Sharpe, 1996), pp. 118–34.
16. See Karimov, op. cit., 1995, pp. 38–49, and *Uzbekistan Human Development Report* (Tashkent: UNDP, 1996), pp. 41–9.
17. See for further discussion, *Uzbekistan Human Development Report* (Tashkent: UNDP, 1996), pp. 41–52.

18 Keith Griffin, 'The Macroeconomic Framework and Development Strategy' in Griffin, op. cit., p. 37. See also World Bank, op. cit., p. 3.
19 Data were taken from the *State Committee for Forecasting and Statistics* in Tashkent, Summer 1996.
20 An excellent account of Uzbekistan's institutional reforms in agriculture is Azizur Rahman Khan, 'Transition to a Market Economy in Agriculture' in Griffin, op. cit., 1996, pp. 75–88. See also *Uzbekistan Human Development Report* (Tashkent: UNDP, 1996), pp. 31–40.
21 This information was provided by the *State Committee for Economic Forecasting and Statistics* in Tashkent in August 1996. See also Karimov, op. cit., 1996, pp. 52–66.
22 Azizur Rahman Khan, in Griffin, op. cit., 1996, p. 76.
23 See Karimov, op. cit., 1995, pp. 57–61.
24 See *Republic of Uzbekistan Decrees and Resolutions, Second Book* (Tashkent: Uzbekiston, 1994); *Republic of Uzbekistan Decrees and Resolutions* (Taskhent: Uzbekiston, 1994).
25 *State Committee for Forecasting and Statistics.* See also *Xalq Sozi*, 28 February 1998, pp. 1–2.
26 See also Asian Development Bank, *Country Economic Review: Uzbekistan* (Manila: Asian Development Bank, 1997).
27 Information obtained at the World Bank Office in Tashkent during my interview with local and foreign experts on the Uzbek economy on 12 July and 14 September 1996, and during my interview with the IMF representative in Tashkent on 3 July 1996.
28 IMF, op. cit., pp. 16–24.
29 Ibid. p. 19.
30 See Islom Karimov's Speech to the National Parliament on the Economic Developments in Uzbekistan, *Xalq Sozi*, 26 July 1996, pp. 1–2, *Ozbekiston Ovozi*, 27 July 1996, pp. 1–2.
31 See Asian Development Bank, *Country Economic Review: Uzbekistan* (Manila: Asian Development Bank, 1997), pp. 11–12.
32 See World Bank, *Commodity Markets and the Developing Countries*, May 1997.
33 International Monetary Fund, *Republic of Uzbekistan: Recent Economic Developments,* Staff Country Report no. 97/98 (Washington, D.C.: IMF, 1997), p. 52.
34 See IMF, *Direction of Trade Statistics Yearbook*, 1997, pp. 457–8. See also IMF, *Direction of Trade Statistics Quarterly,* September 1997 and December 1997.
35 The subject was discussed with Uzbek economists at the World Bank office of Tashkent and during my interview with the IMF representative in Tashkent on 3 July 1996.
36 IMF, op. cit., p. 24; Asian Development Bank, op. cit., p. 4.
37 The subject was discussed with some experts during my interview at the World Bank Office on 4, 5 and 12 July 1996. See also IMF, op. cit., pp. 19–23, and Asian Development Bank, op. cit., pp. 4–5.
38 IMF, op. cit., 1994, p. 5.
39 A detailed account of the agricultural sector is in Asian Development Bank, op. cit., 1996 and 1997. A discussion of the subject is also given by IMF, op. cit., 1997.

40 Several interviews were conducted at the World Bank Office in Tashkent on 4, 5, 6, 12 July, and 11, 19 September 1996.
41 United Nations Development Program, *Uzbekistan Human Development Report* (Tashkent: UNDP, 1996), p. 24.
42 IMF, op. cit., p. 61.
43 Information gathered during an interview at the Ministry of Foreign Economic Relations, on 10 September 1996.
44 Information obtained during discussions with the Tulkun Shayakubov, at the Royal Garden Hotel, London, on 6 November 1997, where he presented a paper to the conference 'Doing Business in Uzbekistan', held by IBC UK Conferences Limited. See also the conference papers presented by Wayne W. Murdy, 'The Zarafshan-Newmont and Angren Gold Projects', Christopher Morgen, 'Progress Report on the Zarmitan Gold Project' and Richard Longstaff, 'Mine Project Risk in Uzbekistan'.
45 State Committee for Forecasting and Statistics.
46 The subject was discussed with the Deputy Chairman of Uzbekneftegas, Ibrat Zainnudinov, who gave a talk on 'New Projects and Approaches of the National Corporation Uzbekneftegas' at the conference held at the Royal Garden Hotel, London, on 6 November 1997. An excellent account of the mining and energy subsectors in Uzbekistan is provided by the Asian Development Bank, op. cit., 1996, pp. 54–61.
47 Asian Development Bank, op. cit., 1996, p. 54.
48 Several discussions regarding transport and communication in Uzbekistan were held with Uzbek officials in the Tashkent districts of Sabir Rakhimov, Pakhtakor, Navoi, Chorsu, Chilanzor and at the main railway station, during March–September 1996.
49 United Nations Development Program, *Uzbekistan Human Development Report* (Tashkent: UNDP, 1996), pp. 55–6.
50 The subject was discussed with officials at the *Telecome Central* at Navoi and the Alaaski districts of Tashkent in July–August 1996.
51 United Nations Development Program, *Uzbekistan Human Development Report* (Tashkent: UNDP, 1996), p. 52.
52 Information was obtained from Hee Choo Chung, Executive Vice President of the Daewoo Corporation, during a discussion with him in London on 6 November 1997. See also *Jahon*, 29 August 1996, pp. 3, 6.
53 See, for further discussion, United Nations Development Program, *Uzbekistan Human Development Report* (Tashkent: UNDP, 1996), pp. 71–84. See also *Uzbekistan Adjusting Social Protection* (World Bank, 1994), for a further discussion of poverty and social protection in the Republic of Uzbekistan.
54 A survey conducted in March 1989 showed that about 45 per cent of the population in Uzbekistan lived with a monthly income of less than 75 roubles, which was the minimum wage at that time.

5

Foreign Policy and External Relations

The formulation of an independent foreign policy in the Republic of Uzbekistan, as in most of the post-Soviet republics, is a new sphere of activity. The republic's external relations were with the countries of the former Soviet Union, and even those were through the central leadership in Moscow. What constituted its national interest, and actual or potential threats to this interest, was shaped by official Soviet ideology.[1] The first six years of activity by the Republic of Uzbekistan in the international arena, however, were a period that saw its acquaintance with and commencement of, integration into the world community. This period also saw the establishment of social, political and economic priorities and the organizing of legal prerequisites for a steady involvement in the world affairs.

Initially, most analysts emphasized several factors such as national character and ethnic and cultural affinity at the expense of other determinants of the republic's external relations, such as the geopolitical situation, economic needs, ideological and bureaucratic factors, and political aspirations. There is no doubt that ethnic, religious, and cultural factors have assisted in shaping the post-independence pattern of the republic's foreign policy priorities, its perception of the world beyond the former Soviet Union, and the republic's place in its region and in the world as a whole. But the relative impact of these has been conditioned by other factors; the determining factors of Uzbek Foreign Policy are geopolitical, political, and economic in nature. In addition to these, the republic's regional and international aspirations have also helped to determine its foreign policy priorities.

The republic's foreign policy doctrine is based on providing political and economic independence, and ensuring the security of the country. The general strategic line of foreign policy since Uzbekistan's expulsion from the rouble zone has been a comprehensive integration into the world community and entry into the system of world trade, communication and information in order to help overcome the previously one-sided orientation to the USSR. Other aims have been to defuse particular states' ambitions over the region and firmly to determine not to become a sphere of someone else's influence; to establish new political and economic connections and to seek self-affirmation in the world arena as a member of the world community enjoying full rights which would in the long run enhance its regional role.

Uzbek foreign policy
Uzbekistan as a sovereign nation emerged in the region after the collapse of the Soviet Union. Despite its commitment to the CIS, the republic has demonstrated a strong sense of independence and a determination to pursue its own interests free from outside direction. Independence confronted the republic with the sudden responsibility for conducting its own foreign relations, a task that Uzbekistan was ill-equipped to perform. With the break-up of the Soviet system, the central authority in Moscow that orchestrated foreign relations for the Union's republics, both with each other and with countries outside the former Soviet Union, disappeared from the scene. Any expectation that its functions would be taken over in substantial form by the CIS did not withstand the test of time and political reality.

Prior to independence, Uzbekistan like other Central Asian republics, had its own 'Ministry of Foreign Affairs' under the old federal system, but its staff and facilities were used largely as a means for enabling Moscow to impart a measure of credibility to the supposed 'autonomy' of the republic. The ministry had no real authority since all foreign relations were handled through Moscow. Even in foreign relations at the federal level, the republic was severely under-represented. This meant that on achieving independence the republic lacked trained and experienced staff capable of administering its foreign relations professionally. Nonetheless, Uzbekistan rushed to exploit its new sovereign status by emerging as an independent actor in the global arena. The establishment of an independent foreign policy was popular in the republic because it symbolized freedom from central control and assisted the political elite's aim to legitimize the republic's government after the takeover of power from the former Soviet system. There was an urgent need to establish new trading ties to replace those that had collapsed with the Soviet Union, and enable the republic to deal directly with foreign governments to solicit economic assistance and political support.

The republic's initial experiment in foreign policy was successful. It resulted in quick recognition by many other countries, including major powers, and saw the establishment of diplomatic ties and the exchange of diplomatic missions. The republic was also accepted with little hesitation into the United Nations and other international organizations. However, many problems remained. Lack of staff, facilities, and funds forced the republic to continue to depend on Russian missions abroad for much of its representation. Russian officials continued to make decisions for the republic on such matters as the issuance of entry visas. Lack of trained and experienced personnel was also an impediment to the development of foreign trade. While entrepreneurs from abroad have been invited to the republic and courted by the president of the republic, they complain about the frustrations of legal ambiguities, overlapping jurisdictions, and grasping and incompetent bureaucracies. Yet despite these difficulties, Uzbekistan is determined to control its own foreign relations without delegating decision-making authority to the CIS, or any other external body. In attempting to advance the security and economic interests of its country, the leadership faces a set of disjunctive, but overlapping areas that are definable in geographical terms: (i) Central Asian states; (ii) CIS states outside Central Asia, mainly the Russian Federation; (iii) the Turkic world; (iv) major countries of Asia and the Middle East; (v) the West: the European Union and the United States.

The Uzbek government initially enunciated its top three priorities as cooperation and integration in Central Asia, integration into the Asian world and cooperation with the CIS, mainly Russia, thereby seemingly ignoring the United States and western Europe in this formulation.[2] Indeed it was not until 1994 that Uzbekistan seriously considered developing its relations with western Europe, and not until spring 1995, with the United States. The main reasons for this were that Uzbekistan had been oriented only to the USSR and had economic, communicational and information connections only with it, and this situation remained largely unchanged after independence. The bulk of connections were with Russia, and this state of affairs continued even after the republic was forced to leave the rouble zone. The interdependent state of affairs was a dominant factor in the decision-making process. Moreover, the Uzbek political elite was still very much dominated by Soviet ideology and this maintained their negative perceptions, a distrust of the West for a while. Because of the lack of experience, the authorities did not feel that they would be able to establish new economic and trade links with countries outside the CIS quickly enough, as the economic situation in the country was deteriorating. Instead of looking for new markets the policy makers preferred improving existing ties. After a period of preoccupation with these options, attention to regional solutions was reduced by a tendency to look also outside the region for assistance: firstly, dealing with such critical multinational problems as reclamation of the Aral Sea basin; secondly, securing large amounts of international capital needed for economic recovery; thirdly, the rise in Russian jingoism towards Central Asia and the decision of the Russian Parliament on 15 March 1996 to vote to re-establish the old Soviet Union by force if necessary. President Karimov condemned this decision during his speech to the regional parliament in Khorezm and considered this as a threat to the integrity and security of independent Uzbekistan. Fourthly, there was a customs union treaty signed between Russia, Kazakstan and Kyrgyzstan; and fifthly, the leadership's desire to gain the United States' backing for a solution to the conflict in Afghanistan.

Towards regional integration
The decision of Central Asian leaders to create a regional union was hardly unexpected. After the disintegration of the USSR the Central Asian states have been in search of a new model of development. They tried to find a new 'big brother' among their neighbours, such as Turkey or Iran, to draw investors' attention, especially with their hydrocarbonate, oil, gas and unique deposits of non-ferrous metals. Meanwhile, they attempted to coordinate their actions within the CIS and international and regional organizations. The states of the region were more insistent in proclamations to remain aligned to the USSR, which seemed to them to guarantee ethno-political stability in the region and provide stable economic relations. At a certain level they understood that the former USSR was not able to restrain fast differentiation of the regions. The idea of the national self-determination of the Central Asian republics was considered by their leaders in all possible versions. It became clear that the main issue was to overcome the historically developed situation of being raw materials adjuncts of the 'Russia-first Empire', a role which has defined the peculiarity of the region's development model. This model

must also fit traditional ways of production, a so-called 'Asian way,' and a mentality where Islamic influence is very strong.

Subsequent events proved that the region could not blindly copy plans of other reforms. The idea of introducing the 'Turkish model' failed; the advice of invited South Korean and American specialists was not carried out. For example, attempts to carry out the privatization programme according to the Russian way slowed down. Traditions of nomadic cattle-breeding, and the division of people into farmers (Uzbeks) and herdsmen (Kazaks and Kyrgyz), prevail in the region, and relations between Central Asian republics are already provided for by their participation in regional organizations such as the Economic Cooperation Organization (ECO), the Black Sea Zone Organization for Economic Cooperation (BSZOEC) and the Organization of Islamic Conference (OIC). At the same time, with these processes came a realization of the deep historical and cultural roots of Central Asian regionalism as an active factor. The rise of nationalist ideas encourages it to move further away from the Soviet past and overcome its inferiority complex.

The search for mutual agreement is being forced by inner processes. In a single year after the USSR dissolved, the republics achieved the first step of becoming separate states and defining their most apparent national interests. They all acquired the necessary status as independent states and were officially confirmed as members of the United Nations. They established control over their own resources and received their share of the Soviet property. The governments of these republics worked out forms of state mechanism that took into account both tradition and contemporary conditions.

The countries of Central Asia, like all the other former Soviet republics, are going through the process of social, political and economic transformation. For the successful completion of this process, it is necessary to have security and stability. This demands that the process involves first of all reforming the very society; secondly, new state-building with the revival of democratic structures; thirdly, the necessity of new strategic attitudes towards the problems concerning the creation of a free economic market system; and finally, strengthening the independence and sovereignty of the Central Asian states. For the fulfilment of these conditions it is necessary to provide conditions for collective security.

The process of transformation in these countries, on the other hand, is accompanied by a number of common conflict-producing problems.

These include, internal-ethnic and inter-clan tensions; economic crisis; conflicts between governments (for the control of natural resources); environmental problems with an international dimension (for example, the drying up of the Aral Sea and its consequences; the narco-business, the transfer of arms, immigration and organized crime). Under the present conditions the process of transformation cannot be completed within a short period of time. For stability, security and sustainable development, it is necessary to have collective action based on viable structures, which would include recognized conceptions of regional integration. It is now a requirement to have a single coordinated policy regarding the settlement of social, economic and political problems in the region, instead of several different views and ideas. This will make it easier to find solutions to the conflicts and problems and can attract greater assistance from the international community. Contemporary tendencies of development in international relations also demand cooperation between nations, at least at the regional level. This would result in the establishment of a system of regional security and cooperation, based on political, military, economic, environmental and other aspects of security which may help further integration.

The stimulus to the search for a new integration model for the Central Asian states of the former USSR was the catastrophic deterioration of the economic situation in the republics. This was caused by the break-up of economic ties and technological chains established, not only throughout the Soviet period, but also during the Russian administration of Turkistan. The republics of Central Asia were so dependent on the Centre, that none of them wanted their independence from the Union. That is why they clung to what remained of the Union for as long as they could, and when it became evident that the Union would collapse, they quickly joined the CIS, hoping to maintain the existing channels until a successful transition to a market economy was completed. Uzbek president Islom Karimov, however, soon realized that the conflicting interests of the various states within the CIS were holding back progress. Instead he opted for the regional integration of the Central Asian republics, while remaining within the CIS. Karimov took the initiative for regional integration and invited the heads of the Central Asian states to Tashkent for the first meeting, to discuss and find a regional solution to the worsening social, political and economic situation in the region.

The five leaders came together for the first time on 4 January 1993 to express their views regarding the problems of the region in amicable terms. After the summit meeting, it was announced that they had agreed to promote cooperation between all countries in Central Asia. The meeting was held in an atmosphere of strict confidentiality because it had been arranged spontaneously and necessitated by the urgent need to find a solution for the escalating disagreements between the neighbours. Later it became clear to the presidents that they needed to utilize their own strength and look for ways out of the economic crisis, not relying on particular states (especially Russia or Turkey), but more within the bounds of closer economic cooperation between the countries of the region. At this summit they agreed to search for joint solutions and coordinate actions in order to solve the economic problems arising from the collapse of the USSR. Kazakstan and Uzbekistan were disturbed by the policies of the Russian Federation regarding economic reform policies since they did not take into account the needs of the Central Asian states when they were members of the rouble zone. They considered Russia rather selfish and irresponsible, and consequently felt forced to leave the rouble zone. But although it was hard for them to leave the rouble zone at that time, it helped the republics to formulate their policies in time according to the region's need. In other words, the republics realized the need to draw on their own strength and look for ways out of the economic crisis without relying on other states.[3]

The statement made by the heads of the member states attending the Tashkent meeting was prudent and could be interpreted as something more than a protocol of intentions. From unofficial sources it became known that the talks of the leaders of the Asian 'five' consisted of mutual claims and reproaches, but they managed to set preconditions for the appearance of a new treaty towards establishing regional unity. The concluding document of the meeting mentioned agreements on the regional economic market, the creation of a single customs union, a common taxation policy and the formation of a joint common defence space. The meeting was also considered as an attempt to pressure Moscow though, ironically, it was Moscow that acted as a catalyst for the Tashkent initiative. On the eve of the meeting there was a cooling of relations between Russia, Kazakstan and Uzbekistan caused by the fact that Russia had refused to take into account the partners' interests in setting financial policy when Kazakstan and Uzbekistan were part of the rouble zone. Meanwhile, Sapar Murad Niyazov, the President of Turkmenistan, still actively supported the idea of integration within the CIS, stressing that Central Asian integration was not an alternative to the CIS at all. Turkmenistan had demonstrated its unwillingness to integrate its economy with its neighbours from the very beginning. Among all the countries, Tajikistan needed the greatest economic support, yet the internal political problems did not help it to adopt a clear position towards the integration programs. Kyrgyzstan needed assistance to a smaller degree. As far as Kazakstan was concerned, its president Nursultan Nazarbayev was known to advocate closer relations with Russia. Nazarbayev, who generated the idea of forming a Euro-Asian Union, stated that he would participate in the moves towards regional integration.

The partners of the new bloc also differed from each other in the character of their political regimes, ranging from authoritarian socialism in Turkmenistan to rudimentary democracy in Kyrgyzstan. Besides, until recently there had been some differences of opinion between president Islom Karimov and Nursultan Nazarbayev *vis-à-vis* Russia and on the question of the possible integration model. Soon after the first meeting, in January 1993, another meeting was organized in Kazakstan. A commission of government experts started examining possible economic links, searching for mutually held views and ideas, deciding on primary tasks, and creating mechanisms for regulating mutual relations within the new bloc. This kind of work went on throughout 1993.

On 9 January 1994 a working party was established in Nukus, comprising the prime ministers of Uzbekistan, Kazakstan, Kyrgyzstan, Turkmenistan and Tajikistan. The meeting was in line with that held on 20 March 1993 in Kizil Orda, Kazakstan where the leaders of the five states, *inter alia*, signed an agreement on joint action regarding the deterioration of the Aral Sea, and drafted documents with a view to creating interstate councils and an executive committee of interstate councils. In Nukus, the prime ministers studied all the previous documents, as well as other questions concerning the introduction of national currencies, without which the regional cooperation would not be practical. The presidents of each country also participated in the second part of the meeting. As a result of the Nukus summit, a treaty was signed on 10 January, though by only two presidents. This created a common economic space between Kazakstan and Uzbekistan, joined shortly thereafter by Kyrgyzstan on 30 April, during a meeting held in Cholpan-Ata. On 8 July 1994, the presidents met again in Almaty where they finalized and signed documents, which provided the basis for economic cooperation between the three states of the region. With these documents they set up interstate councils consisting of the presidents and premiers. These institutions included the Council of the Prime Ministers, the Council of the Foreign Ministers, the Council of the Ministers of Defence, and an executive committee as the working body based in Almaty. The executive body commenced operations immediately after 8 July 1994. Serik Primbetow, a Kazak, was appointed the Committee's first chairman, with Kyrgyzstan and Uzbekistan each represented by one vice-chairman, enjoying the same privileges as ministers. The executive body is expected to resolve problems of economic policy, which the individual states had been unable to resolve on their own.[4] It is unlikely, however, that the executive committee will be able to accomplish such a comprehensive task with the current means available to it. Nonetheless it was formed as a vehicle for promoting sound long-term cooperation and understanding between the states of the region, signalling that these countries were capable of organizing themselves to create more efficient economies.

The signed document envisages cooperation at the economic, social, cultural and military levels: coordinated actions towards credit-debit, budgets, taxation, prices, currency, customs, investment, and licence provisions; immigration, environmental and other spheres of domestic policy coordination; concerted principles in the military and defence spheres; coordinated action against organized crime, terrorism and drug dealers; coordination of the foreign policy of the three states; and the establishment of a central Asian bank for cooperation and development. The parties also intend to provide equal opportunities for all economic subjects and to stimulate business activities. Although the declaration adopted by the three heads of states leaves several unanswered questions relating to important details of a single economic territory, this meeting can be seen as the birth of the 'Union of Three'. The meeting clearly identified the areas of common interest to the three states and laid out the steps to be followed in solving urgent problems. The Almaty declaration also gave special attention to the question of creating an economically viable base for the defence system. This covered areas like material and technical support for military forces, equipment supply, consultation on questions of military defence and common personnel training, and the formation of a joint battalion of peacekeeping forces for Kazakstan, Kyrgyzstan and Uzbekistan. From the outset it was clear that Turkmenistan would remain separate from the process of integration. As for Tajikistan, its internal problems have prevented it from being part of the process. To enable Turkmenistan and Tajikistan to join the alliance in the future, the Almaty declaration emphasized the open nature of the integration process. There are several reasons why Turkmenistan does not want to take part in closer economic or political integration in the region. The main one is that Ashkhabad does not see much to gain from integrating its country's economy with those of its neighbours, and as a small country with a population 20 per cent that of Uzbekistan, Turkmenistan cannot count on playing a leading role among the countries of the region. We must also bear in mind the huge potential of natural gas and oil resources in this country. For example, the Amudarjinski basin is estimated to contain more than 15 trillion cubic metres of natural gas. Turkmenistan is counting on this to help it become a 'second Kuwait'. Furthermore, Turkmenistan's support of the state-owned economic sector sets it aside from other countries in the region, and provides another disincentive to join the integration process.

The next meeting of the prime ministers, in Bishkek in August 1994, centred on the question of mutual debt. By that time, Kyrgyzstan owed Uzbekistan a large sum of money. Kazakstan faced the same problem and, in turn, Tashkent and Almaty were indebted to Kyrgyzstan, while the latter was in need of coal from Kazakstan. These problems were discussed and the participants agreed to settle the issue by means of mutual calculations.

On 6 May 1996, a meeting of the interstate councils headed by the leaders of the three member states was held at Bishkek. It approved a programme for a Central Asian economic cooperation programme until the year 2000. The agreement incorporated such projects as establishing financial–industrial groups; joint development of national economies and a Central Asian Bank, geological and chemical research, development of new transportation routes; and projects to safeguard against environmental and ecological calamities.[5] The projects adopted at this meeting and the direction of the economic integration of the three states, which was also defined in Bishkek, were reviewed by the three Central Asian leaders in Alamty on 23 August 1996. The presidents of Kazakstan, Kyrgyzstan and Uzbekistan, in further discussions regarding economic cooperation, signed a number of documents expanding economic cooperation between their countries. They included agreements on creating a single economic space between the states by 1998 and opening special free economic zones in border areas to increase the turnover of goods. Uzbekistan agreed to give the Central Asian Bank for Cooperation and Development access to its domestic market, which would ease transactions with the Uzbek currency. The meeting also discussed the participation of the Central Asian peacekeeping battalion in exercises involving multinational armed forces under the aegis of the UN. It also decided to admit Tajikistan and Russia as observers to the interstate Council. In the meeting, Kazakstan's term of chairing the Council was extended until the end of 1996. The presidents also heard a report by the Central Asian Bank for Cooperation and Development, set up in 1994, and decided that before the end of September every member nation should pay an additional one million US dollars to the Bank's equity capital in addition to the four million dollars paid earlier. It was further announced that Uzbekistan would not join the Customs Union already set up by Russia and three other former Soviet republics.[6] The Uzbek president has on several occasions stated that Uzbekistan is against the establishment of supranational institutions within the CIS, since they could be used as instruments for centralized control of former Soviet republics. To stress the importance of regional cooperation and to promote integration between the republics, a summit meeting of the presidents of Kazakstan, Kyrgyzstan and Uzbekistan was held in Bishkek on 10 January 1997. At the meeting the three leaders discussed and approved a treaty of eternal friendship and cooperation between their countries. The treaty, which was initiated by Kazakstan, sought to deepen economic cooperation between the three countries and commit them to increased cooperation at all levels, including mutual security by which each country promised to defend the others in the event of an attack by a third party. Considering an attack to any of the states in the region as a threat to the others, this treaty is meaningful, but it can also be considered as a rebuke for Saparmurad Niyazov. President Niyazov has always shown less interest in the Central Asian Union and has been unwilling to cooperate with other leaders in the regional integration process.

On 24–25 July 1997, the Kyrgyzy town of Cholpan-Ata played host to a conference on the Central Asian Union. This was devoted to discussing current issues concerning the region and overcoming differences regarding the sharing of common natural resources, in particular water sharing between the Central Asian republics. The leaders of Kazakstan, Kyrgyzstan and Uzbekistan tried to find solutions to several issues such as the problem of water sharing; furthering integration among their countries; finding a peaceful resolution to the conflict in Afghanistan; expanding economic cooperation; and creating an inter-parliamentary body. They also discussed the progress of the Central Asian Peacekeeping battalion established under the auspices of NATO's partnership for peace. The leaders sought to emphasize the degree of accord among them by agreeing on the above topics and endorsing a Kyrgyzy proposal to hold a conference in Bishkek under UN auspices to discuss the situation in Afghanistan, though they were unable to resolve 'the water sharing crisis'. The task left for the prime ministers of the three countries was to draft a programme for setting up an international consortium to manage energy and water resources before the next summit. At a one-day meeting of the Inter-State Council of the Central Asian Union held in Alamty on 7 August 1997, the Kazak, Kyrgyz and Uzbek Prime Ministers signed several agreements, including regulations on immigration and railroad tariffs. The three prime ministers postponed the signing of agreements on international road haulage and energy and failed to address coordinating their taxation and value added tax provisions. They were also unable to resolve the issue of access to water and this is likely to continue to divide the leaders in the future.[7]

Since Central Asia is an arid or semi-arid region of the globe, the potential for conflicts over water sharing is very high. The issue of water sharing in Central Asia is not the problem of one or two states, but is a regional problem, and must be seen in this broader context. The main water resources are transboundary ones. The five republics mostly use the water they withdraw from their main common rivers, the Amu Darya and the Syrdarya. The problem is serious and could be aggravated if not tackled properly and quickly. There are several points at issue here, including water distribution quotas and principles of water sharing. Under Soviet rule all inter-republic questions on water sharing were defined and imposed mainly by the central authorities in Moscow. With the collapse of the USSR the situation has changed. The newly independent states of Central Asia have faced a set of political and economic problems related to the sharing of common water resources, which need new water management principles, institutions and mechanisms. This has become an issue increasingly dividing the policy makers in the region. While the new pattern is under discussion, some elements of the old system are still used and the old quotas for water usage existing from the Soviet era were re-established in 1995, so as to preclude further escalation of the dispute, which could be exploited by one or more outside powers.

The agreements and arrangements on water sharing and distribution in this region are necessary, but not sufficient. Rapidly expanding populations in the region will inevitably lead certain governments on the one hand to seek to keep whatever water they have, or obtain more from their neighbours; while on the other hand, even more people and politicians will focus on water questions, such as the disappearance of the Aral Sea. Therefore, to find a long-term solution for the problem, and to reduce the chances of conflict, a regional framework is needed for introducing water protection and water-saving technologies, such as improving irrigation technique, and restructuring agriculture. It is necessary for the Central Asian states to share the region's natural resources. Because of the legacy of the communist era, they have similar political and economic circumstances. Moreover they have a historical similarity which reveals itself in common traditions, closeness of languages, cultures and religion. These factors will make it easier for the Central Asian states to increase the level of integration among themselves, tackle the issues dividing them and coordinate their policies. The republics have the potential to integrate, but they also have their own interests. The unresolved disputes will simply add more problems to the existing ones in a region where there are grounds for tension and conflicts.

Finally, it must be stressed that, despite all the disagreements between the leaders in the region, the prospects for integration in Central Asia are meaningful and there is certainly a sincere desire for its success. Central Asia is poised to become a 'natural zone' of economic development, taking into account the great value of natural resources, and the high level of education, qualifications and productivity of 60 million people. From a broader perspective, which incorporates transnational ecological problems and the difficulties encountered during the development of productive economies, it is clear that the possibility of stabilizing the individual national states within Central Asia can be possible only through regional integration. It is, however, important to stress that though there is a sincere desire for the success of the integration process, several fundamental problems, such as internal problems that the transition will precipitate, regional (Tajik and Afghan conflicts and their aftermath) problems, and the Russian influence, are poised to increase divisions among them. The other fundamental problem is that genuine integration will be possible if there are law-based states and if there is genuine democracy in the region. Among Central Asian states, no leader or president currently accepts the rule of law entirely and there is no way that any constitutional court can overrule a president's decision in these states. The Central Asian Economic Cooperation now includes Kazakstan, Kyrgyzstan, Tajikistan and Uzbekistan. The leaders of these four former Soviet republics met for two days in Tashkent on 20 April 2000 and signed a security document. The treaty signed by the four leaders also envisages joint military actions in case of attack. The Central Asian Union founded in January 1994 has, however, produced few results.

Uzbekistan and the Commonwealth of Independent States
When the break-up of the Soviet Union seemed certain towards the end of 1991, the leaders of Russia, Ukraine and Belarus signed a declaration to create a Commonwealth of Independent States (CIS). This would be a body that would enable the republics of the former Soviet Union to conduct relations with one another in an orderly manner and resolve outstanding issues connected with the former Soviet Union. Uzbekistan, along with other Central Asian states, became one of its founding members during a meeting held in Alma-Ata (now Almaty) on 21 December 1991. The CIS now has 12 members: Armenia, Azerbaijan, Belarus, Georgia, Kazakstan, Kyrgyzstan, Moldavia, Russia, Tajikistan, Turkmenistan, Ukraine and Uzbekistan. Its representatives meet regularly to discuss economic, military, political and social issues of common interest. Although all member states are committed to creating a CIS Economic Union, moves towards political and military integration are viewed with varying degrees of intent.

Russia, which plays a leading role in the CIS, makes no secret of its enthusiasm for the closer integration of the organization. It views the key to integration as being economic cooperation and would like the CIS to comprise a common economic space and common security area, and to become a confederation. Some other CIS states, notably Belarus and Kazakstan, see advantages in further integration. Ukraine, however, often attends meetings only as an observer. It acknowledges the need to maintain and develop economic links with other CIS countries, but consistently refuses to participate in attempts to develop the organization's political or military aspects in which Russia would play a dominant role. Its interest is in developing mutually beneficial bilateral relationships with the other CIS countries. As for Uzbekistan, the CIS has a very important role to play in the region that was once part of the former Soviet Union. But this role, according to Uzbekistan, must be limited to economic and cultural issues. It has distanced itself both from proposals for joint protection of frontiers with non-CIS countries, termed by Moscow as external CIS borders, and from suggestions for a unified air defence system. It has, thus far, refused to sign the border protection agreement. Uzbekistan believes further integration within the CIS will lead to a supranational structure, including the unification of military–political structures and a return to a form of the old totalitarian administrative command system. Uzbekistan has ruled out all of this. It wishes the CIS to remain in its current form, but would like to see more cooperation on deepening economic and financial integration, solving payments problems and removing barriers to humanitarian integration within the framework of the approved CIS Charter. According to the Uzbek president, no new agreements need to be signed, especially those of a geopolitical nature.[8] Uzbekistan, therefore, instead of working for further integration within the CIS, has opted for establishing strong bilateral ties with Russia and other individual CIS members. Meanwhile, President Nursultan Nazarbayev of Kazakstan, in an attempt to enable genuinely committed parties to achieve a greater degree of integration, has proposed the creation of a Eurasian Union, consisting of CIS member states that wish to join.

Obviously Uzbekistan's enthusiasm for the CIS reflects its own vision of the organization as a means for preventing economic disruption and providing regional security with Russian assistance. This view is not necessarily shared by others CIS participants who have very different perceptions of its character and mission. These competing blueprints of the various member states of the CIS have failed to transform the organization into a well-integrated, well-functioning multinational economic, political, and security organization, despite the signing of more than 400 agreements on various aspects of intra-CIS relations.[9]

Most of these agreements exist on paper only. Consequently a range of issues facing the CIS and other countries of the former Soviet Union have been dealt with at a bilateral level between Russia and other individual member republics. Lack of a clear purpose, member states' differing perceptions, Russian supremacy, unilateralism and impotence have all plagued the CIS and called into question its future as a supranational entity.

Uzbekistan and Russia

The Russian Federation recognized Uzbekistan's independence on 20 March 1992 and soon after, on 13 July the same year, opened an embassy in Tashkent.[10] Following this, a new relationship emerged between Uzbekistan and Russia. The 'Centre' had disappeared and the republic would no longer be managed from Moscow. Yet the republic's continued political, economic and military dependence on Russia severely restricted Uzbekistan's choices. The Uzbek leadership was well aware of the importance of preserving close ties with Russia, though it sought ways of distancing itself from Moscow and reaffirming its independence. Karimov's initial position was to make Russia's importance for Uzbekistan very clear. He stated: 'We need Russia like the air and like the water.' Therefore, the first years of independence saw Uzbekistan knocking on the doors of the CIS. Uzbekistan was more interested in Russia, mainly for political, security and economic reasons, than Russia was in Uzbekistan. For the Russian Federation the Central Asian republics were a social, political and economic burden, and it tried to rid itself of these, including Uzbekistan. During this time, there were two alternative strategies available to Russia: abandoning the region or becoming more involved in it. During 1992–3, the strategy of leaving was seen as the most appropriate so Russia decided not to get involved in the region. The Republic of Uzbekistan, like other Central Asian republics, was more insistent on maintaining political, economic and military links with Russia. At this stage, Uzbekistan was more dependent on Russia. A perfect example of this is the joint Uzbek–Russian military action to end the Tajik civil war. The Uzbek leadership, concerned at the potential dangers of the Tajik civil war spreading to its own country, was especially keen to see a quick end to the fighting and to restore the *status quo* in Tajikistan. It was mainly active Uzbek diplomacy that convinced

Russia of joint military action in that country. Uzbekistan, therefore, became the principal motor behind the military cooperation with Russia and launched an offensive in support of the National Front forces on 6 December 1992. With the possibility of renewed political challenges and violence in the region, this military cooperation was subsequently formalized into a defence agreement which was extended to include Kazakstan and Kyrgyzstan.

The initiative for a military partnership, realistically speaking, did not come from Russia but had originated from the republic itself. The commitment of Uzbekistan to cooperate with Russia was, however, the result of its colonial legacy, as well as political, economic, and security factors at that time. In many ways the republic depended on the Russian Federation, and regional security factors were making this worse. This unequal dependence was initially taken for granted by Russian policy makers, with Russia consequently behaving arrogantly towards Uzbekistan. It was Russia that imposed its terms on the republic when it was a member of the rouble zone; it was Russia that forced the republic to accept Russian budgetary, financial and monetary policy; it was the Russian Federation that initiated the economic formation of the Slavic troika – Ukraine, Russia and Belarus – in July 1993 with the exclusion of the republics of Central Asia. Although no such Slavic economic union ever came into being, it was, in effect, Moscow's answer to the participation of the Central Asian countries in the ECO, of which Uzbekistan was one. However, for its part, Uzbekistan regarded the announcement as little more than blackmail, which it deeply resented. Moreover, it was Russia's economic and monetary policies undertaken unilaterally and without prior consultation that forced the republic to leave the rouble zone in the fall of 1993. All these factors, together with the power struggle in Moscow between the democratic forces and the neo-communists, the clash between President Yeltsin and the Russian Parliament in October 1993, and the strong showing of the ultra-nationalist Liberal Democratic Party in the Russian elections in December of the same year, encouraged anti-Russian sentiment in Tashkent. Uzbekistan began to move away from Russia's sphere of influence.

Between mid-1994 and early 1995 Moscow abandoned its policy of leaving the region, and shifted to a strategy of presence.[11] It was now Uzbekistan's turn to be the reluctant partner, while Russia insisted on becoming more active in the region. The Kremlin's new policy of fostering better relations with Central Asia can be explained by a number of factors. First, the crisis in Chechnya forced the Russian leadership to compensate for domestic failures by taking effective measures in foreign policy with respect to the near abroad (the former Soviet republics that are now independent states). Second, the threat of NATO's eastward expansion drove Moscow to reinforce its own position in strategically important former Soviet Central Asia. Third, Yeltsin's opponents were calling for the reintegration of the old Russian and Soviet empires by any means. Some like Vladimir Zhirinovskii demanded the reinstitution of the former Russian empire and called for the restoration of Russian rule in Central Asia. Sergei Karaganov and Aleksander Vladislavlev claimed that Russia should send its soldiers to Central Asia. Konstantin Zatulin, a former chairman of the Committee on CIS Affairs in the Russian parliament, remarked that 'one cannot recognize the territorial integrity of states that never existed inside these borders'.[12] A member of the Presidential Council, Andranik Migranian, and Evgeni Ambartsumov, a former chairman of the Committee on Foreign Relations in the Russian parliament, held the view that Russia should declare the territory of the former Soviet Union to be its exclusive sphere of interest and warn other powers not to intervene or to challenge Russia's predominance there.[13] Indeed even the idea of re-establishing the Soviet Union through peaceful means was so popular among a significant part of the Russian population that the issue of reintegration occupied an important place in the election campaign for presidency in late 1996, which President Yeltsin could simply not have afforded to ignore. Fourth, to reinforce its own position in parts of its earlier strategic space, Russia was keen to promote closer political and military cooperation within the CIS framework. There was even some credibility in Russia's plan to create a unified CIS military force. Fifth, in Russia, there was hostility to growing American involvement in the region. Sixth, Russia's security concerns grew, notably over the potential threat of radical Islam, and the risk of inter-ethnic or territorial conflicts in the region and its periphery. Russia was also worried about a potentially large exodus of Central Asia's Russians, including a large number of them from Uzbekistan to the Russian Federation, which would inevitably exacerbate existing problems of job and housing shortages.[14] Seventh, Uzbekistan, Kazakstan and Kyrgyzstan had, early in 1994, agreed to create a Central Asian Union.

In Moscow's view Uzbekistan has already started to distance itself from the Russian sphere and was now towing away two more republics. Having witnessed the Chechen resistance, and faced with problems in other autonomous regions, like Tatarstan, Daghstan and Bashkordstan, Moscow had no desire to see the creation of a hostile bloc of countries to its south. Eighth, Russia's suspicions with regard to Ankara's Turkic policy aroused serious concern in the Kremlin. For instance, the Russian Foreign Ministry characterized the October 1994 Istanbul Turkic summit as a 'brainwashing meeting with pan-Turkist aims'.[15] Surely this characterization is too extreme, but, nonetheless, it bore witness to Moscow's suspicions.

From the Uzbek point of view, in addition to the reasons stated above regarding Uzbekistan's decision to distance itself from the Russian Federation, several other factors also played a crucial role. First, Moscow unilaterally liquidated the rouble zone in November 1993 and this further exacerbated anti-Russian sentiment in Tashkent. Second, the republic became rather suspicious in the face of Russia's policy for the region. Third, political circles in Uzbekistan reacted with indignation to the rhetoric of Moscow jingoists and regarded this as expressing the intentions of the Kremlin itself. President Karimov stated in an interview that he had repeatedly asked President Yeltsin to address Zhirinovskii's comments about Central Asia: 'Tell us to what extent the statements of Zhirinovskii are acceptable, or unacceptable, for you. Express your opinion, Boris Nikolaevich, I earnestly ask this of you.' Yeltsin did not respond. Karimov then said: 'Does Zhirinovskii not reflect views found in the minds of certain state officials? This is a very dangerous symptom.'[16] Fourth, the republic introduced its own currency in 1994 and so was no longer bound by Russian budgetary and financial policies. This gave the country a degree of economic freedom and the government actively sought to divert its market away from the CIS. Russia did not represent a significant or exclusive market for its main export products (cotton and gold). The main transport outlet that linked the republic to the external world did run through Russia, but other alternatives emerged. Moreover the situation in Russia was becoming increasingly unstable and the future of this route was in danger. Fifth, Uzbekistan was concerned that in the event of a neo-imperialist or ultra-nationalist government assuming power in Moscow, Russia would seek to re-establish the former USSR. Andrei

Kozyrev demanded that Central Asian states, including Uzbekistan, grant dual citizenship to its Russian population, treat Russian as an official language and avoid any discrimination. He also claimed that 'there may be cases when the use of direct military force will be needed to defend our compatriots abroad'[17] thus provoking fears that even a non-nationalist Russian government could harbour imperialist aspirations. Sixth, Uzbekistan did not have Kazakstan's worry. The ethnic profile of the republic was less Russified, over 70 per cent of the population being Uzbek. Seventh, Uzbekistan needed capital, a strong private sector and contact with international business, which was exactly what Russia itself needed. By 1995 Uzbekistan had attracted considerable foreign investment and was interested in developing bilateral relations directly with various countries of the world to overcome the economic recession, and strengthen its independence. It developed closer ties with the EU and was looking towards closer ties with the US and NATO. Eighth, Uzbekistan initiated Central Asian integration which gained Kazak and Kyrgyzy support. But Russia forced these two states to agree to a Eurasia economic and customs union on Moscow's terms. Uzbekistan resented this idea and President Karimov regarded it as 'Russia's conspiracy to keep apart the brethren Central Asian republics from one another'.[18] Finally, Uzbekistan was resolved to build its statehood on Uzbek nationalism and to act as a regional power.

Despite its desire to distance itself from Russia, Uzbekistan has maintained strong bilateral relations with the Russian Federation. The republic has signed many agreements with Russia including cooperation in economic, social, political, security, educational, health, communication and transport fields. There are also around 350 Russian–Uzbek joint ventures conducting business in the republic. The republican leadership and its interconnected strong bureaucratic network still find it easier to work with the Russians than with some of their new partners. Russian is still the main language of the executive body in Uzbekistan. For its part, Russia prefers the current Uzbek leadership to any potential alternatives. Although the Russian leadership has encountered some difficulties, the Uzbek leadership is still far more receptive to Russian interests and priorities than any new leadership would likely be. Equally the Uzbek leadership views Russia as a potential ally in its fight against its domestic opposition and disruptive external forces. The Russian and Uzbek leaderships share a number of common security concerns, notably the potential threat of radical Islam and the risk of inter-ethnic or territorial conflicts in the region.[19] The two countries are specifically concerned about future developments in Afghanistan and Tajikistan, and have consistently opposed the Taliban, the Islamist militia running Afghanistan.

On a pre-election visit to Tashkent on 11 December 1999, the then Russian prime minister, and now elected president, Vladimir Putin stated that Uzbekistan is now Russia's 'strategic partner'. Putin visited Tashkent for a second time on 18 May 2000. This was his first foreign visit since his inauguration on 7 May, choosing strategically important Central Asia to try to reassert Russian influence over an area where relations were cooler under his predecessor Boris Yeltsin. During this visit the two sides signed several agreements in the defence and military infrastructure, and energy cooperation spheres. For Uzbekistan, Russia is, in geopolitical and strategic terms, still the most important country in the region and will remain so for a long time to come. The republic recognizes the strategic interests of the Russian Federation in Central Asia, and considers its involvement in regional affairs facilitates the support of a political balance, economic development and the strengthening of security and stability in the region.[20] The Uzbek government feels happier about its own security with some guarantee of Russian military support should it ever be needed. Turkey cannot protect it and the United States' pledge to assist Uzbekistan in building up a military establishment free of Russian influence would be of little use if a crisis were to blow up in the short term. Yet, although Uzbekistan welcomes Russian help against its domestic and foreign enemies, it is also strongly against any attempt to recreate the old 'Centre' or the return of oppressive Russian rule. Its fears that Russian hegemony could return have intensified since early 1994 with the growth of neo-imperialist sentiments in Russia, coupled with a more systemic Russian effort to reintegrate the old Soviet sphere. Having this in mind, the Uzbek leader announced in January 1999 that Uzbekistan planned to pull out of the CIS collective security treaty when it expired in April 2000. But he changed his mind about ending Tashkent's participation in the defence treaty after narrowly escaping death on February 1999 in a series of bomb explosions in Tashkent attributed to radical Muslims. The main challenge for Uzbekistan in its relation with the Russian Federation is how to harness Russian power to advance its own interests without giving in to Russian hegemony. The strategy for reconciling these two contradictory objectives has been to develop alternative economic, political, and security relations with other major powers and neighbouring countries, while maintaining closer ties with the Russian Federation. If the neo-imperialist sentiment in Russia intensifies, so will the republic's strategy of developing these alternative economic, political, and security relations.

Uzbekistan and Turkey
Throughout the Soviet period there were hardly any direct links between Turkey and Soviet Central Asia. This period marked seven decades of economic, social, cultural and political incommunicado between Turkey and this region. All existing political communications were with Moscow, and the relations between Turkey and the Soviet Union covered only the central strategic preoccupation of the East–West bipolar confrontation. Turkish–Soviet relations did enjoy periods of relative warmth, and trade began to grow, but interaction hardly transcended this bipolar enmity. Security considerations always determined relations in all other domains.[21]

This situation, however, ended suddenly and unexpectedly with the break-up of the Soviet Union in late 1991. Four new Turkic republics, each eager to establish a network of external relations beyond the former Soviet Union, emerged in Central Asia. Turkey, for its part, was excited by the changes taking place in its expanding geostrategic space, in particular at what was increasingly perceived as the discovery of long-lost brethren states. It wasted little time in establishing direct relations with Uzbekistan and with the other Central Asian republics. Turkey was not alone in its desire to establish close ties with these republics. For reasons of common historical, linguistic, cultural and ethnic affinity, Turkey became one of the first countries to attract the Turkic republics. The West also actively promoted Turkey's image as the ideal model of an Islamic, but secular and modern, state and urged the Central Asian republics to take Turkey as a role model. The US, for its part, was quick and heavy-handed in pushing the idea of a major role for Turkey in this region as a way of minimizing Iranian influence.[22] Encouraged by the West, Turkey was actively involved with the Central Asian republics to enhance its influence. Initially this idea gained some support in several capitals of these republics, but the period of euphoria soon evaporated, and Turkey realized that there was a limit to how much it could achieve in the region.

Among the Central Asian states, Turkey has attached great importance to Uzbekistan, because of its population, natural resources and geopolitical position in the region. It believes the republic has a promising future. Turkey officially recognized Uzbekistan on 16 December 1991, becoming the first country to do so, and this was followed by President Karimov's visit to Turkey in the same year. The Turkish Embassy was opened in Tashkent on 28 April 1992, followed by the opening of the Uzbek Embassy in Ankara. The Turkish Ambassador appointed to Tashkent became the first foreign ambassador dispatched to the republic. A Turkish–Uzbek business council was set up as early as November 1991. A Turkish Cultural Centre was opened in early 1992. A new body affiliated to the Turkish Ministry of Foreign Affairs, called the Turkish International Cooperation Agency (TICA), opened an office in Tashkent. Direct scheduled flights by the Turkish carrier, Türk Hava Yolları (THY), were established between Turkey and Uzbekistan. Turkey sought to link itself directly with the people of Central Asia via a direct broadcasting system. A special channel, *Avrasya*, was set up with the aim of creating such direct contacts.[23]

Once diplomatic, cultural and business relations were established, high-level diplomatic traffic between two countries intensified. In February 1992, the Turkish Foreign Minister, Hikmet Çetin, paid a visit to Uzbekistan accompanied by a delegation of 140 people, including businessmen and journalists as well as officials.[24] In late April it was the turn of Prime Minister Süleyman Demirel to visit the region. The delegation accompanying Demirel was even larger and included people with different professional perspectives on the emerging relationship.[25] The nature and size of the Turkish delegations that accompanied Çetin and Demirel, were intended to convey the impression that extensive cooperation was taking place on a variety of different levels and ensured that such an impression received maximum publicity. The flow of such diplomatic traffic continued apace with numerous other visits and exchanges in many different spheres. These were also, from the Turkish point of view, intended not to excite the expectation or suspicion that Turkey harboured ambitions of leadership over Central Asia. It did not take long for its neighbours to see through this. In fact it was Turkish officials and ministers who began to speak in expansive terms about Turkey's future role in the area.[26] As early as late September 1991, President Özal had told a Japanese audience that Turkey would enter the twenty-first century as 'the strongest country in the region'; in March 1992 Çetin, on his return from a visit to Central Asia, spoke of the very important and effective role his country could play in the region and it was during this visit that he began citing Turkey as a model country for the Central Asian republics. It was Demirel who indulged in some high-flown rhetoric, speaking of an exclusive bond that existed between Turkey and the Turkic republics. He stated that they 'share the same blood, religion and language'.[27] Some would even argue that the presence of Alparslan Türkeş, the leader of the Pan-Turkist National Action Party, within the Demirel delegation was enough to excite suspicion that Turkey harboured aspirations of becoming a regional hegemon.[28] The rhetoric of Turkish politicians and their comments regarding the Central Asian republics did not cause concern solely to Turkey's neighbours, like Russia. Like other republics in the region, Uzbekistan grew weary and irritated by some of the assumptions and presumptions of Turkish politicians and officials. For example, Turks often assumed that these republics were backward in education and health facilities, whereas rates of literacy and scientific education in Uzbekistan often outstripped those of Anatolia.[29] Moreover, the Republic of Uzbekistan, as a newly independent and sovereign entity, was keen to establish a framework of external relations correspondent with its new status. It wanted to develop relations directly with the principal states of the world. The notion of foreign relations somehow being channelled through Ankara was greatly unattractive. Yet this was persistently implicit and often explicit in Turkish officials' statements. For instance, in late March 1992 during a press conference Süleyman Demirel spoke of Turkey being a 'cultural centre and historic magnet' for the newly independent states, thereby implying that the states themselves were to remain a periphery, with Turkey as the emerging power centre. This openly self-confident tone, which could so easily be perceived as brazen self-interested arrogance, was evident when Demirel went on to say: 'We simply believe we can help these [Central Asian and Azerbaijan] republics in their long overdue attempt to integrate with the world.'[30] In fact, Uzbek officials have considered their own country as a 'cultural centre and historic magnet' for the Turkic people. Such Turkish statements simply exacerbated the republic's resentment toward Turkey. As a newly independent republic, Uzbekistan was also resentful of attempts to close off potentially productive new areas of cooperation because of Western priorities often shared by

Turkey. The republic's suspicions about Turkey's intentions became more obvious after the first Turkic summit meeting convened in Ankara on 30–31 October 1992.

The summit agenda itself was set by Turkey, and consisted of a series of recommendations and extensive cooperation to be pursued rapidly.[31] The blueprint for action that was outlined by Turkish President Özal at the summit was drawn up without adequate consultation with any of the Central Asian republics, simply confirming the earlier impression that Turkey had arrogantly attributed to itself a leadership role within the Turkic world. Uzbek President Islom Karimov made clear his own limited involvement in the exercise. He ruled out any desire to establish a supranational mechanism that would coordinate the Turkic world.[32] Kazakhstan also rejected this idea. Consequently the summit ran into trouble. Turks at all levels had to re-evaluate some of their more fanciful notions of potential cooperation with the Central Asian Turkic republics. Uzbekistan's position clearly showed that it did not have the same interests and priorities as Turkey, while the leadership neither desired nor envisaged an exclusive relationship with that country. Uzbekistan was well aware that other relationships had to be taken into account to overcome severe economic dislocation and maintain security and stability in its region.

It did not take long before the republic developed new relations in other directions. Thus, it re-established close relations with the Russian Federation. It was concerned with the ongoing Tajik civil war right on its own doorstep. The republic was also interested in establishing ties with other countries in the region, such as Iran, China, Pakistan, India and other Asian and south-east Asian countries. The ruling elite in the republic also recognized that Europe would be of crucial economic importance to Uzbekistan, yet Turkey itself was having difficulties gaining entry into the EU. Close identification with Turkey was also recognized to carry the American imprimatur, which in the eyes of the political elite in the country was complicating other options if the commitment were to become too intense. Uzbekistan at this point wished to keep all options open rather than commit itself exclusively to the Turkish connection. Turkey, on the other hand, had also committed itself to many obligations and promises that, realistically speaking, overreached the limits of its capabilities. Initially Uzbekistan was in favour of a Turkish secular model of development, but this soon appeared to be a means of expediting international recognition. Indeed, just before his visit to South Korea, Malaysia, and Indonesia, President Karimov clarified his position towards the so-called Turkish model of development. In an interview, Karimov stated that Uzbekistan would not copy the Turkish model or any other model thoughtlessly, but rather would look for 'its own Uzbek model', borrowing everything valuable from others' experience, including the experiences of Asian countries.[33]

By late 1992, well aware of the limitations of Turkey's resources, and ambitions, Uzbekistan distanced itself from a Turkish vision of external policy and sought to develop extensive bilateral relations with other states in the region. This period prompted Turkey to re-evaluate its relations with the republics of Central Asia as well as convincing Uzbekistan of the need to redesign its relations with Turkey. This period also marked a cooling of relations between Turkey and Uzbekistan. Trouble became evident in 1993 when the political elite in Uzbekistan embarked on a major offensive to silence political opposition in the country. *Birlik* and *Erk* leaders and some of their supporters fled to Turkey. Uzbekistan not only accused Turkey of sheltering its opposition forces, but also accused it of allowing Muhammed Salih, the leader of *Erk* who ran against Karimov in the 1991 presidential elections, to train 'terrorists' in Turkey, alleging that they planned to seize some Uzbek government officials as hostages. Although Turkey denied this, one Turkish official, Namik Emin, stated that there had been training activity for some 'security guards', but that was only for Salih's personal security.[34] Whatever the case, Turkey tried to assure Tashkent that the Turkish government had no intention of supporting the Uzbek opposition. Even so, political relations between the two countries deteriorated further. Uzbekistan recalled its students from Turkey; the only Turkish newspaper published in Central Asia, *Zaman*, was banned in the republic; and the television channel *Avrasya*'s broadcasts were reduced to less than an hour a day.

These events did not, however, precipitate a collapse in Turkish diplomacy. In mid-1994 Turkey launched what it considered to be a serious and constructive diplomacy to develop bilateral relations with the republic. In Ankara it was asserted more coherently than in the past that there had never been any intention to create a sphere of influence in Central Asia with the subordination or exclusion of others.[35] Contrary to its previously heavy-handed idealist diplomacy, Turkey was now pursuing a more cautious policy towards Central Asia due mainly to two factors. Firstly, Russia's suspicions about Ankara's Turkic policy were aroused and from mid-1993 it had been expressing concern over what they described as efforts by Turkey to create a pan-Turkist alliance. Secondly, not only Uzbekistan but other Turkic republics became resentful of Turkey's aspirations and its heavy-handed diplomacy. Mindful of such concerns, Turkey had given extensive support to its private sector which had been active in the region in order to initiate more investment in Uzbekistan to improve its relations with the republic. Although this private sector cannot compete with Western companies in the mining and energy sector, it has nonetheless made significant inroads in the republic, and Uzbekistan has appreciated these efforts. TICA has increased its aid to the republic for this cause and by 1994 it had given Uzbekistan $53 million. The Turkish Eximbank also extended its credit to the republic.

This 'new' Turkish diplomacy coincided with a time when Uzbekistan was trying to distance itself from the Russian Federation because of internal power struggles and instability in that country. The most obvious features of this were the strong showings of the ultra-nationalists and ex-communists in the December parliamentary elections; the increasing role of the military in determining Russia's policy toward the so-called Near Abroad; the republic's expulsion from the rouble zone in late 1993; Uzbekistan's desire to develop cooperation with NATO; and, from spring 1995 onwards, the republic's relations with the US showing signs of improvements. Turkey as a NATO member state had also actively supported Uzbekistan's participation in NATO's 'Partnership for Peace' programme. All these factors undoubtedly contributed to improving strong bilateral relations between Uzbekistan and Turkey. The relationship improved further, first when Kazakstan and Kyrgyzstan signed an economic and customs union agreement with the Russian Federation and Byelorussia in early spring 1996, and second, with the Russian Duma's vote in March 1996 to re-establish the former Soviet Union by force if necessary. This period marked a shift in Uzbekistan foreign policy from a pro-Russian stance to a more pro-Western one. Since then Uzbek–Turkish relations have improved considerably. On 8 May 1996 the republic signed an 'Eternal Friendship' agreement with Turkey during President Süleyman Demirel's visit to Tashkent. Uzbekistan favours close bilateral cooperation, but it does not want Turkish domination. Since late 1991 over 100 agreements in the fields of culture, education, health, politics, economics and military training have been signed between the two countries. Until 1997 there were over 230 Turkish companies conducting business in Uzbekistan and established joint ventures. About 30 major firms had representatives in the country. KOÇ had built a mini-bus plant near Samarkand; GAMA had constructed an oil and gas refinery plant in Bukhara; ALARKO in a joint venture with BAT built a cigarette factory near Samarkand; AY-SEL (Guven SAZAK) construction firm built an Aqua Park and Disneyland, and a five-star hotel with a business centre in Tashkent. Although Turkish construction firms were in general very active in Uzbekistan, major Turkish firms had been investing in the textile industry. Turks had also invested in the catering industry and confectionaries. There were also seven Turkish state and seventeen private Turkish Lycees in Uzbekistan. There had been numerous student exchanges, and Turkey had trained and educated many Uzbek army officers in its institutions.

Uzbekistan has given priority to its future economic development and welcomed any Turkish initiatives in this sphere but it is also determined to limit Turkish political influence over the region. The regional aspirations of the republic,[36] despite its pan-Turkist tendencies made it reluctant to accept a leadership role for Turkey. Following the continuing instability in Turkish domestic politics and Turkey's weakening international image, Uzbekistan sought to distance itself from this country in 1998. After the February 1999 bombing in Tashkent, Uzbek authorities even accused Turkey of having a role. Ankara has played down the resulting strains, but the significance of the Turkish connection to the February 1999 events did not end there. The authorities in Tashkent criticized Ankara, stating that Turkey moved too slowly in extraditing one suspect, Rustem Mametkulov. The Uzbek President then accused Turkey of undermining the secular system in Uzbekistan and trying to overthrow his government. The relations between the two countries deteriorated further and raised tensions. All Uzbek students were called back from Turkey. Turkish schools in Uzbekistan were shut down and many Turks were expelled from Uzbekistan. In response, the Turkish ambassador in Tashkent returned to Ankara. In July, Turkish Prime Minister Bulent Ecevit called the Uzbek ambassador in Ankara to his office. Ecevit later declared to the press that Turkey was interested in again improving its ties with Uzbekistan, but his comments made it clear that tensions still persisted. With the election of Ahmet Necdet

Sezer, the former head of the constitution court, as the new Turkish President in May 2000, Turkish officials are likely to seek ways of reversing the cooling relations between Ankara and Tashkent. Demirel worked hard to preserve the friendly relations established with Uzbekistan during Özal's time, but failed. The series of bomb explosions in Tashkent have provided perfect ammunition for Karimov to counter perceived Turkish ambitions over the region.

The future shape of Uzbek–Turkish relations will, to a large extent, be determined by Russian–Uzbek relations, and by Turkey's own domestic circumstances. Today Turkey is politically, economically and socially unstable. The community is divided along ethnic, religious and ideological lines. The situation in the country continues to be volatile. If present conditions continue much longer they could lead to country-wide civil unrest which would have serious consequences for the state. Under these conditions, an influential future role for Turkey in this region seems unlikely.

Uzbekistan and Asia
Uzbekistan in its foreign policy declaration has always emphasized its position in the region and often stated that it would adopt an Asian mode of development. Therefore, the most important external political event in the second half of 1992 for Uzbekistan was the establishment of diplomatic relations with the countries of south-east Asia and Pacific Asia, personified by official visits by President Islom Karimov to elicit Asian investment in his country.

Given its economic strength, Japan has been rather slow in developing its relations with the republic. Nonetheless, some Japanese firms have recently shown some interest in conducting business in the country. Nishe Ivai is engaged in joint mining of oil and gas deposits in Kokdumalak; Marubei is building an oil refinery plant in the Bukhara oblast; Mitsui is reconstructing the Fergana oil refinery plant and has signed an agreement with Uzbekistan's State Committee for Geology and Mineral Resources to develop the Kyzylalmasai and Kochbulak gold deposits near Tashkent.

South Korea was one of the first countries of the Asian Pacific Region to recognize the independence of Uzbekistan and establish diplomatic relations with it in early 1992. A special relationship was facilitated for the two countries, by the existence of a large Korean minority in Uzbekistan. In June 1992 Islom Karimov paid an official four-day visit to South Korea, during which a number of agreements were signed covering the cultural, political and economic fields. South Korean firms have been active in developing investment opportunities in Uzbekistan. UzDaewoo, a South Korean–Uzbek joint venture has so far been the largest foreign investment project in the republic. It produced 65,000 cars in 1997 and also produces televisions, videos and refrigerators. Uzbekistan–South Korea relations developed further during Islom Karimov's visit to the republic in February 1995, and since then South Korean investment in Uzbekistan has increased considerably. The relationship between the two countries appears to be quite stable despite the economic crisis that hit south-east Asia in early 1998. By late 1997 there were about 66 South Korean companies conducting business in Uzbekistan.

Another country in the region with which Uzbekistan has worked to develop its relations is Indonesia. The relationship between Uzbekistan and Indonesia took off with the visit of the then President Suharto to Tashkent in September 1989, at the time when the USSR still existed. Although this visit did not produce a great deal of tangible benefits between the two countries at the time, it nonetheless established a basis for exploring possibilities for future cooperation. Islom Karimov's visit to Indonesia in June 1992 marked a historical event in Uzbek–Indonesia relations. The two countries signed several agreements in the fields of economy, culture, trade, transport, communications and tourism. Indonesia generously extended to Uzbekistan US$100 million of credit. As the world's fourth largest nation in terms of population and one of the biggest world importers of cotton, Indonesia agreed to import a large quantity of Uzbek cotton fibre. Prima Comensido, an Indonesian company, established joint ventures with local firms and currently works on investment projects in the Uzbek textile and food industries and was interested in developing trade, cement production, chemicals industries, pharmacology, and building new hotels and developing a tourist industry.[37] All these developments undoubtedly contributed to a better relationship between the two countries. But the further development of Uzbek–Indonesia relations will be determined by the ongoing power struggle in Indonesia and political and economic stability in the south-east Asian region.

Among the Asian countries China was the first to engage in relationships with the countries of Central Asia. Immediately after the disintegration of the Soviet Union a Chinese delegation headed by Li Zemin, the Minister of Foreign Economic Affairs and Trade, visited Uzbekistan. The visit itself marked the beginning of Uzbek–China relations. It was the first high-ranking foreign delegation to visit Uzbekistan. The trip led to the signing of trade agreements and the establishment of constructive relations between China and Uzbekistan. Since then the economic ties between the two countries have expanded rapidly. Islom Karimov officially visited China in 1992 and 1994 where he signed several agreements covering transport and communications and an agreement on establishing a China–Uzbek intergovernmental committee on trade and economic partnership. In April 1994 Prime Minister Li Peng, and in July 1996 Jiang Zemin, made trips to Tashkent, further strengthening economic and political ties between Uzbekistan and China.[38] To date there are 87 Uzbek–China joint ventures in various parts of the republic. Although the Chinese leaders' frequent visits to Uzbekistan created businesslike and constructive relations between Beijing and Tashkent, China's immediate concern is its Muslim region of Xinjiang which borders directly with Central Asia and is the home of 10–12 million Uighurs, who are related to the Uzbeks and have several hundred thousand kinsmen living throughout Central Asia. These also have a long history of resistance to Beijing. Therefore Chinese leaders skilfully used growing economic ties to reduce political support for the Uighur separatist movement in its Xinjiang province. This became more obvious in the wake of the fifth Turkic summit held in the new Kazak capital Astana (formerly named Akmola) on 8 June 1998. Prior to the summit, Uzbek President Karimov criticized past rivalries among the Turkic countries, and cautioned that Turkic unity had limits, noting that supporting the Uighurs in China's Xinjiang Province would endanger relations with 'the great China'.[39] Moreover the Uzbek leadership had no intention of provoking confrontation with China. Indeed Central Asian leaders as a whole have enough worries of their own without wishing to antagonize such a populous neighbour.

However, despite improving relations with Uzbekistan, China's security situation along its borders with Central Asia is in general less than satisfactory. A border agreement was signed with Kazakstan, but an agreement with Kyrgyzstan has yet to be signed. Moreover, immediately after the break-up of the Soviet Union, with their frequent visits to Central Asia, the Chinese leaders have increased Beijing's influence in the region. For Uzbekistan, China is a strategically important state and its growing interest in Central Asia cannot be ignored. A significant part of this territory belonged to the Chinese empire in the last century and according to some scholars, China still considers the fertile Fergana Valley to be its own territory.[40] Although Beijing has been careful to avoid publicly mentioning this territorial controversy, it regards the break-up of the Soviet Union as an opportunity to extend its influence over the region. Ironically, Uzbekistan's intention in developing friendly relations with this world's most populous nation was to benefit from the ensuing economic cooperation, yet at the same time it hoped to diffuse Chinese influence in the region. In fact, Beijing's influence over Uzbekistan has increased. Some scholars believe that China has developed a long-term policy that aims to draw Central Asia into the orbit of its own economic and political influence.[41] Indeed there is growing concern within Uzbekistan's political circles about the true intentions of China. There is a view that good relations with China may be temporary, a sentiment coupled with suspicions about Beijing's real intent. Notwithstanding the developing good relations between the two countries, Uzbekistan (like other Central Asian states), nourishes an abiding distrust of Beijing and even a sense of impending doom in the face of its growing power. Nonetheless, relations between China and Uzbekistan will continue to develop, partly due to regional problems and partly due to China's political and economic weight in the international community, but it will be determined by Beijing's growing influence in Central Asia. Beijing's influence and Uzbekistan's distrust are likely to grow in tandem.

Another regional power, India, has also shown a strong interest in developing ties with the Central Asian states. This is due mainly to its security and political concerns in the region. Its competition with Pakistan, the Kashmir problem, the future of Afghanistan, and India's preoccupation with the potential impact of developments in all these regions on its own Muslim population, have increased its anxiety after the break-up of the Soviet Union. India sees any undue expansion of Pakistan's influence or rise in Islamist influence in the region as damaging to its own interests.[42] Despite a recent improvement in its relations with China, India would not be happy for an overexpansion of Chinese influence in Central Asia.[43] Therefore, India's main concern is to prevent regional security threats from developing. In addition to this, It is interested in a potentially important export market in the region and sees Uzbekistan as a state that can play an important role there. Uzbekistan is also concerned with regional security and stability, and as a land-locked country is seeking to develop various trade and transport routes. Access to the Indian Ocean is one transport route in which Uzbekistan has shown great interest. President Karimov noted in this connection that 'the most favourable condition for Uzbekistan's economic development would be access to the Indian Ocean through Afghanistan and Pakistan. You can just imagine the ways in which different parts of the world will be opened for us. We will be able to send loads through the ports of the Indian Ocean and deliver back everything needed for Uzbekistan.'[44] The conflict in Afghanistan and the unstable situation in Tajikistan have so far made Uzbekistan's access to Indian ports impossible and has limited India's economic and political presence in the republic.

Pakistan, though not an immediate neighbour to Uzbekistan, has a deep involvement in Afghanistan, thus making it intensely preoccupied with Central Asia's evolution.[45] It also wants a share of potential economic opportunities in the region. Since the late 1980s, Pakistan has actively presented itself to Uzbekistan as a valuable partner, an alternative model of development to both Iran and Turkey, and an entry corridor to the outside world. Pakistan's influence however has been limited by its inadequate transport infrastructure, its limited financial resources, and its role as a major producer of cotton, and thus a competitor in the textile industry. Its own political and economic difficulties further hinder its chances of being a potential power. Pakistan is also engaged in an impalpable act of competition and limited cooperation with Uzbekistan over Afghanistan's political future. Pakistan and Uzbekistan both oppose any significant role for the Afghan Tajiks and the Hazera Shi'as in any future Afghan government and seek to limit Iran's influence in the region. Pakistan initially favoured the Pashtu Afghan leader Gulbudin Hekmatyar, but has recently been trying to influence Afghanistan's future through the religious militia Taliban, which it formed and has financed. In these goals Pakistan has been supported by Saudi Arabia and the United States.[46] The Taliban consolidated their power in the south and in October 1996 overthrew the Afghan government in Kabul. It now controls two-thirds of the country. The Taliban advanced northwards and almost took control of the northern part of Afghanistan which is under the northern alliance's control; they were initially forced to abandon the region and draw back to Kabul, but in the summer of 1998 they once again took control of the majority of northen Afghanistan with Pakistani assistance. Uzbekistan does not want to see an Islamic government in Kabul and has become increasingly alarmed by the strength of the extremist Taliban, dominated by Pakistan, in Kabul. Before the Taliban's advance to Kabul, there were rumours in Tashkent in mid-summer 1996 that Uzbekistan and Pakistan had, with American approval, drawn up a plan to settle the Afghan problem for good. According to the plan, Afghanistan would become a federal state; Kandahar would join a confederation with Pakistan, and Mazar-i Sharif would join a confederation with Uzbekistan. Thus subject to Pakistani and Uzbek influence, the central government in Kabul would be weakened and Afghanistan would eventually become a confederation, which would probably be divided between Pakistan and Uzbekistan. This would be in the interests of Pakistan, Uzbekistan and the US. The US also wants to enable Uzbekistan to have access to the sea, though not through Iran. For a number of reasons the US has also supported the radical and militarist Taliban movement. The US administration has taken the view that a Taliban victory would end a war that has killed one-and-a-half million Afghans; would act as a counterweight to Iran, whose leadership is fiercely opposed to the Taliban; and would offer the possibility of new trade routes that could weaken Russian and Iranian influence in the region.[47] However, it appears that the US policy makers have incorrectly calculated developments in the region. The militant Taliban has become more extremist and having gained overall control in large parts of Afghanistan, it no longer appears to be listening to either Pakistan or the US. It has expelled almost all non-governmental and international aid organizations from Afghanistan and has shown no respect for basic human rights in the areas under its control. Consequently, the future of Afghanistan as a political entity looks more bleak and more complicated then ever before. Neither Iranian nor Russian influence has diminished. On the contrary, Iran's role in the region has increased. Isolating Iran and Russia does not appear to be practical, and relying on the Taliban is too risky. It may provide temporary stability, but oil and gas pipelines need to be maintained and secured. The Taliban has not explored any form of reconciliation with other ethnic groups either. The situation in Afghanistan has thus become more volatile and is poised to remain so, thus proving deleterious for any type of real investment or other projects.

Nevertheless, Pakistan, like Russia and Uzbekistan, has tried to play a constructive role in resolving the conflict in Tajikistan and hosted one of the intra-Tajik talks sessions in Islamabad. It is actively seeking to extend economic and cultural ties with Uzbekistan and gives a high priority to building up good relations with the republic, since it is the most populated country in the region and politically crucial. Pakistan has signed over forty agreements with Uzbekistan covering transport and communications, trade, education and culture. A branch of the National Bank of Pakistan was opened in 1992. Many businessmen from various parts of Pakistan have investigated commercial opportunities and established a number of joint ventures. Many of these joint ventures are small-scale enterprises, but they have managed to open over 130 joint ventures with their local partners. The Uzbek Foreign Minister Abdulaziz Kamilov's visit to Pakistan in July 1994 and the Pakistani Prime Minister Benazir Bhutto's visit to Uzbekistan in May 1995 paved the way for further cooperation. In October 1996, the Pakistani President Farooq Ahmed Khan Leghari paid a visit to Uzbekistan to enhance bilateral relations and held discussions with President Karimov regarding regional and international issues of mutual concern, most notably, the Afghan conflict. They also signed cooperation accords on organized crime, and the fight against terrorism and illicit drug-trafficking. Bilateral relations between the two states will continue to develop in line with their conflicting interests in the region. Uzbekistan for its part will cooperate with Pakistan in matters that it finds beneficiary, otherwise the republic will regard Pakistan as a competitor. Uzbekistan has also stated its disapproval over the recent nuclear tests by both India and Pakistan in the summer of 1998. The republic has grown increasingly suspicious of Pakistan's intentions in the region as the Taliban has made more gains in Afghanistan.

Uzbekistan and the Middle East

Among the countries of the Middle East it has been the non-Arab states – that is mainly Israel, Iran and Turkey – that have been the quickest and the most enthusiastic to establish ties with the republics of former Soviet Central Asia, including Uzbekistan.[48] Among the Arab states,

Saudi Arabia's involvement with Uzbekistan owed a lot to its Islamic historical legacy. It was concerned about the fate of fellow Muslims in the region as a whole and acted as a source of economic assistance. The Saudi Kingdom is always in search of new opportunities to compete with Iran for strategic dominance in the Persian Gulf and Islamic world. It has therefore been the keenest backer of an Islamic cultural and political resurgence sponsoring religious and cultural activities. Oman and the United Arab Emirates have recently instigated economic and commercial cooperation. Egypt has also established diplomatic ties and opened a large Cultural Centre in Tashkent based in Navoi.

Uzbekistan and Iran

Iran's actual policy towards the Central Asian republics has been guided first and foremost by its national interest and thus its policy appears to be more geopolitical than ideological.[49] It has been careful to maintain good bilateral relations with Uzbekistan, extending economic and commercial cooperation, and establishing firm cultural ties. Iran's attitude towards Uzbekistan has been influenced by this country's size, its potential wealth, its importance as a historical Islamic centre, and its geopolitical proximity.[50] Moreover Uzbekistan has large Persian-speaking Tajik minorities. Tehran is interested in avoiding instability and disorder in the region and wants stable regimes around its borders. It has also been careful not to antagonize Russia. Indeed, Iran avoided early recognition of independence declarations by the Central Asian republics, and recognized their independence only after Moscow had done so. It recognized Uzbekistan's independence in 1992 and established diplomatic relations in early 1993.

Despite Tehran's efforts to establish firm friendly bilateral relations with Uzbekistan, its relations with the republic have been uneasy and unstable. Tashkent initially took the view that Tehran aimed to export its ideology and to interfere in the internal affairs of the countries in the region. It also claimed that Iran was at the root of the civil war in Tajikistan in the name of Islamic revolution. President Islom Karimov's visit to Tehran in November 1992, heading a political and economic delegation, and President Ali Akbar Hashemi Rafsanjani's visit to Tashkent in October 1993, eased Tashkent's fears about Iran's intentions, but did not completely allay its suspicions.

With all its difficulties, Iran has managed to achieve some improvement in its relations with Uzbekistan. In August 1995 the Uzbek foreign minister Abdulaziz Kamilov took part in the opening of the Uzbek Embassy in Tehran, where he disputed reports that Uzbekistan had backed the United States' embargo imposed on Iran at the end of April 1995. The two countries also agreed to establish a joint economic commission to examine possibilities for expanding economic ties. Further discussions on expanding bilateral relations were held during the visit to Tashkent of the Iranian foreign minister Ali Akbar Velaayati. During his meeting with President Karimov on 28 February 1996, Akbar Velaayati stated that Iran would be ready to develop mutually beneficial cooperation with Uzbekistan, especially in the fields of economics, communications and transport. President Karimov agreed that there were possibilities to develop bilateral relations between the two countries and Velaayati's visit provided a space for exchanging ideas about ways of maintaining security and stability in the region, and developing friendly relations between the peoples of Uzbekistan and Iran.[51] As a result, about 100 Iranian–Uzbek joint ventures were established in Uzbekistan. These factors may not have produced a great deal in Uzbek–Iranian relations, but they have been indications of a softening in Uzbekistan's stance towards Iran. The latter for its part has been making every effort to improve its negative image in the republic, while extending economic and commercial ties with other Central Asian countries. It is acting essentially as a nation-state in the region, trying to maintain what it considers to be its legitimate national interest in a rapidly changing and turbulent area. Moreover, from the perspective of Iran's policy-makers it has a lot to gain from the presence of a bloc of friendly states around its borders. Although such expectations are often frustrated by Uzbekistan and some challenges become evident, this still gives Tehran a sense of security and a possible escape from the political isolation it has brought upon itself for the last eighteen years.[52] Because it has elevated its national interest above ideology, Iran has throughout the Tajik civil war pursued a hands-off policy and remained silent in the face of Uzbek–Russian military intervention. It did not allow Uzbekistan's anti-Islamist efforts, or its close ties with Israel, to prevent it from pursuing a conciliatory policy towards Uzbekistan in the hope of improving its bad image.[53] This policy not only softened Uzbekistan's active opposition, but also increased sympathy among Uzbek people in various parts of the country towards Iran.

For its part, Uzbekistan, while pursuing a policy of limiting Iran's influence in the region, also recognizes the important geopolitical advantages that Iran can offer to a land-locked country such as itself. Its direct route to the Persian Gulf and the Indian Ocean is the shortest and cheapest outlet to the outside world, not only for the republic but also for the other Central Asian republics. In addition to this, Iran's reasonably well-developed road and rail systems are the ideal connecting point between Central Asia and Turkey, the Caucasus, China and the Persian Gulf. On 12 May 1996, the rail link of Tejen–Serakhs–Meshkhed–Bandar–Abbas connected the railway system of the republic with Iran's national rail links, which is itself connected to the Turkish railway system, which extends to Europe via Istanbul. However, the character of the Iranian regime and its image as the stronghold of revolutionary Islam are serious liabilities in its bilateral relations with Uzbekistan. Moreover, Iran's Shi'a character and the influence of its civilization in the region are resented by Uzbekistan since the republic considers itself to be the heir to the region's Persian civilization. Uzbekistan's aspirations for regional leadership are not compatible with a strong Iranian presence. It is also aware of Iran's limited financial resources for resolving basic economic problems. It needs capital, a strong private sector and contact with international business, which Iran itself needs. Uzbekistan's desire to elicit badly-needed Western investment and the increasingly close Uzbek–US relations since April 1995 have also limited the republic's bilateral relations with Iran. Although difficulties continue to hamper Uzbek–Iranian relations, Uzbekistan has recognized the crucial importance of Iran as the only land route to the Persian Gulf and, through Turkey, to Europe. At present almost 80 per cent of Uzbekistan's imports go through Iran. In the long run, however, Uzbek–Iranian relations will depend considerably on the developments in Iran itself and its relations with the West. In the absence of political instability, economic breakdown or external aggression, its relations with Uzbekistan could develop further; otherwise they will remain businesslike relations.

Uzbekistan and Israel

Among the Middle Eastern countries, Israel would be expected to have been one of the least active in the Central Asian region, whereas in fact it has been among the most active. The motives behind its ties with Uzbekistan have been both political and economic. In political terms Israel wanted to achieve three goals in the region: (i) to reduce its isolation among the Islamic world by establishing extensive ties with the Central Asian Muslim countries that were largely unaffected either by political Islam or by the Arab–Israeli issue; (ii) to express concern about the emergence of a new bloc of Muslim countries from the East, with the ultimate disposition of nuclear weapons (in Kazakstan), and their possible transfer to such enemies as Iran; (iii) to weaken any attempts by Iran to rally the Islamic world against it. In economic terms, Israel, like many other states, wished to explore the potential commercial benefits in the large mineral-rich republic. Therefore Israel was among the first countries to establish diplomatic ties and open diplomatic representation in Uzbekistan.

The Israeli embassy was among the first to open in Tashkent. In 1994 Shimon Peres, the then Minister of Foreign Affairs, visited Uzbekistan and met with President Karimov. Israeli business has been able to penetrate the region quickly and successfully, and has focused on several areas where Israel has special skills and technology to offer, especially in agriculture. Uzbekistan has been home for a large number of Jews who escaped from the Nazi forces during the Second World War. The republic has also been home to Central Asian Jews for more than 2,000 years. Israeli business received enormous help and guidance from members of Uzbekistan's Jewish community who are well acquainted with the country's economy, and who understand the local norms and customs in business and personal relations. Some of them also have close ties to economic and political circles in Uzbekistan. To make sure that his country received investments from world Jewry, President Karimov assured Peres that ideology played no role in Uzbek–Iranian interaction. Karimov stated that 'Tashkent has a clearly defined position: to establish relations on an equal basis with Tehran, to cooperate honestly in all spheres of economics, science, and culture, but without permitting ideological expansion and the influence of radical Islamic forces'.[54] Uzbekistan has an interest in Israeli products, investment, and technology for developing its agriculture. Therefore the republic intends to expand its ties with Israel.

Uzbekistan and the European Union
To achieve a sound economic, social and political structure, Uzbekistan is eager to integrate into the world community and establish new links with major international economic and political organizations or blocs. Among these, the European Union (EU) occupies a special place in the foreign policy of the country. Uzbekistan's interest in the EU is principally strategic. Being one of the most active regions of the world in international life, Europe is of strategic interest to Uzbekistan which wants to expand into the European market and benefit from European financial, political and military–political institutions that in turn could promote the integration of the republic into the world community. This, however, may not be easy given the current political stance of Uzbekistan.

Nonetheless, several EU member states have shown great interest in Uzbekistan. Their interests are mainly economic in nature, at the base of which are hopes of finding new markets in a region characterized by the availability of rich natural resources and relatively cheap labour. They also want to maintain peace and stability in the Euro-Asian region. Thus, dynamic relations have developed between the Republic of Uzbekistan and the members of the EU since the former's independence. Brussels is the site of one of the four embassies that Uzbekistan has opened so far in Europe (the others are in Bonn, London and Paris).

The political and economic cooperation of Uzbekistan with the countries of the EU also encourages Uzbekistan to work for security in the region, and strengthens and develops the process of state-building. In addition, it provides the country with up-to-date technology, attracts investment in industry, provides opportunities to train specialists in the fields of banking and management, establishes contacts with leading markets in the world and allows a study of foreign experience in the fields of legislation, management, control of economic activity and diplomacy.

In September 1994 diplomatic relations were established between the Republic of Uzbekistan and the EU with the appointment of an official representative of the EU in Tashkent. Official representation from Uzbekistan was established in Brussels in 1995. Owing to the efforts of the Uzbek government, on the one hand, and lobbying by EU governments with major trading interests on the other, relations between Uzbekistan and the EU have developed in two main directions. The first is directly associated with the signing of the Partnership and Cooperation Agreement between Uzbekistan and the EU. The second relates to the benefits from the programme of technical assistance (TACIS), which is directed to supporting the implementation of economic reforms.

The Partnership and Cooperation Agreement
On 26 February 1996 the European Commission adopted a communication to the Council proposing an urgent opening of negotiations with the Republic of Uzbekistan for a Partnership and Cooperation Agreement (PCA). On 7 March 1996 in Brussels, the first round of negotiations were successfully completed and the European Commission adopted a decision to start negotiations with Uzbekistan on reaching a PCA. The exploratory contacts since July 1995 led the Commission to conclude that progress had been made concerning human rights and that the technical assistance projects which were underway for promoting democratic principles and values were progressing satisfactorily. This was, in fact, not the case. The Uzbek government has shown some signs of goodwill, but Uzbekistan's human rights record still remains poor. The EU, although stressing the importance of democracy and human rights to the Uzbek side, for commercial reasons was willing to complete the agreement. As expected, in June 1996 the European Commission in Brussels approved a communiqué to sign a PCA with Uzbekistan even though the EU officials in Tashkent reported that Uzbekistan disregarded the PCA's three main conditions. The first was that the recipient country of the PCA has democracy, the second was that it respects human rights and the third was that the recipient have a convertible currency to facilitate trade.

On his way to the US, President Karimov stopped off at the EU Summit in Florence and signed the PCA between Uzbekistan and the EU on 21 June 1996. The EU views the agreement as a motivation to help Uzbekistan develop the principles of democracy, human rights and a market economy. Uzbekistan, however, views it as a recognition of Karimov's 'successful policies' and of his leadership. Whatever the reason may be, the signature opened the way for Karimov to be accepted at the White House in late June 1996. With the help of the media, this and his meeting with President Clinton certainly enhanced Karimov's place in Uzbek politics. The signing ceremony in Italy and Karimov's meeting with President Clinton at the White House were presented by Uzbek television as an extraordinary event; Karimov's leadership was praised. And Karimov's answers to Abdumanov Pulato's questions in the US at a press conference where Karimov invited the opposition to return to their native country and work for their people if that was their aim, was also seen as a gesture of goodwill. There is no doubt that what was presented by local television was carefully designed to impress people in Uzbekistan.[55]

Without question the importance of the signing of the PCA with the EU was exaggerated in Uzbekistan, but there were good reasons for this. The agreement with the EU will provide for cooperation in a wide range of areas, covering relations in virtually all domains except military and security questions. Based upon a shared commitment to the respect of human rights and the implementation of the principles of the market economy, the PCA provided, *inter alia*, for political dialogue, for a high level of mutual obligations regarding trade in goods, the establishment and operation of companies, the protection of intellectual property rights and the free flow of investment capital. The EU promised to offer assistance to Uzbekistan on a large number of economic questions including transport, energy, financial services, privatization, science and technology, education and training, and the environment. It would also help to prepare Uzbekistan for membership of the World Trade Organization (WTO). The EU would provide political and moral support for Uzbekistan's independence, sovereignty and territorial integrity, and committed itself to assist Uzbekistan in implementing the principles set out in the documents of the OSCE.[56]

However, an early ratification by the European Parliament of the EU's PCA with Uzbekistan faced several problems. Uzbekistan still appeared to have fundamental problems with the three main conditions attached to the document. The Uzbek government promised that by 1997 Uzbekistan would meet the third condition and have a convertible currency. Unfavourable economic conditions, however, prevented it delivering on this promise, and resulted in the government's attempt to further tighten regulations concerning currency convertibility. The

European Commission, on the one hand, tried to revive the PCA, countering an attempt by the European Parliament to postpone its ratification. On the other hand, it pressurized the Uzbek leadership to stand up for what they had signed. The pressure on the European Commission to do this came mostly from lobbying by EU governments with major trading interests in Uzbekistan who wished to ensure that the European Commission persuaded the European Parliament to ratify the agreement as early as possible.

To mark another step in closer relations between the EU and Uzbekistan, an interim agreement was also signed between the EU and the Uzbek government on 14 November 1996 during President Karimov's visit to Brussels. This gave immediate effect to the trade aspects of the PCA, but it did not enter into force for some time. It required formal ratification by the European Parliament and the Council of Ministers. This process was to some extent dependent on progress with the PCA. A high-level delegation of Uzbek trade and economic officials headed by the Deputy Prime Minister, Viktor Chzhen, held talks with the European Commissioner for External Relations, Hans van den Broek, and senior officials on 12 May 1997 to overcome the problems regarding these two agreements. The EU was ready with advice on how to overcome the latest economic problems and the so-called 'convertibility crisis', but stated that Uzbekistan must return to a policy of market reforms, returning to the path of economic 'rectitude' in line with the commitments required under Uzbekistan's application to join the WTO and its relations with the IMF. The EU also urged bank reform on the Uzbek government and offered assistance with its WTO membership bid and a joint committee, under the existing EU relationship with Uzbekistan scheduled for July, to study how the EU could help further. The high-level Uzbek delegation visited Brussels on 12–14 May and signed a number of bilateral trade agreements and consolidated some political contacts. At the end of the visit the head of the delegation was still seeking to convince European audiences that his country's transition efforts deserved a more generous interpretation than they had received so far.[57] It is true that the Uzbek government has adopted several laws and decrees to improve human rights in the country, culminating in the appointment of a human rights ombudsman and the declaration of 1997 as the Uzbek Year of Human Rights, but most of this continues to exist only on paper. It is insufficient to make declarations that are not supported by concrete actions. In September 1997 the European Parliament prepared another critical report on Uzbekistan expressing serious concern over human rights in the republic. This indicated that the PCA would still take some time to be ratified by the Parliament. However, EU Foreign Ministers meeting in Council on 26 January 1998 adopted a decision to bring into effect the Interim Agreement with Uzbekistan, which would allow early implementation of the trade-related provisions of the PCA. This included payments, competition, protection of intellectual property rights, and industrial and commercial property. By 1998 almost all the 15 EU member states had ratified the agreement, and the European Parliament also ratified the PCA document in February 1999.

The TACIS Programme for Uzbekistan
The second level of interaction between the EU and Uzbekistan concerns the realization of the programme of technical assistance (TACIS), which is aimed at supporting the implementation of economic reforms. In January 1994 the Uzbek Bureau of Commission of European Union – UzBureauCEU (UzBuroKES) – was opened in Tashkent in order to realize this program. It defined a set of priorities concerning the restructuring of state enterprises and private sector development, public administration reform, education, agriculture, energy, transport and the rational use of labour resources.

An indicative TACIS programme of technical assistance for 1996–9 was approved by the European Commission with a budget of ECU 57 million. In 1996–7, the programme allocations include ECU 7.7 million for structural and institutional reform, 6.4 million for agriculture and the agro-industry, 5.9 million for infrastructure development and 6 million for policy advice, civil society development, education and enterprise policy. Between 1991 and 1995, ECU 45.5 million was allocated to Uzbekistan under the TACIS programme. For 1991–5, allocations included ECU 7.61 million for restructuring state enterprises and private sector development, 14.31 million for public administration reform (mainly social services and education), 9.63 for agriculture, 5.68 million for energy, 1.97 million for transport, 3 million for policy advice and 3.3 million for other sectors.[58]

The most recent trade figures from the commission show that in 1993, the EU imported goods worth ECU 415 million from Uzbekistan and exported goods to Uzbekistan worth ECU 210 million. Trade between the EU and Uzbekistan developed further in 1994. The EU imported goods worth ECU 518 million from Uzbekistan, mainly precious metals and textiles, and exported goods worth ECU 391 million, mainly machinery, electrical equipment and vegetable products. The value of exported goods to Uzbekistan in 1995 rose to ECU 366.438 million and imports were worth ECU 435.668 million. The figures for 1996 shows further increases in EU exports and imports of goods to and from Uzbekistan. The EU has exported goods worth ECU 590.681 million and imported goods worth ECU 438.137 million.[59]

Uzbekistan's relations with the EU are not limited to these matters. Bilateral relations have also developed with the individual member states. Uzbekistan is actively strengthening its relations with states such as Belgium, Denmark, Holland, Italy, Sweden, Spain, Greece, Finland and Austria, and special attention has been given to Germany, France and the United Kingdom. It is worth looking briefly at each of these states' relations with Uzbekistan.

Uzbekistan and Germany
Relations between Uzbekistan and Germany have developed significantly. Germany recognized Uzbekistan as an independent state on 31 December 1991 and diplomatic ties were established in May 1992. Before the opening of the German Embassy in Tashkent a German–Uzbek Society was set up by the German community living in Uzbekistan with the help of the Uzbek government. Before the break-up of the former Soviet Union there were about 40,000 Germans living in Uzbekistan but this figure had halved by 1996. The majority of those remaining want to return to Germany but the German government wants them to stay in Uzbekistan to facilitate future cooperation. The Germans living in Uzbekistan have been thoroughly Russified, and speak neither German nor Uzbek. Culturally and linguistically they are more Russian than German. The Uzbek government is cooperating with the German government to keep them in Uzbekistan. There is a Protestant Church, closed by Stalin, which Islom Karimov gave to the German community in May 1993.

Germany's relations with Uzbekistan, as with the other states of Central Asia, had achieved all-round development by 1997. This was not only because there was a large number of Germans living in the region, mainly in Kazakstan, Uzbekistan and Kyrgyzstan, but also because the region has great economic and political importance. It can act as a bridge between East Asia and Europe, and the whole region is potentially rich in natural resources. Uzbekistan is a key country in this bridging function. It is the most populous and stable state in the region.

Another official visit by President Karimov to Germany in November 1993, by invitation of the Federal President of Germany, Roman Herzog, underlined the high level of development of Uzbek–German relations. During the visit, President Karimov had talks with Chancellor Helmut Kohl, the Minister of Foreign Affairs, Claus Kinkel, and the Minister for Finance, Shomerus. Uzbekistan and Germany confirmed their joint responsibility along with other member states of the OSCE for strengthening peace, stability and security in the region.

In the course of Karimov's talks with the leaders of Germany, Chancellor Helmut Kohl expressed his readiness to render necessary support to the country in order to overcome the difficulties of the transition period. By creating the scientific research fund, Germany offered its own experience for assistance in the realization of state reform, the creation of budget and tax systems, carrying out privatizations, and furthering the development of the economic law system in order to promote the progress of the reforms in Uzbekistan. From 1993 to late 1996 about ten inter-governmental agreements were signed between the two countries. The agreements included political, economic, social and cultural cooperation. The official visit of President Karimov to Germany in April 1993 and the state visit of Roman Herzog to Uzbekistan in 1995 were the culmination of these bilateral relations. There is also a German society for Technical Cooperation (GTZ) in Tashkent working for cooperation between the two states, and about 86 German firms conducting business in the fields of pharmaceuticals, light industry and food processing. Bayer, Merck, Alkatel, Daimler Chrysler and Siemens AG are among the largest German companies conducting business in the republic. Germany has rendered DM186.5 million to Uzbekistan to implement projects in health care, telecommunications and food processing.

Uzbekistan and France

France was among the first countries to recognize the independence of Uzbekistan. Diplomatic relations between Uzbekistan and France were established in February 1992 and, in May of the same year, the French Embassy was opened in Tashkent marking the start of relations between the two countries. France considers Uzbekistan to be the key state in the Central Asian region with respect to ensuring regional peace and security, and influencing the situation in the region. Paris also closely monitors political developments in the country, and expresses an interest in the preservation of stability and the realization of market reforms in Uzbekistan.

The documents signed during the high-level visits between Uzbekistan and France developed friendship and cooperation between the two countries. In late October 1993, President Karimov visited France and had talks with President Mitterand, the Prime Minister Raymond Balladur and the Minister of Foreign Affairs Alain Juppè. The main result of the talks was the signing of an agreement on friendship and cooperation between Uzbekistan and France. The document sets out relations between the two countries. Each side will give top priority to cooperation in the fields of agriculture, energy, mineral resources, transport, telecommunications, and the military sphere. Another important document is the agreement on cultural, scientific and technical cooperation between the two states. President Mitterand's visit to Uzbekistan in April 1994 gave the first impulse to the relations between Uzbekistan and France. In Tashkent, Uzbek and French officials signed the agreement on cooperation between the ministries of foreign affairs of the two countries, the agreement on the free movement of citizens, and the joint declaration on cooperation in the fields of air services and sports. By late 1996, about ten agreements had been signed between France and Uzbekistan and there were about 39 French firms conducting business in Uzbekistan. The upper chamber of the French parliament, the Senate, approved the agreement on partnership and cooperation between Uzbekistan and the EU on 22 December 1998, making France the last of the 15 countries to complete the procedure of ratification of this agreement.

Uzbekistan and the United Kingdom
The United Kingdom recognized the independence of the Republic of Uzbekistan on 31 December 1991 with diplomatic relations being established on 18 February 1992. A British Embassy in Tashkent opened in May 1993 and in October Douglas Hurd, the Foreign Office Minister, paid a visit to Tashkent, the first such visit by a British minister since

independence. This marked the beginning of relations between the two states. During the visit, intergovernmental agreements were signed on avoiding double taxation of income and property; cooperation in the fields of culture, education and science; and a declaration on mutual understanding between the respective countries' Ministries of Foreign Affairs.

President Karimov's official visit to the UK in November 1993 gave a new boost to the progress of bilateral relations. A number of agreements and treaties were completed and signed. They included agreements on economic cooperation, investment promotion and protection, cooperation in the fields of air services, a memorandum of understanding on unrestricted freedom to travel within Uzbekistan for UK citizens, a memorandum on cooperation with the British company Lonrho Plc, an agreement on scientific, cultural and technical cooperation, an agreement on avoiding double taxation, and a declaration of cooperation between the foreign ministries of the two countries. Later, in January 1995, the Uzbek Foreign Minister Abdulaziz Komilov paid an official visit to the United Kingdom, where he discussed further cooperation with the British government. He paid a further Guest of Government visit in October 1996, where he officially opened the new Uzbek Embassy. An Uzbek Charge d'Affaires was appointed to London in February 1995 but this was replaced by a new Ambassador appointed on 22 July 1997. The then British Foreign Secretary, Malcolm Rifkind, visited Tashkent in January 1996 and HRH the Prince of Wales visited Uzbekistan during 9–12 November 1996. The motive behind the Foreign Secretary's visit was to improve the slow progress of (mainly economic) relations between London and Tashkent, while the Prince of Wales' visit was intended to improve cultural relations between the two countries. In Tashkent the Prince officially opened the British Council's Resource Centre on 12 November. The British Council signed an agreement with the Uzbek government to establish a Resource Centre in Tashkent in 1996 due largely to the intense efforts of Dorothy Bond, the British Council Project coordinator for Uzbekistan. The process of developing relations between the two countries was also assisted by British joint ventures. Up to late 1999 there were about 91 British firms conducting business in Uzbekistan.

An overview of Uzbek–EU relations
The meetings, treaties and agreements which were signed on political, economic, scientific, technical and cultural cooperation with several EU

members states, provided a solid overall basis for furthering relations between the EU and Uzbekistan, leading to the signing of the PCA and an interim agreement between the two parties.

Relations between the EU and Uzbekistan as with other former republics of the Soviet Union are increasingly regulated by the PCA, the scope of which is political, economic, commercial and cultural. The aim is to pave the way for the integration of Uzbekistan into the wider European economy. The EU has important economic interests in Uzbekistan, which is engaged in a process of economic reform with encouraging early results. Uzbekistan has a fast-growing population of over 24 million, and is the region's economic and cultural focus. It is an important partner in view of its geopolitical position between Russia, China and the Islamic world. The republic is also an important trade partner with several EU member states. In terms of natural resources, the country is the world's second largest cotton exporter, the seventh biggest gold producer, and is in the world top ten of producers of natural gas, uranium, copper and silver. Over 3,400 joint ventures with foreign capital have been set up, including a major US involvement in gold mining, the development of indigenous car manufacturing with Daewoo, and a truck assembly deal with Mercedes. The republic has become almost self-sufficient in oil. Hence, it is important for the EU to establish contractual relations with Uzbekistan. With its commitment to reform, and its contribution towards peace and stability in Central Asia, Uzbekistan certainly needs the EU's continuing political and moral support for its sovereignty, independence and territorial integrity as well as assistance for economic reform throughout the transition period.

The improving relations with the EU are significant for Uzbekistan, in providing ideas, development, and new technologies which are needed for economic reform and attracting foreign aid and direct investment. The EU is also an important factor in Uzbekistan's human resources development. EU contacts and input will help the republic to maintain and develop the quality of Uzbek training in science and engineering as well as its cultural and intellectual life. The republic is aware of the benefits of maintaining closer ties in the future with the EU, which occupies an important place in its foreign policy. The EU's political, moral and economic support for Uzbekistan should continue because it will also contribute to the maintenance and development of peace, stability, cooperation and freedom in the region.

Uzbekistan and the US

The US recognized the independence of Uzbekistan on 25 December 1991 and established diplomatic relations in March 1992. Although Uzbekistan and the US have signed several treaties, protocols, agreements and memoranda covering cultural and trade issues, bilateral relations did not produce positive outcomes until 1995. The Uzbek leadership was initially highly suspicious of the United States foreign policy and its attitude towards not just Uzbekistan but Central Asia as a whole. Despite Uzbekistan's severe economic dislocation and its clear need for US aid and broader foreign investment during the early years of independence, the leadership dismissed the US promotion of human rights as unwanted foreign interference. The visit of the US special ambassador for the CIS, Strobe Talbott, to Uzbekistan in September 1993 was concluded after what was described as 'a long and frank conversation with President Islom Karimov'. Karimov himself, however, later bluntly declared that Washington should mind its own business, and let the governments and the people in the region handle the situation as they saw fit.[60]

However, the administration has shown a marked determination to extend its influence over the extraction and transportation of the region's mineral resources, and to defend the interests of US companies investing in the region. It has also sought to prevent the spread of radical Islam in order to contain Iran. It wants to anchor Uzbekistan within the Western security and economic system, and promote democracy and human rights. In addition to these aims, there has been a residual belief in defence circles in the US that Uzbekistan represents a strategic regional core which could act as a regional bulwark against Russia and Iran.[61] Therefore, since October 1994 the US has initiated regular political consultations at ministerial levels. During such consultations a wide range of issues pertaining to regional security and the deepening of bilateral relations have been discussed. However, they did not produce the desired deepening of the bilateral relationship until October 1995 when, during his meeting with Vice-President Al Gore in Washington, President Karimov stressed his readiness to develop mutually beneficial cooperation with the US. This pro-US foreign policy stance of Uzbekistan can be explained by five main factors: first, Russia's insistence on playing a bigger role in the region and Uzbekistan's growing suspicion of Russian intentions in Central Asia; second, the strong showing of the ultra-nationalists and former communists in the Russian Parliament;

third, the increasing role of the military in determining Russia's policy toward the so-called Near Abroad and the military's determination to re-establish Russian control over most parts of the former Soviet Union; fourth, Uzbekistan's growing need to elicit Western aid and major investment which the country desperately needed to overcome the deteriorating economic situation; fifth, Uzbekistan's desire to win US backing in finding ways to settle the conflicts in Afghanistan and Tajikistan. Thus, the meeting between Al Gore and Karimov in Washington marked a new stage in Uzbek–US relations, and prepared the ground for Karimov's meeting with Clinton at the White House on 25 June 1996.

During his first day visit to Washington on 24 June 1996, President Karimov signed a package of agreements on economic cooperation between Uzbekistan and the US. These included an accord with the US Overseas Private Investment Corporation (OPIC) to provide 400 million dollars in credits to a joint venture between the Uzbek state oil and gas company, Uzbekneftgaz, and the Enron Oil and Gas Company for the development of natural gas deposits in Uzbekistan. Under another accord the OPIC undertook to provide support for Uzbekneftegaz to produce lubricants under a licence from another US oil company, Texaco. Another agreement was also signed with the US Trade and Development Agency to grant a $1 million dollar loan to carry out a feasibility study for the joint production of civil aircraft in Tashkent. During the second day of his visit Karimov met the US President Bill Clinton and held talks with Secretary of State Warren Christopher, Secretary of Defence William Perry and Secretary of Energy Hazel O'Leary. The US Defence Secretary described Uzbekistan as an 'important strategic partner of the United States', and their talks with the Uzbek President focused on economic, social and security issues.[62] The issue of Central Asian security and ways of expanding Washington–Tashkent cooperation were also discussed during Karimov's meeting with Clinton. Afterwards, Karimov met congressional representatives and the heads of the National Security Council, the Central Asian–American Enterprise Fund and the World Bank. He also opened the new Uzbek Embassy in Washington.

All these initiatives undoubtedly contributed to improving relations between Uzbekistan and the US and by late 1997 about 199 US companies were conducting business in the republic. Until 1997 Uzbekistan was highly regarded by the US government, because one view of geostrategic issues favoured by some US defence officials was that the republic could become the Central Asian link in a southern chain of ex-Soviet countries coopted to contain Russia.[63] But, under pressure from internal and regional problems, Uzbekistan turned back to Russia for support. During Karimov's visit to Moscow on 5–7 May 1998, Uzbekistan and Russia signed new agreements including one on the 'strategic partnership', to deepen security and economic cooperation between the two countries. This emerging Russian–Uzbek *rapprochement* could further erode the republic's relations with the US. Uzbekistan's stance on the issue of political reforms and its poor human rights record have been a cause of frustration for the US. Russia's position in geopolitical terms is undeniably important for Uzbekistan, but the latter also needs to attract foreign investment. US business can potentially be a source of investment and technical assistance for Uzbekistan's fragile economy. Uzbekistan desperately needs openings into Western economies, and political ties will help cement this. Moreover, Uzbekistan has signed up to join NATO's 'Partnership for Peace' programme. Here the main challenge for Uzbekistan is to find a political balance. For the US the political and economic importance of the region is vast. It can benefit from the emerging commercial opportunities in the whole of Central Asia, in which Uzbekistan can play a pivotal role in the future. The region and several surrounding countries, including Russia itself, are still unstable and there is the potential for future conflicts that could destabilize Eurasia.

Cooperation with international organizations
Among the international organizations, the United Nations (UN) is of particular importance to Uzbekistan, for it is seen as the only important international organization with all-embracing competence to strengthen peace and security as well as to develop cooperation among states of all continents. Uzbekistan's entry into the UN on 2 March 1992 as a member enjoying equal rights in international law was celebrated as an important historical and foreign policy event for the republic.

In accordance with the agreements between the government of Uzbekistan and the UN on 16 November 1992, a UN office was opened in Tashkent in January 1993. The importance of this is that for the first time in Uzbek history a UN office, with its departments such as UNICEF, UNESCO, UNIDO, UNDP, UNISTAR, etc., are working in Uzbekistan. Cooperation with the UN is proceeding in political, economic and social spheres, public health, cultural revival, environmental control and security problems. On the 48th session of the General Assembly of the UN, President Karimov put forward a proposal that the UN Permanent Seminar should be convened in Tashkent to settle problems of security, prosperity and cooperation in Central Asia.[64]

To develop cooperation with NATO, Uzbekistan signed on 13 July 1994 a document officially joining it to the NATO 'Partnership for Peace' programme. Later Uzbekistan signed a second document on 8 August 1995 that set out the aims, tasks and time-terms of its cooperation with NATO and the exchange of information. The 'Partnership for Peace' programme allows Uzbekistan to exchange information about military and political developments around the world and to take part in various NATO events. These include joint military exercises, seminars, research and other work including environmental protection. Uzbekistan considers its participation in NATO's partnership programme to be a means of strengthening its independence and sovereignty.

On 30 January 1992, at the Conference on Security and Cooperation in Europe (CSCE), held in Prague, Uzbekistan was admitted to the organization. The CSCE International Seminar dedicated to problems of security in Central Asia was held in Tashkent in September 1994 and on 5 December the Uzbek delegation took part in the CSCE summit which reorganized the CSCE as the Organization on Security and Cooperation in Europe (OSCE). President Karimov gave a speech at this meeting. Uzbekistan joined the movement of Non-Alignment in September 1992 and in April 1992 was admitted to the International Monetary Fund (IMF) and the International Bank for Reconstruction and Development.

The Organization of Economic Cooperation (OEC) was established in 1964 by Iran, Pakistan and Turkey under the title of the 'Organization of Regional Cooperation with a View of Development' and became the OEC in 1985. It is considered to be one of the influential international organizations in the Asian region. The main tasks of the OEC participant countries consists of the realization of free activity in the common market; expanding the total volume of reciprocal deliveries; carrying out conditions for the increase of living standards as well as the economic development of society; and strengthening and extending the cultural, scientific, spiritual and other relations among the region's nations. It also aims to arrange joint addresses at the international meetings, and to integrate efforts to settle economic problems of great importance for these states. On 6 February 1992, at the OEC meeting in Ankara, Uzbekistan was admitted to the organization along with Kazakstan, Kyrgyzistan, Tajikistan, Turkmenistan, Azerbaijan and Afghanistan. Uzbekistan wants to develop economic and transport opportunities through this organization, and its position on the role of OEC is that it is an economic organization and must not become a political force. However, the disputes and the animosities between the member states have so far failed to accomplish the above-mentioned objectives of the organization.

Uzbekistan's membership of, and activity in, various international organizations is intended to facilitate economic, political, scientific and cultural cooperation between Uzbekistan and the rest of the world. Uzbekistan aims to build partnerships with other states not only within the framework of international organizations, regional alliances and societies, but also through multilateral intergovernmental treaties, and bilateral cooperation.

Conclusion

Uzbekistan's foreign policy is centred around ensuring the political and economic independence and security of the country. The determinant factors in shaping the priorities of its foreign policy are geopolitical, political, and economic in nature. The country's regional and international aspirations have also helped determine its foreign policy priorities. The formulation of an independent foreign policy for Uzbekistan is, however, a new and untrodden path. Throughout the former Soviet era the republic's 'external' relations were restricted to the countries of the former Soviet Union. These relationships were conducted through the central leadership in Moscow while the official Soviet ideology shaped the determination of Uzbekistan's national interest, as well as actual or potential threats to this interest. After the break-up of the Soviet Union and despite its commitment to the CIS, the country has demonstrated a strong sense of independence and a determination to pursue its own interests free from outside direction. Independence left the republic confronted with the sudden and unexpected responsibility for conducting its own foreign relations. This was a task which Uzbekistan was ill-equipped to face as a result of the Soviet legacy. The country had a 'Ministry of Foreign Affairs'under the federal system, but it had no real authority and all its relations with the rest of the union republics were handled through Moscow. The republic lacked funds as well as trained and experienced staff capable of administering the country's foreign relations at a professional level. Nonetheless, Uzbekistan rushed to exploit its new sovereign status by emerging as an independent actor in the global arena and its initial experiment in foreign policy was successful. It resulted in quick recognition by the major powers and many other countries. It established diplomatic ties and exchanged diplomatic missions. It was accepted with little hesitation into the UN and other international organizations.

At the regional level Uzbekistan has sought the regional integration of the five Central Asian republics. In January 1994 Uzbekistan and Kazakstan signed an agreement to create a common economic space between the two countries and were joined shortly afterwards by Kyrgyzstan. The union of the three, despite the difficulties between them, has progressed considerably, so much so that the Tajik republic, which had been reluctant to join at first, changed its mind and joined in March 1998. Uzbekistan's effort to bring these republics together to coordinate their policies to overcome regional social, political and economic problems, is significant. At the international level the republic has acted to establish ties with as many nations as possible and has improved its relations with the world's major powers. Due to its natural mineral resources, its geostrategic position in the region and its desire to develop ties with many countries, Uzbekistan has attracted the attention of numerous states, including Russia, China, India, Pakistan, Iran, Turkey, Saudi Arabia, Israel, the countries of the EU and the US, almost all with conflicting interests in the region. The main challenge for Uzbekistan in its external relations is how to use these powers to advance its own interests without antagonizing others or succumbing to their hegemony. The strategy for reconciling these two opposing objectives has been to try to strike a political balance between the major countries in the region, while nurturing its own ties with countries in different regions.

NOTES

1 See also Hunter, op. cit., 1996, pp. 89–90 and James Critchlow, 'The Ethnic Factor in Central Asian Foreign Policy' in Roman Szporluk, (ed), *National Identity and Ethnicity in Russia and the New States of Eurasia* (Armonk, N.Y: M.E. Sharpe, 1994), pp. 266–72.

2 For Uzbek Foreign Minister Sadik Safaev's remarks on Uzbekistan's foreign policy priorities, see Uzbekistan APN Service in Russian, 15 February 1993, in *FBIS-SOV-93-030*, 17 February 1993, pp. 70–1. See also James Critchlow, in Szporluk et al., op. cit., 1994, p. 268.

3 This subject was discussed during a meeting with a group of academics and journalists in Tashkent in March and April 1996. See also A. Kasimov and I. Vaskin, *Ocnovniye Napravleniya Bneshnyei Politiki Respubliki Uzbekistan (Main Direction of the Foreign Policy of Uzbekistan)* (Tashkent: Uzbekiston, 1994), pp. 30–64.

4 See the statement of the Kazak, Kyrgyz and Uzbek presidents' announcement after the Almaty meeting on 8 July 1994 – unpublished issue held at University of World Economy and Diplomacy, Tashkent. See also Herbert Dieter, 'Regional Integration in Central Asia: Current Economic Position and Prospects', *Central Asian Survey*, 15:3/4, December 1996, pp. 369–86; Sheila Marine and Erik Whitlock, 'Central Asia and Economic Integration', *RFE/RL Research Report*, 2:14, 2 April 1993, pp. 34–44; Bess Brown, 'Three Central Asian States Form Economic Union', *RFE/RL Research Report*, 13:13, 1 April 1994, pp. 33–5.

5 *Ozbekiston Ovozi*, 7 May 1996; *Toshkent Hokikoti*, 8 May 1996; *Vatan*, 8–16 May 1996; *Birlik*, 14 May 1996. See also *Turkiston,* 8 May 1996.

6 *Xalq Sozi*, 24 August 1996; *Ozbekiston Ovozi*, 27 August 1996; *Adolat* 27 August 1996.

7 See also Paul Globe, 'Central Asia: Analysis from Washington: A Watershed in Central Asia', *Turkistan-N Newsletter* (27 July 1997), *RFE/RL Research Report* (25 July 1997).

8 See Islom Karimov's speech to the foreign diplomatic corpus and journalists in Tashkent on 12 April 1996.

9 An excellent discussion of the causes of CIS failure is Hunter, op. cit., 1996, pp. 107–23.

10 Russian–Uzbek relations were discussed during an interview with Russian Embassy officials on 23 August 1996 in Tashkent and during my talks with Uzbek officials at the Uzbek Ministry of Foreign Affairs, as well as with local experts on Uzbek Foreign Affairs at the Institute of Strategic Studies.

11 Interview 23 August 1996.

12 For S. Karaganov's and A. Vladislavlev's remarks, see *Nezavisimaia gazeta*, 17 November 1992, p. 5. For K. Zatulin, see Ibid. 5 May 1994, p. 9.

13 *Izvestiia*, 7 August 1994, pp. 2–3. Cited in Rumer, op. cit., 1996, p. 19.

14 See 'Russia's Over-friendly Squeeze', *The Economist*, 16 April 1994, p. 69.

15 See 'Foreign Minister Responds to Russian Statement', *FBIS/WEUN*, 19 October, 1994, p. 76, cited in Hunter, op. cit., 1996.

16 U. Kasenov, '"Doktrina Kozyreva" – Rossiikii variant "Doktriny Monro"', *Nezavisimaia gazeta*, 12 March 1994, p. 43, cited in Rumer, op. cit., 1996, p. 21.

17 See John Thornhill, 'Kozyrev Remarks on the Use of Force Fuel Fears in ex-Soviet States', *Financial Times*, 21 April 1995.
18 On 15 March 1996 during his speech to the Khorezm regional parliament, President Karimov expressed his concern and regret about the 'Eurasia Union' agreement signed by Russia, Belarus, Kazakstan and Kyrgyzstan. He stated that it was Russia that had initiated this to hamper Central Asian integration and set Central Asian countries against one another.
19 See also Hunter, op. cit., 1996, pp. 122–3.
20 *Ozbekiston Ovozi*, 10 May 1998, *Xalq Sozi*, 9 May 1998.
21 Uzbekistan–Turkey relations were discussed during an interview with Turkish Embassy officials in Tashkent in early September 1996. This issue was also discussed with Uzbek officials at the Uzbek Ministry of Foreign Affairs in Tashkent on 10 September 1996, and with Uzbek foreign policy experts at the Institute of Strategic Studies on 29 August 1996. For an excellent discussion of relations between Turkey and Central Asian republics see Philip Robins, 'Turkey's Ostpolitik, Relations with the Central Asian States' in David Menashiri (ed.), *Central Asia Meets The Middle East* (London: Frank Cass & Co Ltd, 1998), pp. 129–47. Another interesting discussion of this subject is Graham E. Fuller and Ian O. Lesser with Paul B. Henze and J. F. Brown, *Turkey's New Geopolitics: From the Balkans to Western China* (Boulder: Westview Press, 1993), pp. 66–76. An interesting discussion of Turkey–Central Asia relations is Mustafa Aydin, 'Turkey and Central Asia: Challenges of Change', *Central Asian Survey*, 15:2, June 1996, pp. 157–77. For Turkey's objectives in Central Asia, see Stephen J. Blank, 'The Eastern Question Revived; Turkey and Russia Contend for Eurasia' in Menashri, op. cit., 1998, pp. 168–84.
22 See also Philip Robins, in Menashri, op. cit., 1998, pp. 135–6; and Hunter, op. cit., 1996, p. 137.
23 Blaine Harden, 'Turkey Builds a Muslim Empire in the Air, via Satellite', *The Washington Post* National weekly edition, 30 March–5 April, 1992, p. 18.
24 *Milliyet*, 27 February 1991.
25 *Turkish Daily News*, 27 April 1992.
26 See also Philip Robins in Menashri, op. cit., 1998, p. 133.
27 For President Özal's statements see *Newspot*, 3 October 1991; for Çetin's words see *Newspot*, 12 March 1992; and see *Newspot*, 7 May 1992 for Demirel's statements.
28 See, for example, Philip Robins in Menashri, op. cit., 1998, p. 132.
29 Ibid. p. 134.
30 *Newspot*, 9 April 1992. See also Philip Robins, in Menashri, op. cit., 1998, p. 135.
31 For this and the speeches and statements from the summit, see *British Broadcasting Corporation, Summary of World Broadcasts, The Middle East (SWB)*, 2 November 1992.
32 *Turkish Daily News*, 1 November 1992.
33 *Xalq Sozi*, 25 May 1992. See also Karimov, op. cit., 1993.
34 Interview with Abdumanov Poulatov, in Tashkent, 20 September 1996.
35 See 'Turkish States Grow Closer', *Financial Times,* 20 October 1994; and 'Turkish Republics Summit', *Milliyet*, 23 October 1994.
36 See, for example, Islom Karimov, *Turkistan Umumiy Uyimiz (Turkistan, Our Common Home)* (Tashkent: Uzbekiston, 1995), and op. cit., 1993.

37 See *Adolat*, 10 February 1996, *Xalq Sozi*, 9 February 1996 and *Ozbekiston Ovozi*, 9 February 1996.
38 See *Xalq Sozi*, 4 July 1996, *Ozbekiston Ovozi*, 4 July 1996.
39 *RFE/RL Newsline*, 2:110 P. I, 10 June 1998.
40 An excellent discussion of China–Central Asia relations is Boris Rumer, 'Disintegration and Reintegration' in Rumer, op. cit., 1996, pp. 6–9. Another interesting discussion is Peter Ferdinand, 'The New Central Asia and China' in Ferdinand, op. cit., 1994, pp. 95–107.
41 See, for example, Rumer, op. cit., 1996, p. 9.
42 Uzbek–Indian relations were discussed during my meetings with officials at the Ministry of Foreign Affairs in Tashkent, and with a group of specialists at the Institute of Strategic Studies Tashkent in late August 1996, where I had the opportunity to discuss various issues in the region. Another interesting discussion of Indian and Central Asia relations is Hunter, op. cit., 1996, pp. 139–41.
43 For a more detailed study of India's attitude towards Central Asia and its interests in this region, see Anita Inder Singh, 'India's Relations with Russia and Central Asia', *International Affairs*, 71:1, January 1995, pp. 69–8. An interesting discussion of Indian–Pakistani–Central Asian interaction is Anthony Hyman, 'Central Asia's Relations with Afghanistan and South Asia' in Ferdinand, op. cit., 1994, pp. 75–90.
44 *Xalq Sozi*, 4 November 1995.
45 Pakistani–Uzbek–Afghan–Indian relations were discussed during an interview with officials at the Pakistani Embassy in Tashkent, on 10 September 1996. These issues were also discussed with officials at the Afghan Embassy in Tashkent on 10 September 1996; and with the officials at the Ministry of Foreign Affairs in Tashkent.
46 On the Taliban, see George Aligiah, 'Victorious Warlords Fight to the Death over Ruins of Afghanistan', *Independent on Sunday*, 5 March 1994. On Pakistani and Saudi Support see Kenneth Cooper, *New York Times*, 4 June 1997. On US support see Tribunal News Service, *New York Times*, 26 May 1997; and also *US Department of State 97/05/27, Daily Press Briefing, Office of the Spokesman*, Briefer John Dinger, 12 June 1997.
47 Tribunal News Service, *New York Times*, 26 May 1997.
48 Interviews with Uzbek officials at the Ministry of Foreign Affairs and at the Institute of Strategic Studies in Tashkent in August–September 1996. For an interesting discussion on the Middle East and Central Asia, see Philip Robins, 'The Middle East and the Central Asia' in Ferdinand, op. cit., 1994, pp. 55–74. For Central Asia–Israeli relations see also Rumer, op. cit., 1996, p. 5 and Hunter, op. cit., 1996, pp. 143–6.
49 Iranian–Uzbek relations were discussed during an interview with Iranian diplomats at the Iranian Embassy in Tashkent on 13 September 1996. The subject was also discussed during my talks with several Uzbek Foreign Policy experts at the Institute of Strategic Studies in Tashkent. For a detailed discussion of Iran's relations with the Central Asian states, see Menashri, op. cit., 1998, pp. 73–94. Two other interesting discussions of this subject are Hunter, op. cit., 1996, pp. 129–35, and Anthony Hyman, *Power and Politics in Central Asia's New Republics* (London: Research Institute for the Study of Conflict and Terrorism, 1994), pp. 12–14.

50 See Menashri, op. cit., 1998, p. 88.
51 *Ozbekiston Ovozi*, 29 February 1996.
52 See Farhad Kazemi and Zohreh Ajdari, 'Ethnicity, Identity and Politics' in Menashri, op. cit., 1998, pp. 60–62.
53 See also Hunter, op. cit., 1996, pp. 132–3.
54 *Aziia*, 1994, no. 27, p. 2, cited in Rumer, op. cit., 1996, p. 5.
55 For the aims of President Karimov's visit to the United States, see Jayhun Molla-Zade and Joanne Neuber, 'Uzbekistan: Reproving the Ancient Silk Road; An Interview with the Uzbek Ambassador Fatih Teshabaev', *Caspian Crossroads Magazine*, 2:1, US-Azerbaijan Council, Spring–Summer 1996.
56 See also *Xalq Sozi*, 2 July 1996; *Ozbekiston Ovozi*, 2 July 1996.
57 See also *European Report*, no. 2174, 13 November, 1996, no. 2181, 7 December, no. 2100, 20 January, 1996 and *European Report*, no. 2223, 14 May, no. 2224, 17 May, 1997.
58 The information was gathered at the EU office at 4 Tarasa Shevchenko Street, Tashkent. See also *European Report*, no. 2161, 28 September and *European Report*, no. 2175, 16 November, 1996, *Tacis Annual Report 1994*, Brussels, 18 July, 1995, Com (95) 349 final pp. 42–59 and *The Tacis Programme Annual Report 1995-96*, Brussels, 22 July 1996 Com (96) 345 final pp. 42–59.
59 See *European Report*, no. 2175, 16 November, 1996. My gratitude also goes out to Anad Hadi from the DTI in London for providing me with the statistics (from Eurostat Extra & Intra EU Trade) about EU exports and imports of goods from Uzbekistan. See also *Adolat*, 18 November 1995, *Xalq Sozi*, 18 November 1995, *Ozbekiston Ovozi*, 18 November 1995.
60 See reports of 15 and 16 September 1993 by BBC, Reuters and UPI. See also Anthony Hyman, *Political Change in Post-Soviet Central Asia* (London: The Royal Institute of International Affairs, 1994), p. 16.
61 See also Hunter, op. cit., 1996, pp. 157–9. EIU *Uzbekistan Country Report*, 1st and 2nd quarters 1998, pp. 6–7.
62 *ITAR-TASS news agency (World Service)*, Moscow, in English, 18:47 (GMT) June 1996. Uzbek radio second programme, Tashkent, in Uzbek, 13:00 (GMT) 26 June 1996.
63 EIU *Uzbekistan Country Report*, 1st quarter 1998, pp. 6–7.
64 *Pravda Vostoka*, 28 November 1992, 19 October, 27 March, 6 May 1993.

6

Conclusion

After the demise of the Soviet Union, Uzbeks asserted full control over their own state and sought to establish a commanding position in the politics of Central Asia. The name 'Uzbek' goes back to the middle ages. It was the name of the Golden Horde Khan, Ghiyath ad-Din Muhammad Ozbeg(k) (Uzbek). Following the conversion of the Golden Horde to Islam by Uzbek Khan, his subjects were called Uzbeks. Until 1420, the early Uzbeks, were neither psychologically nor geographically true Central Asians. The significance of their history to contemporary Uzbekistan is that the present-day Uzbeks are heirs to their new name and they held power with few lapses until the Tsarist Russian rule. The present-day Uzbeks are, however, descendants of various Turkish tribes that began moving to Maverannahr between the fifth and tenth centuries AD who intermingled with the original inhabitants, predominantly the Tajiks of Persian stock, and descendants of a conglomerate of Turkic-Mongol tribes that had migrated to the region with Muhammad Shaybani Khan around AD 1500. It was only after the arrival of Muhammad Shaybani and his subjects that this land was first called Uzbekistan.

Throughout their entire history, the people of Uzbekistan have experienced many social, political and economic changes. The land that today is known as Uzbekistan has itself undergone substantial change. All the empires formed there had an impact on the people's lives, but none attempted to build a serious civil society. The two most recent empires that extended themselves to the region were Tsarist Russia and the Soviets. Although Tsarist rule permitted the people of Uzbekistan a significant degree of political and cultural autonomy, it paid little attention to the concept of a pluralist democracy. Russian rule broke up the old order and, to some extent, paved the way for further progress and put an end to the constant feudal wars between the various khans and emirs. But the real changes under this rule were mainly territorial organizations.

After the Russian revolution, the Soviet regime undertook major changes in Uzbekistan. The first important reform came with the creation of Uzbekistan as a 'nation-state,' and was followed by a comprehensive campaign to modernize, but at the same time 'Sovietize', the republic. The key mobilizing factors in Uzbekistan were secularization, collectivization, industrialization and intensive education. Mass education contributed to rising literacy levels. In the early Soviet period, the average literacy rate was 2–3 per cent, but by the early 1980s it was virtually 100 per cent. The local population was drawn into the party organization, the central and regional administration and legal apparatus. Women were given equal rights with men before the law, in education and in the work place, and were encouraged to play an active role in the socio-political life of the community. The formation of collective farms, the development of irrigation and the establishment of new industries also changed the face of the country. Cotton planting and cultivation were mechanized. Electric power production commenced with the construction of new thermal power stations and hydroelectric plants in the major cities. Under Soviet rule, the appearance of Uzbek cities, towns and villages underwent enormous changes. Medical centres and hospitals were built, with special attention being given to maternal and infant welfare. New communication and transport networks were developed. In essence, Soviet policies transformed Uzbekistan from a traditional society into a modern one. The infrastructure put in place provided the Uzbek people with a framework to eliminate not only economic, but also cultural backwardness.

However, alongside the efforts to establish new norms and values and bring about a modern society, a concerted campaign was undertaken to remove every visible vestige of the pre-Soviet culture. Local intellectuals and leaders were either executed, imprisoned, forced to flee abroad or coopted into the services of the Soviet regime. Little attention was devoted to the development of manufacturing industry and Uzbekistan became highly dependent on inter-republican trade. The process of social transformation was hastened by the purges of the 1930s which, though they did not eliminate all potential sources of opposition, created a climate of mass terror that resulted in self-censorship. The education system transmitted Soviet ideology, and other aspects of the modernization campaign were similarly activated by ideological concerns. The system engendered ignorance among the Uzbeks of their culture and history with the Communist Party and its ideology becoming the only guiding force of society in all spheres. Uzbekistan suffered in full measure from the shortcomings of the Soviet system. Patchy development followed from inefficiency and inadequate technical maintenance while catastrophic environmental problems followed from unsustainable and excessive use of the irrigation system and natural resources.

Throughout the decades of Communist rule in Uzbekistan, the key factors in Moscow's policies towards the republic were its desire to dictate policy, control its implementation and control the republic's leadership. It asserted its power to mandate who would serve in which posts and remove those who no longer served the centre's needs. Many of these changes and removals were often brutally enforced. During the Stalin era, they took the form of national purges, summary imprisonment, public trials and executions. The terror and the oppressive character of the Soviet regime were such that it generated tremendous hatred towards the regime in the republic, but at the same time a sense of fear that led people to be silent about what was going on around them. The Kremlin took advantage of this situation to tighten its grip on the staffing of the Party and the state *apparat*, especially at the crucial *oblast* (region) and *raion* (district) levels where policies were implemented. For a while, this provided the Moscow leadership with full control of the party and state activity in Uzbekistan. However, the decades after Stalin's death witnessed a quiet transfer of power in the republic away from Moscow towards the republic's Party organs. By 1983, large numbers of people had been assigned to higher positions to the republic-wide bureaucratic elite, whether in the Party, government, and economic or cultural institutions. These recruitments and promotions were carried out not in line with who was best suited to given jobs, but rather who was willing to work in line with the republican Party organs. This was also a policy executed by the Soviet authorities in Moscow, which failed to achieve the loyalty sought. Rather, the cadre policy led to widespread corruption, discrimination and abuse of power by those in the office, as well as unsatisfactory performance at almost every level of the state *apparat*. In 1986, the new leader of the Soviet Union, Mikhail Gorbachev, introduced his reform programme policies – *glasnost* and *perestroika* – to address the corruption, inefficiency and incompetence of the Soviet system throughout the Union. In one of his speeches to the Moscow Communist Party Congress in 1986, Gorbachev also addressed the Uzbek question and stated that shortcomings in Uzbekistan had not 'occurred all at once', but were the 'accumulations of years', and he called for a thorough investigation. Thus, the anti-corruption purges, which had been running since 1984, were stepped up and in early 1986 they penetrated deep into the lower levels of the Party and government departments. By 1988, the number of persons guilty of crimes against the state was conceivably in the 'tens of thousands' at every level of the state authorities, including collective farms and law-enforcement institutions. The lawlessness and abuse of power ran so deep that corrupt cadres ended up being replaced by other corrupt colleagues, or those ousted resurfaced in other responsible posts. The impact of *glasnost* and *perestroika* on Uzbekistan and its people was two-fold. On the one hand they introduced the idea of freedom and 'electability' which meant contributing to bringing out all sorts of corruption by giving people more say in public affairs. On the other hand, it led to a new measure of autonomy and a 'national awakening', promoted by anger at the manner in which Uzbekistan was treated as the 'scapegoat' for corruption. *Glasnost* and *perestroika* policies also unleashed violent ethnic riots in the Fergana Valley.

The cadre campaign at the regional and district levels provoked a storm of resistance. In its efforts to defeat the Uzbek elites, Moscow encouraged the masses to use *glasnost* and *perestroika* to criticize officials and unmask their shortcomings and misdeeds in the name of 'democratization'. People used the occasion to express their anger towards the political elite and its corrupt managers. Letters and telegrams were sent to Moscow, and critical articles appeared in journals and newspapers when they perceived something to be wrong. Workers began to disobey their directors and managers, and the central authority in Tashkent came under immense pressure. Local leaders who remained in office were harassed and humiliated in the media by Moscow. But Moscow's efforts to use the Uzbek masses to pressure the elites from below backfired. The political elite in the republic successfully enlisted the country's cultural figures (e.g. writers, artists, scholars and scientists) in rallying national opinion to oppose Moscow's policies and directives and defeated Moscow in its attempts to turn the masses against them. Many articles began to appear in the Uzbek media full of resentment towards Moscow, claiming that much of the criticism of their country in Moscow newspapers was unjustified and an insult to Uzbek honour. They noted indignantly that the rewards of corruption had ended up not in Uzbekistan but in Moscow. Therefore, the wounded feelings of all Uzbeks produced a national consensus of resistance to Moscow in the late 1980s. The manner and style in which *glasnost* and *perestroika* policies were conducted in Uzbekistan alienated the republic from the Central Soviet authorities. In the end, the Moscow leadership tried, though largely failed, to regain control of cadre policy in Uzbekistan. Moscow relied on traditional authoritarian methods, operating through the party command system, but corruption was entrenched even there. Consequently, while *glasnost* and *perestroika* policies failed to transform Soviet Uzbekistan, movements for independence gained impetus in the republic, and the Uzbek leadership could not reverse these in the early 1990s. In order not to leave the agenda to his opponents, Islom Karimov declared Uzbekistan's political independence in August 1991, and after the demise of the Soviet Union, the leadership took steps to consolidate its power in the republic. However, the political environment did not change much in post-Soviet-era Uzbekistan. The government concentrated on the concepts of stability, security and peace, and economic conditions in the country, paying little attention to the concept of a pluralist democracy for the republic. Fighting between various ethnic and political forces worsened in Tajikistan, Uzbekistan experienced ethnic clashes in the Fergana Valley early in 1989, and smaller outbreaks in 1990 demonstrated the potential for violence in the country. The Karimov government was hostile towards the opposition forces in the country, fearing that political instability would endanger national integrity. Therefore, all potential opposition forces in Uzbekistan were banned, and the transition to democracy in Uzbekistan became authoritarian. As a result, political, ethnic, cultural and other differences and grievances were pushed underground and silenced, rather than being alleviated or resolved, and the political system of the old *iron curtain* was replaced by new *glass curtains*.

However, these early measures taken by the government to silence its opponents were not meant to prevent the emergence of a pluralist democracy in Uzbekistan. The initial goal of the leadership was to prevent a social explosion and total anarchy during the first years of independence. The authorities were familiar with only one method – totalitarian rule – a legacy of the Soviet system in which the Communist party oppressed anyone disagreeing publicly with its own policies and ideology. They had only ever operated in a society without a political history of free democratic opposition. The state authorities did not have experience of engaging in civilized dialogue with opponents, but instead had traditionally relied on smashing them.

In the post-Soviet era, Uzbekistan, as an independent state, has also sought a new orientation, one to inspire the sense of national pride and confidence that was destroyed during the Soviet rule. To achieve this, the state has used many of the same mechanisms of the Soviet period to take the initiative in shaping a new ideology fit for an independent Uzbekistan. The national ideology performs two basic functions, sociocultural and political. The sociocultural function includes: strengthening the feeling of patriotism and independence; national culture, traditions and customs revival; nation consolidation; and the establishment of new types of social relations. The political function involves: the restructuring of political institutions; the establishment of a new political system corresponding to the spirit of the national ideology; protecting and strengthening the sovereignty and independence of the republic. The goal of the state in pursuing these is to build a 'new nation' based on the values of national identity and national consciousness, which Soviet policy had attempted to eradicate. To initiate the new nation-building, the political elite has revived three main cultural landmarks: the recreation of Uzbek history and a redefinition of the historical personalities of Maverannahr; the reintroduction of the Uzbek language as the official national language; and the revival of Islam and its values in Uzbekistan.

In response to his opponents who accused him of being a product of the Communist nomenclatural system, and in an effort to improve his public image as a defender of the Uzbek nation, President Karimov has actively sponsored the revival of Islam in the republic. This is because Islam has had a significant impact on the lives of the majority of the people of Uzbekistan. While the people of present-day Uzbekistan followed various religions for many centuries, since the Arab conquest the majority of the population has been Muslim and, up to the establishment of the Soviet regime, Islam was unquestionably the strongest and most durable cultural influence to have taken root in the area. Before the coming of the Russians, Islamic culture not only survived but was also embraced by all non-Muslim invaders. The Tsarist regime adopted a fairly tolerant and indifferent attitude towards Islam, although from time to time it became rather hostile towards Islam and its followers. Even the openly hostile Soviet attitude towards the Islamic creed and the way of life by no means eradicated Islamic influence. Therefore, Islam and the formation of social organizations around it has had enormous political importance in post-Soviet Uzbekistan. During Tsarist rule, Islam played a mobilizing role for various ethnic groups to unite in one force and organize resistance movements against colonial Russian rule. This prevented the wholesale Russifying of the local population. For the 'Soviet Islam', Uzbekistan was of exemplary importance.

Tashkent was the biggest seat of the four spiritual heads of Muslims in the Soviet Union and the director of these was the Mufti of Tashkent. He was the highest representative of state-controlled 'official Islam'. The only two Islamic universities in the Soviet Union were located here. Uzbekistan was also an important centre of non-official 'parallel' or 'shadow' Islam. The most important role that Islam played during Soviet rule was when the Soviet regime made efforts to establish new norms and values, and to bring about a modern society with its concerted campaign to remove every visible vestige of pre-Soviet culture. Islam was not only able to survive this onslaught but to prosper. It led to family neighbourhood cells, but within this neighbourhood network, relationships provided a degree of protection against the arbitrary excesses of the system and thus provided some counterbalance to the enormous changes that were taking place in the public domain. These networks became a safety valve, enabling high levels of social transformation to take place while providing some degree of stability.

After the collapse of the Soviet system, the liberalization of the religious sphere saw the convergence of 'official' and 'non-official' Islam. The post-Soviet Uzbek government supported this and tried to put itself at its head. In contrast, the current government in Tashkent is focusing on the opposite, destabilizing the elements of 'Islamic rebirth'. It has declared 'ethnic and religious extremism' the main enemies of the state and tends to label all movements as potentially 'dangerous extremists'. Thus, it appears that what is problematic for the state is not the religious content of Islam but rather its expression as a social and political catalyst. Therefore, the government is intolerant of Islamic movements not under government control, and there is the danger that in adopting this stance the authorities might unintentionally turn devoted believers into criminals.

Uzbekistan at the time of its creation as a Soviet Socialist Republic was a multi-ethnic state. Ethnic diversity was, however, greatly increased starting from the last decade of Tsarist rule to the 1950s. Initially, hundreds of thousands of immigrants, mostly from the Slav republics, were moved there. There were also political exiles. During the Second World War, there was another wave of immigration, most of these people being placed in the industrial enterprises that were relocated from the endangered western republics to Uzbekistan. The larger group of the next migration, however, was the 'punished peoples' – entire populations who were accused of treason by the Soviet State. Today, there are about 100 ethnic groups living in Uzbekistan. The main historical and cultural divide between ethnic minority groups in the republic was, and still is, between the 'immigrant' and the 'indigenous' communities. During the Tsarist administration, the settlers did not arrive in the area until the beginning of the twentieth century. Nevertheless, despite the small numbers involved, the scarcity of good land created conflicts between Russians and the local population. The Russians did not mix with the local population but, instead, purely Russian towns sprang up in various parts of the country. Throughout the Soviet period, although inter-ethnic relations in Uzbekistan were in general cordial, social boundaries between the immigrants and the indigenous groups were strongly maintained. Informal socialization, too, was comparatively low, and mixed marriages were rare. Although most small groups were assimilated, the deported people, to a large extent, retained their original social structures. There were tensions between the indigenous peoples and different immigrants, but this remained at a low level. There were instances of discrimination and harassment, but there was no institutionalized racism. The regime was successful in providing scope for advancement for a sufficiently wide range of people for there to be a general perception of ethnic equality.

In the last decade of Soviet rule, when the power of the central government was beginning to diminish and economic and environmental conditions were deteriorating, hitherto latent ethnic tensions unexpectedly exploded into open conflict: in the Fergana Valley, between Uzbeks and Meskhetian Turks in spring 1989, and between Uzbeks and Kyrgyz in 1990, when hundreds of people were murdered. On the eve of the demise of the Soviet Union, ethnic relations in Uzbekistan were quite tense. In the post-Soviet era, there appeared an immense confusion not only at the public level but also at governmental level about how to tackle the exploding ethnic problems. The system that held them together had collapsed. Law and order was also on the verge of collapse. The political elite, however, had inherited from the former Soviet regime a single method to solve any sort of unrest in the country, namely the use of force. Several cultural movements were banned; political parties that had just begun to emerge were also closed down. All opposition movements were repressed. Today, the confusion and instability have to a great extent subsided. Several national associations dedicated to develop and further the ethnic minorities' cultures were granted official registration. The Uzbek government has largely managed to preserve the social accord while introducing new changes. The prospects for ethnic minorities in Uzbekistan appear brighter than they were during the break-up of the Soviet Union. After independence, Uzbekistan sought to initiate its policies of nation-building, an idea based on strengthening the Uzbek national identity in order to foster patriotism and to affirm the legitimacy of the new state as the protector of the culture that suffered under Soviet rule. This effort can be justified as long as it is not initiated at the expense of making those with 'subnational' identities outsiders. Uzbekistan has always been a multinational state and there is tremendous cultural diversity. Contemporary Uzbekistan, therefore, would be better off preserving the rich ethnic diversity in the country.

The present period is witnessing the demolition of the old political system, the rejection of the former ideology, the establishment of new relations in the economic, political and spiritual spheres of society, and the formation of democracy and democratic institutions in Uzbekistan. The ideas of modern democracy and the forms of democratic systems that developed in the course of the development of European civilization are alien phenomena to the newly independent republic, so the problem is complicated and requires careful analysis. Among the local political scientists there is disagreement as to how the problem should be understood. Historically, these problems in Soviet sociology were understood within the confines of Marxist–Leninist principles with their classical approach to almost all social phenomena. The belief about a special Soviet democracy as the highest form of democratic development standing much higher than 'Western bourgeois democracy', the unwillingness to see general aspects of mankind in understanding democracy, rejecting the right of existence of Western liberal democracy and ignorance of its achievements, led Soviet sociologist into a *cul-de-sac*. Therefore, the primary task of modern political science in Uzbekistan is to study and understand the problems of democratic development. It needs new approaches to shift Uzbekistan away from Marxist dogmas and provide its political system with a sound structure.

The idea of democracy in its modern form in the pre-Soviet Central Asian societies was rarely developed and cultivated. More than seventy years of Soviet totalitarianism only thwarted the development of democracy in the lifestyle and consciousness of the whole society. Today, Uzbek politicians need pragmatic and sober approaches to reform the political system, taking into consideration the particular features of historical development and national psychology. The idea of building a genuine democracy in Uzbekistan is developing in an ambivalent way. On the one hand the authorities want to develop the principle of democracy in a country that has no democratic heritage, just to please or gain international legitimacy; on the other hand, the state wants to forge a nation based on a top-down national ideology that foresees a single means of national development. The idea of forging a nation according to a single ideology was attempted by the Soviet regime, but it failed. The simple existence of democratic organs and institutions does not necessarily amount to democracy, particularly if there is no social base for it. There are trends towards establishing the foundations of democracy against a background of acute political struggle in a number of countries in the region, but these developments could actually slow the transition to democracy in the republic. Uzbek authorities appear to be committed to establishing a democratic society where pluralism and social justice will prevail. The problem with democracy in Uzbekistan is that time is required to transform and adjust the old establishments into newer relations, norms and institutions. Rapid and unplanned political moves to a liberal democracy in a society that has never had a democratic history might lead to an accumulation of social problems. But this should not be used as an excuse for the authorities to maintain authoritarian rule. Bearing in mind the geopolitical and strategic location of Uzbekistan at the heart of Eurasia with a population of 24 million people, and a significant natural resource base, a pluralist democracy would enhance its position in this region and strengthen Uzbekistan's influence among neighbouring countries. In the domestic sphere, the official institutions through which ordinary citizens effectively participate in the political process would give the state a strong bulwark on which to rely for survival, especially in times of crisis.

In the economic sphere, after the demise of the Soviet Union, conditions drove the Uzbek economy into recession. The deterioration in the country's economy was, however, not due to specific government policies, but rather to the effects of more than seventy years of Soviet-era development and disrupted patterns of economic, trade, and financial relations within the former Soviet Union. Economic reforms in the early stage also contributed to this decline, but because Uzbekistan has adopted its own model of economic reform, which is based on gradual step-by-step transformation of the old economic relations into a multi-sectoral market economy with the state being the main reformer, the economic dislocation has been less severe in comparison with other CIS countries. Although the Uzbek economy is still going through a period of transition and strong macroeconomic stabilization is yet to be achieved, the Uzbek model of economic development deserves credit for its success in the initial stage of the economic transformation and the improvements achieved in macroeconomic stability in a fairly short period of time. However, it may still be too early to draw a final conclusion about the merits and demerits of this model since it has been applied for only a few years.

The formulation of an independent foreign policy for the republic of Uzbekistan is one of the new trends of activity. The most influential factors in determining Uzbek foreign policy and shaping its priorities are geopolitical, political and economic factors. In addition to these, the republic's regional and international aspirations have also been determinants of its foreign policy priorities. The character of the leadership also plays an influential role. The doctrine of the foreign policy of Uzbekistan is based on providing political and economic independence and security for the country. The general strategic line of its foreign policy since expulsion from the rouble zone has been a comprehensive integration into the world community and entry into the system of world trade, communication and information which will help overcome the former one-sided orientation. This will not only defuse particular states' ambitions over the region and indicate a firm determination not to become a sphere of someone else's influence but also help establish new political and economic connections and promote self-affirmation on the world arena as a member of the world community enjoying full rights which would, in the long run, enhance its regional role. In the external relations sphere, Uzbekistan is poised to have an independent voice without antagonizing or succumbing to foreign domination. But the regional problems and the republic's own economic difficulties have so far made this option difficult to achieve. Due to its natural mineral resources, its strategically sensitive position at the crossroads of several major powers and its desire to establish links with many countries, the republic has attracted the attention of several states and major powers such as Russia, China, India, Pakistan, Iran, Turkey, Saudi Arabia, Israel, the countries of the European Union and the United States, almost all of which have conflicting interests in the region. In this situation, Uzbekistan seeks to develop a political balance between using these powers to advance its own interests and nurturing its own links with the countries in various regions.

Appendix A

MAP 1
Post-Soviet Central Asia

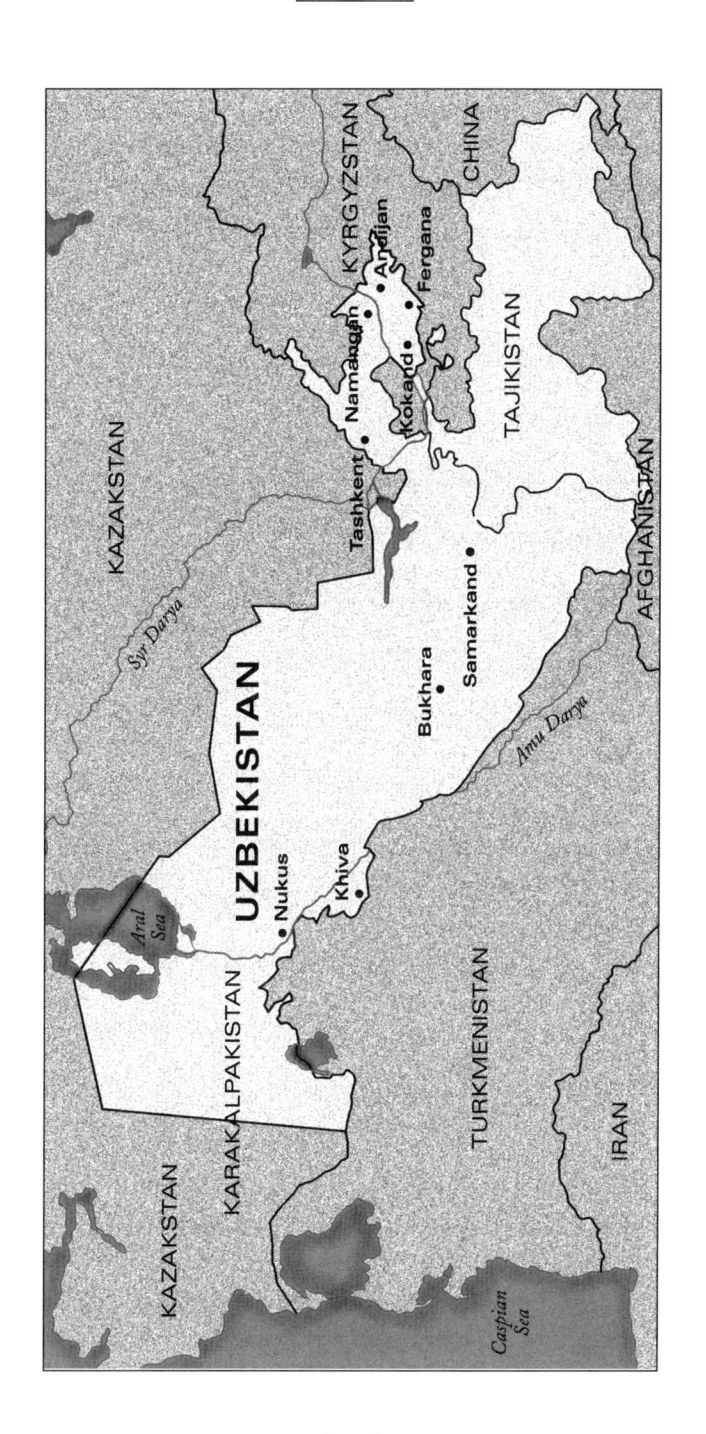

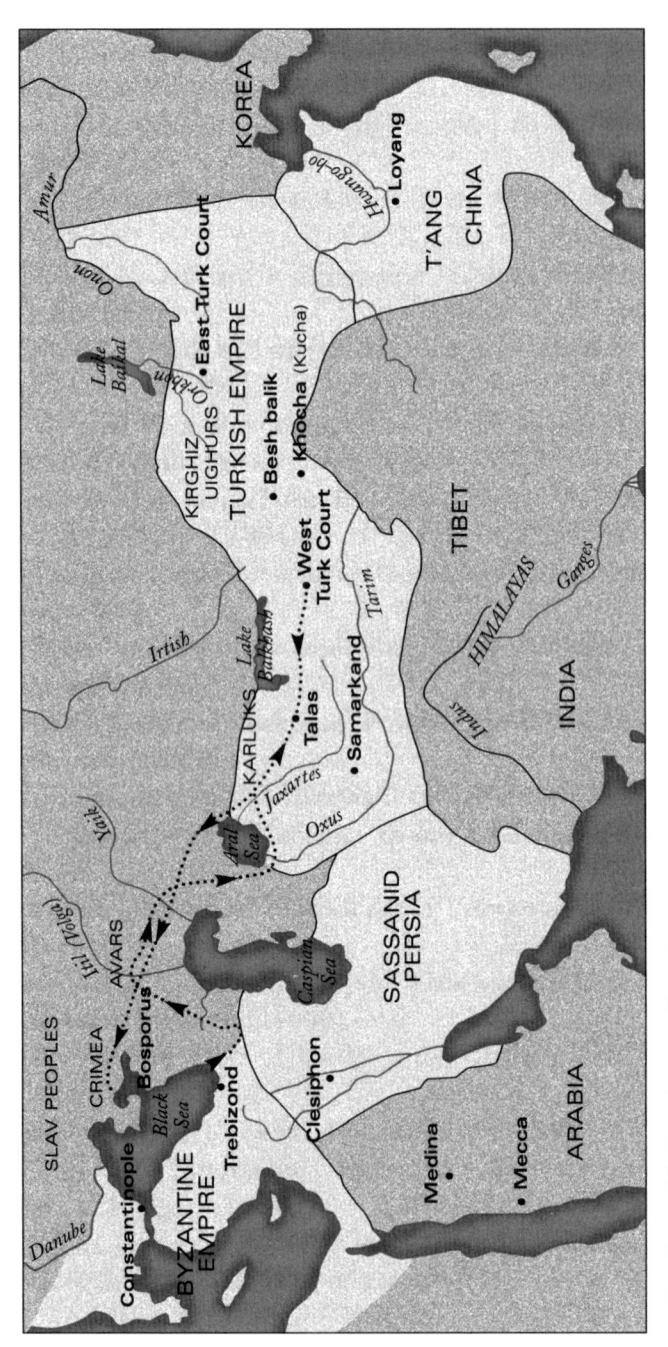

MAP 2
The first Turkish Empire about AD 600

⋯⋯▶ Route of the Byzantine envoy Zemarchus

APPENDIX A

Map 3
The first Turkish Empire about AD 600

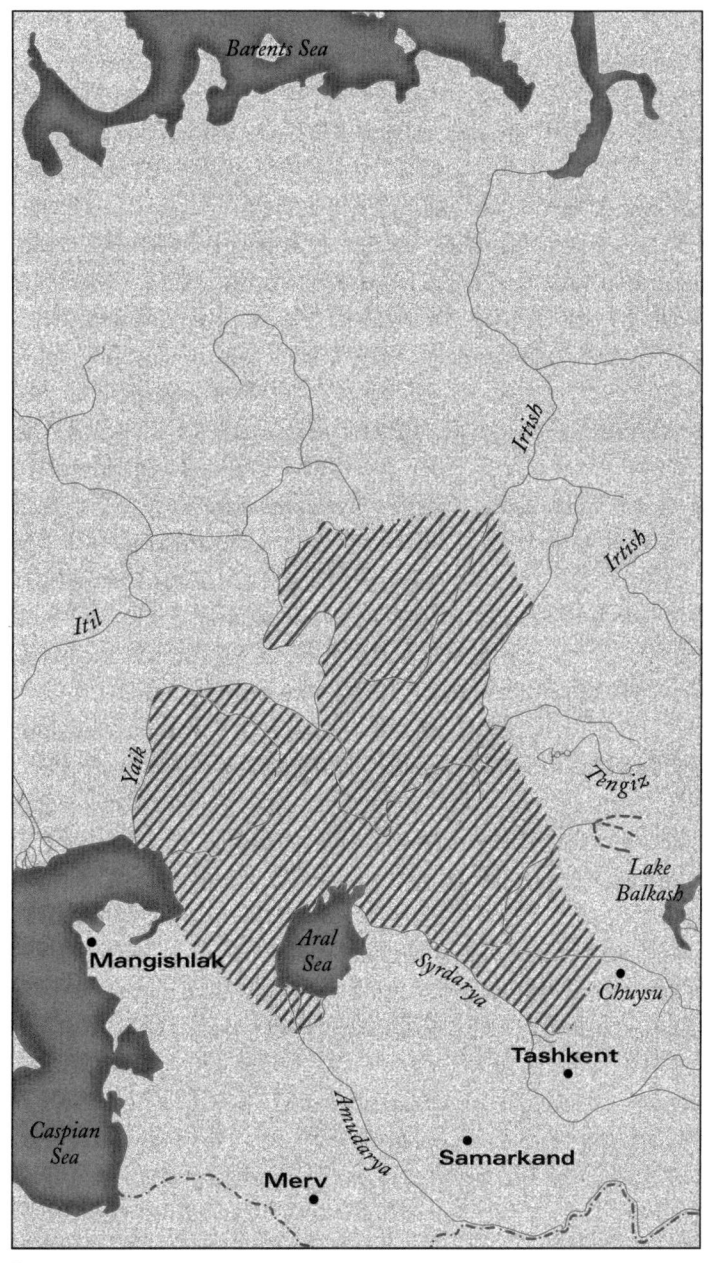

The first Uzbek homeland ca.1400

Appendix B

THE DYNASTIES DESCENDED FROM CHINGGIS KHAN

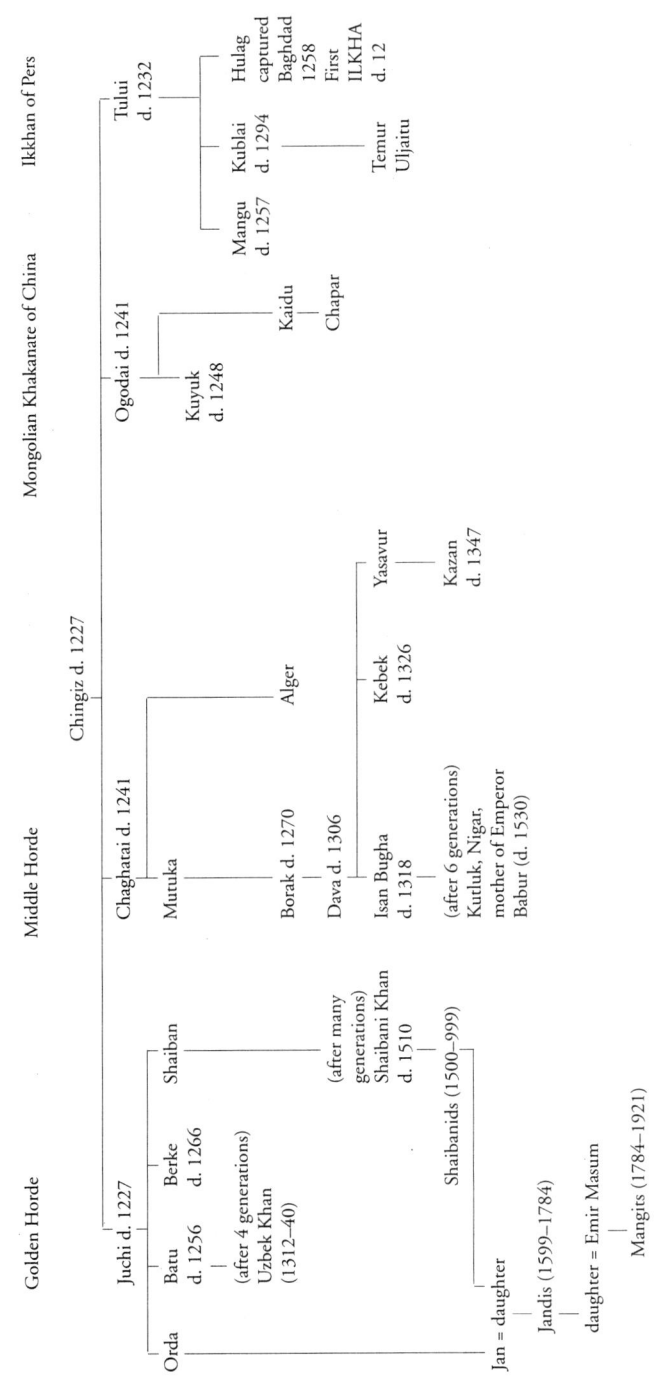

Chingiz d. 1227

Golden Horde

Juchi d. 1227
- Orda
- Batu d. 1256
- Berke d. 1266
- Shaiban

(after 4 generations) Uzbek Khan (1312–40)

(after many generations) Shaibani Khan d. 1510

Shaibanids (1500–999)

Jan = daughter

Jandis (1599–1784)

daughter = Emir Masum

Mangits (1784–1921)

Middle Horde

Chaghatai d. 1241
- Mutuka
  - Borak d. 1270
  - Dava d. 1306
  - Isan Bugha d. 1318
  - (after 6 generations) Kutluk, Nigar, mother of Emperor Babur (d. 1530)
- Alger
  - Kebek d. 1326
  - Yasavur
  - Kazan d. 1347

Mongolian Khakanate of China

Ogodai d. 1241
- Kuyuk d. 1248
- Kaidu
  - Chapar

Ikkhan of Pers

Tului d. 1232
- Mangu d. 1257
- Kublai d. 1294
  - Temur
  - Uljaitu
- Hulag captured Baghdad 1258 First ILKHA d. 12

Sources: J.J. Saunders, *The History of the Mongol Conquests* (London: Routledge & Kegan Paul, 1971); John Andrew Boyle, *The Mongol World Empire, 1206-1370* (London: Variorum, 1977).

Interviews

Shaikh Abdoulgani Abdullah, Head of the International Islamic Research Centre, Tashkent, 27 August 1996. Several discussions were held with the local Muslim heads, and representatives of the *Adolat* (Justice) banned Islamic movement, during my visits throughout the region. Several visits were also made to the Tashkent Board of Muslims.

Bakhodir Alaniyazov, Chairman of the Karakalpak Cultural Centre, Tashkent, 21 August 1996.

Mikhail Ardzinov, Human Rights Society of Uzbekistan, Deputy Chairman, 20 August 1996.

Mehmet Arslan, General Director of the private Uzbek–Turkish Lycee, Tashkent, 5 May 1996.

Alisher A. Atakhodjaev, Director of the Immovable Property Exchange of Tashkent region, 24 August 1996.

Dr Sergey M. Bozhko, Advisor to the UN Representative Administrative Officer, Tashkent, 22 May 1996.

Chad Breckinridge, American Business Centre Manager, Tashkent, 19 August 1996.

Michael B. Dan, Project Manager of the European Union's Tacis Programme, Tashkent, 7 August 1996.

Professor Abdu-Kadir Ergashev, Sustainable Development Advisor to the United Nations Development Programme (UNDP), Momir Vranes, Technical Officer, UNDP project 'Aral Sea Basin Capacity Development', 12 August 1996.

Tursunmat Halbayev, Chairman of the Kazak Cultural Centre, Tashkent, 24 June 1996. Many discussions were also held with Kazak students and workers in the Tashkent and Gulistan regions.

Aziz Kayumov, leader of the *Milli Tiklanish Party*, (National Rebirth Party), Tashkent, 1 May 1996.

Dilovar Khabilova, Deputy chair of the Women's Committee of Uzbekistan, 20 August 1996.

A.K. Khalikova, Chairwoman of the Tatar Cultural Centre, Tashkent, 3 July 1996. Several visits were also made to the Tatar Information and Documentary Centre in Chilanzor-Tashkent throughout the summer of 1996.

Umaiyeh Khammash, United Nations Population Fund, Regional Officer for Central Asia, Azerbaijan and Kazakstan, 11 August 1996.

Peter Kim, Chairman of the Korean Cultural Centre, Tashkent, 27 April 1996. Discussions were held with several other Uzbek Korean intellectuals on 21 June 1996.

Jumen Niyozi Komilcan, one of the party chairmen of the Uzbekistan *Khalk Demokratic Party* (People's Democratic Party – former Communist Party), Tashkent, 16 April 1996.

Tairov Komunar, Chairman of the Uighur Cultural Centre, Tashkent, 25 May 1996. Several discussions were also held with Uighur intellectuals at the Uzbek State University.

G. A. Leventul, a representative of the Jewish Cultural Centre in Tashkent, 10 August 1996. Discussions were held with members of the Uzbek Jewish community in Bukhara, 14 August 1996.

John MacLeod, representative of the Human Rights Watch/Helsinki in Tashkent, 15 September 1996.

Mir Botir Mirabdulaev, Secretary of the *Vatan Taraqiyot* (Homeland Progress) Party, Tashkent, 4 March 1996.

Tulanbay Kurbanov Mirzakuloglu, Chairman of the Krgyzy Cultural Centre, Tashkent, 21 June 1996.

Elmira Muratova, World Bank Human Resources Resident Mission in Uzbekistan, Tashkent, 4 July 1996.

Nabiyev Tokhta Murod, Chairman of the Tajik Cultural Centre, Tashkent, 27 July 1996. Extensive discussions were held with Tajik intellectuals, workers, drivers, students, farmers, etc. in Tashkent, especially

Interviews

the Bostanlik district, Fergana city, Namangan, Khokand, Samarkand and Bukhara.

Mirhan M. Nazmutdinov, Universal World League of Tatar Press, Political, Scientific Documentation and Researches, Tashkent, 15–16 July 1996.

Mark B. O'Brien, Resident Representative, International Monetary Fund, Tashkent, 3 July 1996.

Officials at the Embassy of the Islamic State of Afghanistan, 10 September 1996.

Officials at the Chinese Office of the Counsellor for Trade–Economic Affairs, 22 March 1996 and 4 September 1996.

Officials at the Embassy of France, 4 September 1996.

Officials at the Embassy of the Federal Republic of Germany, 28 August 1996.

Officials at the Embassy of the Islamic Republic of Iran, 13 September 1996.

Officials from the Embassy of the Republic of Korea, 21 June 1996.

Officials at the Embassy of the Kyrgyz Republic, 3 September 1996.

Officials at the Embassy of Pakistan, 10 September 1996.

Officials at the Embassy of the Russian Federation, Tashkent, 23 August 1996.

Officials at the Embassy of the Turkish Republic, 9 August 1996.

Officials at the Uzbek Ministry of Foreign Affairs, 17–18 September 1996.

Abdoumannob Poulatov, one of the leaders of the banned opposition party, *Birlik*, (Unity), Tashkent, 20 September 1996.

Haydarov Rawshan Rasuloglu, Chairman of the *Adolat* (Justice) Social Democrat Party of Uzbekistan, Tashkent, 11 April 1996.

Werner Roider, Deputy Chief, Resident Mission, the World Bank, Tashkent, Abdulaev M. Bahtier, Economist, Macroeconomic Unit World

Bank Mission in Central Asia, Anatoly Krutov, Operations Officer, Tashkent, 10–12 July 1996.

Mehmedov Ismail Rustamoglu, Chairman of the Azerbaijani Cultural Centre, Tashkent, 21 June 1996.

C. Zihni, Chairman of the Russian Cultural Centre, Tashkent, 8 July 1996. Many discussions were also held with Russian intellectuals, workers, business people, drivers and students throughout the country, especially in Tashkent, Chirchik and Navoi.

Participated and held discussions with Uzbek Government officials at the Sub-Regional Workshop on 'Socio-Economic Consideration of Democratic Transition of Central Asia', held at the University of World Economy and Diplomacy, Tashkent, 27–30 November 1995.

Discussions were held with a representative of the Meskhetian Turks, Tashkent, 8 September 1996 and in Almaty 25 July 1996.

Discussions were held at the Embassy of Israel, 1 August 1996.

A representative of the TICA – Turkish International Cooperation Agency, 8 August 1996.

An expert on the economic and industrial issues in Uzbekistan, Ministry of Foreign Economic Relations of the Republic of Uzbekistan, 20 August 1996.

Discussions were held with a group of experts in regional issues and Uzbek foreign policy at the Institute of Strategic Studies, Tashkent, 29 August 1996.

Representatives of the Women's Resource Centre, 25 July 1996, and Mahbuba Ergasheva, a national expert on women's issues in Uzbekistan, at the Centre for Young Women, 5 September 1996.

A lengthy discussion of the political system and internal developments in Uzbekistan, with a group of experts from the Department of International Affairs, University of World Economy and Diplomacy, 2 March 1996, and with several academics at the Institute of Oriental Studies, on 15 September 1996.

Discussions were held in London, at the Royal Garden Hotel, with Dr Rustam S. Azimov, Chairman of the Board of the National Bank for Foreign Economic Activity of the Republic of Uzbekistan; Zakirov Alimjohn Abdurakhimovich, Deputy Minister of the Republic of Uzbekistan; the Deputy General Director of the state Joint-Stock Company National Corporation 'Uzbekneftegaz'; and Hee Choo Chung, Executive Vice President the Daewoo Corporation, 6 November 1997.

Bibliography

Books and papers

Adshead, S. A. M. (ed.), *Central Asia in World History* (New York: St. Martin's Press, 1993).

Akhmedov, B. *Amir Temur* (Tashkent: Abdulla Kodiriy Nomidagi Khalkh Merosi Nasriyoti, 1995).

—*Sokhibkiron Temur* (Tashkent: Abdulla Kodiriy Nomidagi Khalkh Merosi Nasriyoti, 1996).

—(ed.), *Temur Tuzuklari* (Tashkent: Ghafur Ghulam Nomidagi Adabiyot va Sanoat Nasriyoti, 1996).

Akhmedov, E. and E. Saidaminova. *Uzbekiston Respublikasi: Khiskhacha Malumotnoma* (Tashkent: Uzbekiston, 1995).

Akiner, S. *Central Asia: Conflict or Stability and Development?* (London: Minority Rights Group, 1997).

—(ed.), *Cultural Change and Continuity in Central Asia* (London: Kegan Paul International, 1991).

—*Islamic Peoples of the Soviet Union* (London: Kegan Paul International, 1986).

Allison, R. (ed.), *Challenges for the Former Soviet South* (Washington, DC: Brookings Institution, c. 1996).

Allworth, E. (ed.), *Central Asia: 130 Years of Russian Dominance, A Historical Overview* 3rd edn (Durham: Duke University Press, 1994).

—*The Modern Uzbeks: From the Fourteenth Century to the Present: A Cultural History* (Stanford: Hoover Institution Press, 1990).

—(ed.), *The Nationality Question in Soviet Central Asia* (New York: Praeger, 1973).

—(ed.), *The Tatars of Crimea: Return to Homeland: Studies and Documents* (Durham: Duke University Press, 1998).

—*Uzbek Literary Politics* (The Hague: Mouton, 1964).

Amsden, Alice H., J. Kochanowicz, L. Taylor. *The Market Meets Its Match: Restructuring the Economies of Eastern Europe* (Cambridge: Cambridge University Press, 1994).

Anderson, J. *The International Politics of Central Asia* (New York: Manchester University Press, 1997).
Asian Development Bank. *Country Economic Review: Uzbekistan* (Manila: Asian Development Bank, 1997).
—*Economic Report on Uzbekistan* (Manila: Asian Development Bank, 1996).
Atabaki, T. and J. O'Kane (eds), *Post-Soviet Central Asia* (Leiden, London, N.Y.: Tauris Academic Studies, The International Institute for Asian Studies, 1998).
Azimova, D. *Youth and the Cultural Revolution in Soviet Central Asian Republics* (Moscow: Nauka, 1988).
Bacon, E. *Central Asians Under Russian Rule: A Study in Culture Change* (Ithaca, New York: Cornell University Press, 1966).
Bailey, F. M. *Mission to Tashkent* (London: Jonathan Cape, 1946).
Barfield, Thomas J. *The Perilous Frontier: Nomadic Empire and China* (Oxford: Basil Blackwell, 1989).
Bartold, V. V. *Four Studies on the History of Central Asia, I* (Leiden: 1956).
—*Four Studies on the History of Central Asia, II* (Leiden: 1958).
Becker, S. *Russia's Protectorates in Central Asia: Bukhara and Khiva, 1865–1924* (Cambridge, MA: Harvard University Press, 1968).
Behar, B. E. (ed.), *Bagimsizligin Ilk Yillari: Azerbaijan, Kazakistan, Kirgizistan, Ozbekiston, Turkmenistan* (Ankara: T.C. Kultur Bakanligi, 1994).
Benningsen, A. and S. Wimbush. *Muslim National Communism in the Soviet Union* (Chicago: Chicago University Press, 1979).
Benningsen, A. and Marie Broxup. *The Islamic Threat to the Soviet State* (New York: St. Martin's Press, 1983).
Bobokhonova, L. T. and S. D. Bektuganova. *Uzbekistan va Uzbeklar* (Tashkent: Uzbekiston, 1996).
Boinazarov, F. *Urta Osiyaning Antik Davri* (Tashkent: Uzbekiston, 1991).
Bremmer, I. and R. Taras. *Nations and Politics in the Soviet Successor States* (Cambridge: Cambridge University Press, 1993).
—*New States New politics: Building the Post-Soviet Nations* 2nd edn (Cambridge; New York: Cambridge University Press, 1996).
Buranov, M. K. *Tarakkiyot va Khamkorlik Iyullarida; Uzbekiston Tashki Siyosati va Diplomatiyasi* (Tashkent: Uzbekiston, 1993).

Buronov, K. and V. Kolyeova. *Birinci Chakirik Uzbekiston Respublikasi Oliy Majlisining Deputatlari* (Tashkent: Uzbekiston, 1995).
Canfield, R. (ed.), *Turko-Persia in Historical Perspective* (Cambridge: Cambridge University Press, 1991).
Caroe, O. S. *Soviet Empire: The Turks of Central Asia and Stalinism* 2nd edn (London: Macmillan, 1967).
Carrere d'Encausse, H. *Islam and the Russian Empire: Reform and Revolution in Central Asia* translated by Quentin Hoare (London: Tauris, 1987).
Central Asia: On The Path of Security and Cooperation, Materials of Tashkent Meeting-Seminar on the Issues of Security and Cooperation in Central Asia (September 15–16, 1995) (Tashkent: Uzbekiston, 1995).
Coates, Z. and W. P. *Soviets in Central Asia* (London: Lawrence and Wishart Ltd., 1951).
Crawshaw, S. *Goodbye to the USSR: The Collapse of Soviet Power* (London: Bloomsbury, 1992).
Critchlow, J. *Nationalism in Uzbekistan: A Soviet Republic's Road to Sovereignty* (Boulder: Westview Press, 1991).
Curzon, G. N. *Russia in Central Asia in 1889 and the Anglo-Russian Question* (London: Frank Cass & Co. Ltd, 1967).
Dallin, A. and G. W. Lapidus (eds), *The Soviet System in Crisis: A Reader of Western and Soviet Views* (Boulder: Westview Press, 1991; 1st edn); *The Soviet System: From Crisis to Collapse* (Boulder: Westview Press, 1995; 2nd edn).
Dannreuther, R. *Creating New States in Central Asia: The Strategic Implications of the Collapse of Soviet Power in Central Asia* (London: International Institute for Strategic Studies, 1994).
Dawisha, K. and B. Parrott. *Russia and the New States of Eurasia: The Politics of Upheaval* (USA: Cambridge University Press, 1994).
Duverger, M. *Political Parties* (Cambridge: Cambridge University Press, 1954).
Eastern Europe and the Commonwealth of Independent States 3rd edn (Europa Publications Limited, 1997).
Economist Intelligence Unit. *Central Asian Republics: Industrial Reform and Restructuring Industrial Development* Review Series (London: The Economist Intelligence Unit for UNIDO, 1996).

Ehteshami, A. (ed.), *From the Gulf to Central Asia: Players in the New Great Game* (Exeter: Exeter University Press, 1994).

Eickelman, D. F. (ed.), *Russia's Muslim Frontiers: New Directions in Cross-Cultural Analysis* (Bloomington: Indiana University Press, 1993).

Federal Institute for East European and International Studies. *The Soviet Union 1987–1989: Perestroika in Crisis* (London: Longman, 1990).

Ferdinand, P. (ed.), *The New Central Asia and Its Neighbours* (London: Pinter Publishers, The Royal Institute of International Affairs, 1994).

Fierman, W. (ed.), *Soviet Central Asia: The Failed Transformation* (Boulder: Westview Press, 1991).

Fuller, G. E. *Central Asia: The New Geopolitics* (Santa Monica, California: Rand Corporation, 1992).

Fuller, G. E. and Ian O. Lesser. *Turkey's New Geopolitics: From the Balkans to Western China* (Boulder: Westview Press, 1993).

Geography Department, Lerner Publications Company. *Uzbekistan: Then and Now* (Minneapolis: Lerner Publications Company, 1993).

Goldenberg, S. *Pride of Small Nations: the Caucasus and Post-Soviet Disorder* (London: Zed Books, 1994).

Griffin, K. (ed.), *Social Policy and Economic Transformation in Uzbekistan* (Geneva: International Labour Office, 1996).

Gross, J. (ed.), *Muslims in Central Asia: Expressions of Identity and Change* (Durham: Duke University Press, 1992).

Hambly, G. *Central Asia* (London: Weidenfeld and Nicolson, 1969).

Hayit, B. *Turkestan in XX Jahrhundert* (Darmstatt: C.W. Leske Verlag, 1956).

Heywood, A. *Political Ideologies: an Introduction* (London: Macmillan, 1992).

Hiro, D. *Between Marx and Muhammad: The Changing Faces of Central Asia* (London: HarperCollins, 1994).

Human Rights Watch/Helsinki. *Uzbekistan: Persistent Human Rights Violations and Prospects for Improvement* (1996).

Hunter, Shireen T. *Central Asia Since Independence (The Washington Papers/168)*. (Washington D.C.: The Centre for Strategic and International Studies, 1996).

—*Turkey at the Crossroads: Islamic Past or European Future*, CEPS Paper no. 63 (Brussels: Centre for European Policy Studies, 1995).

Huntington, Samuel P. *The Clash of Civilizations and the Remaking of World Order* (New York: Simon and Schuster, 1996).
Huttenbach, H. (ed.), *Soviet Nationality Policies: Ruling Ethnic Groups in the USSR* (New York: Mansell, 1990).
Hyman, A. *Political Change in Post-Soviet Central Asia* (London: The Royal Institute of International Affairs, 1994).
—*Power and Politics in Central Asia's New Republics* (London: Research Institute for the Study of Conflict and Terrorism, 1994).
Ibrahimova, D. *The Islamization of Central Asia: A Case Study of Uzbekistan* (Leicester: Islamic Foundation, 1993).
Independent Uzbekistan Today: A Reference Book (Tashkent, 1993).
International Monetary Fund. Direction of Trade Statistics Yearbook (1997).
—Direction of Trade Statistics Quarterly (1997).
—*Economic Review: Uzbekistan* (Washington, DC: IMF, 1994).
—*IMF Directory of Trade Statistics Yearbook, 1997* (Washington, DC: IMF, 1997).
—*Republic of Uzbekistan: Recent Economic Developments*, Staff Country Report no. 97/98 (Washington, DC: IMF, 1997).
—*Republic of Uzbekistan: Recent Economic Developments*, Staff Country Report no. 00/36 (Washington, DC: IMF, 2000).
—*Uzbekistan Country Economic Review* (Washington, DC: IMF, 1992).
Investment Projects of the Republic of Uzbekistan (Tashkent: Uzbekiston, 1994).
Jabbarov, I. *Uzbek Khalki Ethnografiyasi* (Tashkent: Uzbekiston, 1994).
Jalalov, J. *Bozor Iktisodiyoti: Turkiya Modelining Siri* (Tashkent: Adolat, 1994).
Jalilov, S., *Davlot Khokimiyati Makhalliy Organlari Islokhoti: Tajriba va Muammolar* (Tashkent: Uzbekiston, 1994).
—*Makhalla Yangilanish Davrida* (Tashkent: Mekhnat Nashriyati, 1995).
Johnson, S. and B. Islomov. *Property Rights and Economic Reform in Uzbekistan* (Helsinki: WIDER Working Papers WP90, 1991).
Kabirov, M. N. *Pereselenie Iliiskikh Uigur v Semirechie* (Alma-Ata: A.N. Kazakhskoi SSR, Izd., 1951).
Karimov, Islom. *Building The Future: Uzbekistan – Its Own Model for Transition to a Market Economy* (Tashkent: Uzbekiston, 1993).
—*Buyuk Maksad Yolidan Ogishmailik* (Tashkent: Uzbekiston, 1993).

—*Our Road – The Road to Independent State and Progress* (Tashkent: Uzbekiston, 1994).
—*Rodina Svyashenna Dlya Kajdogo* (Tashkent: Uzbekiston, 1995).
—*Turkistan Umumiy Uyimiz* (Tashkent: Uzbekiston, 1995).
—*Uzbekistan: The Road of Independence and Progress* (Tashkent: Uzbekiston, 1992).
—*Uzbekistan XXI Asr Bursaghasida; Khafsizlikka Taghdid, Barkororlik Shartlari va Tarakkiyot Kafolatlari* (Tashkent: Uzbekiston, 1997).
—*Uzbekistan: A Country with a Great Future* (Tashkent: Uzbekiston, 1992).
—*Uzbekistan: Along the Road of Deepening Economic Reform* (Tashkent: Uzbekiston, 1995).
—*Uzbekistoning Milli Istiklol Mavkurasi* (Tashkent: Uzbekiston, 1993).
—*Uzbekistoning Siyosi-Ictimayi va Itktisodiy Istikbolining Asosiy Tamoyillari* (Tashkent: Uzbekiston, 1995).
Kaser, M. and S. Mehrotra. *The Central Asian Economies After Independence* (London: The Royal Institute of International Affairs, 1992).
Kasimov, A. V. *Ocnovniye Napravleniya Bneshnyei Politiki Respubliki Uzbekistan* (Tashkent: Uzbekiston, 1994).
Khalfin, N. A. *Russia's Policy in Central Asia 1857–1868* (Oxford: Central Asian Research Centre in association with St. Anthony's College, 1964).
Kirkwood, M. (ed.), *Language Planning in the Soviet Union* (London: Macmillan, 1989).
Kul'chik, I. U. G. *Central Asia After the Empire* (London: Pluto Press in association with the Transnational Institute, 1996).
Landau, J. M. *Pan-Turkism: From Irredentism to Cooperation* (London: Hurst and Co., 1995).
—*Pan-Turkism in Turkey: A Study of Irredentism* (London: Hurst and Co., 1981).
—*The Politics of Pan-Islam: Ideology and Organization* (Oxford: Clarendon, 1984).
Lewis, A. *Economic Development with Unlimited Supplies of Labor* vol. 20 (New York: The Manchester School, 1954).
Lewis, R. A. (ed.), *Geographic Perspectives on Soviet Central Asia* (London: Routledge, 1991).
Lindner, R. P. *Nomads and Ottomans in Medieval Anatolia* (Bloomington: Research Institute for Inner Asian Studies, Indiana University, 1983).

Lubin, N. *Labour and Nationality in Soviet Central Asia: An Uneasy Compromise* (London: Macmillan in association with St. Anthony's College Oxford, 1984).

Malik, H. (ed.), *Central Asia: Its Strategic Importance and Future Prospects* (Basingstoke: Macmillan, 1994).

Mandelbaum, M. (ed.), *Central Asia and the World: Kazakhstan, Uzbekistan, Tajikistan, Kyrgyzstan and Turkmenistan* (New York: Council on Foreign Relations, 1994).

—(ed.), *The Rise of Nations in the Soviet Union: American Foreign Policy and the Disintegration of the USSR* (New York: Council on Foreign Relations Press, 1991).

Manz, B. F. (ed.), *Central Asia in Historical Perspective* (Boulder: Westview Press, 1994).

Marine, S. *Poverty in Pre-Reform Uzbekistan: What Do Official Data Really Reveal?*, EUI Working Paper, ECO no.93/95 (Florence: European University Institute, 1993).

Marshall, G. *What Went Wrong with Perestroika?* (New York: Norton, 1991).

Martin, S. *Ideology and Politics* (London: Allen and Unwin, 1976).

Medin, W. K., W. M. Cave and F. Carpenter. *Education and Development in Central Asia: a Case Study of Social Change in Uzbekistan* (Leiden: Brill, 1971).

Menashri, D. (ed.), *Central Asia Meets the Middle East* (London: Frank Cass & Co. Ltd, 1998).

Mesbahi, M. (ed.), *Central Asia and the Caucasus after the Soviet Union: Domestic and International Dynamics* (Gainesville: Florida University Press, 1994).

Mirolimov, S. *Makhalla Mekhri* (Tashkent: Navruz, 1994).

Miyamoto, A. (ed.), *Natural Gas in Central Asia: Industries, Markets and Export Options of Kazakstan, Turkmenistan and Uzbekistan* (London: The Royal Institute of International Affairs, 1997).

Morgan, D. *The Mongols* (New York: Basil Blackwell, 1986).

Naumkin, V. (ed.), *State, Religion and Society in Central Asia: A Post-Soviet Critique* (Reading: Ithaca Press, 1993).

Nekrich, A. *The Punished Peoples* (New York: Norton, 1978).

Olcott, M. B. *Central Asia's New States: Independence, Foreign Policy, and Regional Security* (Washington, DC: Institute of Peace Press, 1996).

Open Society Institute. *Crimean Tatars: Repatriation and Conflict Prevention* (New York: 1996).

Özbekistan Cumhuriyeti Kanun ve Kararnameleri (Tashkent: Uzbekiston, 1993).

Pale, K. *Mission to Turkestan* (London: Oxford University Press, 1964).

Park, A. G. *Bolshevism in Turkestan 1917–1927* (New York: Columbia University Press, 1957).

Parrott, B. (ed.), *State Building and Military Power in Russia and the New States of Eurasia* (Armonk, N.Y.: M.E. Sharpe, 1995).

Peimani, H. *Regional Security and the Future of Central Asia: the Competition of Iran, Turkey, and Russia* (Westport, Conn: Praeger, 1998).

Pierce, R. A. *Russian Central Asia 1867–1917: A Study in Colonial Rule* (Cambridge: California University Press, 1960).

Pomfret, R. W. T. and K. H. Anderson. *Uzbekistan: Welfare Impact of Slow Transition* (Helsinki: WIDER Working Papers no. 135, 1997).

Pope, H. *Turkey: Expanding Influence,* MEI Report no. 418, 7 February 1992.

—*Turkey, The U.S. and Central Asia: Wooing the Republics,* MEI Report no. 419, 21 February 1992.

Prawdin, M. *The Mongol Empire: Its Rise and Legacy* (London: George Allen & Unwin Publishers Ltd, 1940).

Przeworski, A. *Democracy and the Market; Political and Economic Reforms in Eastern Europe and Latin America* (USA: Cambridge University Press, 1991).

Rashid, A. *Resurgence of Central Asia: Islam or Nationalism?* (London: Zed Books, 1994).

Republic of Uzbekistan Decrees and Resolutions (Tashkent: Uzbekiston 1994).

Republic of Uzbekistan Decrees and Resolutions, Second Book (Tashkent: Uzbekiston, 1994).

Riasonovsky, V. A. *Fundamental Principles of Mongol Law* (The Hague, 1965).

Ro'i, Y. (ed.), *Muslim Eurasia: Conflicting Legacies* (London: Frank Cass & Co. Ltd, 1995).

Rorlich, A. A. *The Volga Tatars: A Profile in National Resilience* (California: Hoover Institution Press, 1986).

Rumer, B. Z. (ed.), *Central Asia: Dilemmas of Political and Economic Development* (Armonk, N.Y: M.E Sharpe, 1996).

—*Soviet Central Asia: 'A Tragic Experiment'* (Boston: George Allen & Unwin, 1989).
Rywkin, M. *Moscow's Muslim Challenge: Soviet Central Asia* (Armonk, N.Y.: M.E. Sharpe, 1982).
Sartori, G. *Parties and Party Systems* (Cambridge: Cambridge University Press, 1976).
Saunders, J. J. *The History of the Mongol Conquests* (London: Routledge and K. Paul, 1971).
Shashenkov, M. *Security Issues of the Ex-Soviet Central Asian Republics* (London: Brassey's for the Centre for Defence Studies, 1992).
Sheehy, A. *The Crimean Tatars and Volga Germans: Soviet Treatment of Two Nationalities* (London: Minority Rights Group, 1977).
Sixsmith, M. *Moscow Coup: The Death of the Soviet System* (London: Simon & Schuster, 1991).
Smith, G. (ed.), *The Nationalities Question in the Post-Soviet States* 2nd edn (London: Longman, 1996).
Spoor, M. *Agrarian Transition in Former Soviet Central Asia: A Comparative Study of Uzbekistan and Kyrygzstan*, EUI Working Paper no. 202 (The Hague: Institute of Social Studies, 1995).
Star, Frederick S. (ed.), *The Legacy of History in Russia and the New States of Eurasia* (Armonk, N.Y: M.E. Sharpe, 1994).
Szporluk, R. *National Identity and Ethnicity in Russia and the New States of Eurasia* (Armonk; N.Y: M.E. Sharpe, 1994).
Tajfe, H. *The Psychology of Minorities* (London: Minority Rights Group, 1992).
Technical Cooperation Centre For Europe and Central Asia. *CIS Migration Report 1996* (Geneva: International Organization for Migration, 1997).
Togan, Zeki V. *Turk ve Tatar Tarihi* (Istanbul: Enderun, 1982).
—*Turkili Turkistan ve Yakin Tarihi* 2nd edn (Istanbul: Enderun, 1981).
Turan, U. *Turkiy Khalklar Mafkurasi* (Tashkent: Cholpan Nashriyoti, 1995).
Undeland, C. and N. Platt. *The Central Asian Republics: Fragments of Empire, Magnets of Wealth* (New York: The Asian Society, 1994).
United Nations Development Program. *The Aral Sea in Crisis* (Tashkent: UNDP, 1995).
—*Uzbekistan Human Development Report* (Tashkent: UNDP, 1995).

—*Uzbekistan Human Development Report* (Tashkent: UNDP, 1996).
Uzbekiston Fanlar Akademiyasi. *Uzbekistan Khalklari Tarikhi* vols. I & II (Tashkent: FAN Nashriyoti, 1993).
Uzbekiston Respublikasining Konuni: Latin Yozuvga Asoslangan Uzbek Alifbosini Jorii Etish Tughrisida (Tashkent: Uzbekiston, 1993).
Uzbekiston Respublikasining Sailov Tughrisidagi Konunlari (Tashkent: Uzbekiston, 1994).
Uzbekiston Respublikasining Konstitusiyasi (Tashkent: Uzbekiston, December 1992).
Walker, R. *Six Years that Shook the World: Perestroika, the Impossible Project* (New York: Manchester University Press, 1993).
Ware, A. *Political Parties and Party Systems* (Oxford: Oxford University Press, 1996).
—*Political Parties: Electoral Change and Structural Responses* (Oxford: Basil Blackwell, 1987).
Webber, M. *The International Politics of Russia and the Successor States* (Manchester, New York: Manchester University Press, 1996).
Wheeler, G. *The Modern History of Soviet Central Asia* (London: Weidenfeld & Nicolson, 1964).
—*The Peoples of Soviet Central Asia: A Background Book* (London: Bodley Head, 1966).
White, S. *Gorbachev and After* (Cambridge: Cambridge University Press, 1991).
Whiting, Allen S. and General Sheng Shih-ts'ai. *Sinkiang: Pawn or Pivot?* (USA: Michigan State University Press, 1958).
Wilson, A. *The Crimean Tatars: A Situation Report* (London: International Alert, 1994).
Winrow, G. M. *Turkey in Post-Soviet Central Asia* (London: The Royal Institute of International Affairs, 1995).
Wright, M. *Soviet Union: The Challenge of Change* (Harlow: Longman Group UK, 1989).
World Bank. *Country Report; Uzbekistan Economic Memorandum: Subsidies and Transfers* (1994).
—*Commodity Markets and the Developing Countries* (1997).
—*Country Study: Russian Economic Reform* (1992).
—*Memorandum of the President of the International Bank for Reconstruction and Development to the Executive Directors on a Country Assistance Strategy of the World Bank Group for the Republic of Uzbekistan* (1995).

—*Uzbekistan: Adjusting Social Protection* (1994).
—*Uzbekistan: An Agenda for Economic Reform* (1993).
—*Uzbekistan: Creating Financial Markets: A Review of the Financial Sector* (1997).
Yongjin, Z. and R. Azizian (eds), *Ethnic Challenges Beyond Borders: Chinese and Russian Perspectives of the Central Asian Conundrum* (Oxford: Macmillan, 1998).
Zenkovsky, S. A. *Pan-Turkism and Islam in Russia* (Cambridge, MA: Harvard University Press, 1960).

Articles
Ahmar, M. 'Pakistan and the Power Struggle in Afghanistan', *Eurasian Studies*, 3 (Fall 1996).
Akbarzadeh, S. 'Nation-building in Uzbekistan', *Central Asian Survey*, 15:1 (1996).
—'A Note on Shifting Identities in the Ferghana Valley', *Central Asian Survey*, 16:1 (March 1997).
—'The Political Shape of Central Asia', *Central Asian Survey*, 16:4 (December 1997).
Akchurin, M. 'Uzbekistan: The Quest For Economic Independence', *Central Asia Monitor*, 2 (1993).
Alici, D. M. 'The Role of Culture, History and Language in Turkish National Identity Building: An Overemphasis on Central Asian Roots', *Central Asian Survey*, 15:2 (June 1996).
Aligiah, G. 'Victorious Warlords Fight to the Death over Ruins of Afghanistan'. *Independent on Sunday*, 5 March 1994.
Alimov, K. 'Are Central Asian Clans Still Playing a Political Role?', *Central Asia Monitor*, 4 (1994).
Allworth, E. 'The Cultural Identity of Central Asian Leaders: The Problems of Affinity With Followers', *Central Asia Monitor*, 6 (1993).
Altan, M. B. 'A Brief History of the Crimean Tatar National Movement', *The Crimean Review*, special issue, Boston, MA (1995).
Apostolou, A. 'The Mistake of the Uzbek Economic Model', *Central Asia Monitor*, 2 (1998).
Aras, B. and I. Colak. 'American–Central Asian Relations', *Eurasian Studies*, 3 (Fall 1996).

Aydin, M. 'Turkey and Central Asia: Challenges of Change', *Central Asian Survey*, 15:2 (June 1996).
Benningsen, A. 'Pan-Turkism and Pan-Islamism: History and Today', *Central Asian Survey*, 3:3 (1985).
—'Soviet Islam since the Invasion of Afghanistan', *Central Asian Survey*, 1:1 (July 1982).
—'Unrest in the World of Soviet Islam', *Third World Quarterly*, 10:2 (April 1988).
Biezans, L. 'Volga-Ural Tatars in Emigration', *Central Asian Survey*, 11:4 (December 1992).
Bilge, S. 'Commonwealth of Independent States and Turkey', *Eurasian Studies*, 4 (Winter 1995).
Brown, B. 'Central Asia: Economic Crisis Deepens', *RFE/RL Research Report*, 10 (2 April 1988).
—'Three Central Asian States Form Economic Union', *RFE/RL Research Report*, 13:13 (1 April 1994).
Broxup, M. 'Islam in Central Asia since Gorbachev', *Asian Affairs*, 18:74 (October 1987).
Budak, M. 'The Origin of Ottoman–Uzbek Relations', Eurasian Studies, 4 (Winter 1995/96).
Cashel, J. and C. Kedzie. 'Uzbekistan: Programs and Prognosis', *Central Asia Monitor*, 1 (1993).
Cavanaugh, C. 'Histography in Uzbekistan', *Central Asia Monitor*, 1 (1994).
Critchlow, J. 'Central Asia's Challenge to our Understanding', *Central Asia Monitor*, 1 (1992).
—Futher Repercussions of the "Uzbek Affair", *Report on the USSR*, 2:18 (1990).
—'Did Faizulla Khojaev Really Oppose Uzbekistan's Land Reform?', *Central Asian Survey*, 9:3 (1990).
—'Uzbekistan And the West: Time for a new departure', *Central Asia Monitor*, 5 (1993).
—'Uzbekistan's Prospects', *Central Asia Monitor*, 4 (1998).
—'What Is the U.S. Interest in Central Asia's Future?', *Central Asia Monitor*, 1 (1992).
Crow, S. 'Russia Promotes the CIS as an International Organization', *REF/RL Research Report*, 3 (11 March 1994).
Daulet, S. 'The First All-Muslim Congress of Russia, Moscow, 1–11 May 1917', *Central Asian Survey*, 8:1 (1989).

Dieter, H. 'Regional Integration in Central Asia: Current Economic Position and Prospects', *Central Asian Survey,* 15:3/4 (December 1996).
Ehteshami, A. and E. C. Murphy. 'The Non-Arab Middle East States and the Caucasian/Central Asian Republics: Turkey', *International Relations,* XI:6 (1993).
—'The Non-Arab Middle East States and the Caucasian/Central Asian Republics: Iran and Israel', *International Relations,* XII:1 (1994).
Fierman, M. 'Glasnost in Practice: The Uzbek experience', *Central Asian Survey,* 8:2 (1989).
Fierman, W. 'The Communist Party, Erk and the Changing Uzbek Political Environment', *Central Asian Survey,* 10:3 (1991).
Foltz, R. 'The Tajiks of Uzbekistan', *Central Asian Survey,* 15:2 (June 1996).
Fragner, B. G. 'Central Asian Aspects of Pre-Modern Iranian History (Fourteenth to Nineteenth Century)', *Central Asian Survey,* 12:4 (1993).
Freedman, R. O. 'Israel and Central Asia: A Preliminary Analysis', *Central Asia Monitor,* 2 (1993).
Fuller, G. E. 'The Emergence of Central Asia', *Foreign Policy,* 78 (Spring 1990).
Gidadhubli, R. G. 'Economic Transition in Uzbekistan', *Economic and Political Weekly,* 29:6 (1994).
Globe, P. 'Central Asia: Analysis from Washington: A Watershed in Central Asia', *Turkistan-N Newsletter* (27 July 1997), and *RFE/RL Research Report* (25 July 1997).
—'Ten Issues in Search of a Policy: America's Failed Approach to the Post-Soviet States', *Current History,* 92:576 (October 1993).
Gretsky, S. 'Uzbekistan Open Forum on Human Rights: A Report', *Central Asia Monitor,* 3 (1996).
Gumpel, W. 'Economic Development and Integration in Central Asian Republics', *Eurasian Studies,* no. 13, Spring 1998.
Haghayeghi, M. 'Islamic Revival in the Central Asian Republics', *Central Asian Survey,* 13:2 (1994).
Heitman, S. 'The Soviet Germans', *Central Asian Survey,* 12:1 (1993).
Hunter, S. T. 'Central Asia and the Middle East: Patterns of Interaction and Influence', *Central Asia Monitor,* 6 (1992).

—'Central Asia and the Middle East: Patterns of Interaction and Influence', *Central Asia Monitor*, 1 (1995).
—'Closer Ties for Russia and Iran', *Transition*, 1:24 (29 December 1995).
—'The Muslim Republics of the Former Soviet Union: Policy Challenges for the United States', *Washington Quarterly*, 15:3 (Summer 1992).
Huttenbach, H. R. 'The Soviet Koreans', *Central Asian Survey*, 12:1 (1993).
Jalolov, A. 'Kuch Khalk Bilan Birgalikda', *Mulokot*, (Spring 1995).
Juan, L. and S. Alfred. 'Political Identities and Electoral Sequences', *Deadalus*, 121:2 (1992).
Kangas, R. 'Recent Developments with Uzbek Political Parties', *Central Asia Monitor*, 4 (1992).
—'Uzbekistan – Evolving Authoritarianism', *Current History*, 93:582 (1994).
Karpat, K. 'The Old and New Central Asia', *Central Asian Survey*, 12:4 (1993).
Kasenov, U. 'Problems of Cooperation and Integration', *Central Asia Monitor*, 6 (1997).
Kaser, M. 'Economic Transition in Six Central Asian Economies', *Central Asian Survey*, 16:1 (March 1997).
—'Stabilization and Growth in Central Asia, 1990–8', Seminar on Central Asia in the 1990's: Oxford Centre for Islamic Studies, Oxford (20 October 1998).
Keller, S. 'Islam in Soviet Central Asia, 1917–30: Soviet Policy and the Struggle for Control', *Central Asian Survey*, 11:1 (March 1992).
Khazanov, A. M. 'Meskhetian Turks in Search of Self-Identity', *Central Asian Survey*, 11:4 (December 1992).
Khyasov, B. 'Uzbekistan Diplomatiyasi: Ilk odimlar', *Guliston*, 4 (1996).
Kirimli, M. 'Uzbekistan in the World Order', *Central Asian Survey*, 16:1 (1997).
Kubicek, P. 'Managing Inter-Ethnic Relations in Central Asia: Theory and Practice', *Eurasian Studies*, 3 (Fall 1996).
Lepingwell, J. W. R. 'The Russian Military and Security in the Near Abroad', *Survival*, 36:3 (Autumn 1994).
Linder, R. P. 'What was a Nomadic Tribe', *Comparative Studies in Society and History*, 24:4 (1982).
Lipousky, I. 'The Central Asian Cotton Epic', *Central Asian Survey*, 14:4 (1995).

Mahmood, T. 'Pakistan and Central Asia', *Eurasian Studies*, 4 (Winter 1996/97).
Marine, S. and E. Whitlock. 'Central Asia and Economic Integration', *RFE/RL Research Report*, 2:14 (2 April 1993).
Martin, K. 'Central Asia's Forgotten Tragedy', *RFE/RL Research Report*, 3:30 (29 July 1994).
—'China and Central Asia: Between Seduction and Suspicion', *RFE/RL Research Report*, 3:25 (24 June 1994).
McCray, T. 'Complicating Agricultural Reforms in Uzbekistan: Observations on the Lower Zaravshan Basin', P. I, *Central Asia Monitor*, 1 (1997).
—'Complicating Agricultural Reforms in Uzbekistan: Observations on the Lower Zaravshan Basin', P. II, *Central Asia Monitor*, 2 (1997).
Mesamed, V. 'Inter-ethnic Relations in The Republic of Uzbekistan', *Central Asia Monitor*, 6 (1996).
Mesbahi, M. 'Russian Foreign Policy and Security in Central Asia and the Caucasus', *Central Asian Survey*, 12:2 (1993).
Minrow, G. M. 'Turkey and Former Soviet Central Asia: National and Ethnic Identity', *Central Asian Survey*, 11:3 (September 1992).
Nettleton, S. 'Uzbek Independence and Educational Change', *Central Asia Monitor*, 3 (1992).
Oztas, A. 'The Role of Women in the Making of the New Uzbek Identity', *Eurasian Studies*, 3 (Fall 1996).
Pamir, P. 'Turkey, the Trans-Caucasus and Central Asia', *Security Dialogue*, 24 (1 March 1993).
Polat, A. 'Trying to Understand Uzbekistan's Dilemma', *Central Asia Monitor*, 1 (1998).
Puri, M. M. 'Central Asian Geopolitics: The Indian View', *Central Asian Survey*, 16:2 (June 1996).
Rahr, A. 'Is Gorbachev Finished? Report on the USSR', *RFE/RL Research Institute*, 3:51 (December 1991).
Sabol, S. 'The Creation of Soviet Central Asia: The 1924 National Delimitation', *Central Asian Survey*, 14:12 (1995).
Sadri, H. A. 'Integration in Central Asia: From Theory to Policy', *Central Asian Survey*, 16:4 (December 1997).
Saltmarshe, D. 'Civil Society and Sustainable Development in Central Asia', *Central Asian Survey*, 15:3/4 (December 1996).

Sander, O. 'Turkey and the Turkic World', *Central Asian Survey*, 13:1 (1994).
Schoeberlein-Engel, J. 'The Prospects for Uzbek National Identity', *Central Asia Monitor*, 2 (1996).
Shahrazarov, B. 'Cultural Pluralism in Uzbekistan', *Eurasian Studies*, 4 (Winter 1996/97).
Shakoor, A. 'Central Asia: The US Interest-perception and its Security Policies', *Eurasian Studies*, 2 (Summer 1995).
Sheehy, A. 'The CIS: A Shaky Edifice', *RFE/RL Research Report*, 2 (1 January 1993).
—'Commonwealth Emerges From a Disintegrating USSR: Report on the USSR', *RFE/RL Research Institute*, 1:1 (3 January 1992).
—'Commonwealth of Independent States: An Uneasy Compromise', *RFE/RL Research Institute*, 1:2 (10 January 1992).
—'Major Anti-Corruption Drive in Uzbekistan', *Radio Liberty Research Bulletin*, RL 324/84 (30 August 1984).
—'The Union Treaty: A Further Setback', *RFE/RL Research Institute*, 3:49 (December 1991).
Singh, A. 'India's Relations with Russia and Central Asia', *International Affairs*, 71:1 (January 1995).
'Statement by Muhammad Salikh Chairman of Erk (Freedom) Party of Uzbekistan', *Central Asia Monitor*, 3 (1996).
Tarock, A. 'Iran's Policy in Central Asia', *Central Asian Survey*, 16:2 (June 1997).
Teague, E. 'The CIS: An Unpredictable Future', *RFE/RL Research Report*, 3:1 (7 January 1994).
Teague, E. and V. Tolz. 'CPSU, Report on the USSR', *RFE/RL Research Institute*, 3:47 (22 November 1991).
Thurman, M. 'Leaders of the Communist Party of Uzbekistan in Historical Retrospect: The "class of '38", P.I, *Central Asia Monitor*, 6 (1995).
—'Leaders of the Communist Party of Uzbekistan in Historical Retrospect: The "class of '38", P.II, *Central Asia Monitor*, 1 (1996).
Tyson, D. 'The Role of Unofficial Audio Media in Contemporary Uzbekistan', *Central Asian Survey*, 13:2 (1994).
Yaacov, R. 'Central Asian Riots and Disturbances, 1989–90: Causes and Context', *Central Asian Survey*, 10:3 (1991).

Yavuz, H. M. 'The Patterns of Political Islamic Identity: Dynamics of National and Transnational Loyalties and Identities', *Central Asian Survey*, 14:3 (1995).

Serials
Adolat
Aral Sea Basin Monitor
Avrasya Dosyasi
BBC World Summary Broadcasts
Caspian Crossroads Magazine
Central Asia Monitor
Central Asian Review
Central Asian Survey
Current History
Economist
Eurasian Studies
European Commission, TACIS Annual Report, 1994, 1995, 1996, 1997
Guliston
Inside Central Asia (BBC Monitoring)
International Affairs
International Relations
Khalk Suzi
Milliyet
Mulakat
Milli Tiklanish
Ozbekiston Adabiyoti va Sanaati
Ozbekiston Ovozi
RFE/RL Research Reports
TACIS Uzbekistan Economic Trends Quarterly
The Economist Intelligence Unit Country Report
Toshkent Khokikoti
Turkiston
Vatan
The Washington Post
The World Today
Xalq Sozi

Index

A

Abdurakhim   165
Abdurakhmanov, Abduljabbar   38
Abu-l-Ala'Mawdudi   99
Abu Said   32
Achaemenid Dynasty   1, 25
administration *see* Government
Adolat Sosial Demokratik Partyasi   97, 153–4, 172, 174
Afghanistan   9, 60, 65, 99, 100, 104, 238, 246, 248, 255, 266–9, 285, 288
agriculture   7, 10–11, 12, 18–20, 24–5, 61, 73, 77, 82, 128, 140–1, 165, 179, 182–3, 186, 188, 192–6, 205, 210, 212–16, 229–30, 273, 278, 281, 296
   see also names of crops
Agzamov, Yurii (Gen.)   61
aid   13, 21, 238, 261, 268, 270, 283, 284, 285
airports   222–3, 229
Ak Horde *see* White Horde
Akhmedov, Rustam   56
Alexander the Great   4, 25–6
Alexander II, Tsar   126
Allworth, Edward A.   63
Alma-Ata *see* Almaty
Almalyk   219
Almatov, Zakijon   56
Almaty   48, 243, 244, 246, 248
alphabet   15, 82, 84, 93, 112
Altin Orda *see* Golden Horde
aluminium   13

Ambartsumov, Evgeni   252
Amu Darya river   9, 11–12, 18, 19, 20, 26, 33, 73, 118, 213, 246
Amudarjinski   244
Andijan   10, 101, 125, 130
Angren   101
Ankara   253, 257, 259, 260, 261, 262, 263
apparat   49, 50, 297
Aq Mechet   35
Aq Tagh (Akdag)   26
Arabic   14, 15, 82
Aral Sea   9, 12, 13, 17–21, 23, 61, 118, 144, 213, 224, 238, 240, 242, 247
armed forces   2, 45, 46, 48, 80, 122, 123, 149, 161, 165, 245, 276, 285
Armenia   46, 48–9, 248
Ashkhabad   244
Asia   264–5
Asia, Central   1–6, 8, 9, 11–13, 21, 25, 34–7, 52, 65, 107, 115–16, 121–2, 123, 133, 145, 165, 166, 225, 247, 295
   and China   72, 265, 266
   and CIS *see* regional co-operation and integration
   economy *see* economy
   geography   17–19
   and Germany   279–80
   and India   266–7
   and Iran   271
   and Israel   273
   languages *see* languages

regional cooperation and integration
    48, 59, 237–9, 243–50, 252, 255,
    260, 263, 265, 280, 281, 283, 287,
    289, 304
  and Russia, Tsarist   78–81, 111,
    116–17, 129, 162
  and Soviet Union   37–8, 82, 96–9,
    189, 240, 246
  and Turkey   74, 256, 257–8, 259,
    260–1
  and US   252, 256
  water *see* water
Astrakhan   31, 35
auls   83, 156
aviation   179–80, 222, 223, 257, 281,
    282, 285
Avicenna   17, 66
Azerbaijan   30, 48–9, 124, 248, 258, 288
Azim, Usman   165

B
Babor   32–3, 66, 76
Bactria-Sogdiana   1, 25, 26
Bahadur, Abul Ghazi, Khan   62
Balkh   33
Balladur, Raymond   281
Baltic Republics   42, 46, 165
  see also names
Baltic Sea   2, 27
banks and banking   185, 228–9, 243,
    244, 245, 261, 274, 287
Banna, Hassan Al   99
Barlas tribe   30, 64
Bartold   63
Bashkordstan   253
Bashkurt   63
Basmachi Movement   37, 63
Batken   60
Batu   28–30, 72, 75
Bayazid II, Sultan   34
Bayqara, Husayin, Sultan   78
Bekovich-Cherkasskii, Prince   35
Belarus   46, 47, 48, 104, 125, 248–9, 251
Berke   29, 72, 75
Al-Beruni, Abu-Raikhan   17
Bhutto, Benazir   269
Birlik (Unity) Party   54, 55, 56, 110, 143,
    165, 166, 171, 260

Bishkek   244, 245, 246
Black Sea   26, 29, 31
Black Sea Zone Organization for Economic
    Cooperation (BSZOEC)   239
Bolsheviks   1, 2, 37, 163
  see also Soviet Union
bombs   58–9, 255, 262
Bond, Dorothy   282
borders   5, 9, 27, 37, 91, 127, 249, 265,
    270, 271
Brezhnev, Leonid   49
broadcasting   222, 257, 260
Buddhism   16, 17, 26, 32, 119
budget   39, 41, 150, 157, 181, 186, 202,
    203, 205, 211, 212, 243, 280
buildings   30
  see also housing
Bukhara   5, 12, 16, 17, 23, 24, 27, 31,
    33, 36, 37, 38, 71, 79, 81, 94, 101,
    111, 112, 113, 117, 119, 124, 125,
    195, 198, 213, 220
Bukhara, Khanate of   5, 34, 35, 78, 128,
    163
Bukhari, Ishmail Muhammad Al-   66, 94
Bukholz   35
Burunduk, Khan   33
business   23, 171, 254, 257, 262, 269,
    273
Business Women's Association, The   22–3
Byelorussia   261

C
Cabinet   43, 60–1, 93, 97, 146, 149,
    150, 153, 166, 220
camels   11, 73
canals   12, 19, 179
capitalism   86, 164
caravan routes   5, 26, 34, 77
Caspian Sea   26, 29, 73
Catherine the Great   126
Catherine II   116–17
Caucuses   29, 30, 35, 71, 104, 126
censorship   36, 41, 58, 83, 88, 296
census   105, 106, 107, 108, 114, 119,
    124, 127, 128, 130
Central Asian Union   245, 246, 248, 252
Cetin, Hikmet   257, 258
Chagatai   28–32, 30, 75, 77, 78

[338]

INDEX

Chechnya 252, 253
Cherniev, General 35
children 22, 83
China 5, 26, 28, 31, 72, 73, 77, 119, 128–9, 208, 306
  and Central Asia 72, 265, 266
  and Uzbekistan 259, 265–6
Chinese Empire 1, 26, 28
Chinggiskhanid tribes 29, 32
Chirchik 11, 12
Chon-Alai 60
Christianity 16, 17, 102, 116, 119, 127, 279
Christopher, Warren 285
Chzhen, Viktor 277
Cihan, Numan Celebi 115
Cilnkurgan 12
citizenship 36, 110–11, 120, 121, 122, 123, 145, 161, 254
climate 7, 10–12, 17, 19, 62
Clinton, Bill 276, 285
coal 179, 198–9, 219, 220, 244
Commonwealth of Independent States (CIS) 4, 11, 14, 23–8, 48, 56, 63, 105, 107, 183, 184, 189, 190, 192, 230, 235, 240, 242, 245, 248–50, 284, 288
  see also Russia and Soviet Union
Communism 66, 86, 87, 88, 89, 90, 92, 149, 155, 163, 164, 170, 225
Communist Party 36, 39, 41–4, 46, 53, 98, 115, 121, 142, 145, 151, 159, 164–5, 167, 175, 180, 296, 299, 300
  Central Committee 37, 39, 51, 148
  Congress of 50, 51
  General Secretary 39, 44
  Uzbek 38, 39, 46, 49–50, 53, 93, 143, 148, 151, 164–5, 167–9, 297–8
community, international 235–6
conflict and unrest 3, 36, 40, 53, 55, 59, 97–9, 113–14, 131–3, 167, 181, 188, 298–9
  see also ethnic relations
constitution 22, 43, 61, 93, 144, 145–7, 149, 150, 151, 153, 157, 161
constitutional court 149, 151, 153
construction industry 223–4, 230, 262

contraception *see* family planning
copper 13, 179, 219, 283
corruption 39, 40, 50–2, 55, 60, 97, 131, 297, 298
cotton 1, 11, 14, 17, 18, 19, 20, 49, 52, 61, 80, 83, 122, 165, 179, 182, 192–5, 201, 205, 206–8, 210, 212–17, 224, 227–8, 253, 267, 283, 296
Council of Ministers 39, 56, 150
crime 39, 243
Crimea 31, 46, 81, 104, 114–16, 126
  War *see* War
Crimean Tatar National Movement 115
culture 1, 7, 15, 16, 22, 80, 83, 86, 89–90, 92, 93, 96, 99, 110, 111, 113, 114, 116, 122, 123, 125, 127, 130, 150, 174, 183, 184, 186, 187, 188, 282, 296
currency 8, 54, 94, 183–6, 196, 199, 219, 228, 229, 242, 243, 253
  exchange 110, 185, 196, 202, 207, 229, 245, 275, 276–7
  see also rouble zone
customs 203, 238, 241, 243, 245, 254, 261
Cyrillic alphabet *see* alphabet
Cyrus, King 25

D

Daghstan 35
Dalimov, Turabek 173
Daminov, Turghunpulat Obidobic 172
Dasht-i Qipchaq 29, 72, 75
defence 95, 205, 241, 243–6, 248, 251, 252, 255
dekhan 193
Demirel, Süleyman 257, 258, 261
democracy 3, 7, 4, 42, 54–5, 137–44, 145, 149–50, 151–2, 153, 155, 156, 158, 159, 160, 166, 176, 275, 299, 303–4
demographic *see* population
demonstrations and riots *see* conflict and unrest
deportation *see* migration
deputies 24, 41, 150, 152–3, 155, 156, 157–8

dervish   30, 36, 77–8
divorce   22
Djurabaev, Anvar   172
Djuraev, S.   88
Duverger, Maurice   159

E
earthquakes   10
ecology *see* environment
Economic Cooperation Organization (ECO)   239
economy   3, 21, 36, 43, 47, 48, 54, 56, 60, 77, 80, 86, 95–6, 107, 110, 131, 133, 140, 145, 147, 157, 180, 182, 212–13, 223, 227–8, 229, 253, 282, 299, 305
    European and world   184, 187, 283
    and foreign policy   235, 238, 272, 274
    Gross Domestic Product (GDP)   180, 182, 183, 192, 197, 199–200, 202–3, 205, 206, 208, 214, 217
    market   4, 8, 24, 57, 132, 137, 138, 139, 142, 143, 144, 152, 156, 158, 164, 170, 174, 187, 188, 209, 240, 275, 305
    planned   4, 39, 41, 83, 137, 138, 144, 181, 188
    privatization   4, 8, 132, 150, 170, 181, 186–7, 190–1, 195–6, 210, 239, 276, 280
    reform of   57, 58, 80, 139, 143, 144, 150, 152, 158, 166, 170, 171, 173, 175, 180–1, 183, 184, 186–92, 194, 197, 224, 225, 228, 277, 278, 280, 281, 283, 305
    regional   239–41, 243–5, 247, 249, 259, 274, 283
    role of agriculture *see* agriculture
    subsidies   183, 184, 186, 188, 192, 200, 205, 213
education   16, 21, 23, 24, 77, 80–4, 93, 94, 96, 98, 99, 101, 102, 111, 112, 114, 117, 122, 123, 163, 205, 226, 230, 262, 276, 278, 282, 296
Egypt   75, 270
elections   42, 44, 53, 56, 60, 137, 144, 147, 148, 151, 153, 154, 162, 166, 170, 180, 255, 262, 284

electoral system   8, 22, 23, 41, 53, 145, 148, 154
electricity   12, 14, 83, 179, 198, 205, 221, 296
elite   17, 49, 51, 52, 53, 79, 90, 91, 92–3, 132, 143, 146, 150, 158, 236, 237, 259, 260, 297, 298, 302
emigration *see* migration
Emin, Namik   260
empires   1, 25, 71, 252, 295
employment   22, 24, 82–3, 109, 119, 132, 179, 183, 187, 210, 213, 217, 224, 226–7, 252
energy   7, 12, 14, 60, 182, 192, 195, 198–9, 217, 219, 220, 221, 246, 261, 276, 278, 281
environment   11, 17–21, 61, 84, 131, 157, 165, 224, 240, 243, 244, 276, 297
    see also pollution
Ergasheva, Mahbuba   23
Erk (Freedom) Party   54–8, 110, 165, 166, 167, 260
Esenbuqa   32
Estonia   48
ethnic and ethnic relations   7, 104–14, 118, 119, 124, 128, 130–3, 153, 166, 167, 171, 173–4, 188, 235, 240, 254, 279, 298, 299, 301–3
EU *see* European Union
Europe   5, 16, 26, 77
European Union   208, 254, 259, 274–6
European Union and Uzbekistan   237, 254, 259, 275, 276–8, 282–3, 306
exports   14, 180, 196, 206–8, 213, 217, 218, 220, 279
extradition   120

F
families   22, 130–1
family planning   23
Family Planning Association of Karakalpakistan   23
Farsi   14, 15, 28, 62, 76, 79, 112, 124, 270
fascism   86, 159, 164
Fergana Valley   9, 10, 11, 18, 23, 63, 65, 66, 78, 79, 101, 102, 111, 116, 128, 130, 179, 198, 213, 220, 224, 263

conflict and unrest   36, 37, 40, 53, 55, 58–60, 99, 124, 131, 298, 299, 302
history   33, 65, 266
Fetullah Hoca's group   101
Fidokorlar Milliy Demokratik Partiyasi   148, 154, 168, 174
finance   181, 183–6, 195, 201–3, 205, 251, 276
food and drink   73, 185, 192, 206
Foreign Internal Affairs, Ministry of   97
Foreign Ministers, Council of   243
foreign policy   4, 5, 7, 8, 57, 75, 85, 90, 91, 149, 151, 235–6, 254, 259, 260, 261, 268, 288–9, 305
   European   237, 254, 261, 274, 276, 283
   Middle East   269–73
   regional   237, 243–50, 252, 254, 255, 263, 265, 266, 269, 272, 286, 289, 305
   as part of Soviet Union   164, 236, 237
   and trade   236–7
   and USA   237, 254, 284
France   222, 279, 280–1
fruit   11, 14, 179, 212, 213, 214
fur trade   11, 14

G

gas   13, 14, 20, 198–9, 199, 219–21, 238, 244, 262, 268, 283, 285
Gaspirinski, Ismail Bey   36, 115
geography   71, 79, 121, 140, 235, 246, 283, 304
Georgia   46, 48–9, 104, 123, 248
German(s)   104, 107, 126–7
Germany   107, 127, 163, 216, 222, 279–80
Ghaznavid State   28
glasnost   2, 6, 40, 41, 46, 51, 297–9
Gobi Desert   72–4
Gofurov, Ibrahim   173
gold   13–14, 179, 182, 184, 206, 207, 218–19, 225, 253, 263, 283
Golden Horde   28, 29, 30–1, 62, 63, 64, 71, 75, 114, 116, 295
Gorbachev, Mikhail   2, 39–48, 50, 51, 52–3, 100, 168, 297–8
Gore, Al   284, 285

government
   local   138, 141, 146, 149, 155, 156–9
   national   32, 56, 60, 76–7, 87, 96, 103, 132, 139, 140, 144, 160, 236, 298, 303
grain   49, 179, 180, 192, 194–5, 201, 205–6, 210, 213–17, 227
Greek(s)   104
Gross Domestic Product (GDP) *see* economy

H

Hambly, Gavin   63
Herzog, Roman   280
history   5, 6, 7, 24, 30, 34, 65, 66, 71, 84, 86, 92–4, 111, 140, 151, 164, 295, 296, 300
horses   11, 73, 74
hospitals   83, 98, 230, 296
hostages   60, 103, 260
housing   109, 190, 223, 226, 252
Human Rights Watch   57, 97, 314, 322
human rights   58, 143, 268, 275, 276, 277–8, 284, 286
Hungary   28, 29
Hurd, Douglas   281
hydrocarbonate   13–14, 238

I

Ibn Sina, Abu Ali (Avicenna)   17
Ibrahimov, Veli   115
identity   5, 7, 36, 40, 62, 66, 76, 84, 91, 92, 93, 95–6, 99, 102, 130
ideology   3, 38, 66, 84–92, 138, 143, 149, 155, 164, 170, 172, 175, 180, 235, 237, 271, 288, 296, 299, 300, 303
Idiku   31
Ikramov, Akmal   38
Ikrom Utbosarov   87
Ilias-Hodi   30
IMF *see* International Monetary Fund
immigration *see* migration
imperialism   86, 164
imports   14, 180, 195, 199, 206, 207, 208–9, 213–14, 217, 272, 279
income *see* wages
independence   2–3, 14–16, 26–32, 34–5, 37, 38, 42–3, 47–9, 53–4, 57, 85, 86,

87, 88, 89–91, 130, 144, 145, 151, 156, 158, 166, 172, 192, 210, 220, 226, 235, 238, 239, 250, 258, 283, 284, 299–300, 303, 305
India   53, 77, 259, 266–7, 306
Indonesia   260, 264
industry   7, 13, 20, 83, 84, 89, 179–80, 182, 188, 191, 197–8, 212, 217–18, 229, 296
inflation   132, 182, 183, 184, 185, 199–200, 205–6, 226, 228
Internal Affairs, Ministry of   53
International Cultural Centre   122
International Monetary Fund (IMF)   202, 206, 228, 287
international relations   7, 151, 235, 240, 266, 274, 304, 305–6
   see also foreign policy
investment   21, 188, 195, 196–201, 225, 228, 229, 238, 243, 254, 261, 264, 271, 273, 276, 282–6
Iran   25, 62, 267, 268, 271, 272, 306
   Uzbekistan   238, 259, 269, 270–2, 273
Iraq   31
irrigation *see* water
Irtysh   28
Ishmail, Shar   33–4
Islam   5, 16, 27, 29, 30, 33, 36, 55, 58, 62, 75, 76, 78, 80–1, 83, 94, 95–103, 117, 119, 123, 129, 239, 252, 255, 265, 266, 268, 270, 272, 273, 284, 300–1
Islamic Conference, Organization of   239
Islamic Movement of Uzbekistan (IMU)   59–60, 103
Islamic Renaissance Party   55, 97, 167
Islamist(s)   58, 60, 103
Israel   125, 126, 216, 269, 271, 273–4, 306
Istemi   26
Ivan IV   116
Izzetullah, Mir   65

J

Jadid movement   15, 37, 38, 81, 162
Jalolov, Abdulhafiz (Prof.)   60, 86, 148, 170
Janibek   32, 33

Japan   119, 120, 121, 263
Jews   104, 107, 124–5, 273
Jiang Zemin   265
Jochi Ulus   28–30, 63, 64
Jonibeck   30
Judaism   16, 17
judges   24, 79, 149, 153, 161
Jungaria   29
Justice, Ministry of   60, 161–2, 166

K

Kalmuyks   33
Kamalov, Sabir Kamalovich   39
Kamilov, Abdulaziz   269, 271
Kaqin tribe   64
Karaganovr, Sergei   252
Karakalpak(s)   117–18
Karakalpak Autonomous Republic *see* Karakalpakistan
Karakalpakistan   12, 20, 21, 23, 25, 38, 61, 118, 119, 146, 172, 174, 202, 220, 224
Karakalpak language   118
Karakhandis   28
Karimov, Islom Abdughanievich   3, 53–5, 56, 57–9, 60, 87, 89, 91, 92, 93, 94, 95, 96, 103, 143, 147–50, 158, 165, 166, 168, 170, 173, 189, 195, 238, 240, 242, 250, 253, 254, 257, 259, 260, 263, 264, 265, 267, 269, 270, 273, 275–6, 277, 279, 280, 281, 282, 284, 285, 287, 299, 300
Kashgaria   28, 128
Kashkadarya   10, 102, 112
Kasym   33
Kayumov, Aziz   173
Kazak Culture, National Association of   114
kazaks   113, 118, 119, 122
Kazakstan   9, 12, 17–18, 20, 279, 288
   history   28, 31, 114, 129
   post-Soviet   48, 59, 100, 124, 127, 208, 214, 238, 248–9
   Soviet rule   61
   and Uzbekistan   241–2, 244–6, 248–9, 251, 252, 254, 259, 265, 273, 289
Kazak tribe(s)   33, 35, 64, 76, 77, 81
Kazan Khanate   31, 104, 116

INDEX

Kerki region 38
KGB 2, 53
Khalilov, Erkin 153
Khamidov, Bakhtoyor 56
Khan, Chinggis 62, 73–5, 76
Khan, Haci Giray 114
Khan Leghari, Farooq Ahmed 269
Khatun, Bibi 94
Khayr, Abu-l, Khan 31–3, 62, 63, 76
Khiva 27, 35, 36, 37, 71, 79, 81, 125, 195
Khiva, Khanate of 5, 34, 35, 78, 128, 163
Khodja-Ilgar 30
Khojaev, Faizulla 37, 38
Khojaev, Tursun 36
Khokand 71, 101, 125, 163
Khokand, Khanate of 5, 34, 35, 36, 78, 128
Khorezm 10, 12, 24, 25, 27, 28, 31, 33, 63, 65, 66, 101, 102, 119, 220, 238
Al-Khorezmi, Muhammed 17
Khosrau Anoshirvan I 26
Khruschev, Nikita 39, 115
Khwarazm 32
Kim, Peter 122
kishlaks 83, 156
Kohl, Helmut 280
kolkhozy 192–3
Komilov, Abdulaziz 6, 282, 282
Koray 32, 33
Korea 120, 123, 189, 208, 260, 263–4
Korean(s) 17, 104, 118, 119–21, 123
Korean cultural centre 122
Korean language 123
Kozyrev, Andrei 253–4
Kravchu, Leonid 45
Kravchuk 48
Kremlin 49, 50, 52, 69, 252–3, 297
Kryuchkov, Vladimir 45
Kucha 26
Kushan empire 1, 26
Kyrgyz language *see* Turkish
Kyrgyzstan 9, 17, 18, 37, 49, 59, 60, 76, 103, 124, 127, 128, 130, 214, 220, 238, 242, 244, 246, 248, 251, 252, 254, 261, 265, 279, 288, 289
Kyrgyzy(s) 118, 127, 131, 133, 302

Kyrgyzy Republic *see* Kyrgyzstan
Kzyl Kum (Red Sands) 9, 18

L

labour 80, 89, 126, 130, 140, 179, 186, 215, 224
  see also employment
Labour, Ministry of 210
land 140–1, 144, 166, 192–6, 213, 226
language(s) 14–15, 28, 62, 63, 81, 82, 105, 111–12, 125, 254, 258
  see also names
Lashkari Islami 60
Latin alphabet *see* alphabet
Latvia 48
law 22, 28, 61, 74, 79, 91, 143, 151, 155, 156, 157, 160, 161, 170, 189, 286, 302
lead 179
Lenin, Vladimir Illyich 2–3, 36, 92, 121
Liao dynasty 28
Liberal Democratic Party 251
Li Peng 265
literature 6, 14–15, 28, 78–9
Lithuania 48
livestock 11, 193, 194, 212, 213
Li Zemin 265

M

Macedonian empire 1
Madali, Ihsan 36
Madrassah 101, 117
mahallas 23, 141, 156, 170, 226, 230
Mahrnudek Khan 63
Malikov, Mukhed Bobir 56
Mametkulov, Rustem 262
Mamluk alliance 29, 75
Manchuria 121
mangit tribe 64
Maracanda 25
Maritime Province 104, 119, 120–1
marriage 22, 72, 112, 117, 125, 130–1, 302
Marx, Karl 86, 92
Marxist 86, 138, 164, 303
Maverannahr 1, 9, 28, 31–2, 33, 62, 66, 76, 79, 93, 295, 300

[343]

medals 94–5
Medea 1, 25
media 51, 56, 57, 66, 98, 145, 298
 see also names
medicine 17, 83, 296
Merv 33
Meskhetia 40, 123
Meskhetian Turks 104, 123–4, 131, 133, 302
Middle East 16, 26, 77, 270, 273
Migranian, Andranik 252
migration 104, 105, 107–12, 117, 118–22, 125, 127, 129–30, 132, 243, 252, 302
military *see* armed forces
Milli Tiklanish Demokratic Partiyasi 154, 168, 172, 173, 174
minerals 13, 281, 306
mining 13–14, 217, 218, 229, 261, 283, 284
Ministers, Council(s) of 39, 43, 50, 57
Minsk 48
Mirsaidov, Shukrulla 55–6
missionaries 101–2, 116
Mitterand, François 281
Moldavia 46, 48, 248
monarchy 140–1, 151, 163
Mongke-Ternur 29–30
mongol(s) 1, 16, 28, 64
Mongol Empire 1, 16, 26, 28–30, 32, 33, 71–2, 75–6, 129
Mongolia 29, 72, 73, 128
Moscow 37, 38, 39, 44, 46, 51, 52, 53, 143, 152, 163, 168, 180, 182, 184, 188, 246, 251, 252, 270, 297
Mucaheddin 100
Mufti 96, 101
Mugholistan 31, 32, 62
Mukhiddinov, Nuriddin Akramovich 39
Mulakat 170
murder 58–9
Muslim(s) *see* Islam
Muslim Board 101, 103
Muslim Board for Central Asia 100
'Muslim Bureau' 36
Muslim Spiritual Assembly of Orenburg 36
Mutalov, Abdulkhasim 56, 57

N
Nagorno Karabakh 126
Namangan 36, 101, 112
Namangani, Juma 59
Naqshbandi 94, 101
Nasqhi-bandis, Sufi Brotherhood of 36
national independence *see* ideology
National Revival Party *see* Milli Tiklanish
National Security Council 285
National Women's Committee, The 22, 23, 24
nationalism 5, 37, 39, 40, 44, 51–2, 66, 81, 85, 87, 88–90, 91, 92, 95, 111, 131, 239, 251, 254, 298
NATO 246, 252, 254, 261, 286–7
Navoi, Mir Alisher 24, 66, 78, 94
Navoi province 111, 219
Nazarbayev, Nursultan 242, 249
New Sarai 75
newspapers *see* Press
Nikolay, Tsar 162
Nishanov, Rafik 53
Niyazov, Amin Irmatovich 38, 39
Niyazov, Sapar Murad 242
Nogay 31, 64
nomads 7, 72–5, 77
Norbutaev, Erkin 174
Novo-Ogarevo 44
Nukus 2, 21, 42
Nuri, Sayid Abdullah 57

O
oblast 24, 49, 50, 297
Ogetei 28
oil and petroleum 13, 20, 179, 198, 199, 206, 210, 219, 220–1, 238, 244, 262, 263, 268, 283, 285
Oirats 32, 33, 35
O'Leary, Hazel 285
Olima, National Association of 23
Oliy Majlis *see* Parliament
opposition 54–8, 60, 97, 103, 110, 154, 165–7, 171, 175
Organization of Economic Cooperation (OEC) 287–8
Oriental Studies, Institute of 122
Osh 128
Otayev, Valery 60

INDEX

Overseas Private Investment Corporation 285
Ozal, President 257, 259
Ozbekiston Ovozi 161
Ozbeks *see* Uzbeks

P

Pakistan 259, 266, 267, 268, 269, 306
Palvan-Zade, Abdusamat 60
parliament 24, 56, 61, 122, 137, 138, 143, 144, 147, 148–55, 157, 159, 161, 174
patriotism 66, 88, 89, 90
 see also nationalism
Pavlov, Valentin 45
peace 57, 286, 287, 299
Peking, Treaty of 119
Peoples' Democratic Party (PDP) 4, 58, 88, 147, 148, 152, 153, 154, 159, 167, 168–70, 171, 172, 175–6
People's Deputies, Congress of 42, 43, 46–7
Peres, Shimon 273
perestroika 2, 6, 40, 42, 51, 52, 142, 144, 165, 226, 297–9
Perovskii, General 35
Perry, William 285
Persia 25, 29, 31, 33, 34, 62, 72, 73, 76, 272
Persian empire 1, 25
Persian language *see* Farsi
Peter the Great 35
poetry *see* literature
Poland 28, 29, 166
police 46
Politburo 52, 53
political parties 6, 55, 57, 58, 132, 137, 138, 153, 159–75
 see also names
political science 138, 303–4
political system 6, 23–4, 39, 43, 49–50, 77, 79–80, 82, 83, 84, 85, 87–92, 103, 137, 138, 140–1, 146, 148, 151, 152, 155, 161, 172, 174, 299, 303
 and foreign policy 235
 reform 2, 40, 41, 42, 53, 58, 85, 139, 142, 144, 304
 see also Constitution

politicians 139
pollution 12, 17–20
Popular Front 42
population 4, 18, 19, 21, 24, 52, 80, 98, 105–10, 112, 113, 114, 118, 119, 124, 127, 128, 130, 187, 188, 191, 210, 224, 227, 247, 279, 283, 304
postal services 222
poverty 8, 52, 109, 186, 187, 191, 225–7
President
 Soviet 44, 45, 48
 Uzbek 3, 53, 60, 138, 143, 146, 147–9, 152, 154, 156, 157, 161, 175, 255
press 57–8, 99, 111, 147, 161, 162, 163, 170, 171, 172, 174, 260, 298
prices 54, 181, 182, 183, 191, 205, 210, 217, 224, 243
Primbetow, Serik 243
Prime Minister 38, 45, 60, 149
Prime Ministers, Council of the 243
Prime Minister, Deputy 24, 220
prisoners 57, 59
privatization *see* economy
property 22, 46, 126, 140, 142, 195, 277
Pugo, Boris 45
Pulato, Abdumanov 165, 276
purge(s) 38, 49, 50, 51, 59, 83, 98
Putin, Vladimir 255

Q

Qara-Khitay 28
Qarshi 33
Qimiz 73
Qunduz 33
Qurultai 74
Qutb, Sayyid 99

R

radio 57, 118
Rahmanov 57
railways 36, 80, 222–3, 272
raion 49, 50, 297
Rashidov, Sharef 39, 52
Rashidova, Sayora 24
Rasulovich, Rasulov Karim 173
Red Army 37

[345]

Red Crescent 23
referendum(s) 45, 48
  see also elections
refugees 58
religion 7, 15–17, 96–9, 101, 258
  see also names
retailing 224
Rifkind, Malcolm 282
rivers 11–12, 17–19
roads 83, 222–3, 272
rouble 8, 54, 56, 110, 183–5, 202
rouble zone 235, 237, 241, 242, 251, 253, 261, 305
RSFSR 44, 45, 46, 47
Russia 15, 16, 28, 29, 30, 31, 33, 48, 59, 104, 105, 107, 110, 118, 124, 125, 151, 165, 213, 219, 245, 248, 261, 306
  Bolshevik Revolution see Soviet Union
  and Central Asia see Asia, Central
  cotton see cotton
  economy 241, 254
  and Iran 270
  Tsarist 1, 3, 7, 16, 36, 37, 81, 108, 119, 120, 121, 129, 163, 182, 295
  and Turkey 253, 261
  and Uzbekistan
    post-Soviet Union 8, 132, 208, 237, 242, 250–6, 261, 263, 284, 286
    Tsarist rule of 79–82, 88, 98–9, 109, 162, 182, 300–2
  see also RSFSR and Soviet Union
Russia, Central Bank of (CBR) 184
Russian Cultural Centre 108, 110, 111
Russian Federation see Russia
Russian language 14, 15, 107, 110, 111, 119, 125, 127, 254
Russian-Orthodox Church 17, 100
Russian Soviet Federative Socialist Republic see RSFSR
Ryskulov, Turar 36
Ryzhkov, Nikolai 37, 43

S
Safavid Dynasty 33, 34, 76
Saidov, Akmal 88
Salih, Muhammad 52, 55, 260
Samanid Dynasty 1, 16, 27

Samarkand 5, 11, 17, 23, 24, 25, 27, 31, 33, 35, 38, 71, 79, 94, 101, 111, 112, 113, 119, 124, 125, 195, 213
Sarai 75
Sartori 160
Sarts 63
Sasanian Dynasty 1, 16, 26, 27, 73
Satimov, Khokim 97
Saudi Arabia 99, 267, 270, 306
savkhozy 192–3
science and technology 17, 30, 210, 273, 276, 282
script see alphabet
Second Secretary 50
security 59, 61, 90, 98, 149, 235, 239, 249, 252, 254–5, 259, 265, 267, 271, 274, 276, 284, 285, 286, 287, 299, 305
Security and Cooperation in Europe, Organization for (OSCE) 148, 287
Seleucian Kingdom 26
Seleucus 26
Seliger, Martin 85
Semipalatinsk 35
Semirechie 28, 79, 129
Sezer, Ahmet Necdet 262–3
Shahrisabz 30, 94
Shamanism 16
Shamil, Imam 35
Shatalin, Stanislav 181
Shaybani Dynasty 31, 32, 33, 34, 66, 79
Shaybani, Muhammad, Khan 32, 33–4, 62, 66, 76, 79, 295
Shaybani, Ubaydullah 79
sheep 11, 25, 73, 74, 194
Shushkevich, Stanislav 48
Sibagan 31
Siberia 28, 32, 71, 73, 115, 120, 126, 127, 130
Sighnaq 32
silk 11, 14, 179
Silk Road 5, 26, 27, 77
silver 13, 179, 219, 283
social security 22, 203, 227, 230
social services 78, 188, 226–7, 230, 278
society 3, 32, 53, 61, 71, 74, 84, 89–90, 99, 132, 137, 140, 144, 155, 167, 187, 278, 299, 304

[346]

Index

sociology 138
Sodiq, Muhammad Yusuf Muhammed (Mufti) 97, 103–4
Sogdiana 1, 25, 26, 65
Solih, Muhammad 165, 166
sovereignty 2, 42, 43, 45, 46, 47, 54, 61, 89, 91, 118, 143, 151, 168, 172, 239, 258, 283, 300
Soviet Union 1, 4, 17, 39–40, 44, 46, 63, 121, 126, 142, 168, 180–1, 187, 206
  Bolshevik Revolution 2, 36, 71, 82, 114, 120, 144, 162, 163, 295
  and Central Asia see Asia, Central
  Communist Party see Communist Party
  cotton see cotton
  demise 2, 21, 39–48, 53, 54, 84, 86, 100, 133, 137, 138, 142, 144, 157, 181–2, 189, 208, 218, 235, 241, 248, 299
  economy see economy
  elections see elections
  KGB 2, 45, 46
  President 44, 45, 46
  and Turkey 256
  and Uzbekistan see Uzbekistan
Stalin, Josef 2, 121, 123, 126, 130, 164
steppes 32, 33, 35, 62, 72, 73, 74, 75, 76
sufism 36, 77, 94, 99, 101
Suharto, President 264
Sultanov, Uthkir 57, 60
sum(s) 8, 54, 94, 185–6, 197, 205, 211, 216, 217, 228
Supreme Council see Parliament
Supreme Court 146, 149, 153, 162
Supreme Soviet(s) 39, 41, 42, 43, 45, 47, 48, 52, 55, 56, 152, 180
Surkhandarya 10, 23, 102, 112, 213
Switzerland 208
Syrdarya 9, 11–12, 31, 32, 33, 35, 38, 62, 63, 72, 79, 118, 130, 213, 246
Syria 31, 75

T
Taiwan 189
Tajik(s) 62, 65, 73, 76, 77, 107, 112, 122, 124, 295
Tajikistan 9, 17–18, 38, 49, 57, 65, 78, 104, 107, 220, 242, 244, 245, 248, 255, 259, 270, 271, 288
  political unrest 55, 57–60, 97–9, 104, 250–1, 267, 269, 299
Taksonov, A. 88
Talbott, Strobe 284
Taliban 255, 267–9
Tang Dynasty 26
Taraghai 30
Tashkent 10, 11, 23, 24, 27, 33, 36, 37, 38, 39, 51, 52, 57, 59, 66, 71, 79, 94, 96, 97, 100, 101, 103, 108, 109, 110, 111, 112, 114, 116, 117, 118, 119, 122, 125, 128, 130, 156, 164, 170, 172, 173, 174, 180, 190, 195, 221, 222, 223, 224, 240–1, 244, 248, 250, 253, 255, 257, 261, 263, 264, 265, 270, 281, 287, 301
Tatar(s) 30, 31, 36, 63, 72, 73, 81, 104, 114–17, 118, 119
Tatarstan 253
taxation 45, 77, 140, 151, 157, 181, 185, 192, 195, 202–3, 205, 207–8, 241, 243, 246, 280, 282
telecommunications 222, 223, 229, 281, 296
television 57, 118
Temur, Amir 30–2, 66, 75, 93–4
Temurid Dynasty 16, 29–33, 75, 76, 77, 78
Termez 27, 101
Tilyabuguz 12
Timurlane see Temur, Amir
Tobolsk 31, 35, 62
Togan, A. Zeki Velidi 63–5
Tore Khan 36
Toshmukhamedov, Bekh 165
totalitarianism 3, 87, 90, 138–9, 142, 156, 249, 299, 304
tourism 195, 264
towns and cities 9, 13, 38, 61, 71, 80, 83, 245, 296, 302
trade 4, 5, 25, 26, 32, 34, 56, 77, 83, 117, 180, 181, 182, 184, 196, 201, 203, 206, 207–8, 213, 223–4, 228, 235–6, 238, 245, 264–5, 267, 268, 275, 276–9, 283, 296, 305

see also Silk Road and caravan routes
Transoxiana   1, 9, 63
transport   221–2, 244, 246, 253, 267, 272, 276, 278, 281, 296
Treaty, Union   44, 45, 46, 47, 48
tribe(s)   5, 31, 62, 63–5, 71–2, 75, 76–7, 78, 118, 295
see also names
Tsar Alexander II   119
Tuglug-Temur   30
Tu-men   26
Tuqtamush   30, 31
Tura   63
Turkestan   5, 18, 27, 28, 34–7, 79, 129, 130, 162–3, 240
Turkestan National Liberation Movement   63
Turkey   15, 16, 59, 63, 208, 222, 238
  and Central Asia   256, 257–8, 259–61
  and Russia   253, 261
  and Soviet Union   256
  and US   256, 259
  and Uzbekistan   256–63, 267, 269, 306
Turkic see Turkish language
Turkish empire   1, 16, 26–8, 35, 73, 81, 115
Turkish language   15, 75, 76, 78–9, 117, 123, 127
Turkmen(s)   118, 119, 122
Turkmenistan   9, 19, 49, 219, 220, 242, 244, 248, 288
Turks, Meskhetian see Meskhetian Turks
Tursunov, Ahtam   171

U
Uighurs   27, 73, 128, 265
Uiguristan see Turkestan
Ukraine(s)   1, 45, 46, 48, 105, 107, 118, 125, 126, 213, 248–9, 251
ukus   94, 101, 118
Ulugbek, Muhammed   17, 66, 94
Ulus   28, 29
UN see United Nations
United Kingdom   34, 216, 222, 279, 281
United Nations (UN)   237, 239, 245, 286
United States (US)   8, 13, 56, 57, 107, 125, 208, 216, 267
  and Central Asia   252, 256, 268, 284

  and Turkey   256, 259
  and Uzbekistan   237, 238, 268, 272, 275–6, 284–6, 306
universities   96, 111
Ural Mountains   115, 126
Ural river   62
Uranium   13
Urgench   32
Utaev, Abdulla   55, 97
Uzbek(s)   2, 4, 5, 6, 7, 16, 25, 61–6, 71, 75, 76, 77, 79, 107, 111, 119, 122, 124, 133, 167, 171, 295
see also tribes
Uzbek Empire   1, 30–3, 34, 62, 77, 78
Uzbekistan   1, 5–6, 8, 25, 31, 37, 46, 49, 64, 116, 122, 123, 125, 160, 173, 241, 244, 248, 252, 288
  and European union   237, 254, 259, 282–3
  and Germany   107, 126–7, 163, 216, 222, 279–80
  independence see independence
  and India   266–7
  and Iran   238, 259, 269, 270–2, 273
  Mongol rule see Mongol Empire
  and Pakistan   267, 268, 269
  people see Uzbeks
  post-Soviet   53–7, 84–5, 86–90, 91–2, 93, 138, 139, 141, 144, 150, 188, 189, 235, 295, 299, 300, 303
  and Russia
    post-Soviet relations   8, 132, 208, 237, 250–6, 259, 261, 263, 284, 286
  Soviet rule   2–3, 7–8, 15, 16, 36–9, 49–53, 81–4, 87, 91, 93, 98, 99, 109, 114, 127, 139, 144, 150, 188, 264, 288–9, 295–301
  Tsarist Russian rule   79–82, 88, 98–9, 109, 162, 182, 295, 300–2
  and Turkey   256–63, 267, 269
  and US   237, 238, 272, 275–6, 284–6
Uzbekistan, Central Bank of   94, 149, 184, 201, 202, 205
Uzbekistan, People's Democratic Party of see PDP
Uzbek Khan   62, 295
Uzbek Khanate see Uzbek empire

[348]

Index

Uzbek language 14–15, 82, 84, 92, 93, 110, 111, 112, 117, 119, 124, 127, 128, 165, 300

V

Vatan Taraqiyoti Party 66, 95, 152, 154–8, 167, 168, 170–2, 174
Verniy 35
Vitold of Lithuania, Grand Duke 31
Vladislavlev, Aleksander 252
Vladivostok 119
Volga 29, 31, 36, 75, 81, 104, 114
Volga German Autonomous Republic 126

W

wages 24, 132, 183–4, 186, 199, 203, 210–11, 225–6, 230
Wahhabis 58, 99
Wales, Prince of 282
War 149, 164
 Crimean 35
 First World 126
 Second World 40, 104, 109, 115, 123, 125, 126–7, 180, 273, 302
Ware, Alan 159, 160
water 7, 9, 11–13, 17–20, 78, 82, 84, 118, 140, 166, 179, 205, 213, 246–7, 296
weather 12
West, the 40, 55, 75, 86, 238, 256, 258, 272, 284
Wheeler, Geoffrey 62
White Horde 30
White Huns 1, 26

women 7, 21–4, 82, 171, 172, 173, 174, 296
women's issues 22, 23, 24, 316
Women's Resource Centre, The 23
World Bank 13, 206, 285
World Trade Organization (WTO) 276, 277

X

Xalq Birligi Xarakoti 173–4
Xalq Demokratik Partiyasi *see* People's Democratic Party
Xinjiang 265

Y

Yanayev, Gennadi 45
Yangiabad 60
Yazev, Dmitrii 45
Yeltsin, Boris 44, 45, 46, 47, 152, 251, 252, 253, 255
Yildirim Beyazid I, Sultan 31
Yoldashev, Abdulvali 60
Yoldashev, Anvar 171
Yoldashev, Tohir 59–60
Yunus Khan 2
Yusupov, Usman 38
Yuzhno-Surkhandarya 12

Z

Zaravshan 10, 11, 12, 63, 66
Zatulin, Konstantin 252
Zerabulak 35
Zhirinovskii, Vladimir 252, 253
zinc 179
Zoroastrianism 16, 17, 25

Also available

Durham Middle East Monograph Series

The Yemen in the 18th and 19th Centuries
Vol. 1 • 1985 • 228pp • 215 x 135 mm • Cased £20.00 • ISBN 0 86372 033 1

Underdevelopment and Rural Structures in Southeastern Turkey: The Household Economy in Gisgis and Kalhana
Vol. 2 • 1986 • 300pp • 215 x 143 mm • Cased £30.00 • ISBN 0 86372 034 X

Yemen in Early Islam 9–233/630–847: A Political History
Vol. 3 • 1988 • 264pp • 222 x 143 mm • Cased £30.00 • ISBN 0 86372 102 8

Syria and the New World Order
Vol. 4 • 1999 • 376pp • 235 x 155 mm • Cased £35.00 • ISBN 0 86372 249 0

Iran and Eurasia
Vol. 5 • 2001 • 228pp • 235 x 155 mm • Cased £35.00 • ISBN 0 86372 271 7

Lebanon's Renaissance: The Political Economy of Reconstruction
Vol. 6 • 2001 • 276pp • 235 x 155 mm • Cased £35.00 • ISBN 0 86372 252 0

Unfolding the Orient: Travellers in Egypt and the Near East
Vol. 7 • 2001 • 324pp • 235 x 155 mm • Cased £35.00 • ISBN 0 86372 257 1

Interpreting the Orient: Travellers in Egypt and the Near East
Vol. 8 • 2001 • 284pp • 235 x 155 mm • Cased £35.00 • ISBN 0 86372 258 X

Available from your local bookshop; alternatively, contact our Sales Department on +44 (0)118 959 7847 or email on **orders@garnet-ithaca.co.uk** to order copies of these books.

DATE DUE

RETURN TO:
LIBRARY
Room 1E41 OHB
For Renewals Call:
482-2239 or x 52525

MAR 2 4 2004